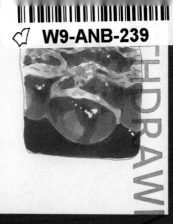

I go to Osaka about once a year. I never really considered that I liked Osaka, but maybe I do. The kushiage was really good.

—Tite Kubo

BLEACH is author Tite Kubo's second title. Kubo made his debut with *ZOMBIEPOWDER.*, a four-volume series for *WEEKLY SHONEN JUMP*. To date, *BLEACH* has been translated into numerous languages and has also inspired an animated TV series that began airing in the U.S. in 2006. Beginning its serialization in 2001, *BLEACH* is still a mainstay in the pages of *WEEKLY SHONEN JUMP*. In 2005, *BLEACH* was awarded the prestigious Shogakukan Manga Award in the *shonen* (boys) category.

BLEACH
VOL. 65: MARCHING OUT THE ZOMBIES
SHONEN JUMP Manga Edition

STORY AND ART BY
TITE KUBO

Translation/Joe Yamazaki
Touch-up Art & Lettering/Mark McMurray
Design/Kam Li
Editor/Alexis Kirsch

Printed in the U.S.A.

Published by VIZ Media, LLC
P.O. Box 77010
San Francisco, CA 94107

10 9 8 7 6 5 4 3 2 1
First printing, November 2015

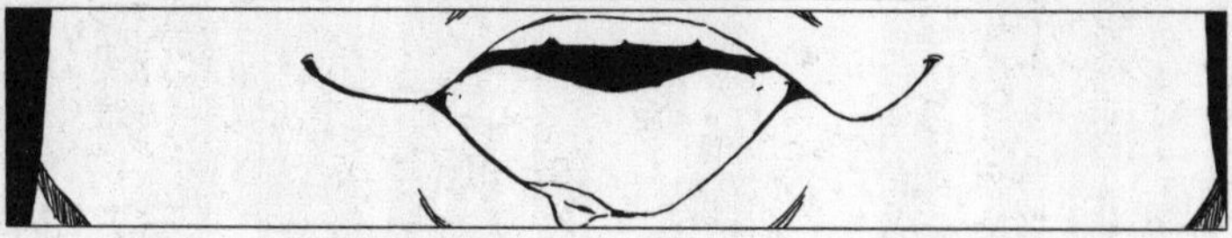

Love you to death

BLEACH 65

MARCHING OUT THE ZOMBIES

Shonen Jump Manga

ALL STARS ★
AND

キャンディス・
キャットニップ

**CANDICE
CATNIPP**

**KENPACHI
ZARAKI**

更木剣八
ザラキケンパチ

石田雨竜
イシダウリュウ

**URYU
ISHIDA**

plot

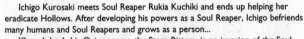

Ichigo Kurosaki meets Soul Reaper Rukia Kuchiki and ends up helping her eradicate Hollows. After developing his powers as a Soul Reaper, Ichigo befriends many humans and Soul Reapers and grows as a person...

Yhwach leads his Quincy army, the Stern Ritters, in an invasion of the Soul Society. The Court Guards stand in their way, but against the mysterious power of the Quincies even the Soul Reaper captains are in for the fight of their life. As the battle continues, Kenpachi goes up against the mysterious Gremmy. Against Gremmy and his ability to turn his imagination into reality, Kenpachi reveals the full power of his sword for the first time and achieves victory. However...

BLEACH

GISELLE GEWELLE

ジゼル・ジュエル

ミニーニャ・マカロン

MENINAS MCALLON

LILTOTTO LAMPERD

リルトット・ランパード

STORIES

BLEACH 65

MARCHING OUT THE ZOMBIES

CONTENTS

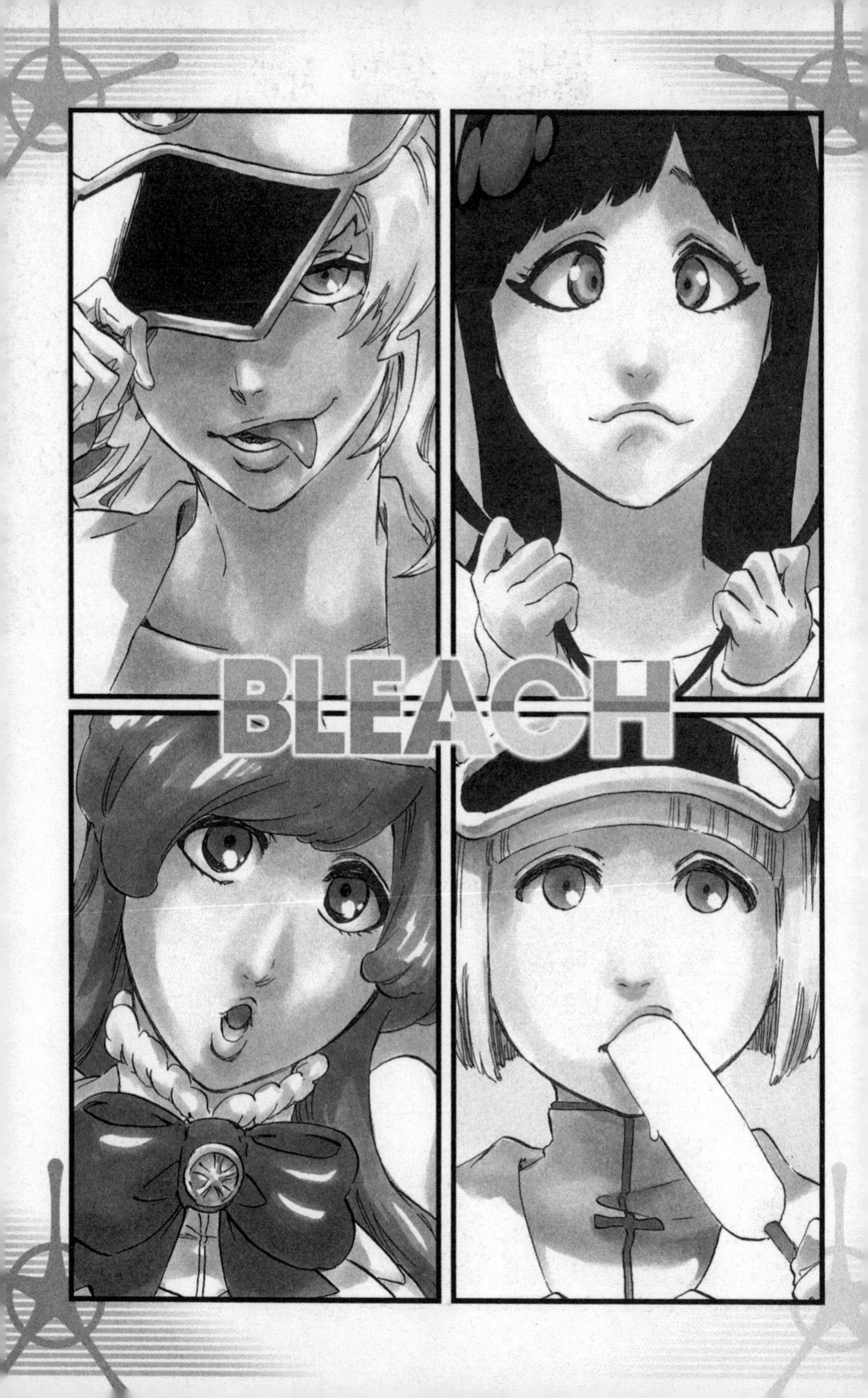
BLEACH

BLEACH

ブリーチ

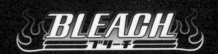

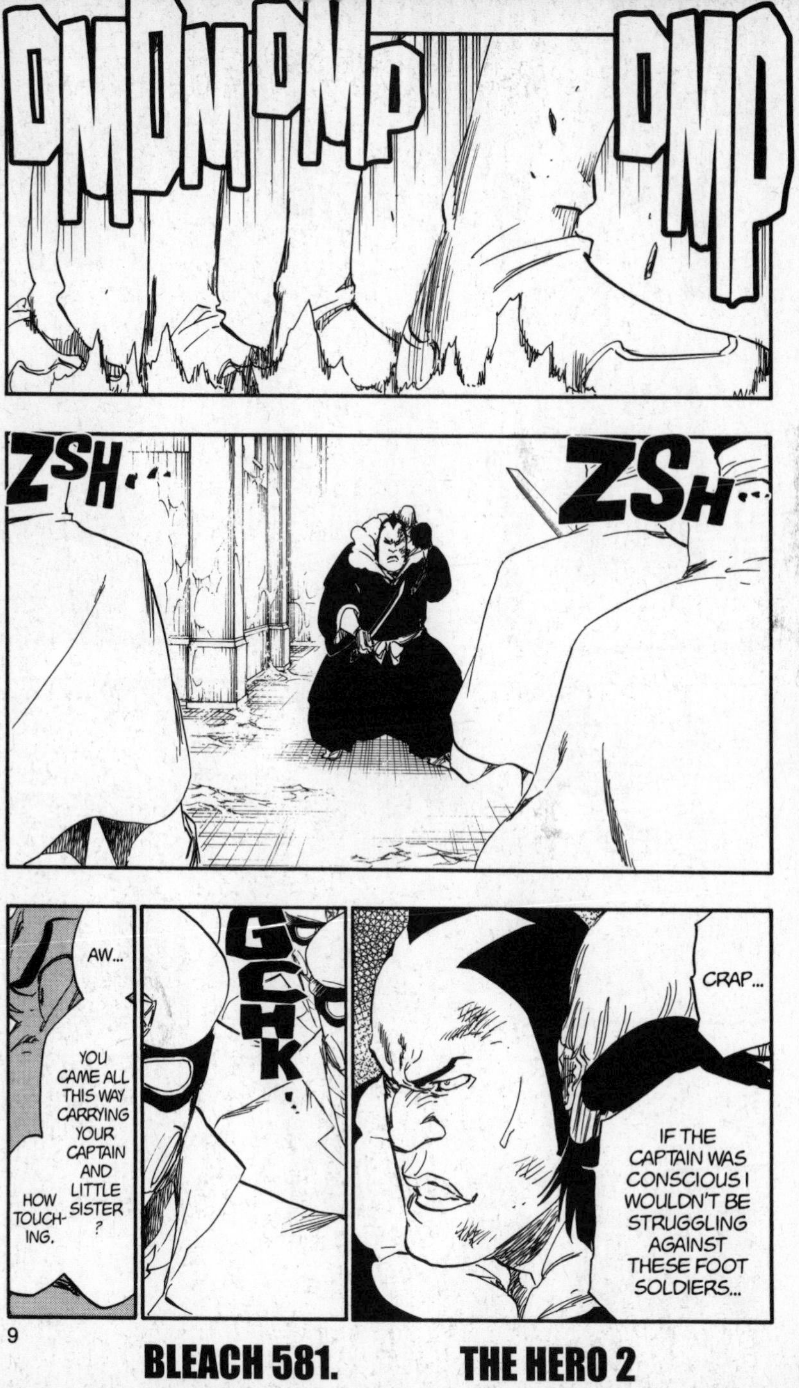
DMP
DMDMDMP
ZSH...
ZSH...
CRAP...
IF THE CAPTAIN WAS CONSCIOUS I WOULDN'T BE STRUGGLING AGAINST THESE FOOT SOLDIERS...
GCHK
AW...
YOU CAME ALL THIS WAY CARRYING YOUR CAPTAIN AND LITTLE SISTER?
HOW TOUCH-ING.

BLEACH 581. THE HERO 2

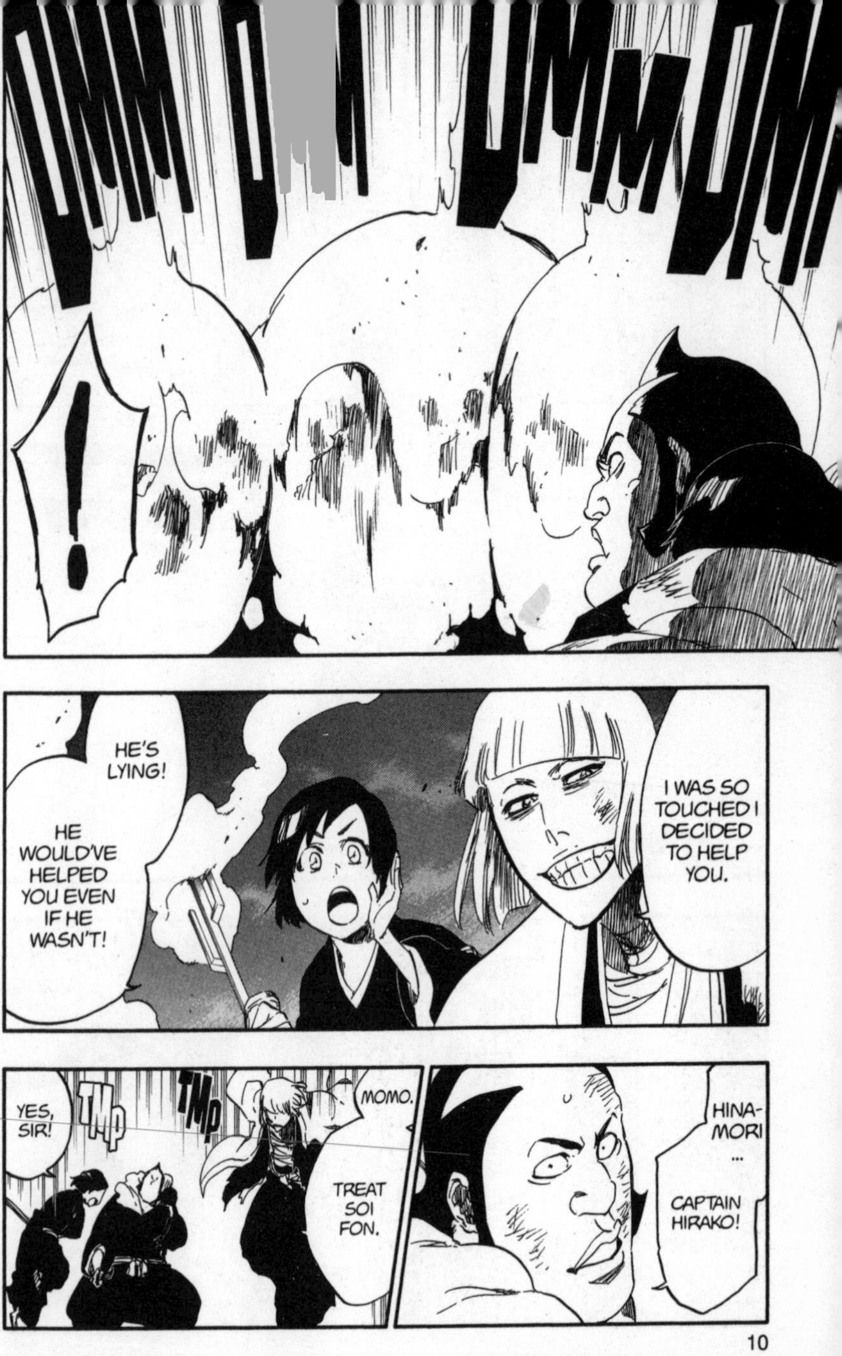
!
I WAS SO TOUCHED I DECIDED TO HELP YOU.
HE'S LYING!
HE WOULD'VE HELPED YOU EVEN IF HE WASN'T!
HINA-MORI ...
CAPTAIN HIRAKO!
MOMO.
TREAT SOI FON.
TMP
TMP
YES, SIR!

READ THIS WAY

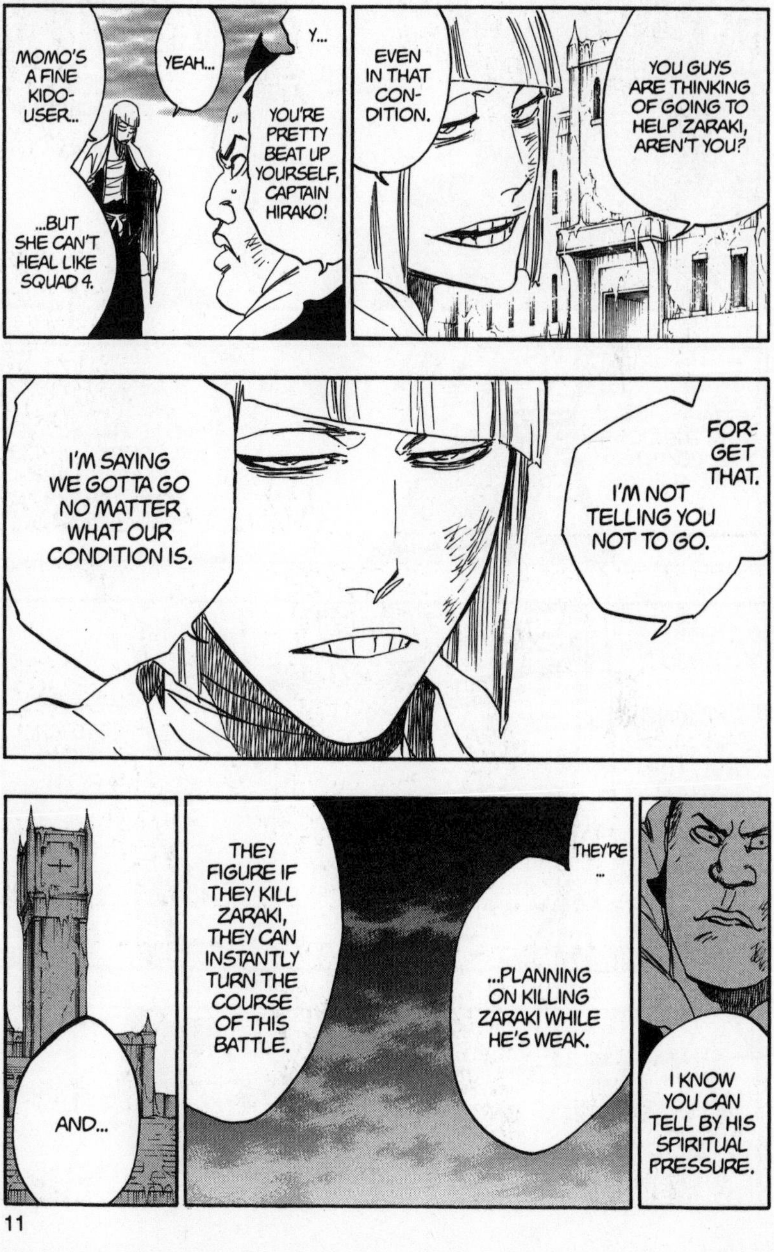
YOU GUYS ARE THINKING OF GOING TO HELP ZARAKI, AREN'T YOU?
EVEN IN THAT CON-DITION.
Y...
YOU'RE PRETTY BEAT UP YOURSELF, CAPTAIN HIRAKO!
YEAH...
MOMO'S A FINE KIDO-USER...
...BUT SHE CAN'T HEAL LIKE SQUAD 4.
FOR-GET THAT.
I'M NOT TELLING YOU NOT TO GO.
I'M SAYING WE GOTTA GO NO MATTER WHAT OUR CONDITION IS.
I KNOW YOU CAN TELL BY HIS SPIRITUAL PRESSURE.
THEY'RE...
...PLANNING ON KILLING ZARAKI WHILE HE'S WEAK.
THEY FIGURE IF THEY KILL ZARAKI, THEY CAN INSTANTLY TURN THE COURSE OF THIS BATTLE.
AND...

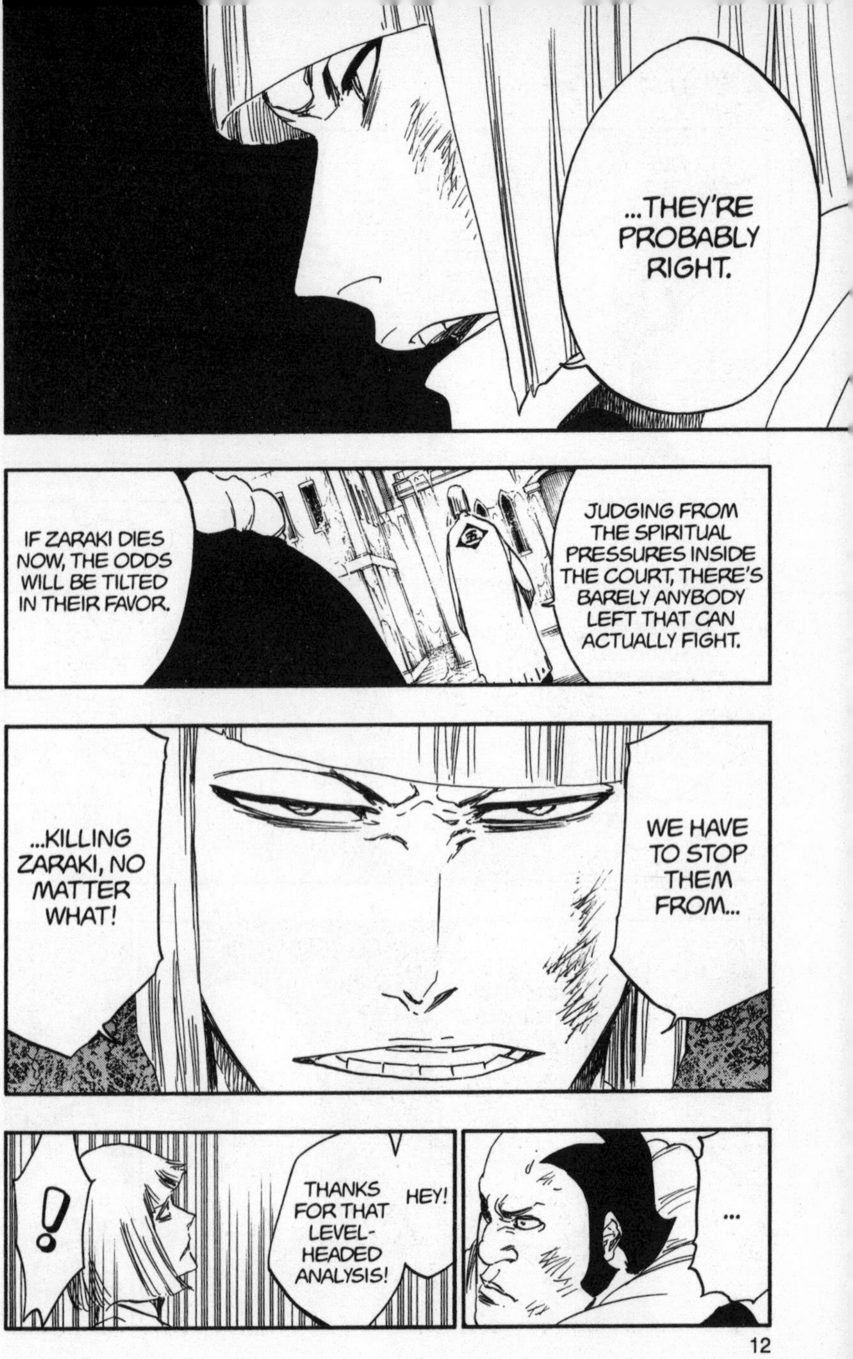
...THEY'RE PROBABLY RIGHT.
JUDGING FROM THE SPIRITUAL PRESSURES INSIDE THE COURT, THERE'S BARELY ANYBODY LEFT THAT CAN ACTUALLY FIGHT.
IF ZARAKI DIES NOW, THE ODDS WILL BE TILTED IN THEIR FAVOR.
WE HAVE TO STOP THEM FROM...
...KILLING ZARAKI, NO MATTER WHAT!
...
HEY!
THANKS FOR THAT LEVEL-HEADED ANALYSIS!
!

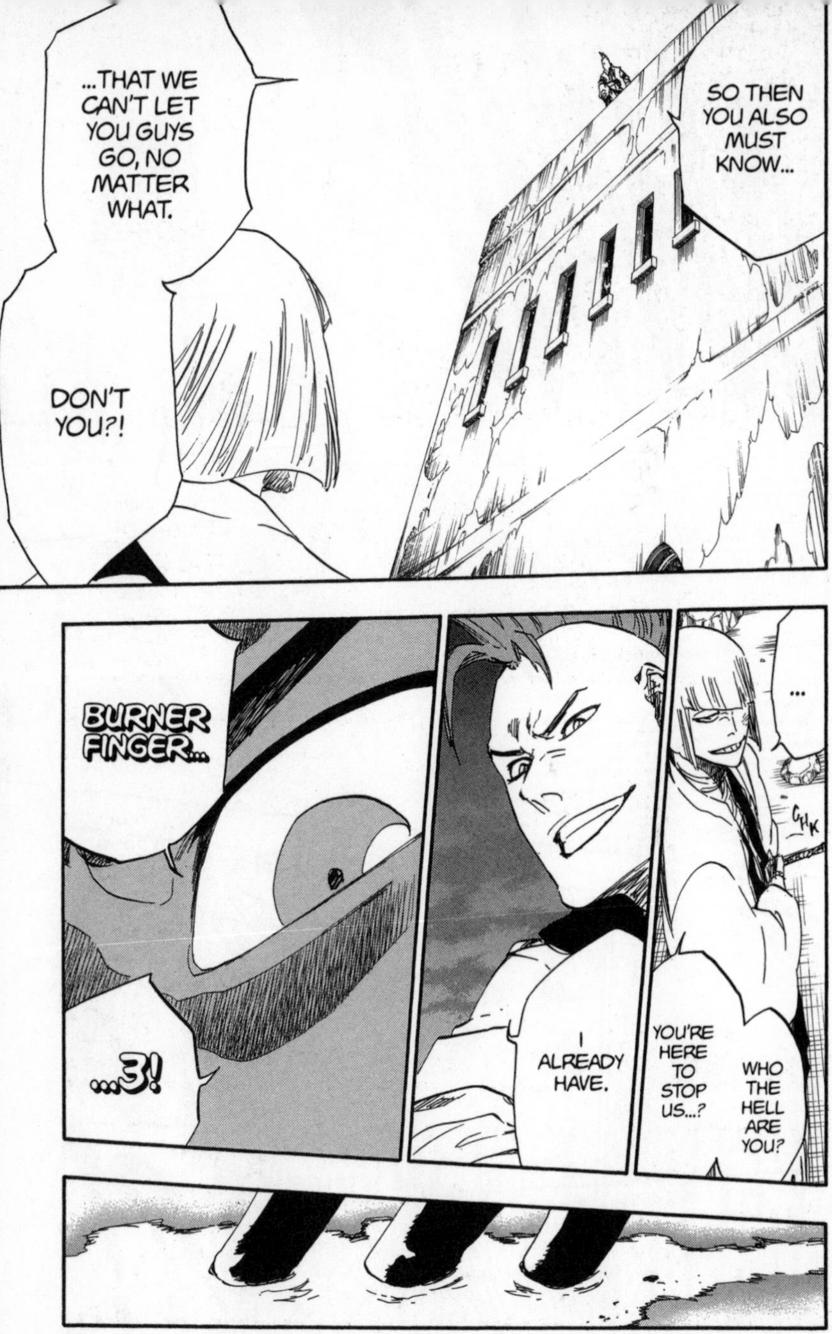
SO THEN YOU ALSO MUST KNOW...
...THAT WE CAN'T LET YOU GUYS GO, NO MATTER WHAT.
DON'T YOU?!
...
CHK
WHO THE HELL ARE YOU?
YOU'RE HERE TO STOP US...?
I ALREADY HAVE.
BURNER FINGER...
...3!

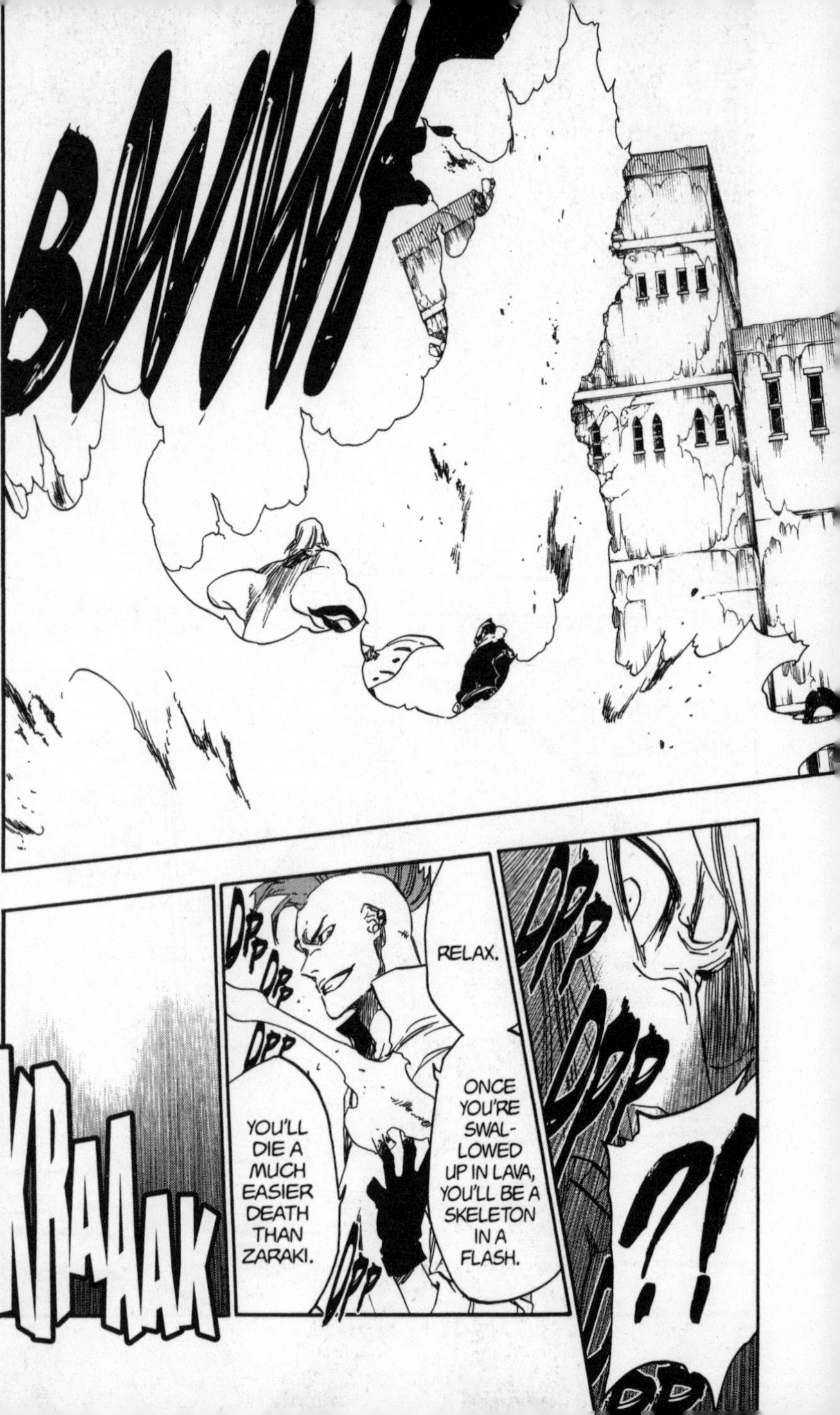
BWWF
?!
RELAX.
ONCE YOU'RE SWAL-LOWED UP IN LAVA, YOU'LL BE A SKELETON IN A FLASH.
YOU'LL DIE A MUCH EASIER DEATH THAN ZARAKI.
KRAAAK

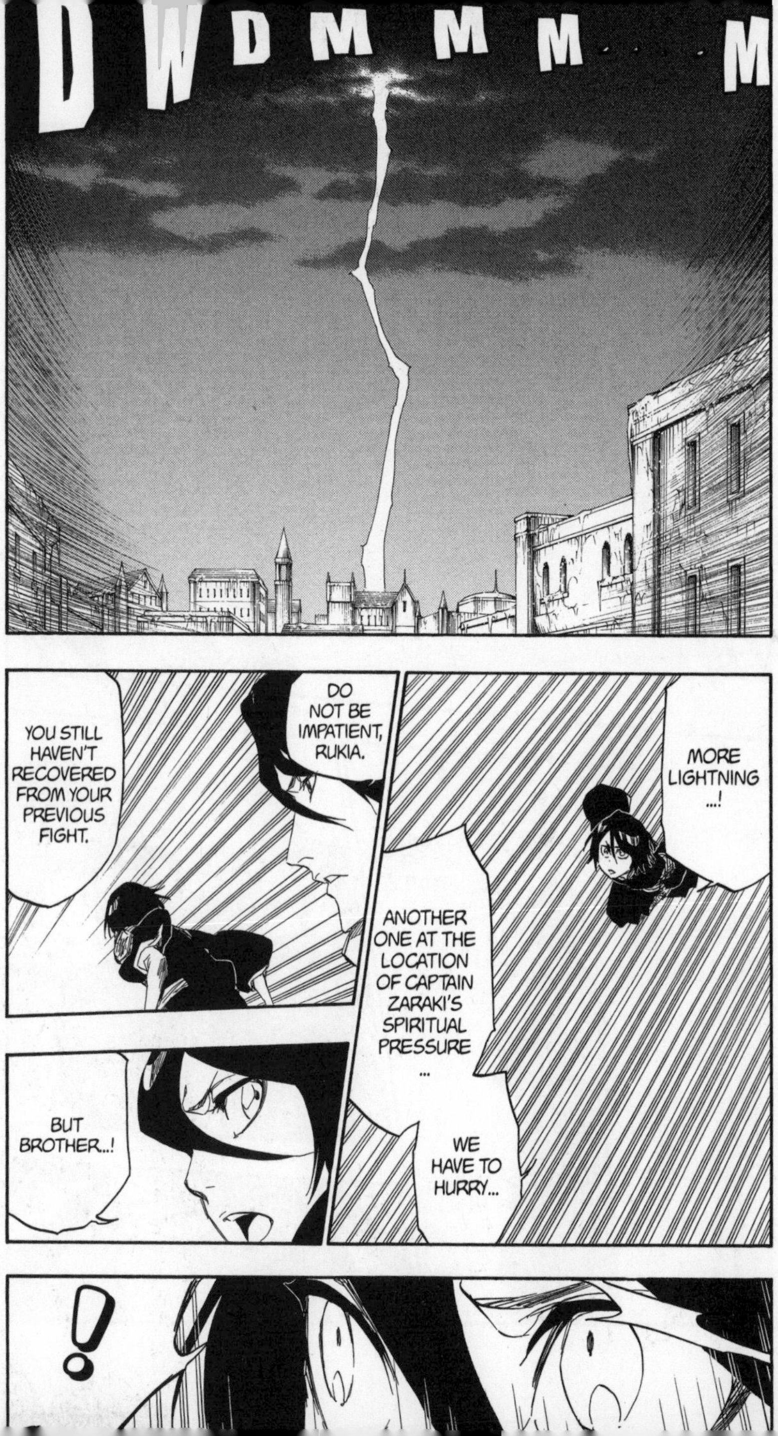
DWDMMM...M
MORE LIGHTNING ...!
ANOTHER ONE AT THE LOCATION OF CAPTAIN ZARAKI'S SPIRITUAL PRESSURE ...
WE HAVE TO HURRY...
DO NOT BE IMPATIENT, RUKIA.
YOU STILL HAVEN'T RECOVERED FROM YOUR PREVIOUS FIGHT.
BUT BROTHER...!
!

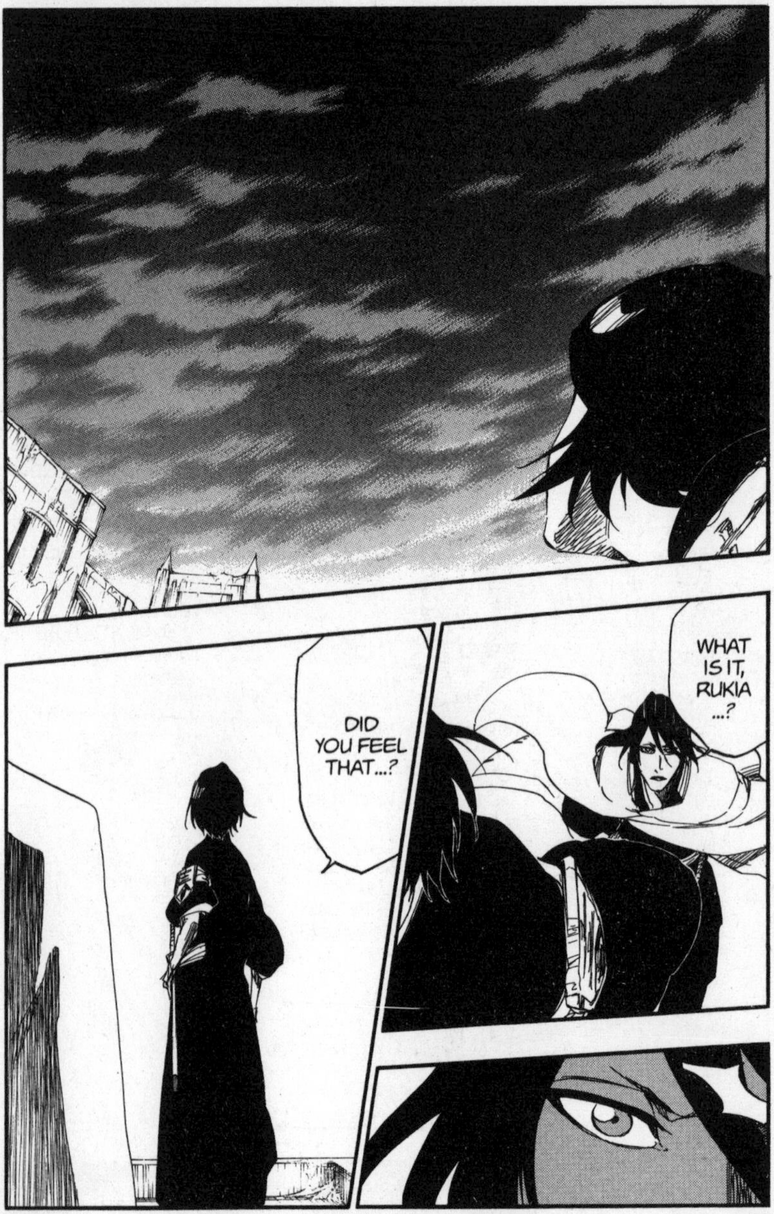
WHAT IS IT, RUKIA ...?
DID YOU FEEL THAT...?

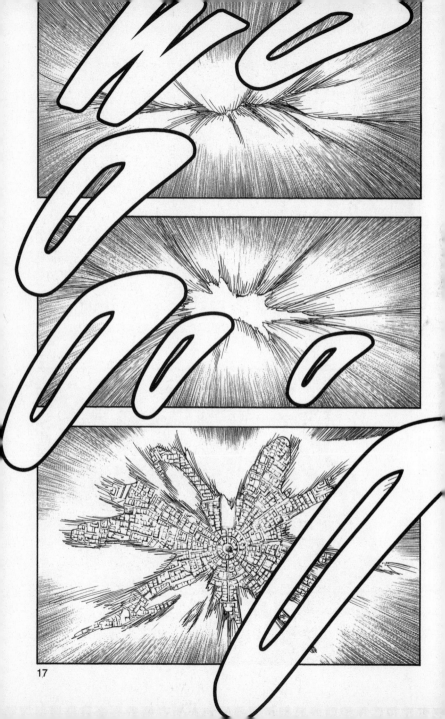

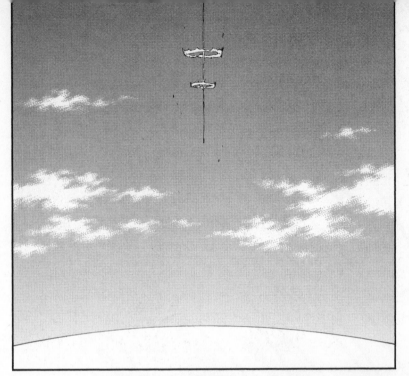

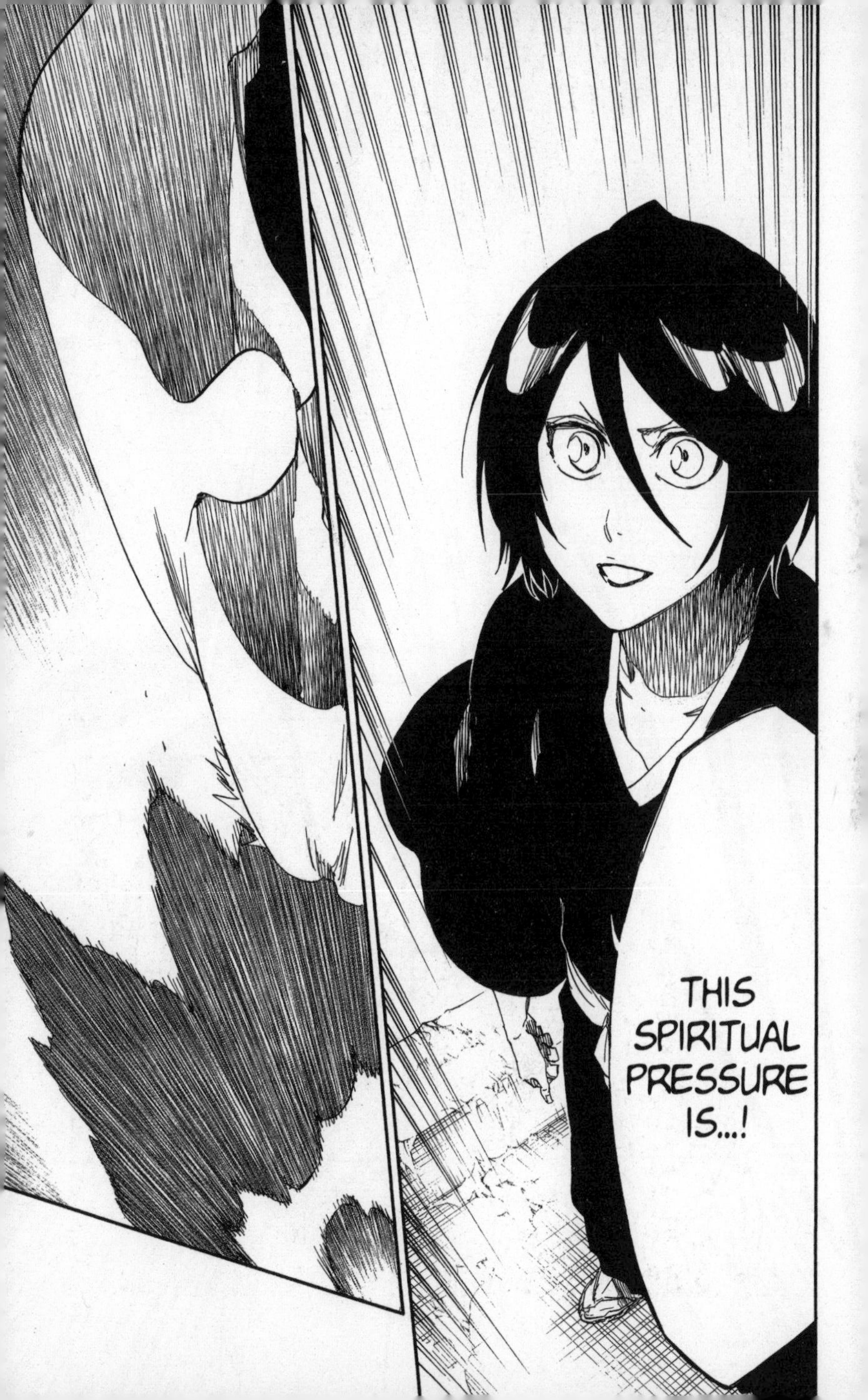
THIS SPIRITUAL PRESSURE IS...!

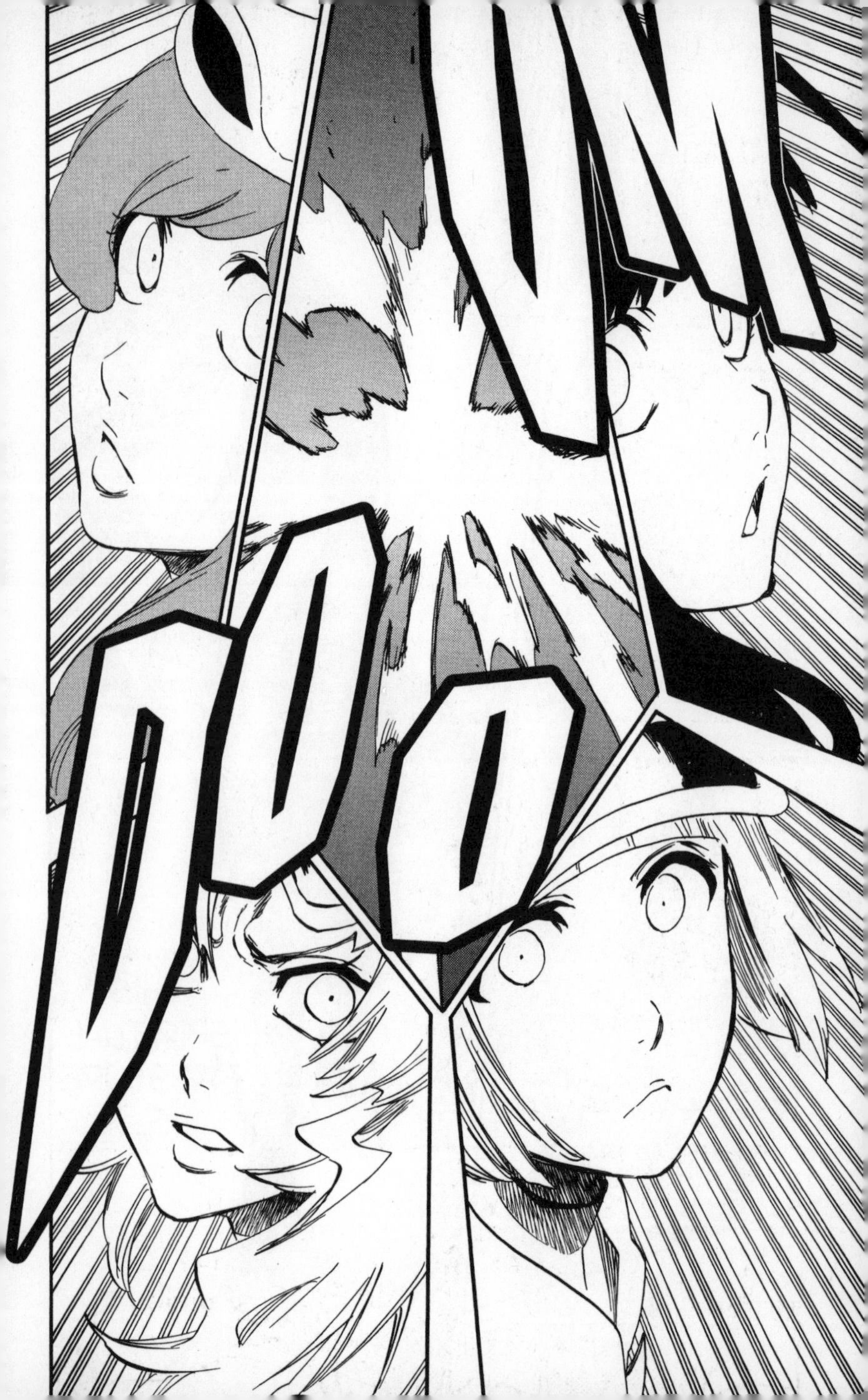
DOOM

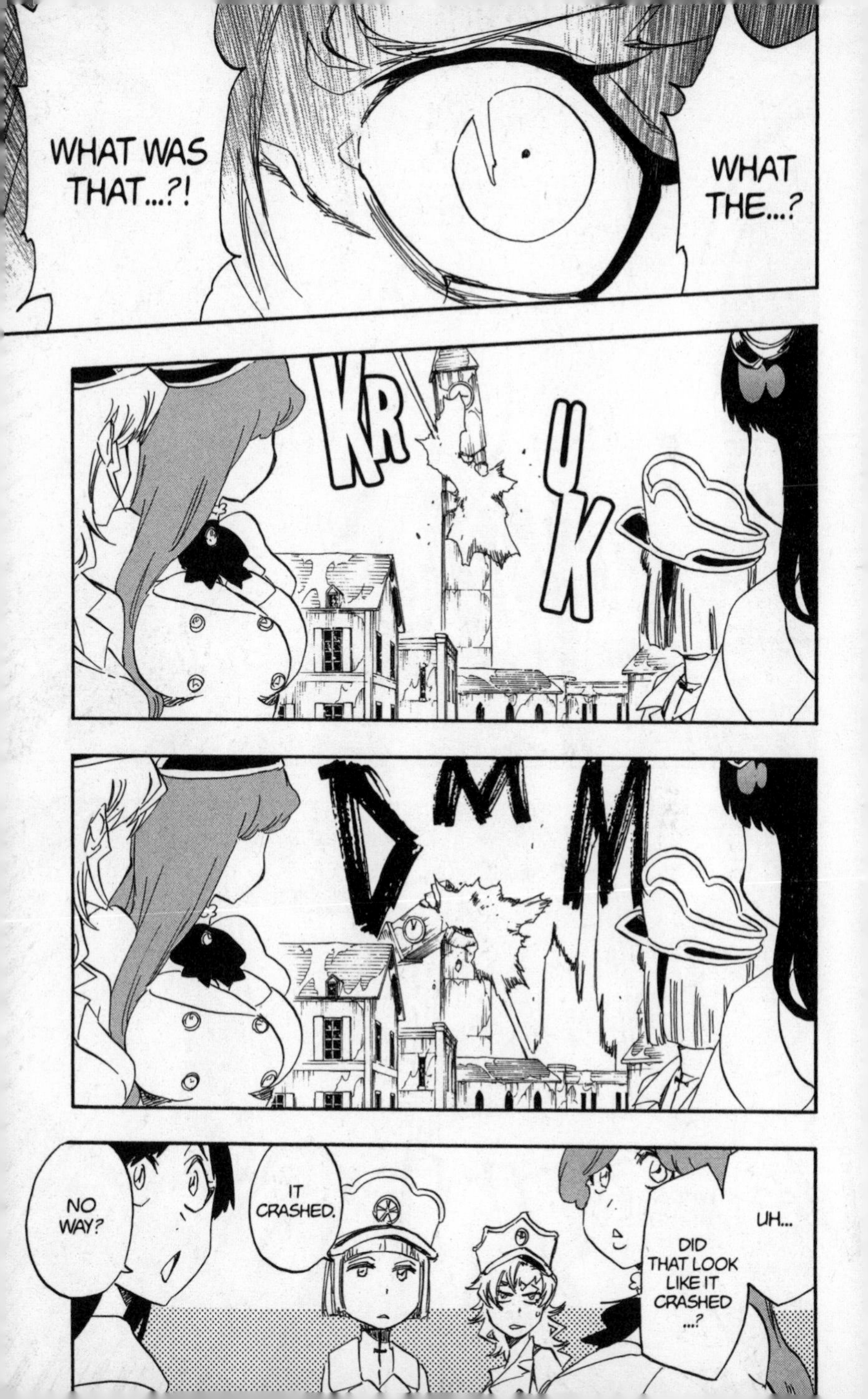

WHAT THE...?
WHAT WAS THAT...?!
KRUK
DMM
UH...
DID THAT LOOK LIKE IT CRASHED ...?
IT CRASHED.
NO WAY?

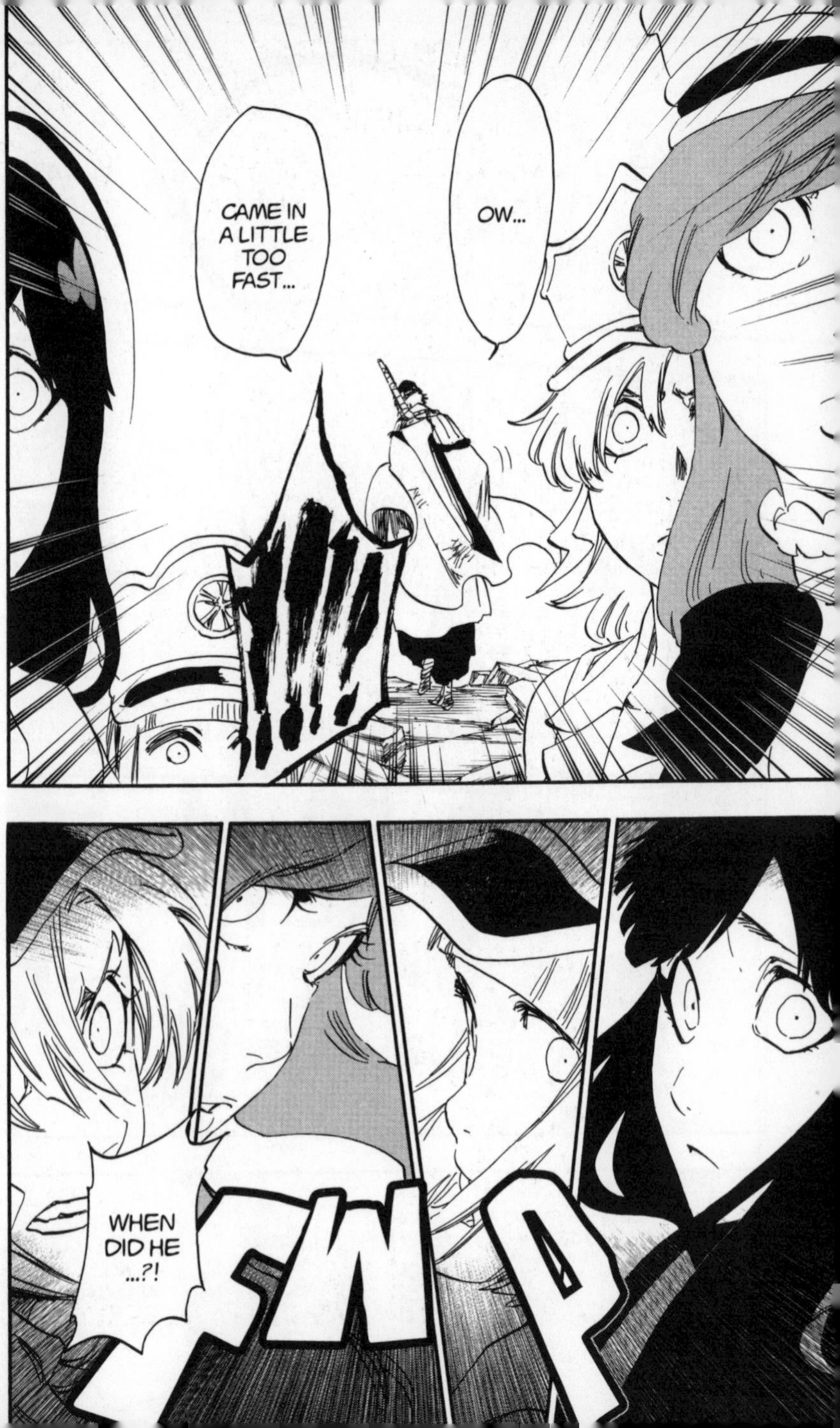
OW...
CAME IN A LITTLE TOO FAST...
WHEN DID HE ...?!

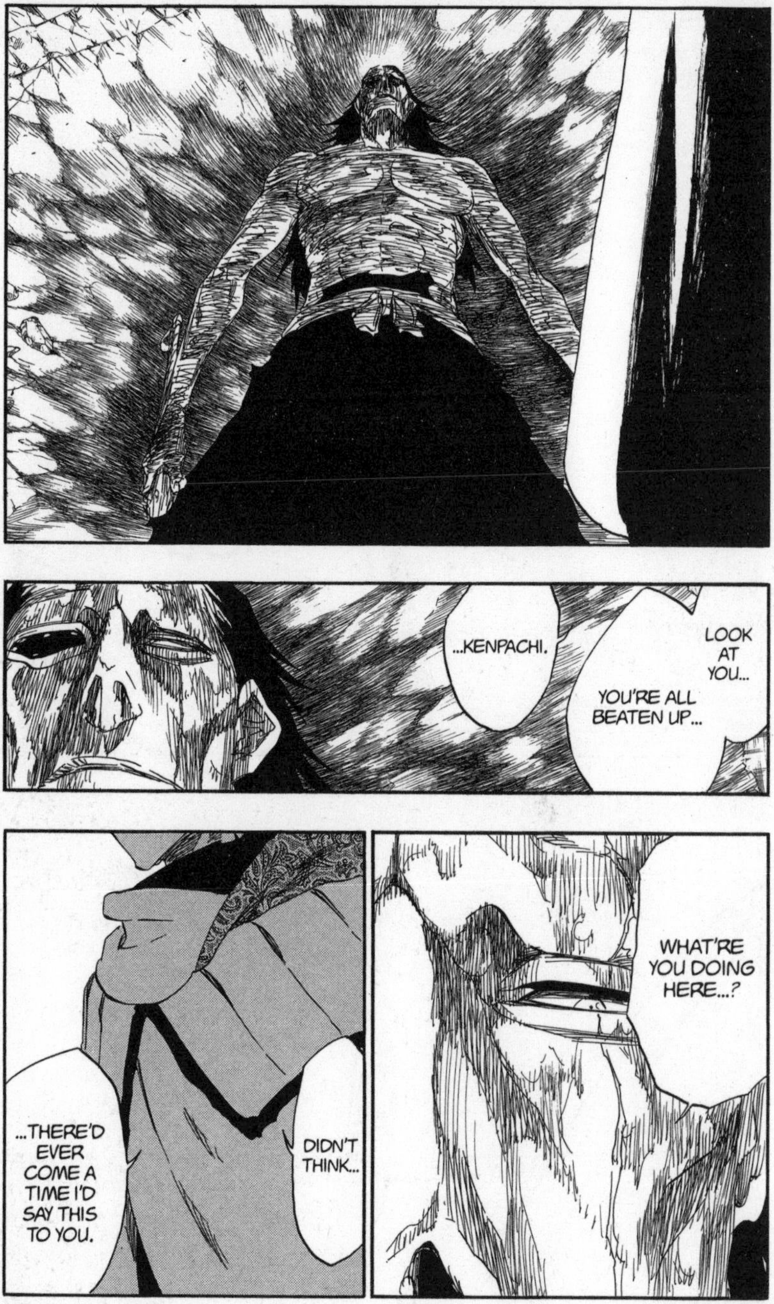
LOOK AT YOU...
YOU'RE ALL BEATEN UP...
...KENPACHI.
WHAT'RE YOU DOING HERE...?
DIDN'T THINK...
...THERE'D EVER COME A TIME I'D SAY THIS TO YOU.

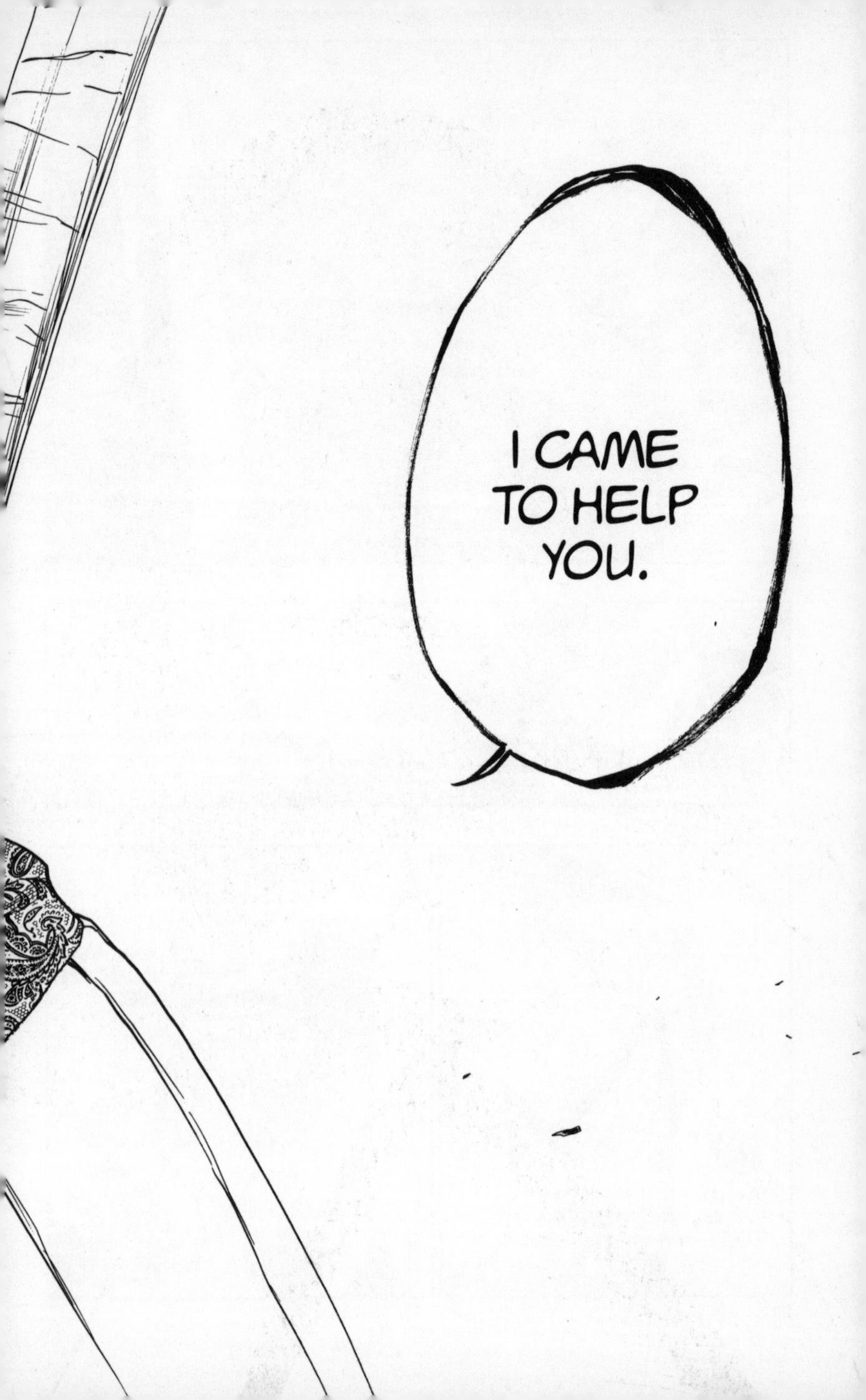
I CAME TO HELP YOU.

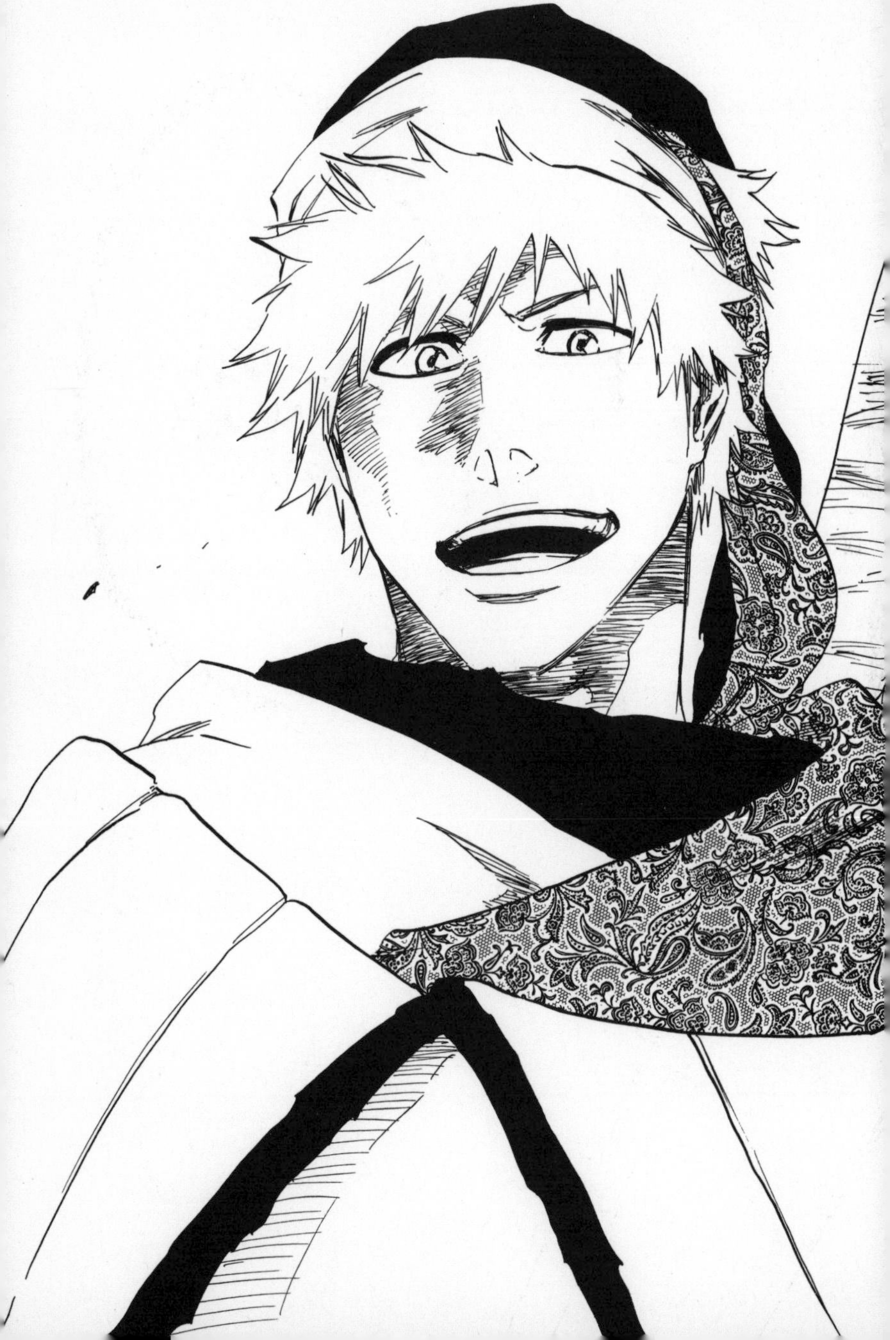

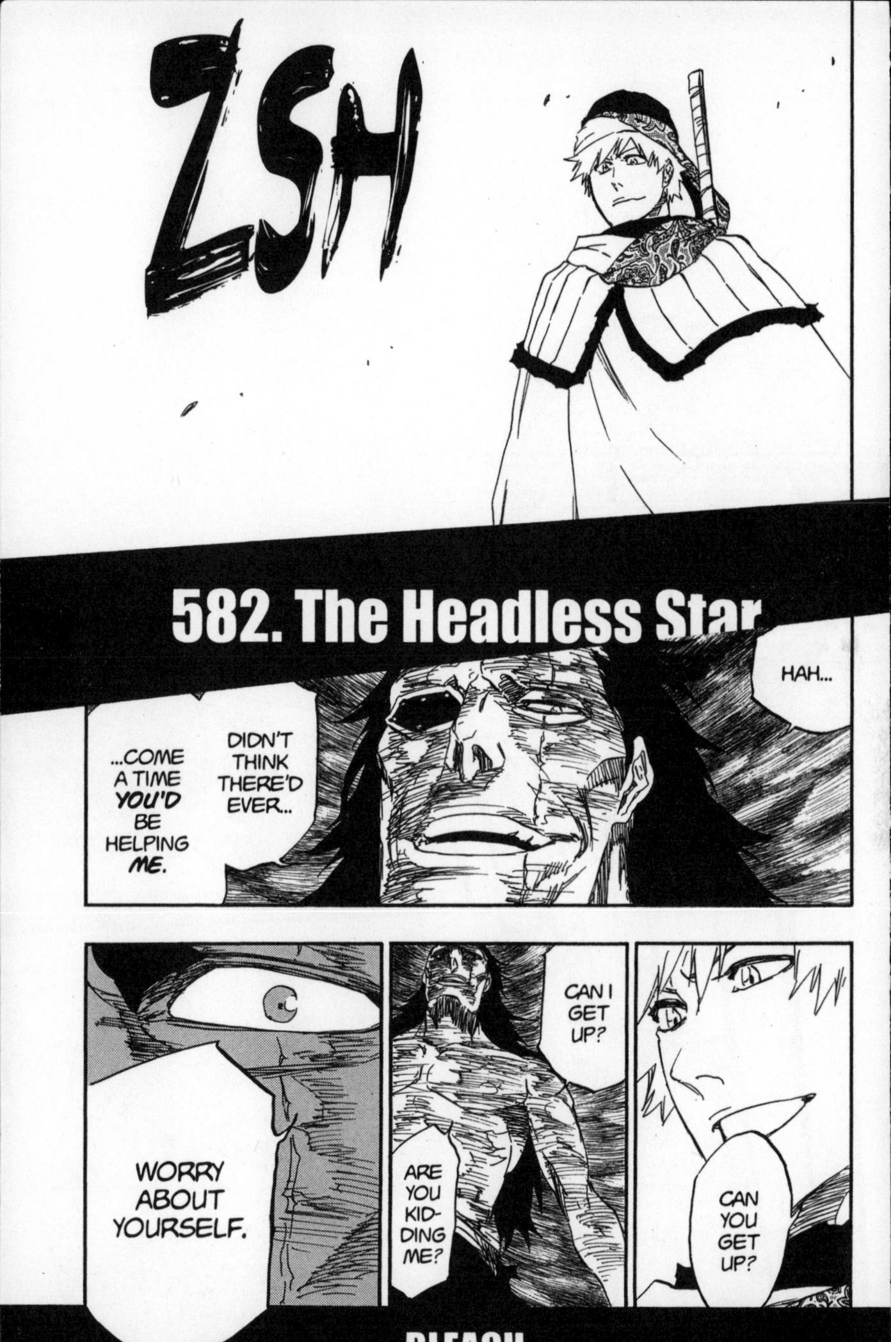
ZSH
582. The Headless Star
HAH...
DIDN'T THINK THERE'D EVER...
...COME A TIME *YOU'D* BE HELPING *ME*.
CAN YOU GET UP?
CAN I GET UP?
ARE YOU KID-DING ME?
WORRY ABOUT YOURSELF.

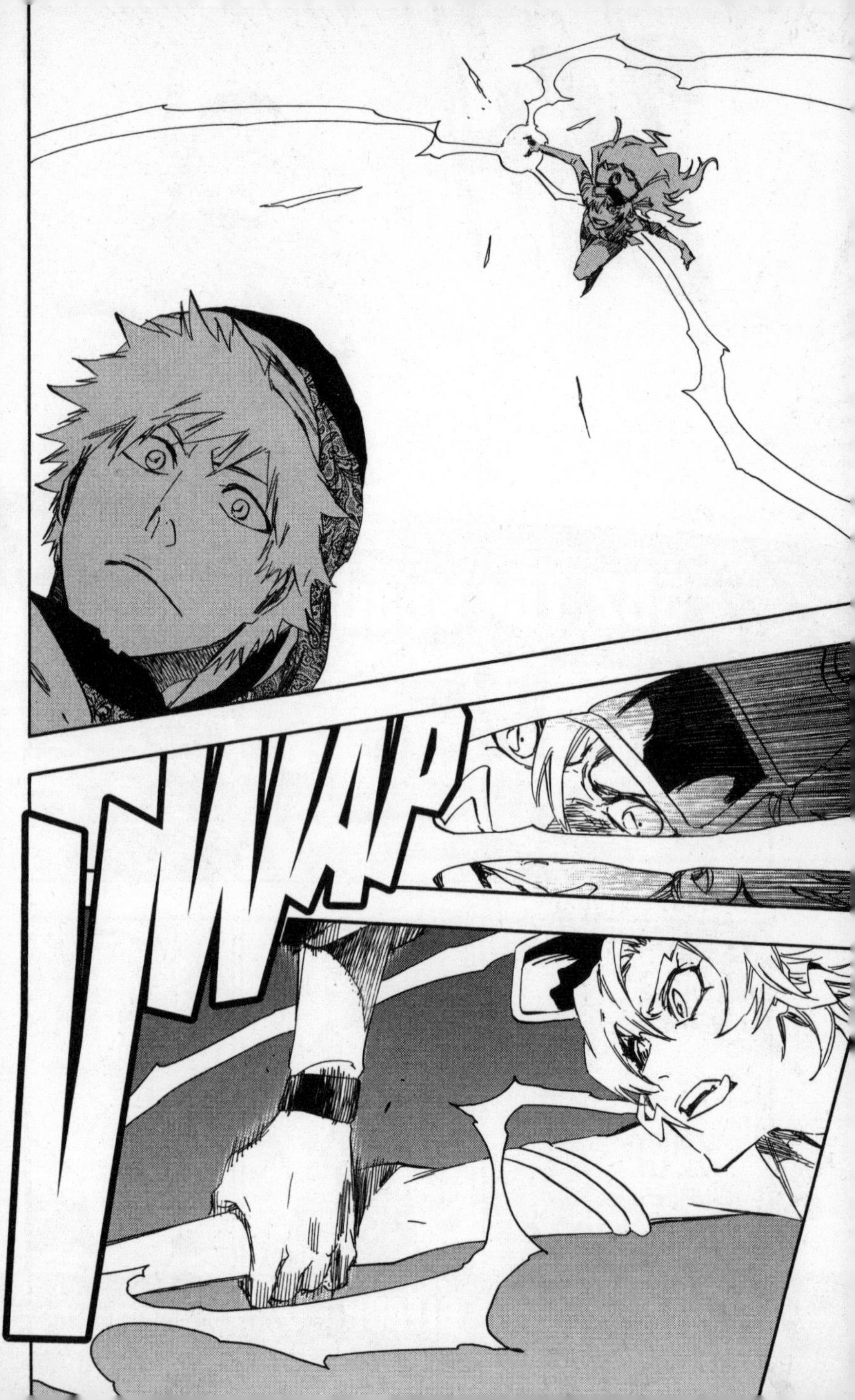
WAP

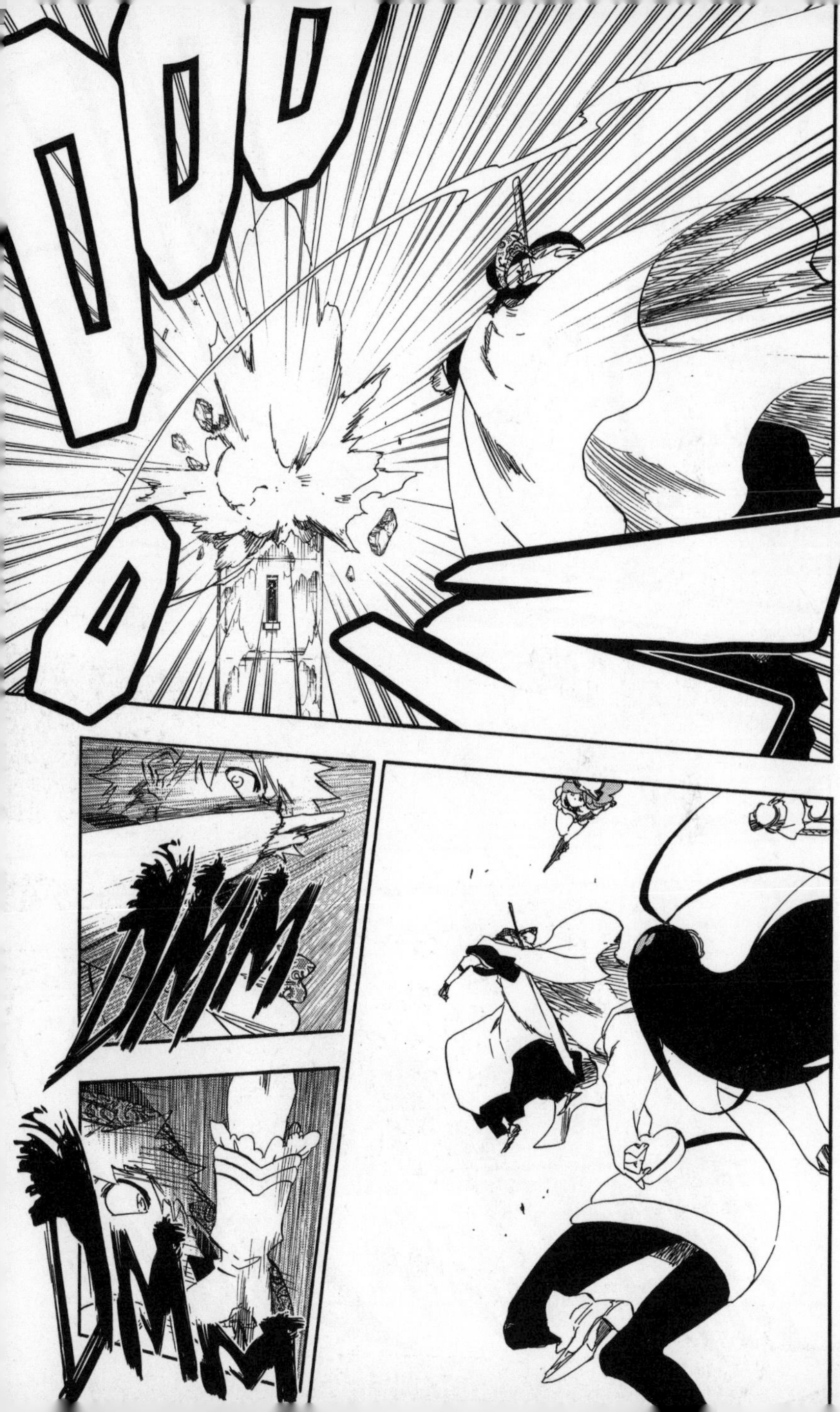
DMM
DMM

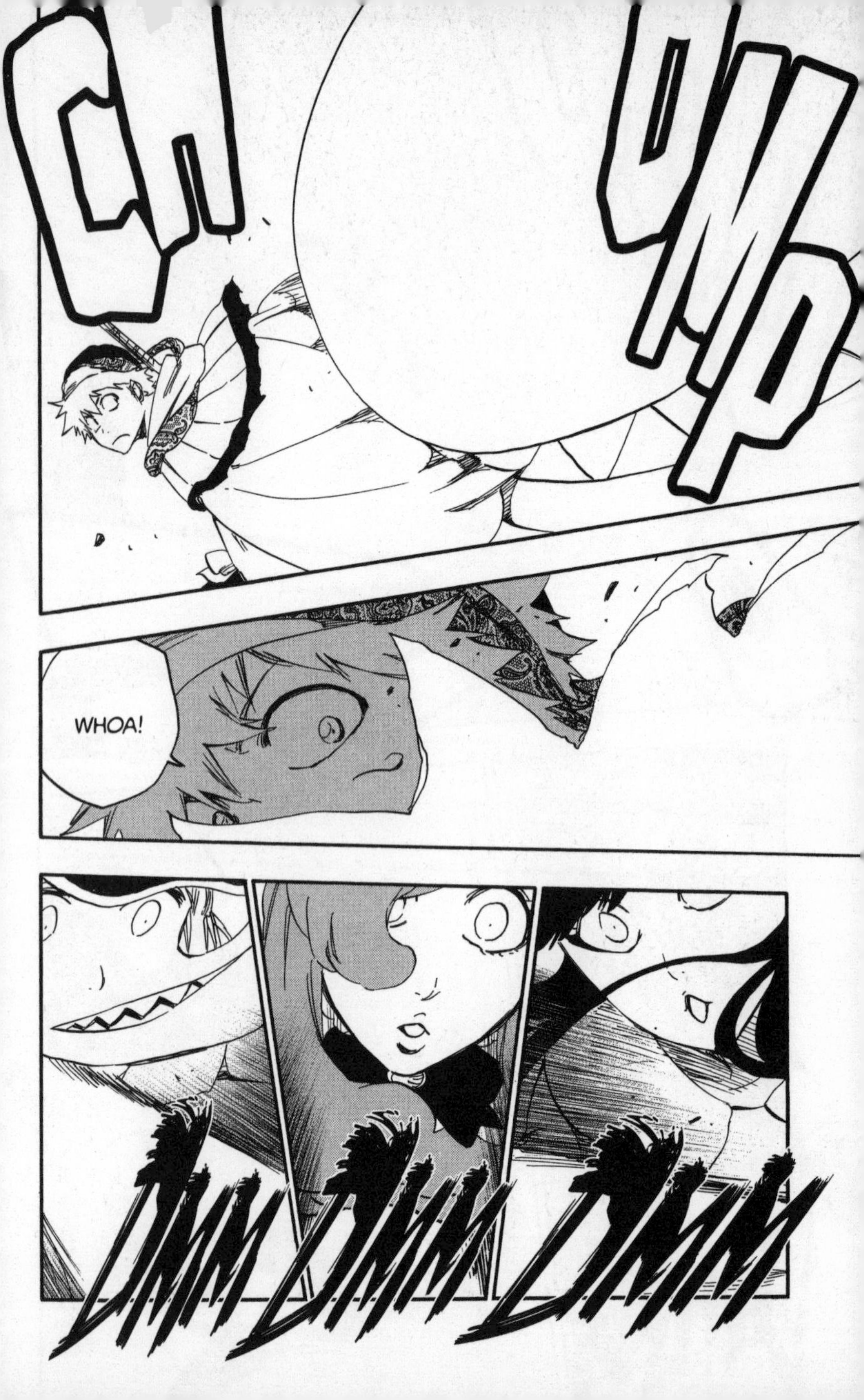
CH
OMP
WHOA!

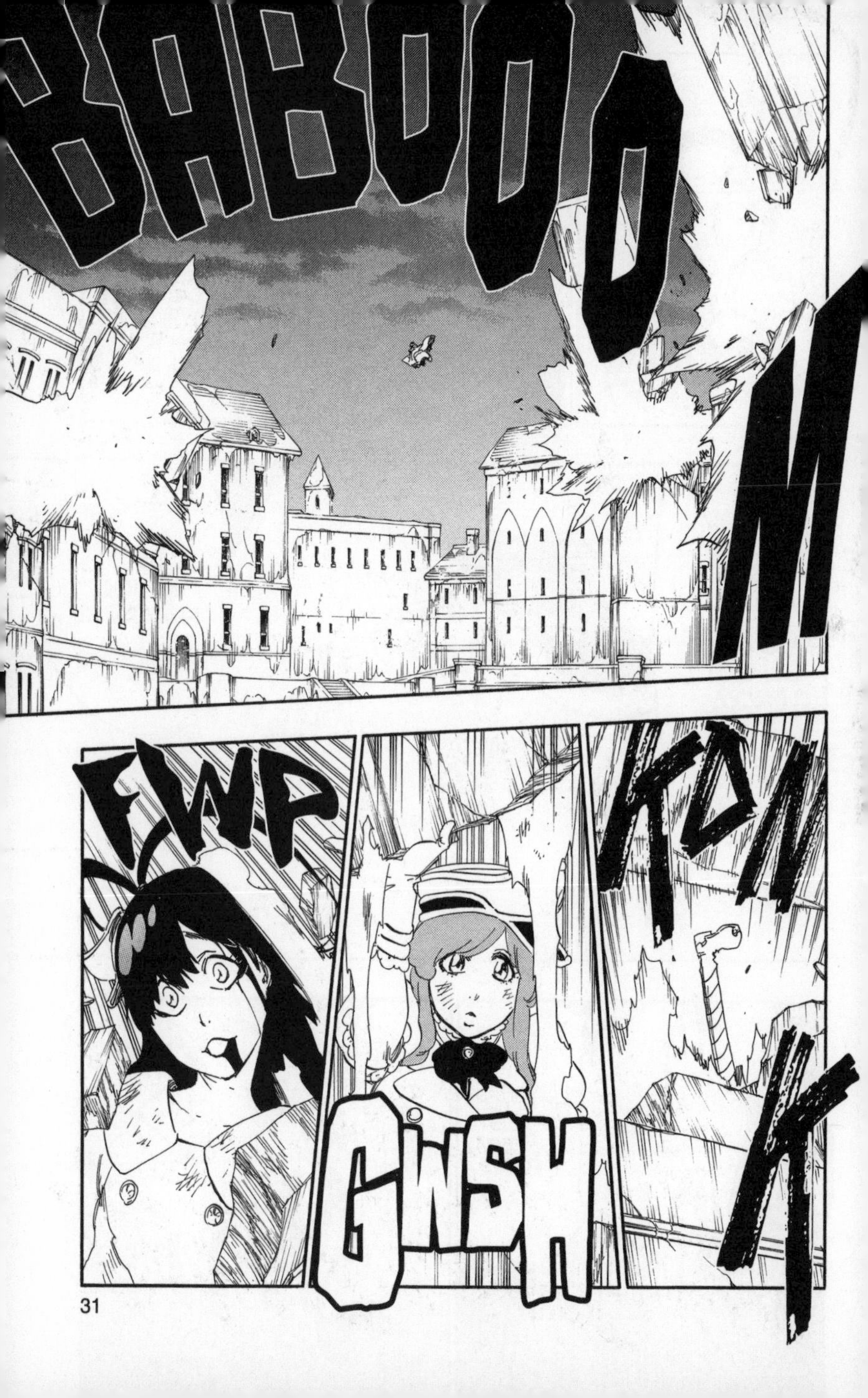
BABOOOM
KRNK
GWSH
FWP

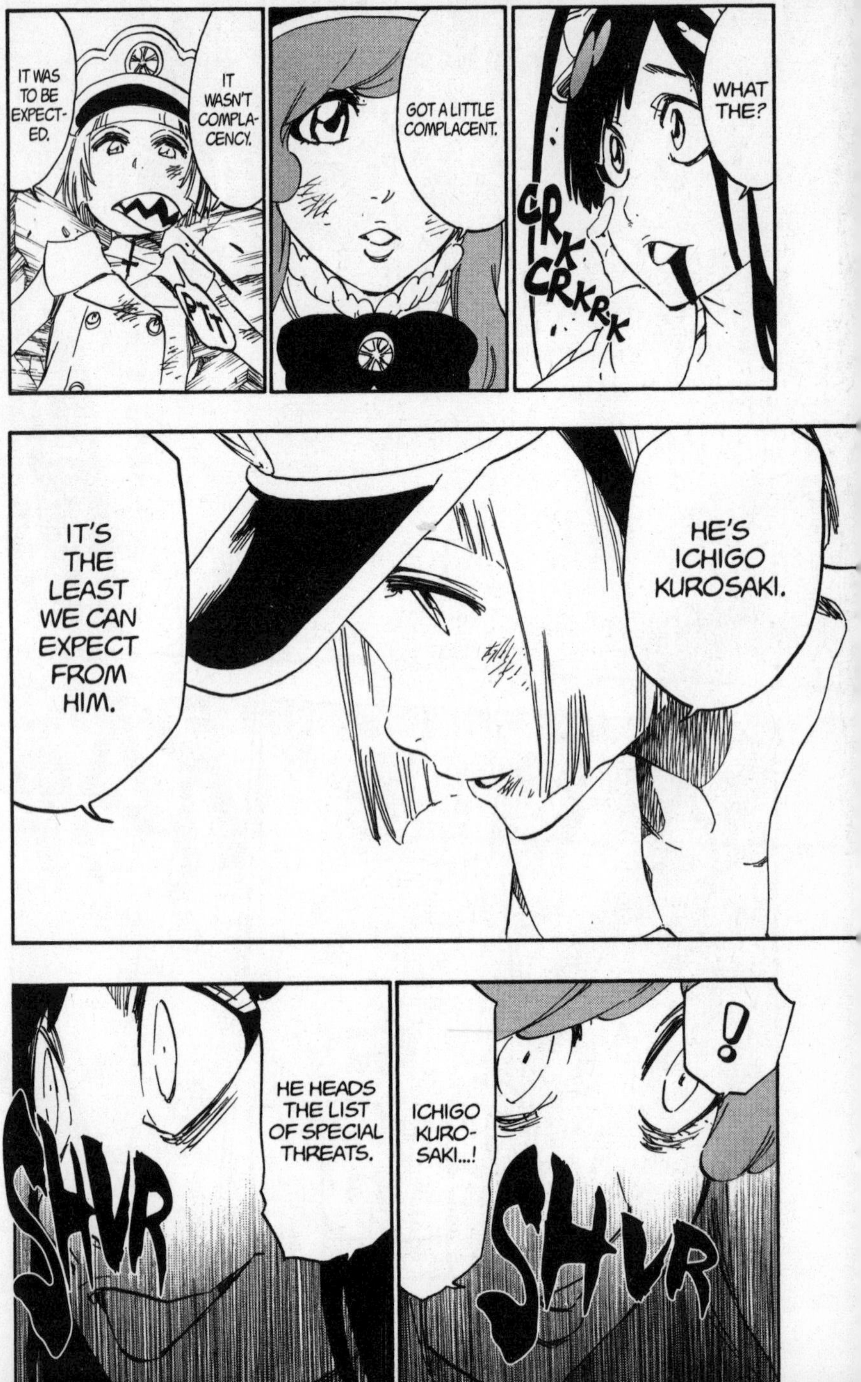
WHAT THE?
CRK
CRKRKRK
GOT A LITTLE COMPLACENT.
IT WASN'T COMPLA-CENCY.
IT WAS TO BE EXPECT-ED.
PTT
HE'S ICHIGO KUROSAKI.
IT'S THE LEAST WE CAN EXPECT FROM HIM.
!
ICHIGO KURO-SAKI...!
SHVR
HE HEADS THE LIST OF SPECIAL THREATS.
SHVR

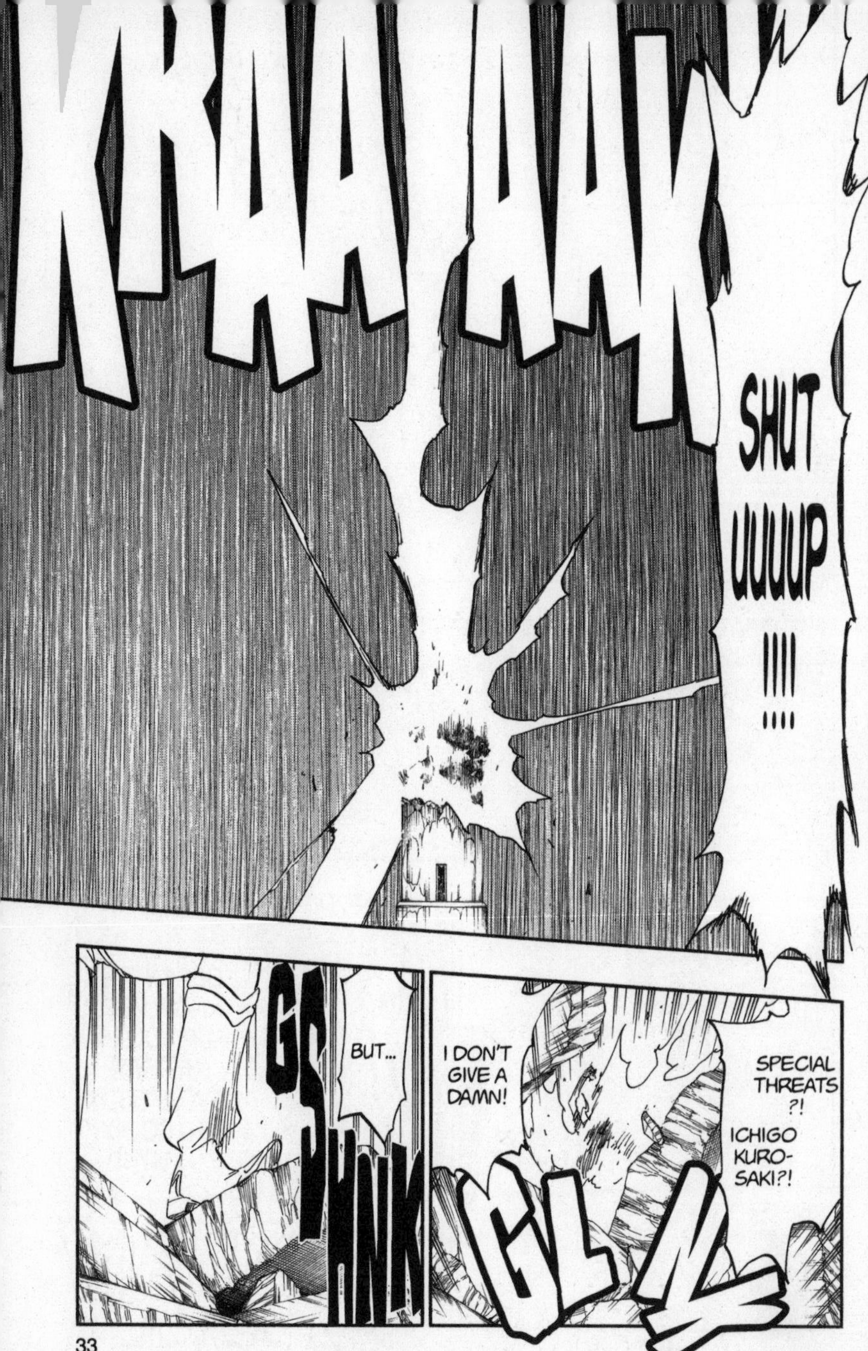
KRAAAK
SHUT UUUUP!!!!!!!!
SPECIAL THREATS?!
ICHIGO KURO-SAKI?!
I DON'T GIVE A DAMN!
GLNK
BUT...
GSHNK

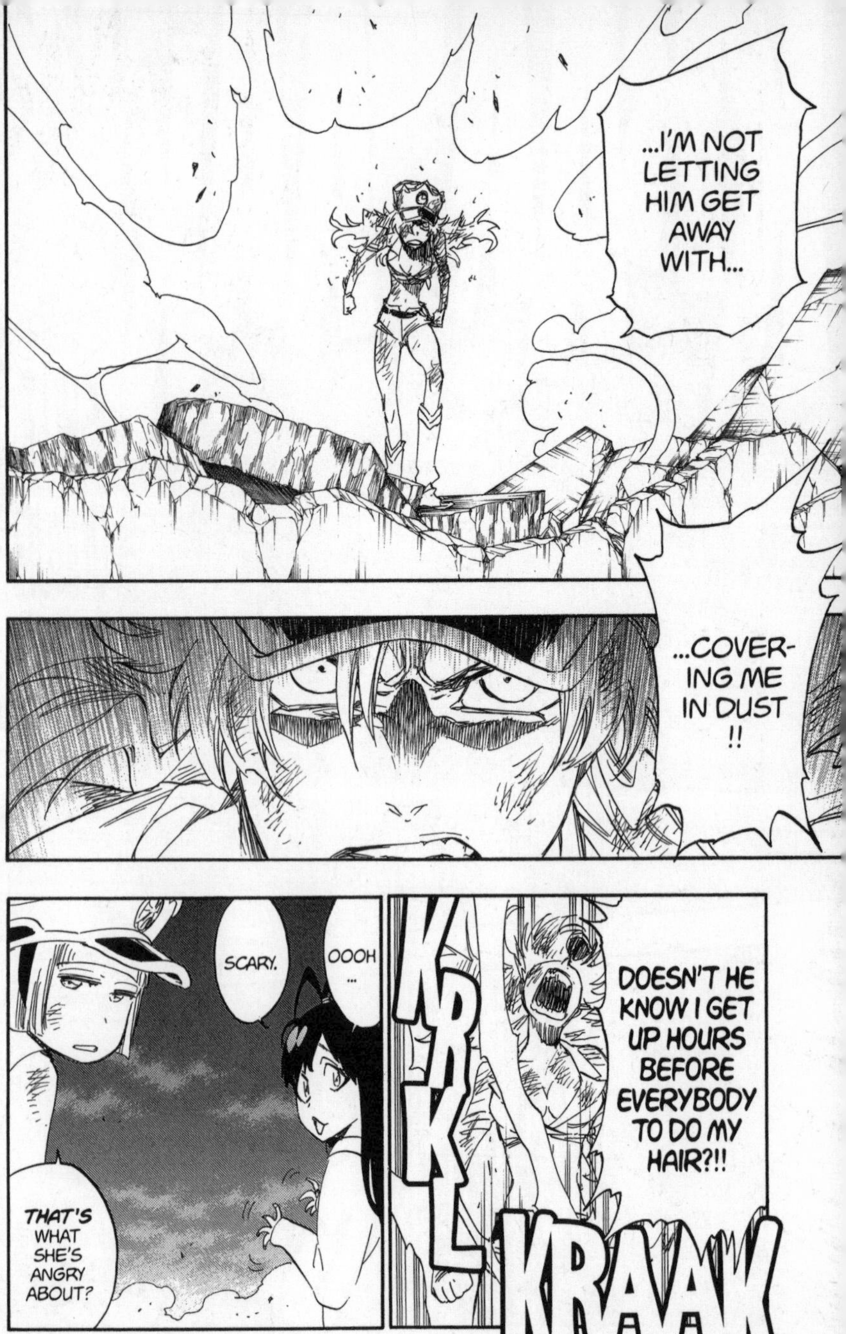
...I'M NOT LETTING HIM GET AWAY WITH...
...COVERING ME IN DUST !!
KRKL
DOESN'T HE KNOW I GET UP HOURS BEFORE EVERYBODY TO DO MY HAIR?!!
KRAAK
OOOH ...
SCARY.
THAT'S WHAT SHE'S ANGRY ABOUT?

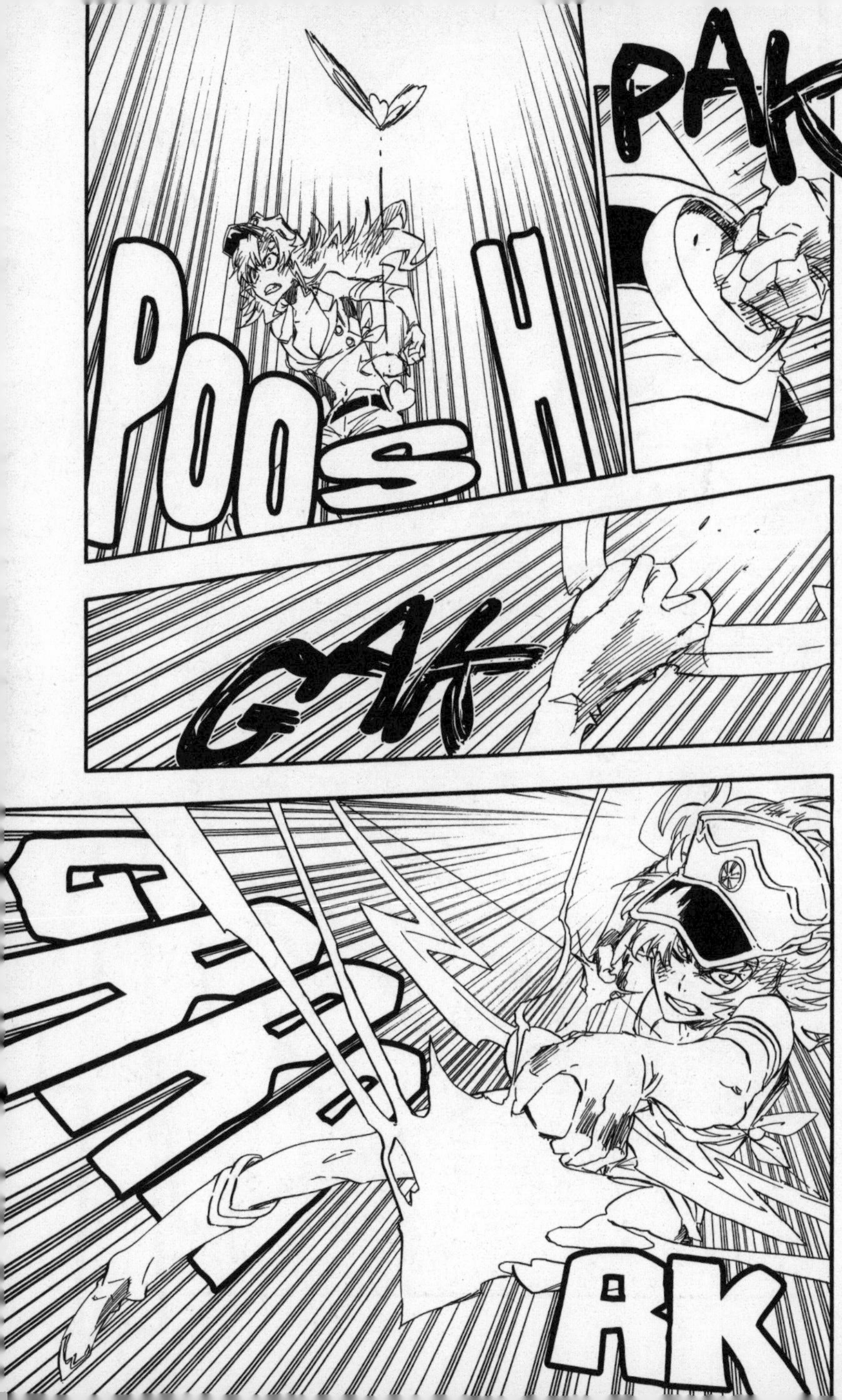
PAK
POOSH
GAH
AK

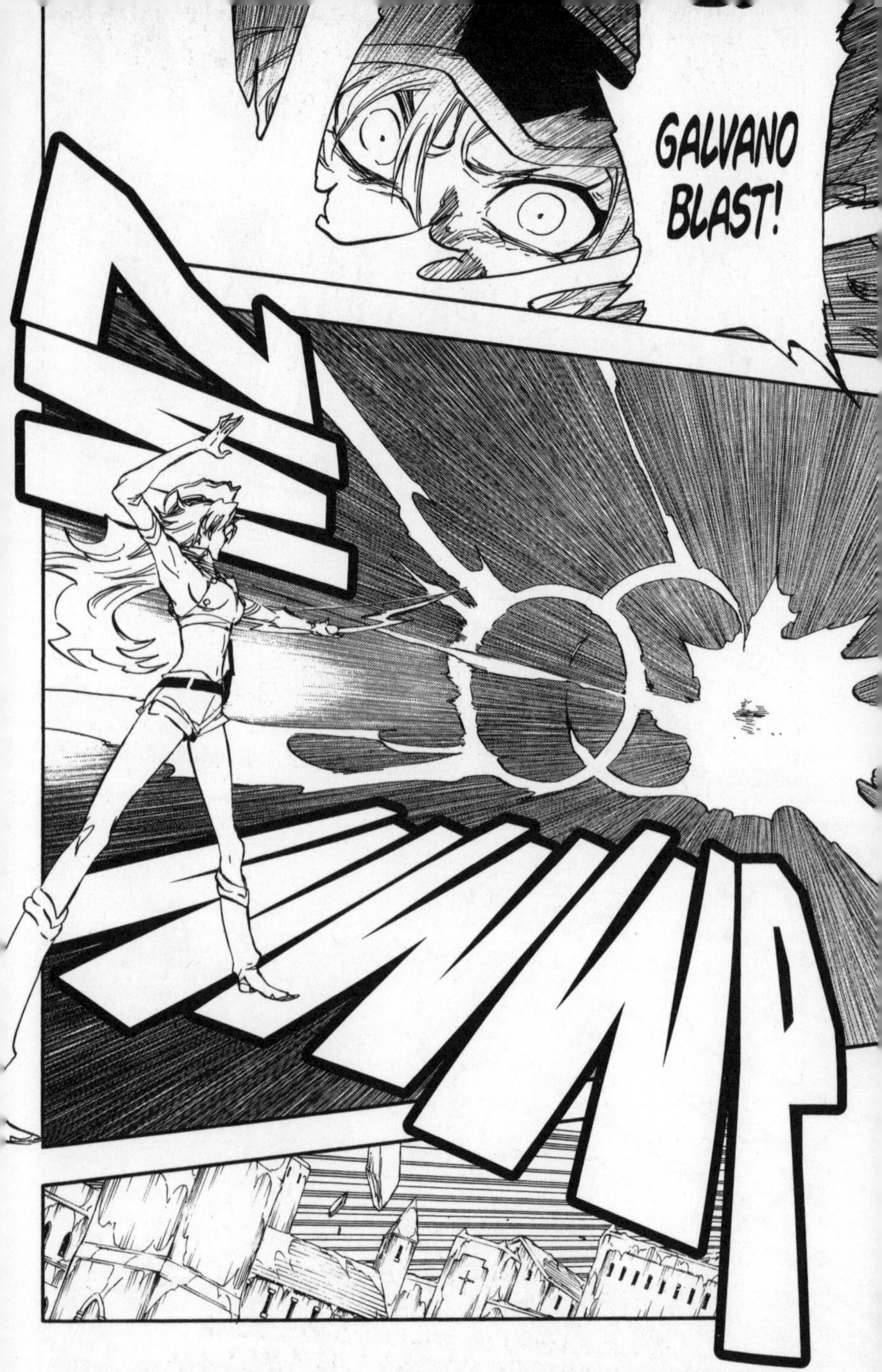
GALVANO BLAST!

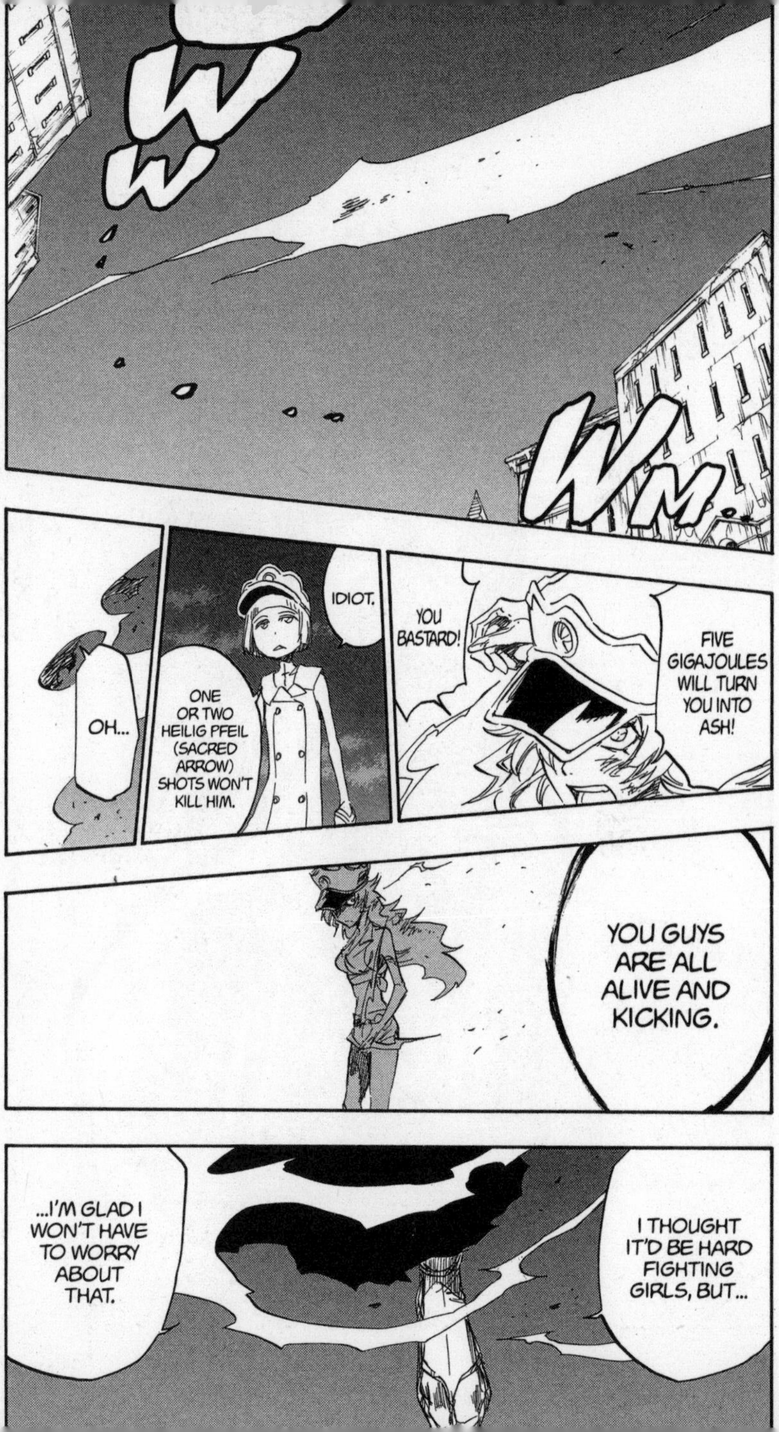
WWW
Wm...
FIVE GIGAJOULES WILL TURN YOU INTO ASH!
YOU BASTARD!
IDIOT.
ONE OR TWO HEILIG PFEIL (SACRED ARROW) SHOTS WON'T KILL HIM.
OH...
YOU GUYS ARE ALL ALIVE AND KICKING.
I THOUGHT IT'D BE HARD FIGHTING GIRLS, BUT...
...I'M GLAD I WON'T HAVE TO WORRY ABOUT THAT.

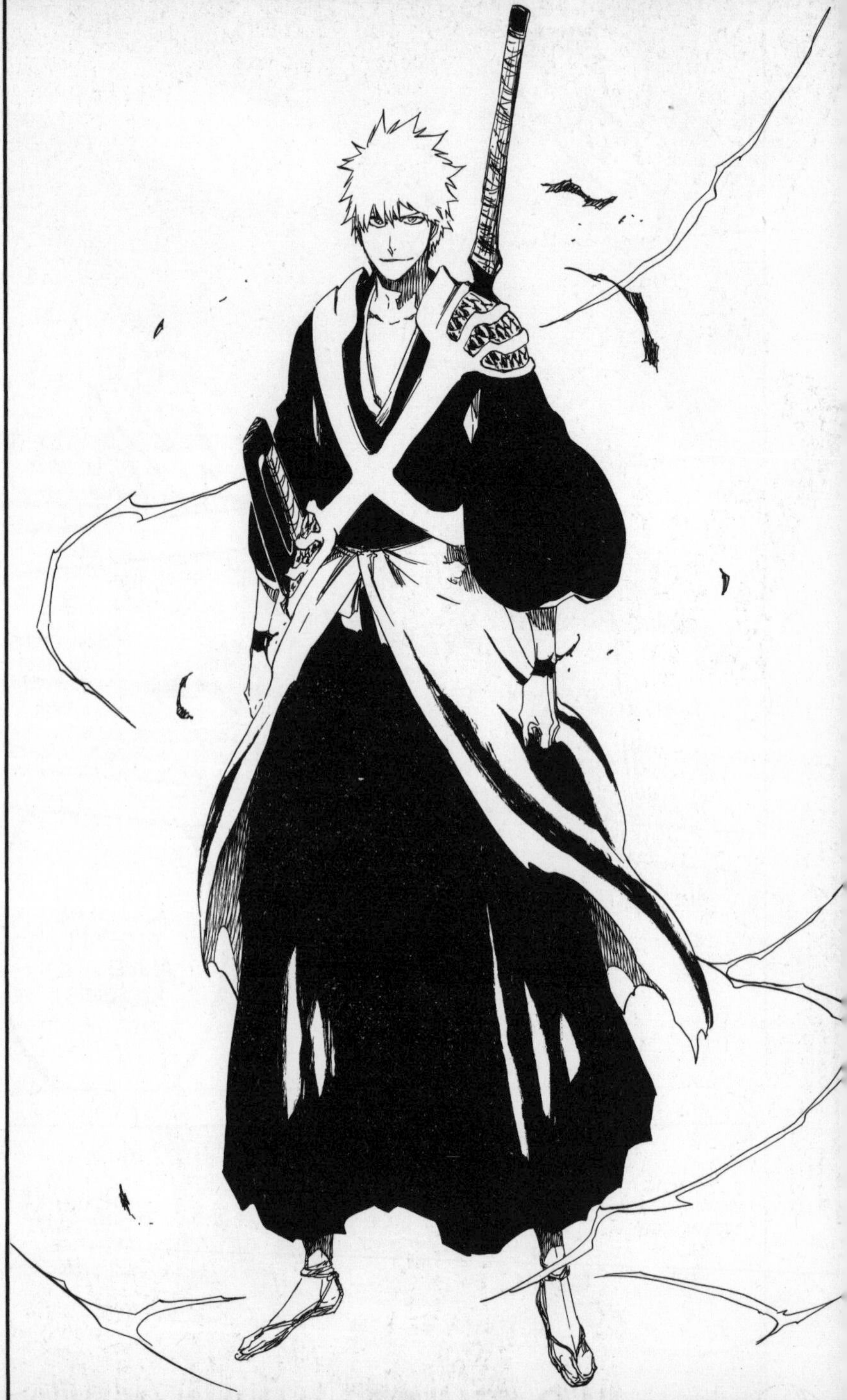

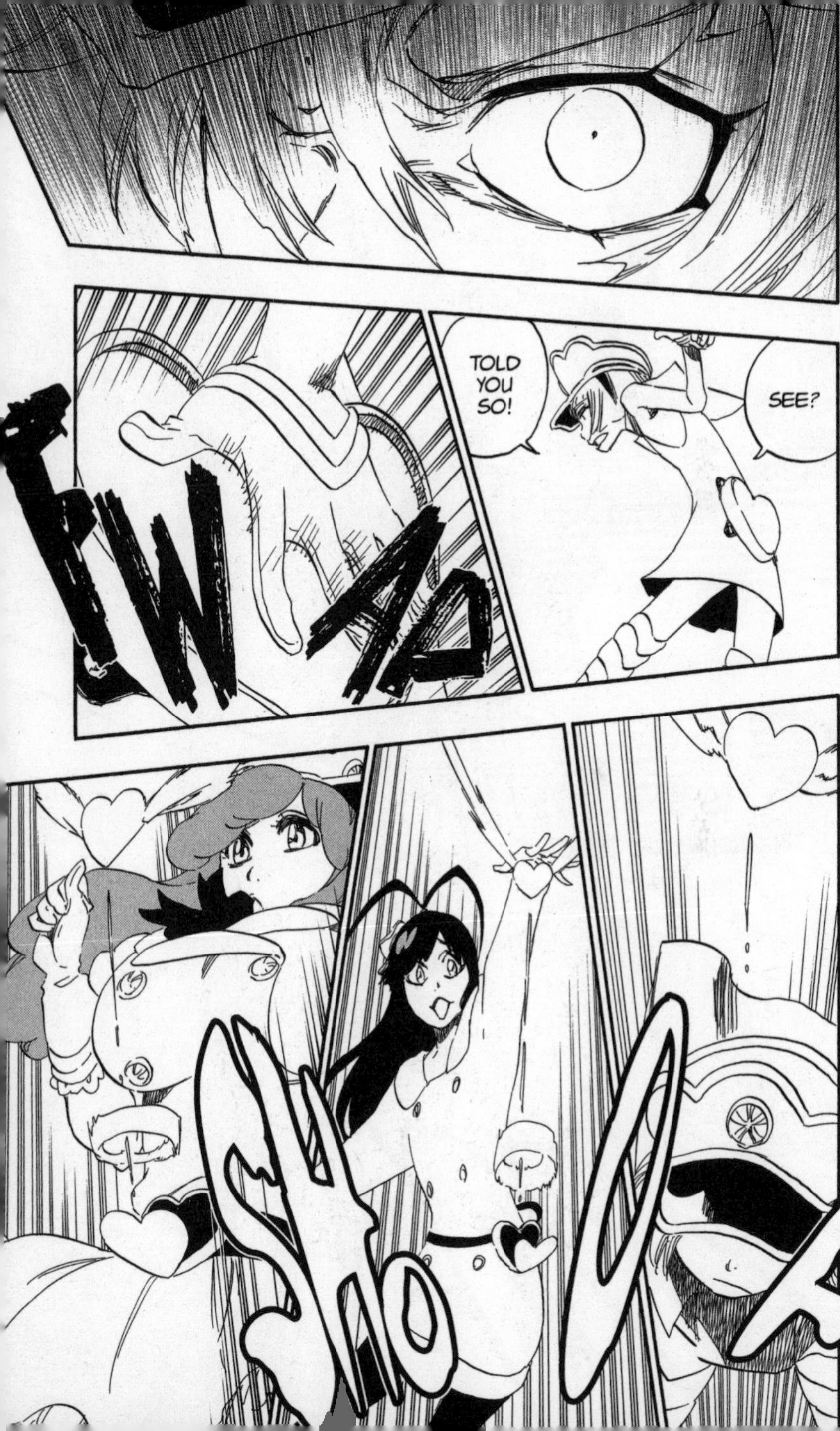
SEE?
TOLD YOU SO!
FWAP
!
SHOOP

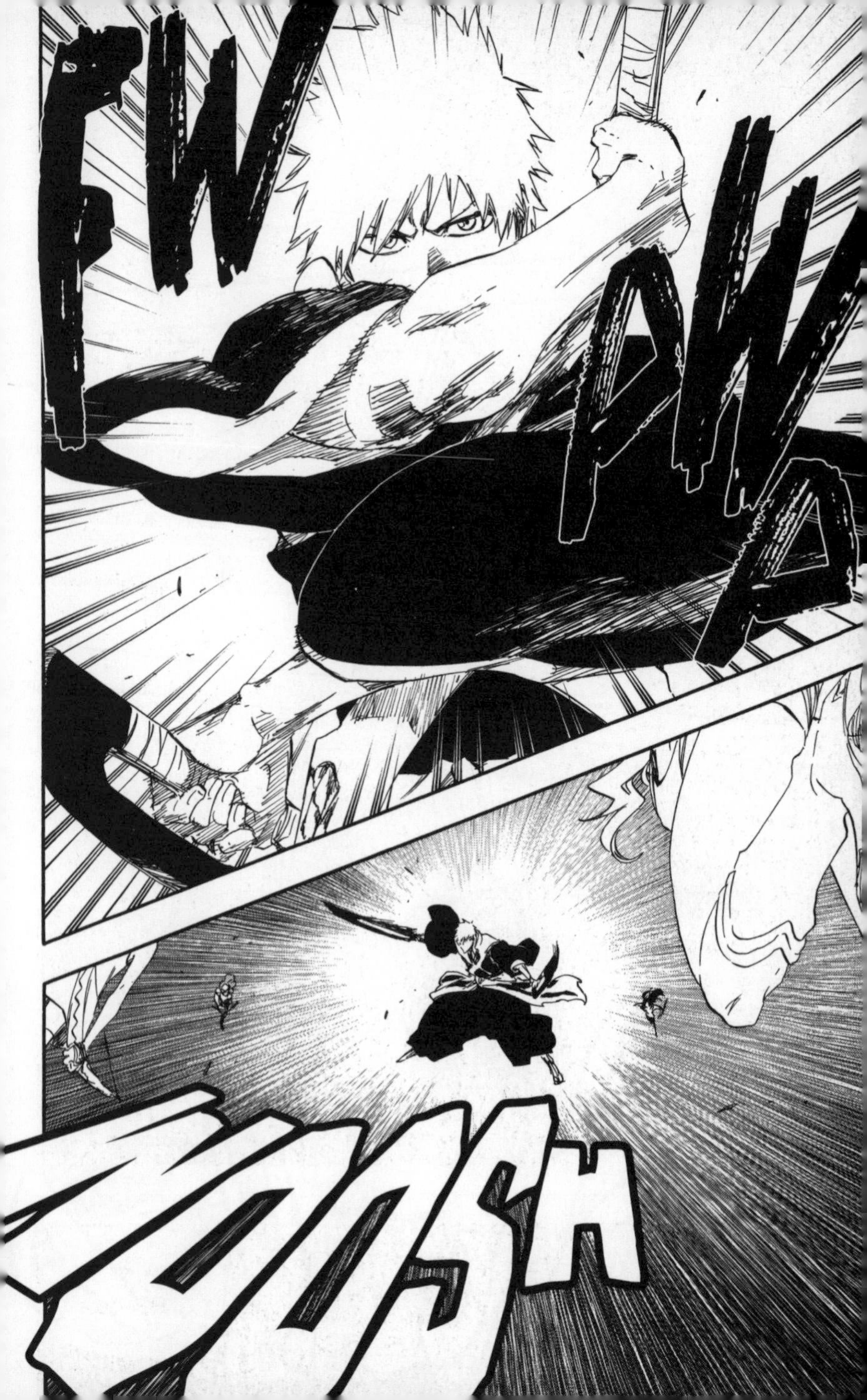

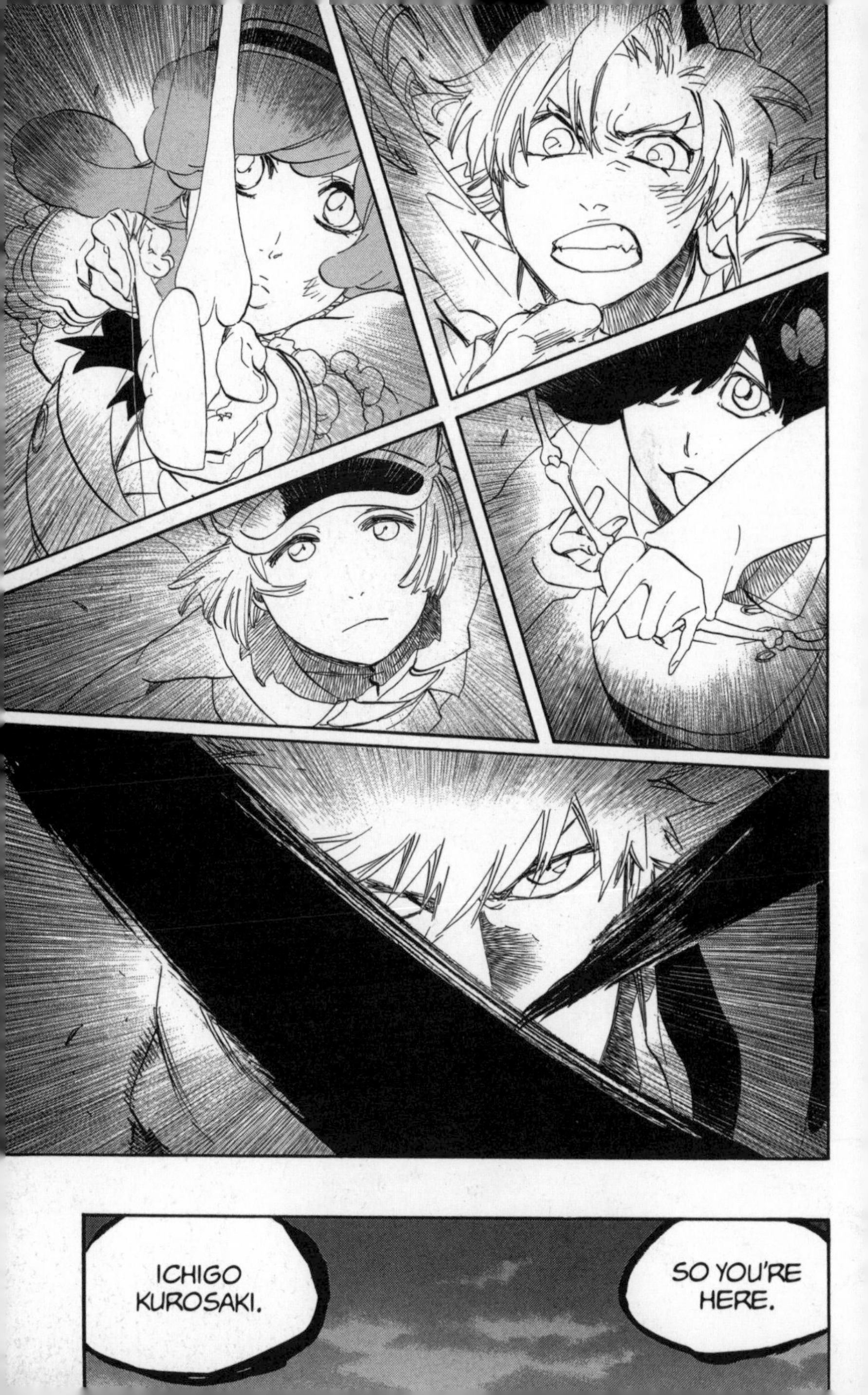
SO YOU'RE HERE.
ICHIGO KUROSAKI.

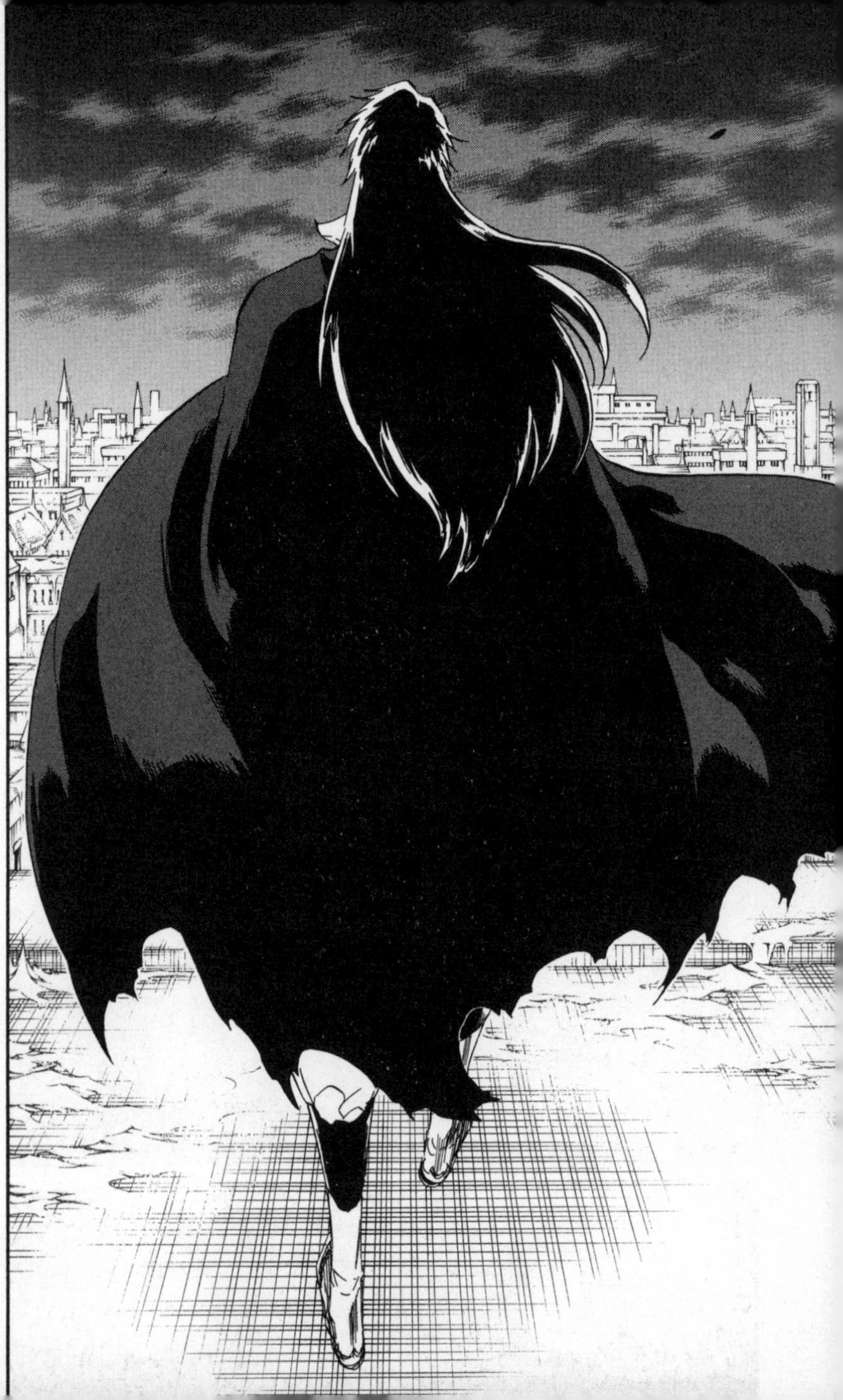

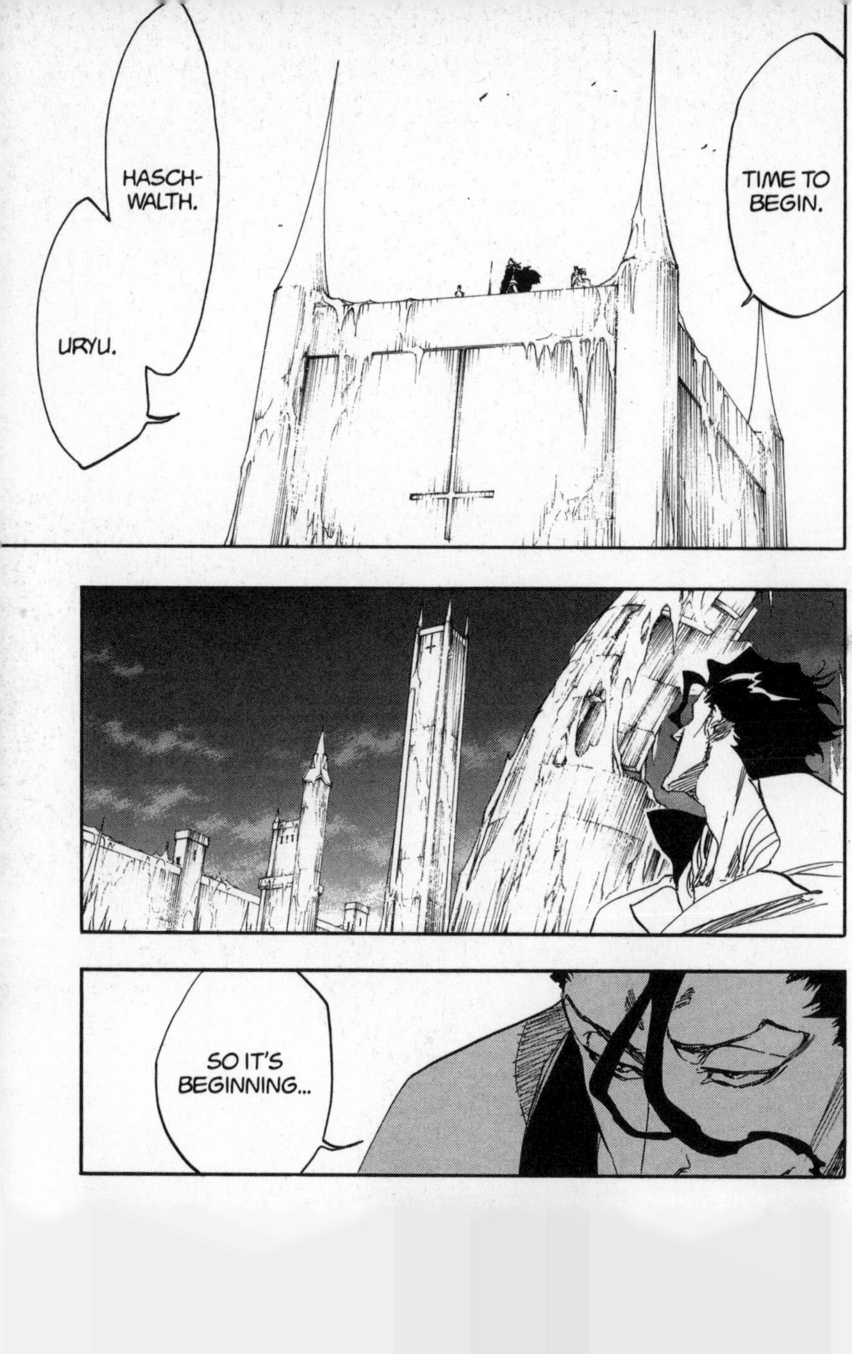
TIME TO BEGIN.
HASCH-WALTH.
URYU.
SO IT'S BEGINNING...

583. THE HEADLESS STAR 2

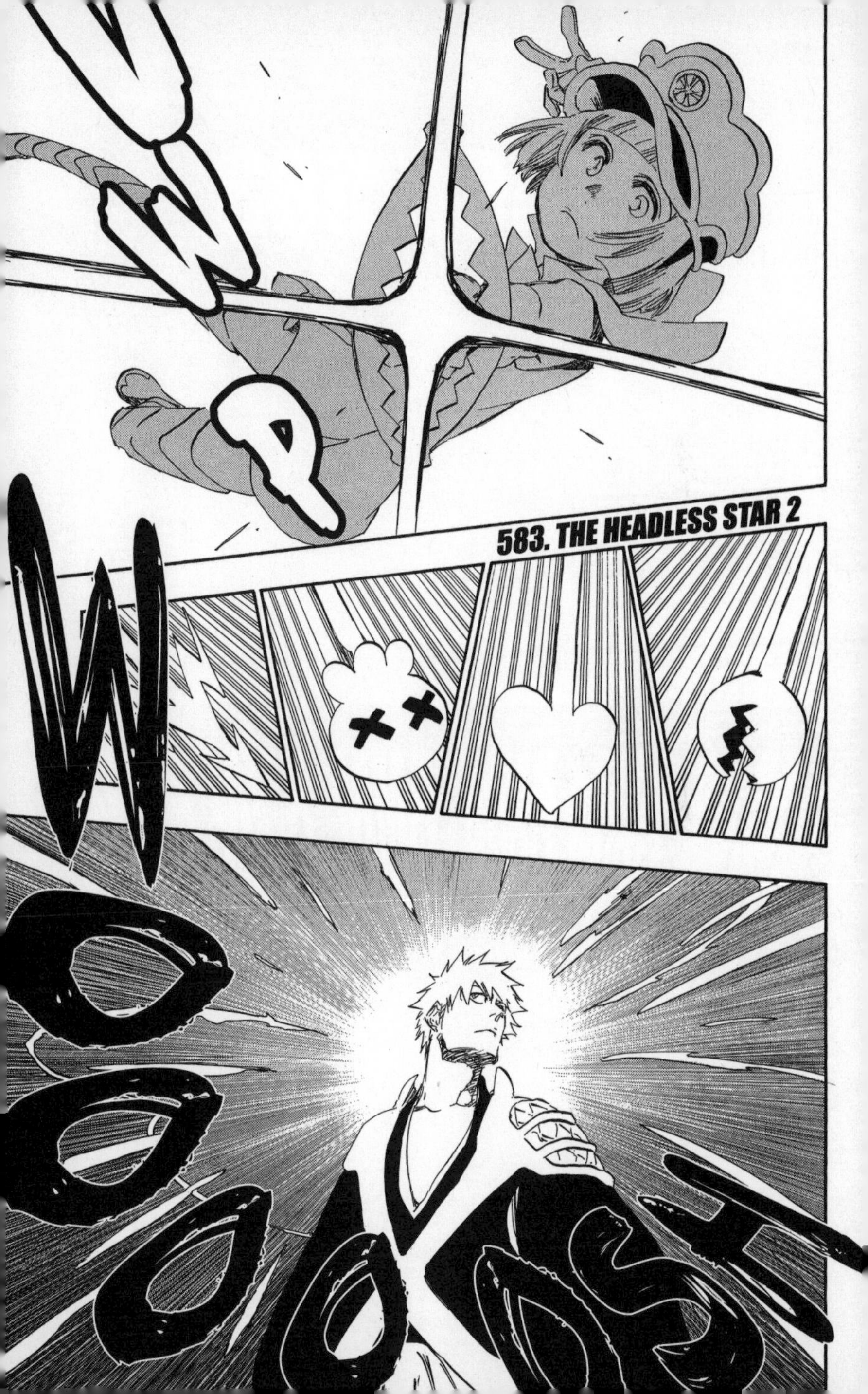

BLEACH 583.

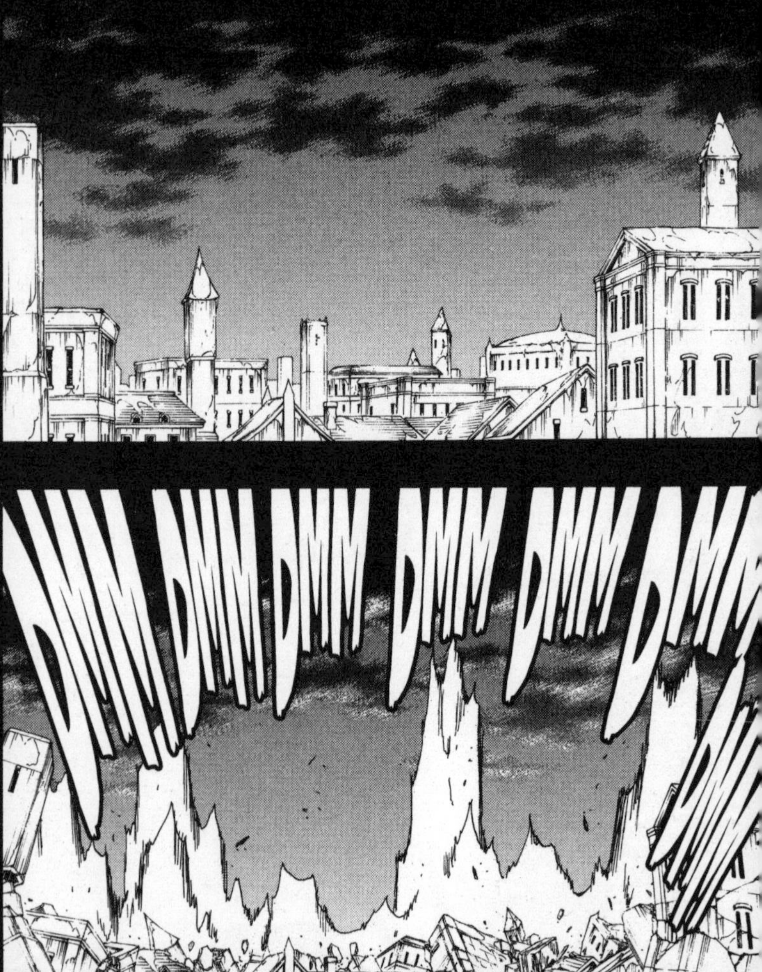
DMM DMM DMM DMM DMM

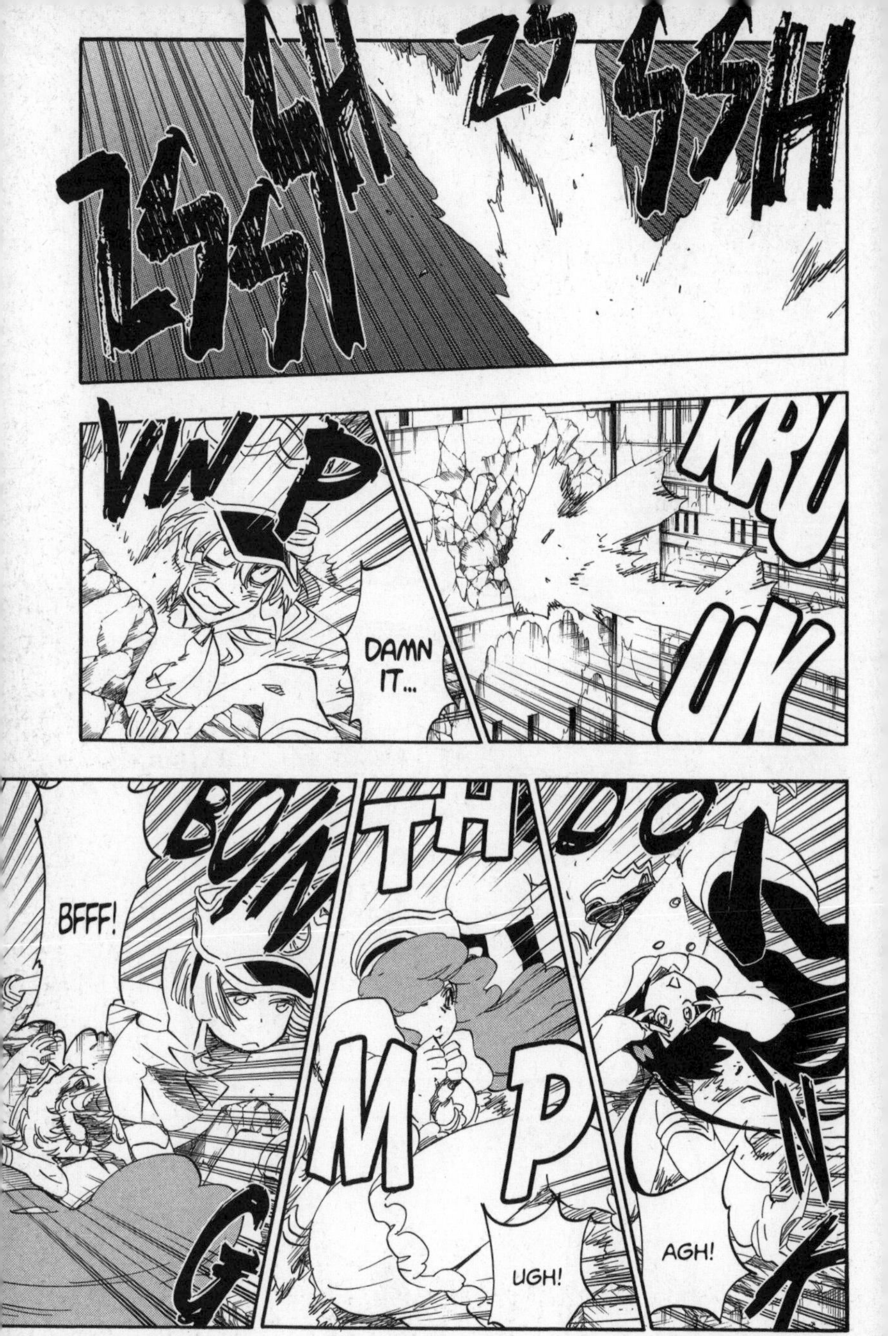
SSH
ZS
ZSSH
KRU
UK
VWP
DAMN IT...
DO
NK
AGH!
TH
MP
UGH!
BON
G
BFFF!

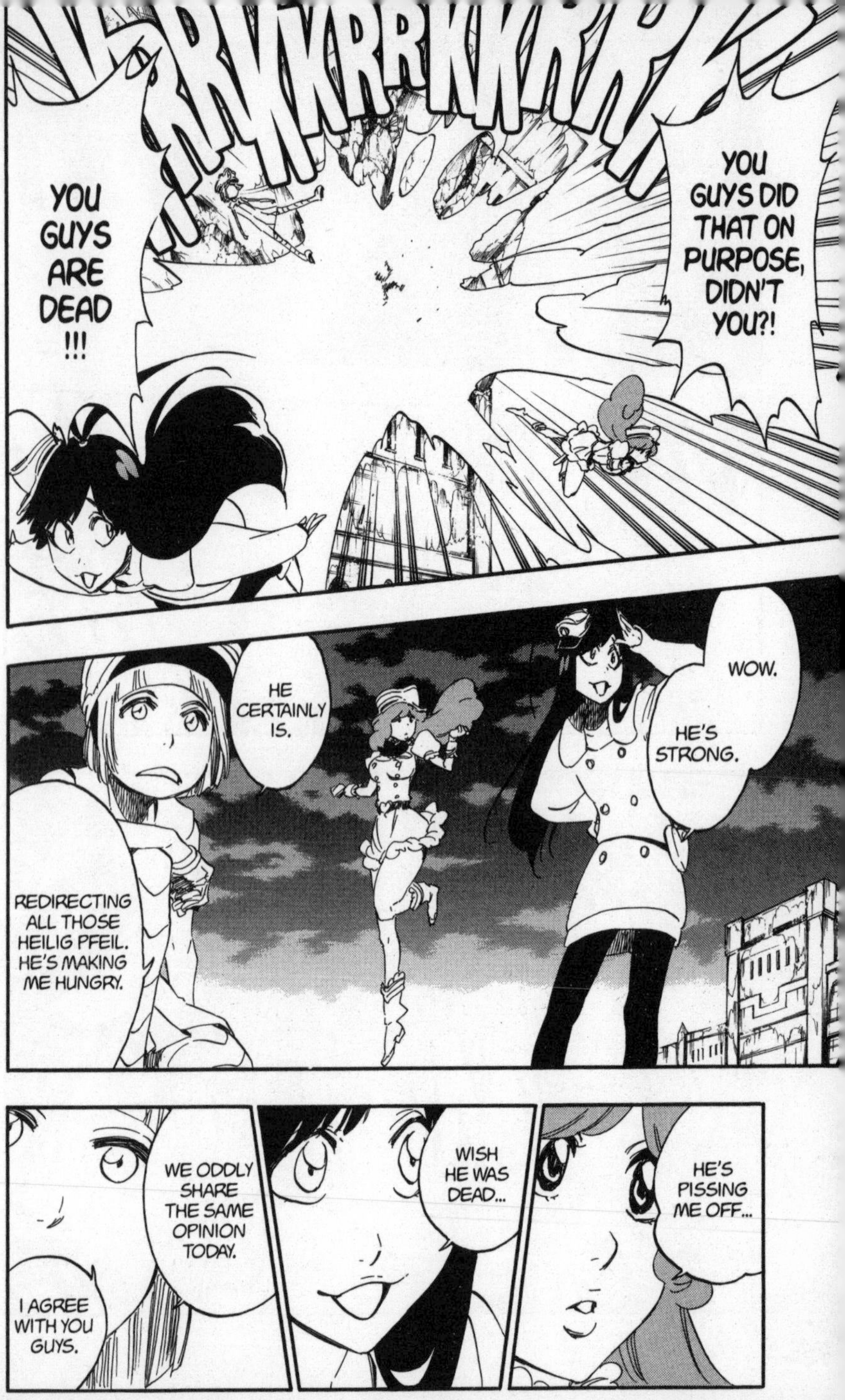
YOU GUYS DID THAT ON PURPOSE, DIDN'T YOU?!
YOU GUYS ARE DEAD!!!
WOW.
HE'S STRONG.
HE CERTAINLY IS.
REDIRECTING ALL THOSE HEILIG PFEIL. HE'S MAKING ME HUNGRY.
HE'S PISSING ME OFF...
WISH HE WAS DEAD...
WE ODDLY SHARE THE SAME OPINION TODAY.
I AGREE WITH YOU GUYS.

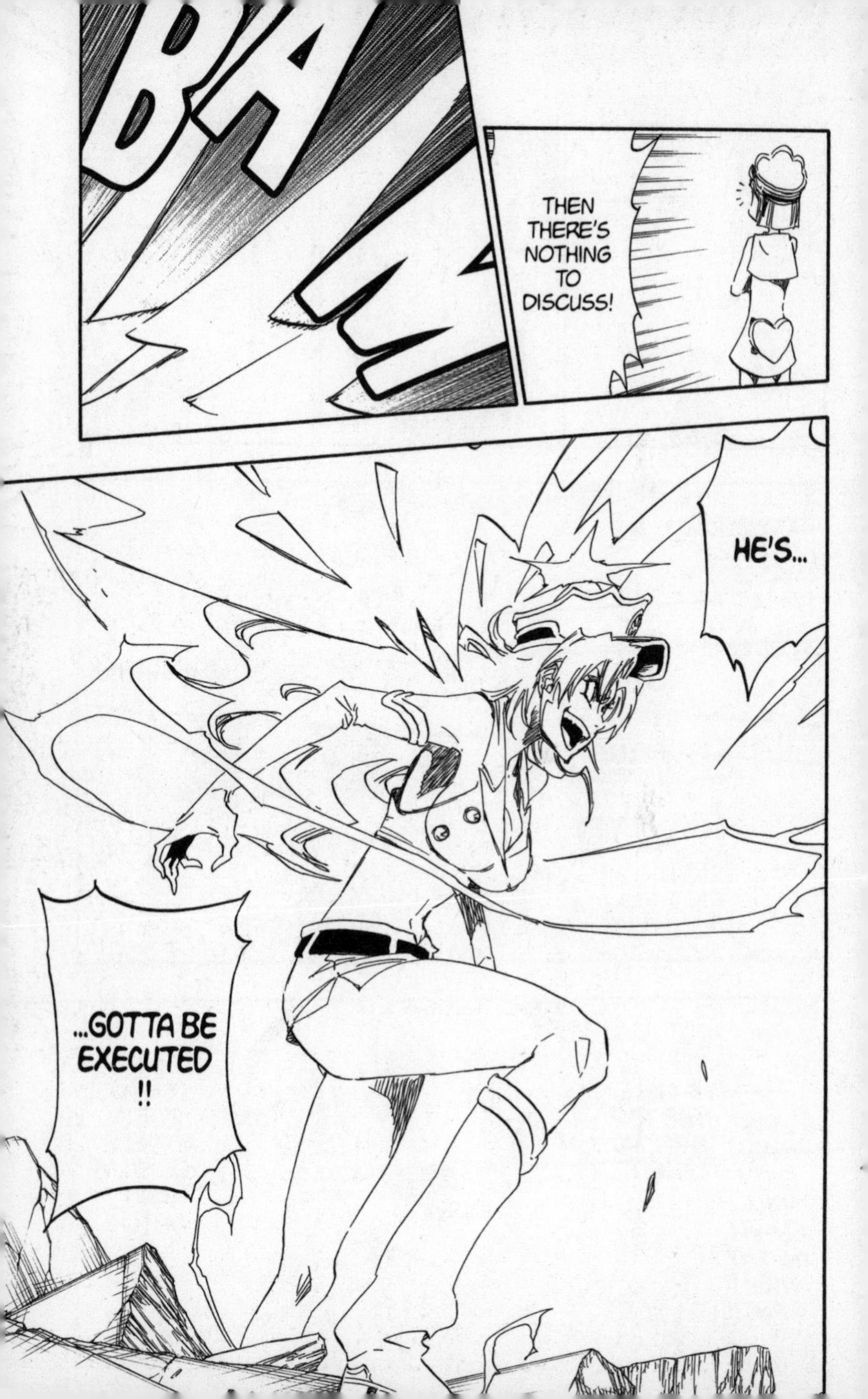
THEN THERE'S NOTHING TO DISCUSS!
BA
HE'S...
...GOTTA BE EXECUTED !!

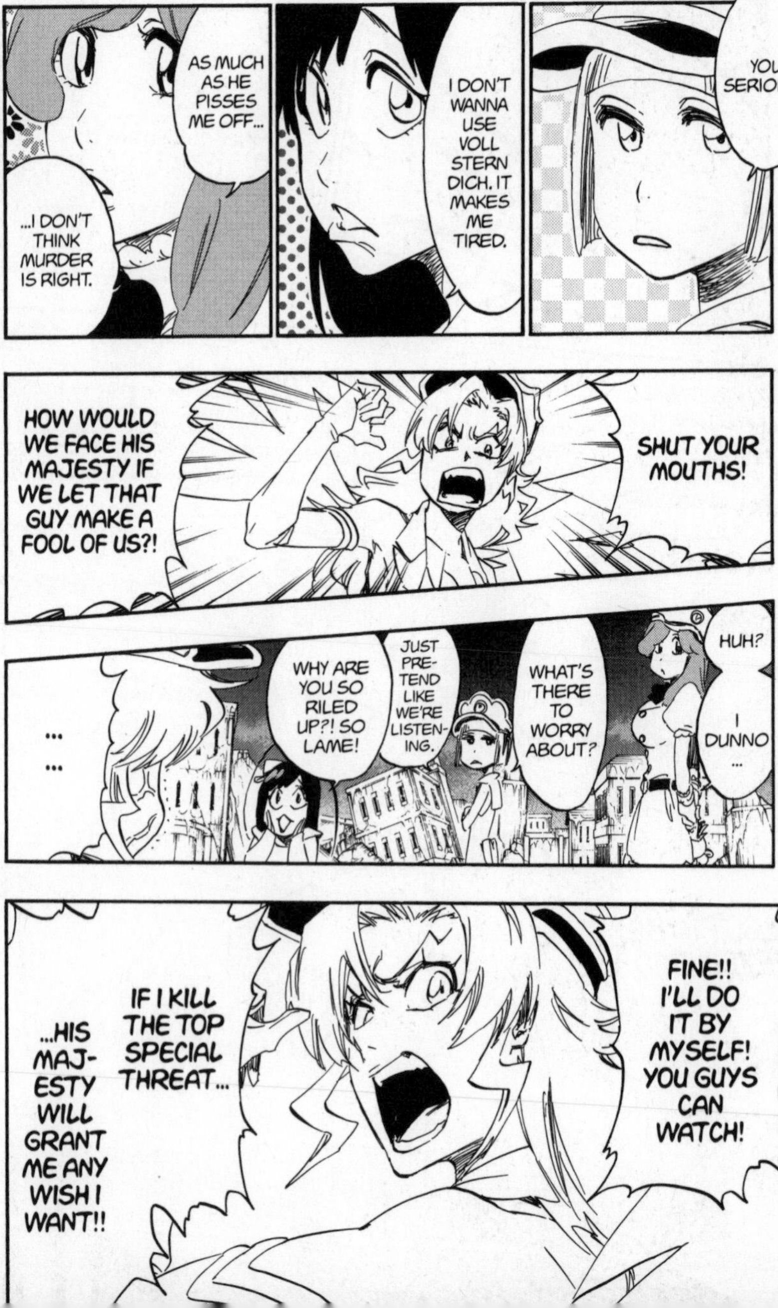
YOU SERIOUS?
I DON'T WANNA USE VOLL STERN DICH. IT MAKES ME TIRED.
AS MUCH AS HE PISSES ME OFF...
...I DON'T THINK MURDER IS RIGHT.
SHUT YOUR MOUTHS!
HOW WOULD WE FACE HIS MAJESTY IF WE LET THAT GUY MAKE A FOOL OF US?!
HUH?
I DUNNO ...
WHAT'S THERE TO WORRY ABOUT?
JUST PRE-TEND LIKE WE'RE LISTEN-ING.
WHY ARE YOU SO RILED UP?! SO LAME!
... ...
FINE!! I'LL DO IT BY MYSELF! YOU GUYS CAN WATCH!
IF I KILL THE TOP SPECIAL THREAT...
...HIS MAJ-ESTY WILL GRANT ME ANY WISH I WANT!!

READ THIS WAY

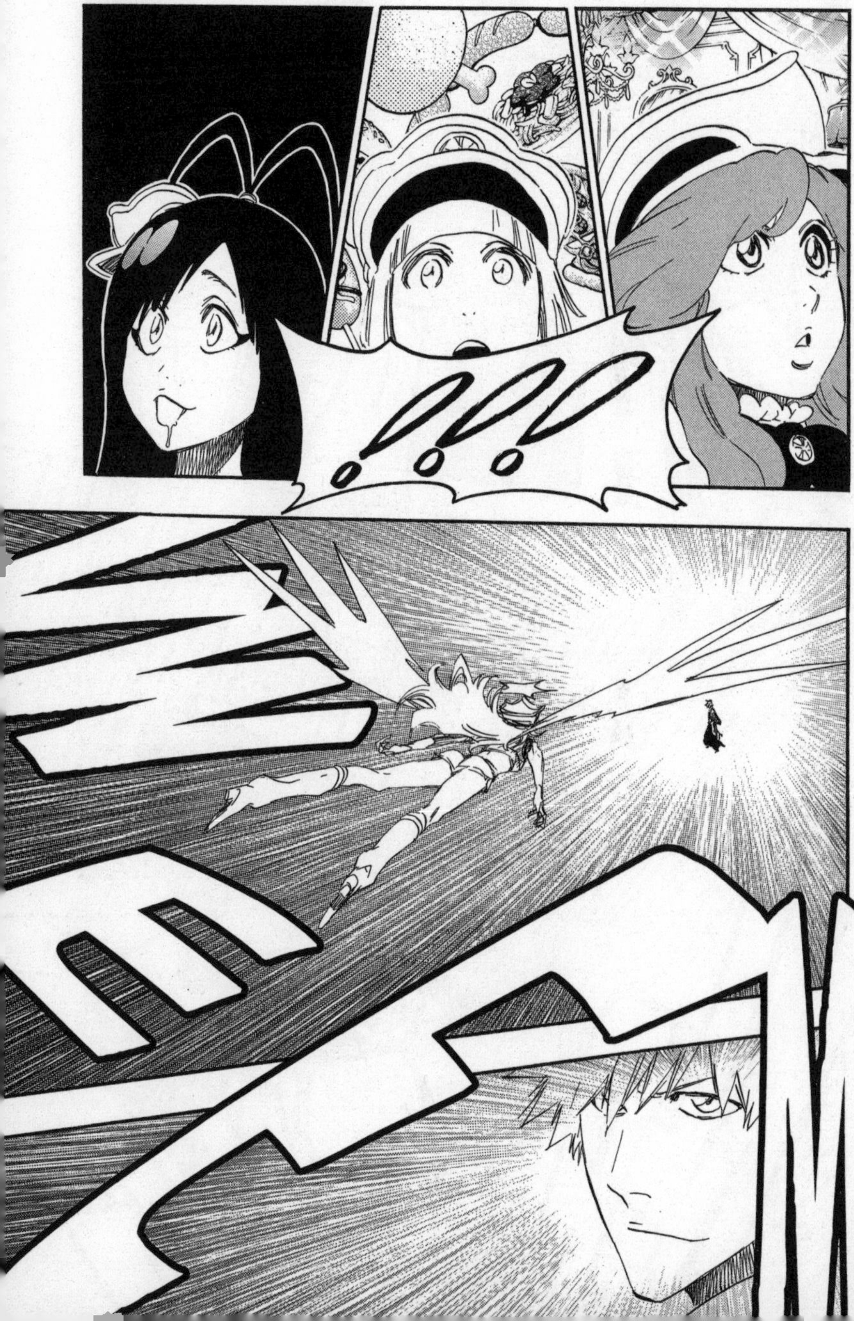
!!!

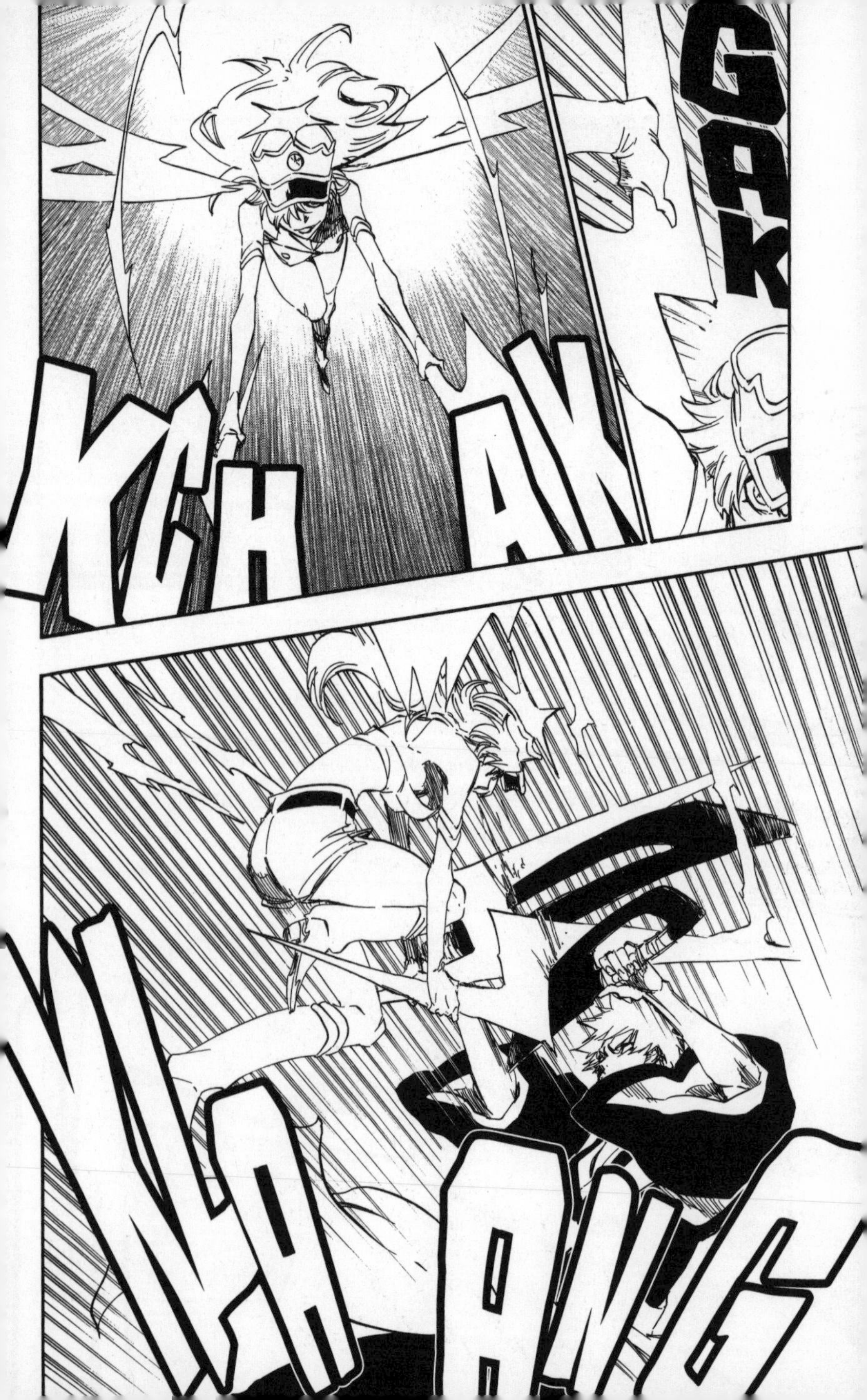
GAK
KCHAN

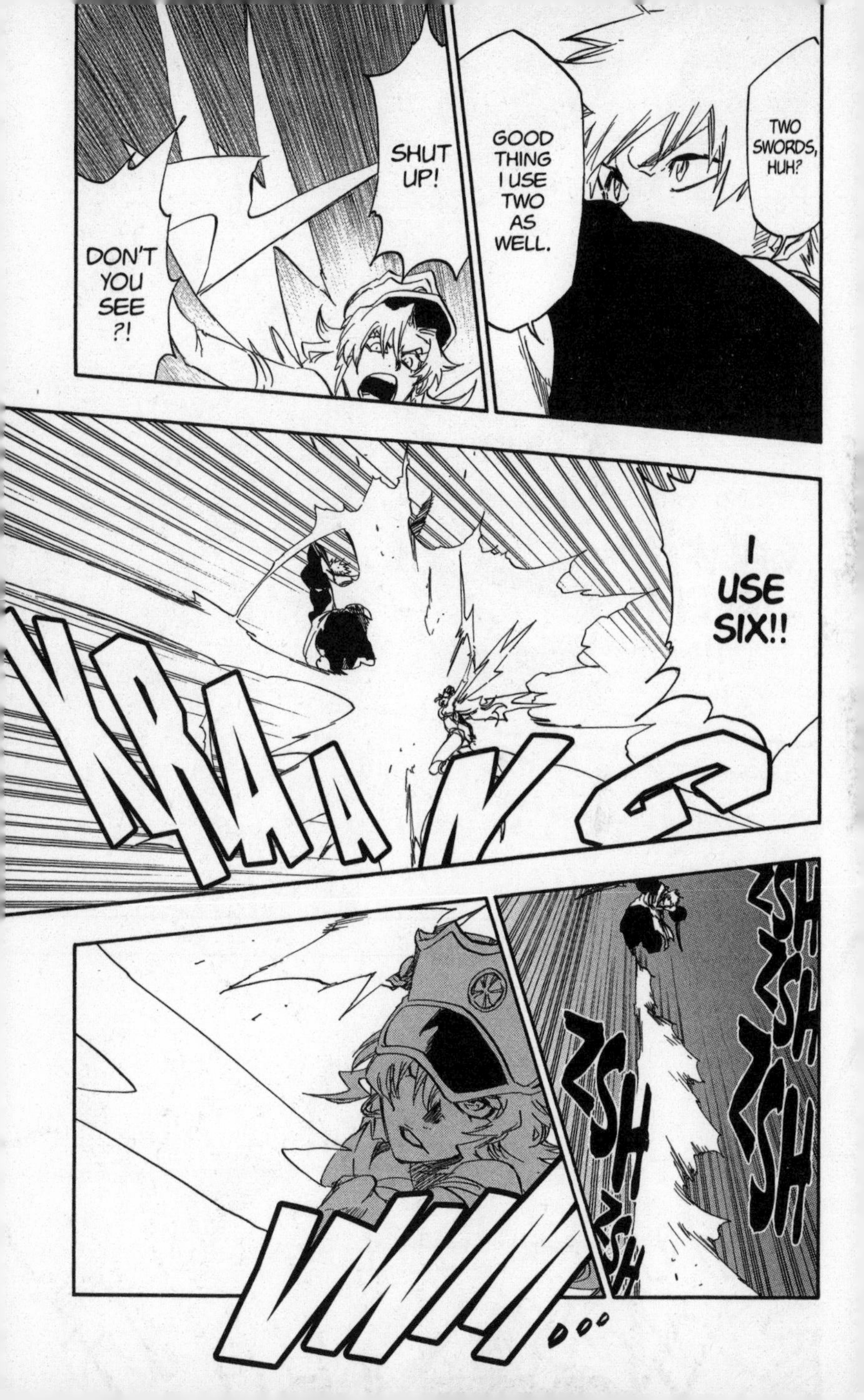

TWO SWORDS, HUH?
GOOD THING I USE TWO AS WELL.
SHUT UP!
DON'T YOU SEE ?!
I USE SIX!!
KRAANG
ZSH ZSH ZSH ZSH

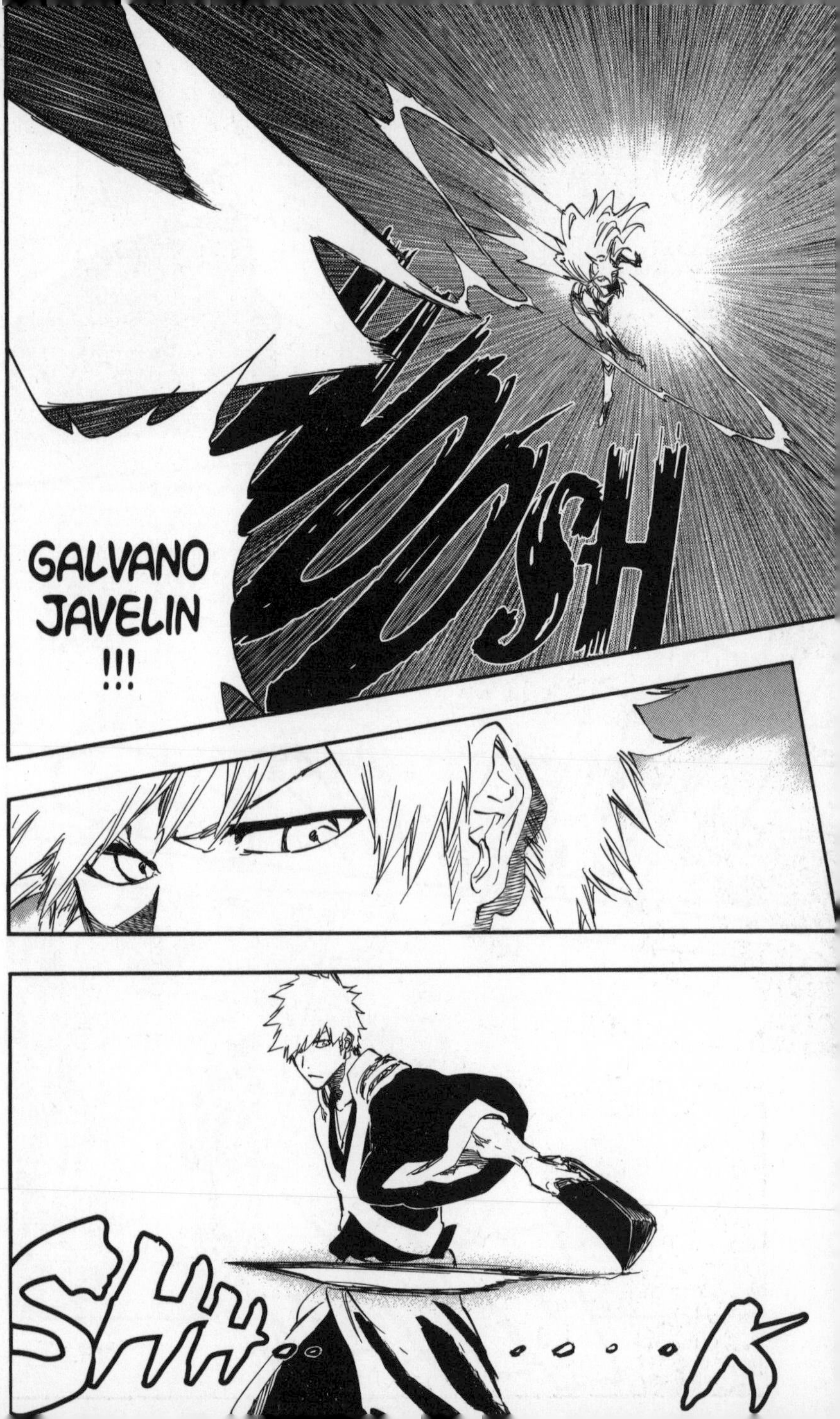
WHOOSH
GALVANO JAVELIN !!!
SHH....K

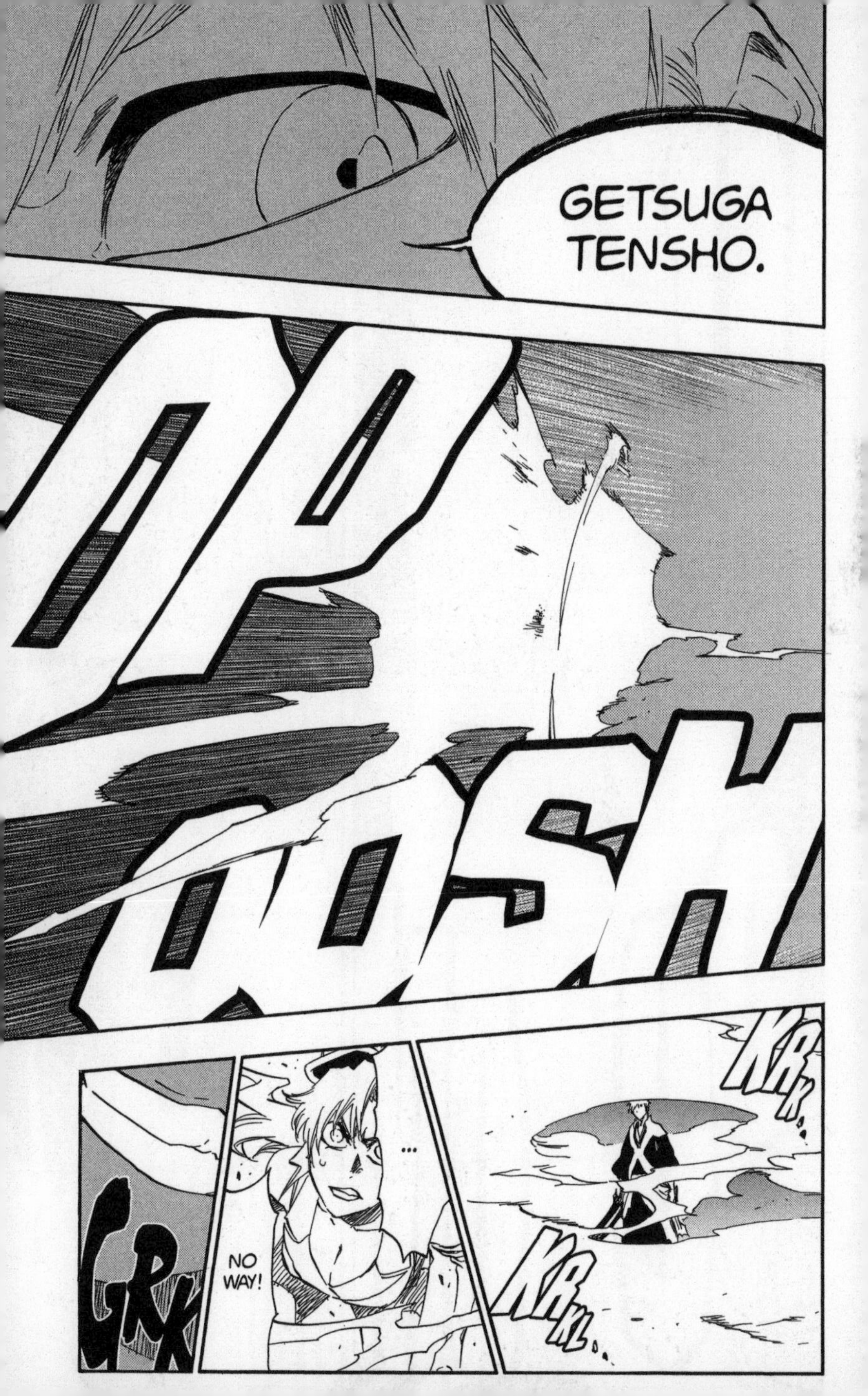
GETSUGA TENSHO.
KRK..
KRKL..
...
NO WAY!
GRK

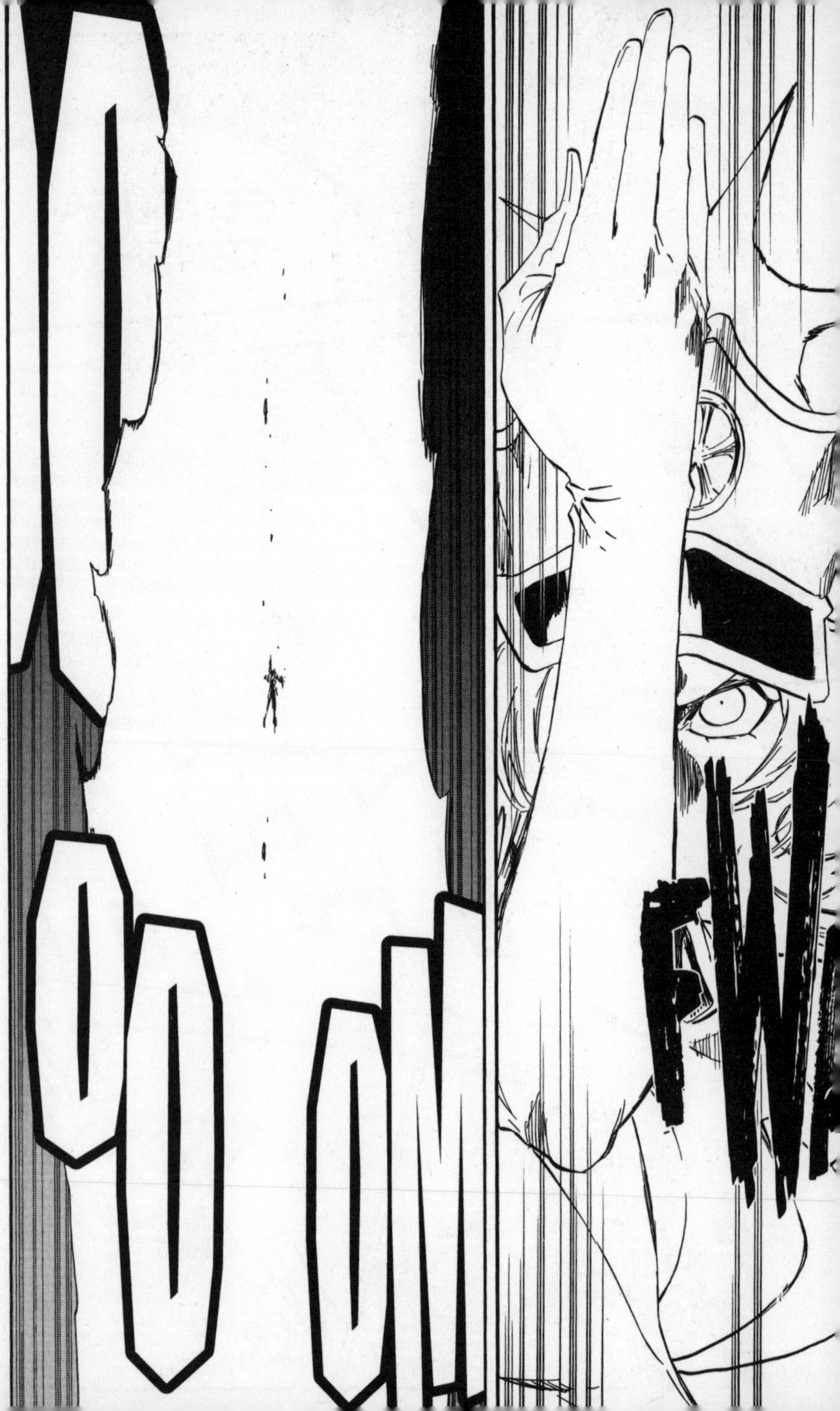

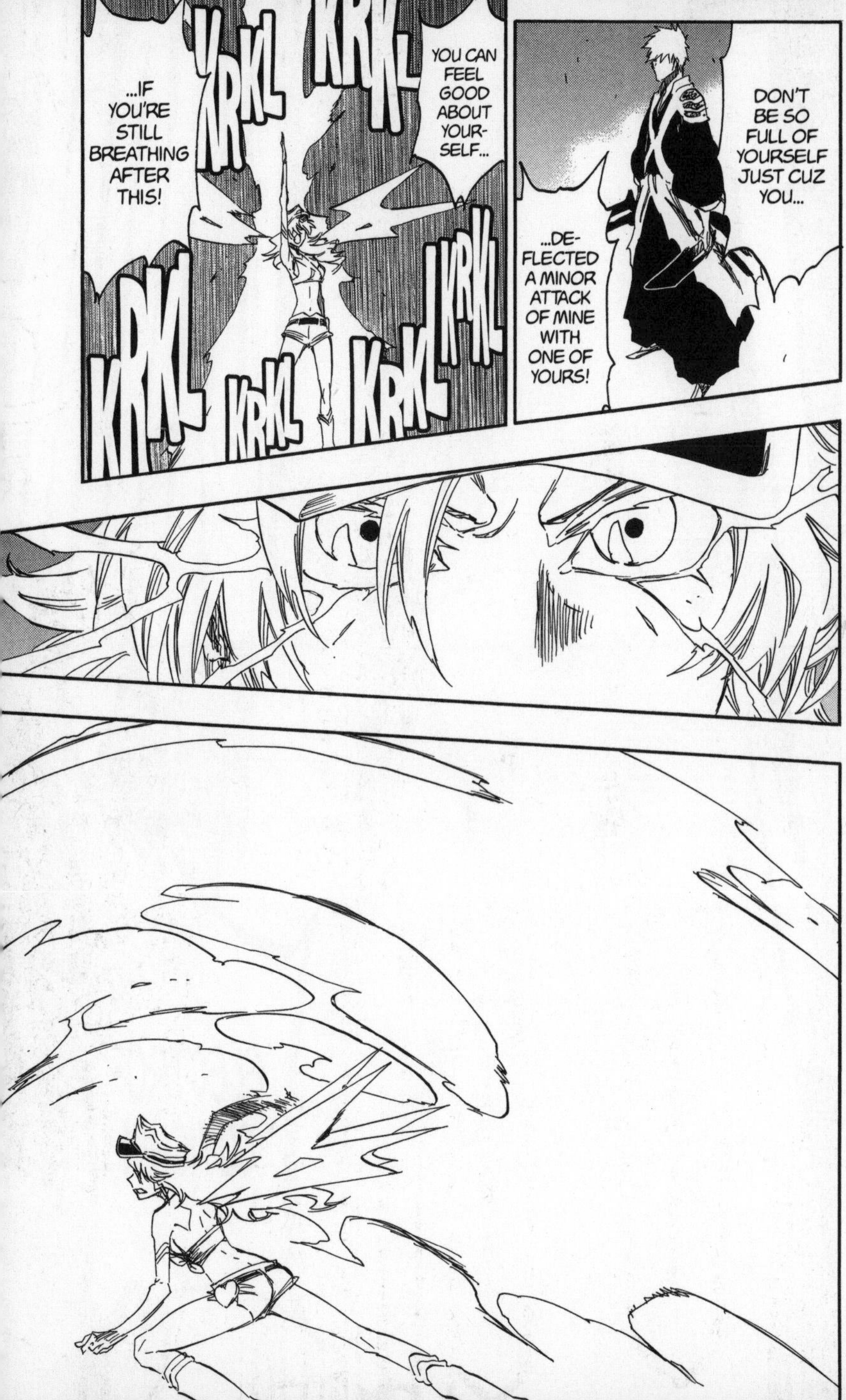
DON'T BE SO FULL OF YOURSELF JUST CUZ YOU...
...DE-FLECTED A MINOR ATTACK OF MINE WITH ONE OF YOURS!
KRKL
YOU CAN FEEL GOOD ABOUT YOUR-SELF...
KRKL
...IF YOU'RE STILL BREATHING AFTER THIS!
KRKL
KRKL
KRKL
KRKL
KRKL

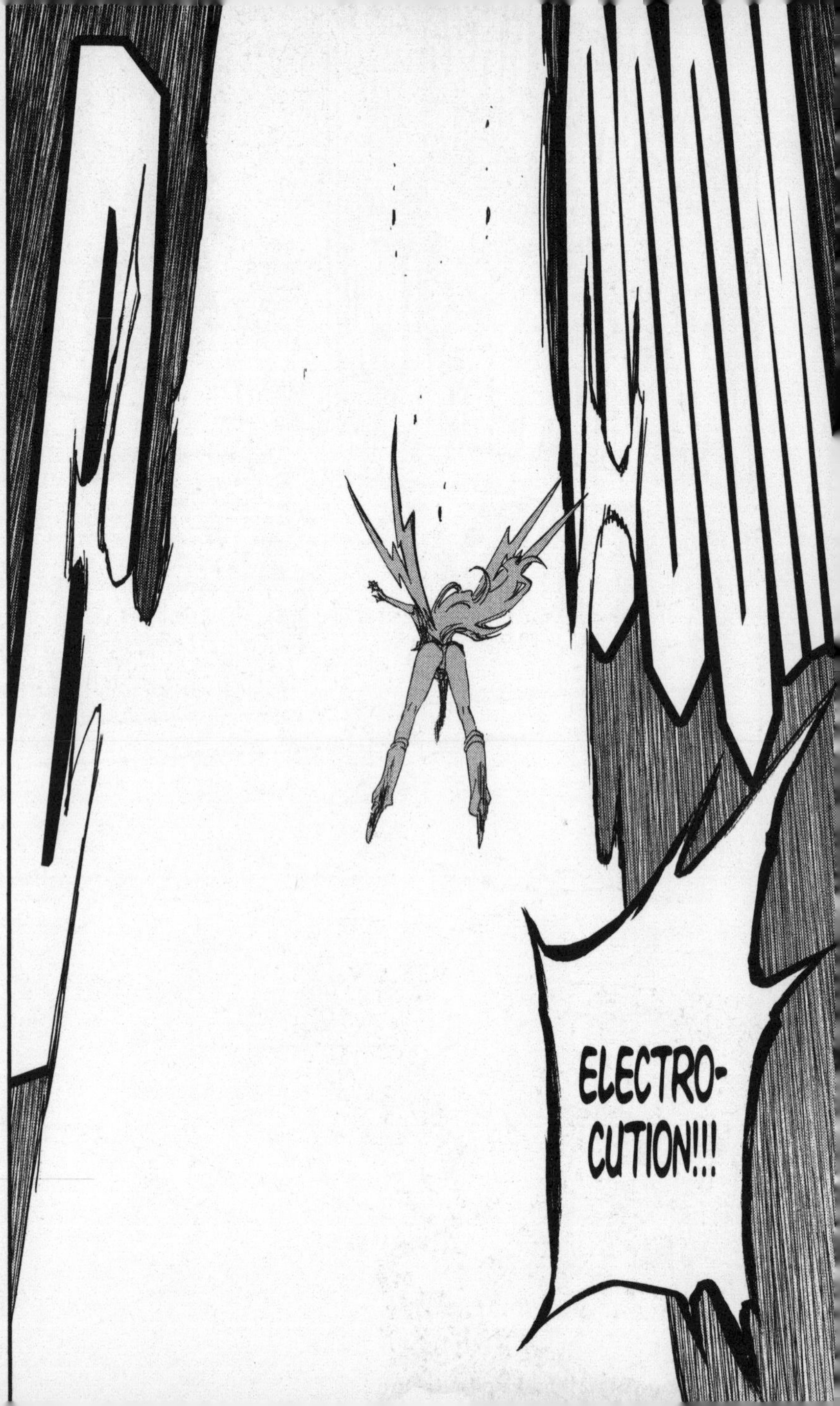
ELECTRO-
CUTION!!!

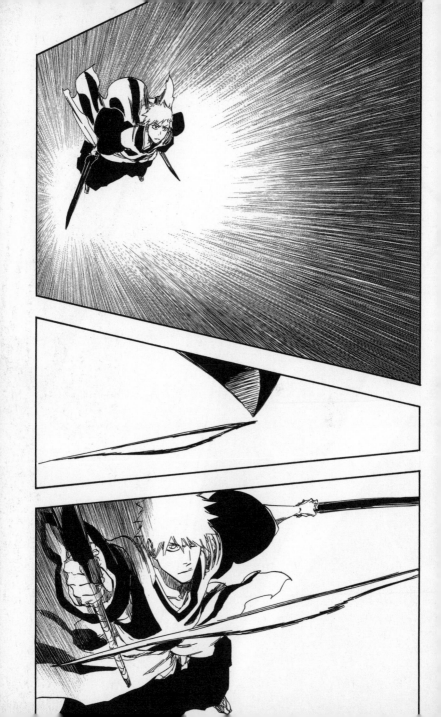

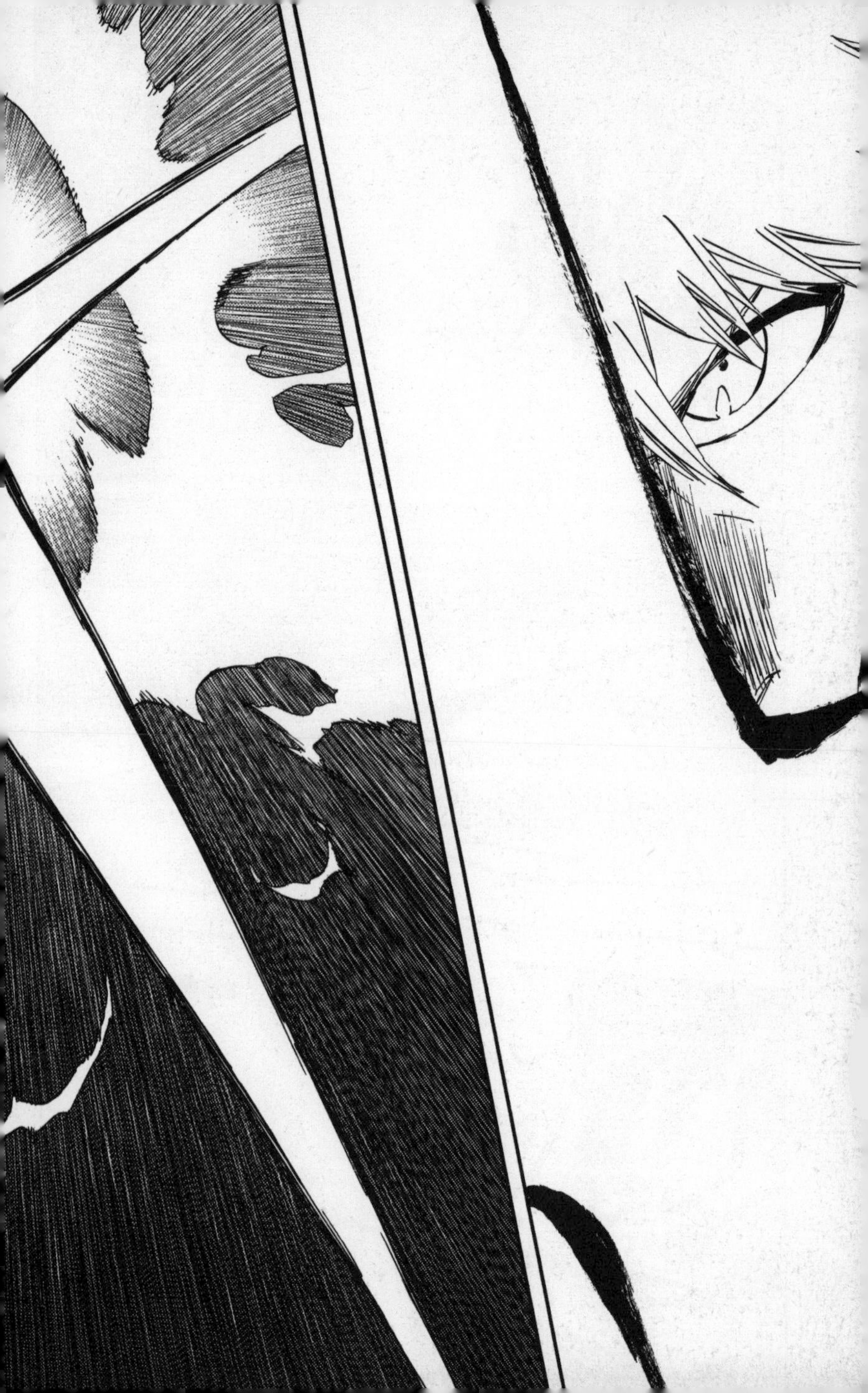

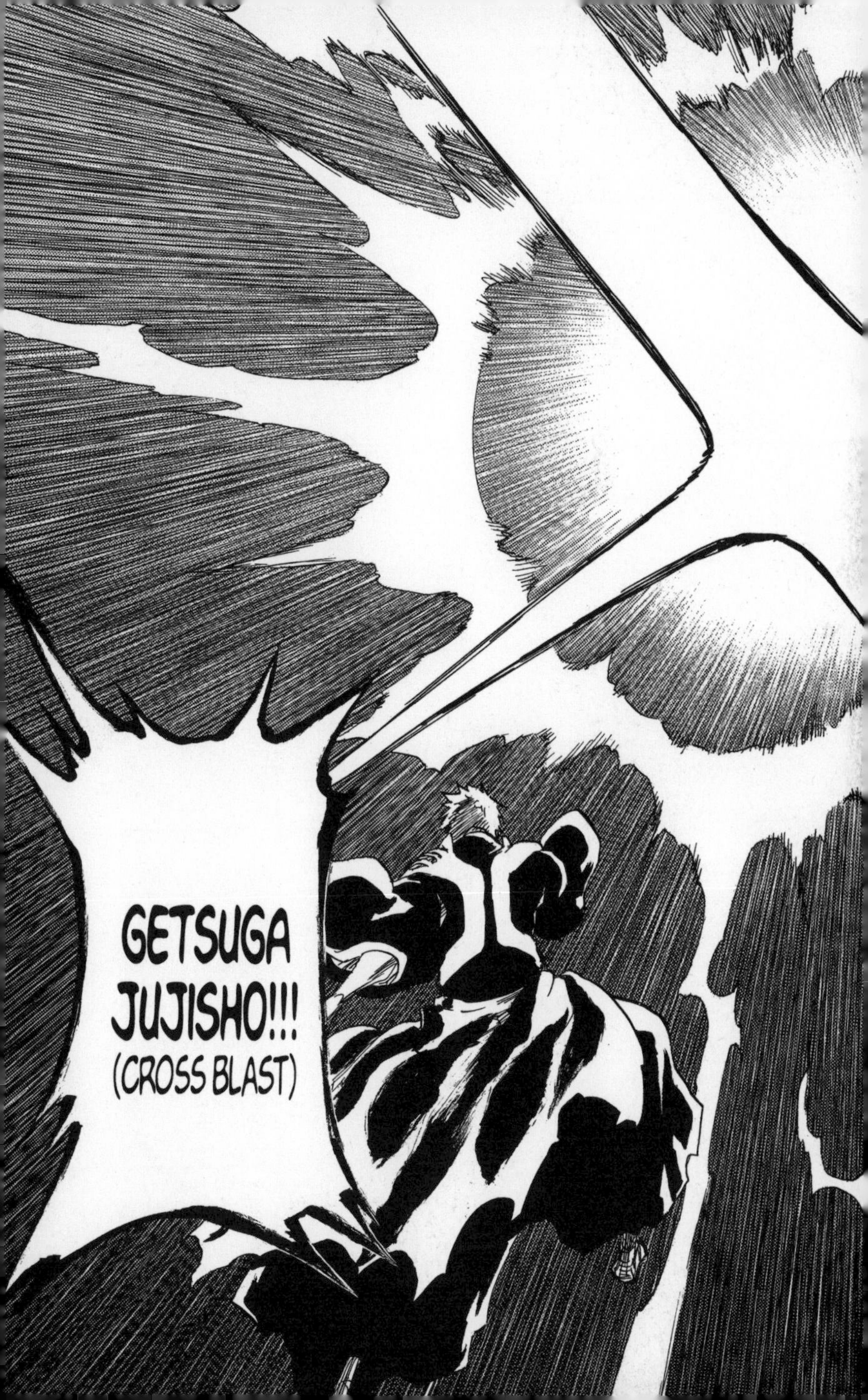
GETSUGA JUJISHO!!!
(CROSS BLAST)

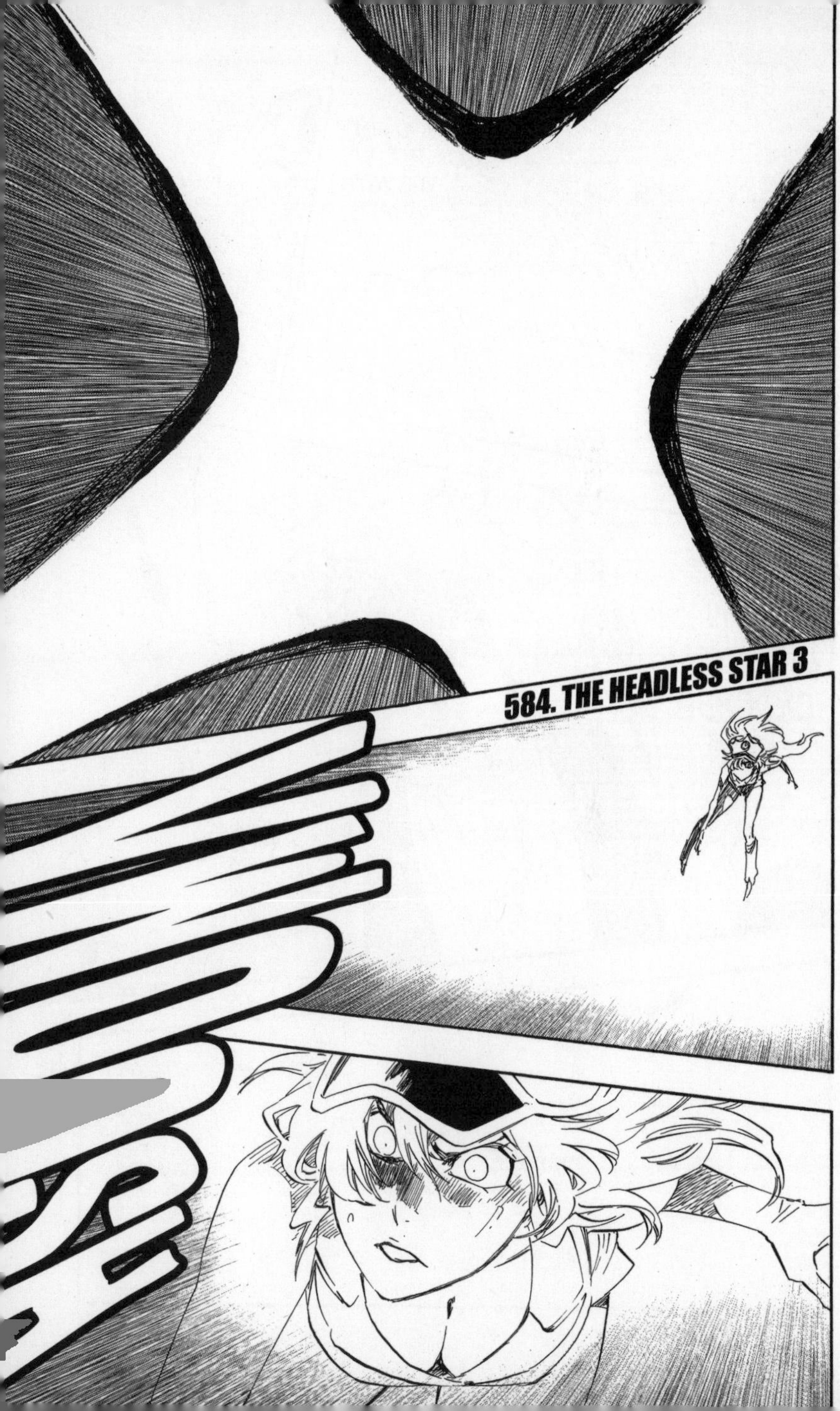
584. THE HEADLESS STAR 3

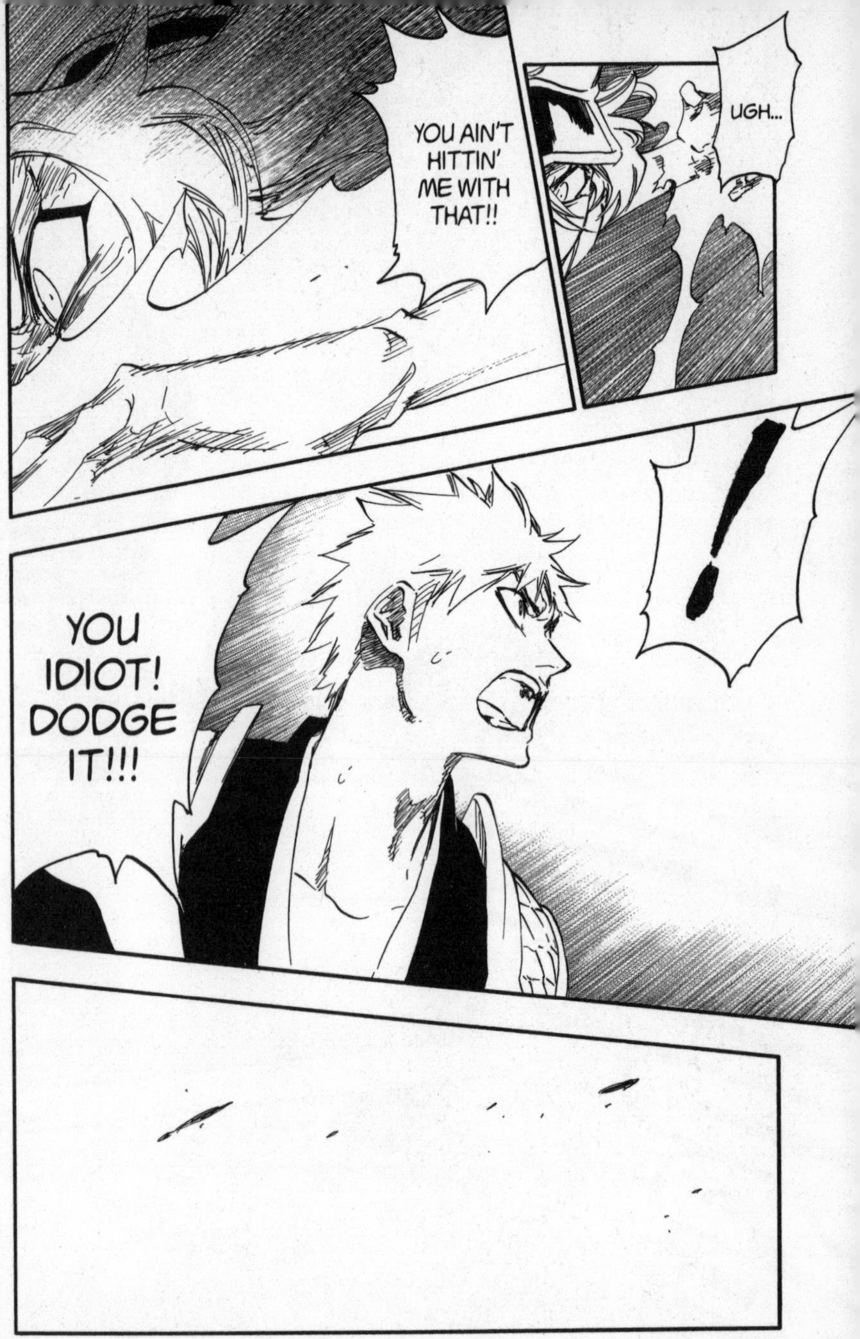
UGH...
YOU AIN'T HITTIN' ME WITH THAT!!
!
YOU IDIOT! DODGE IT!!!

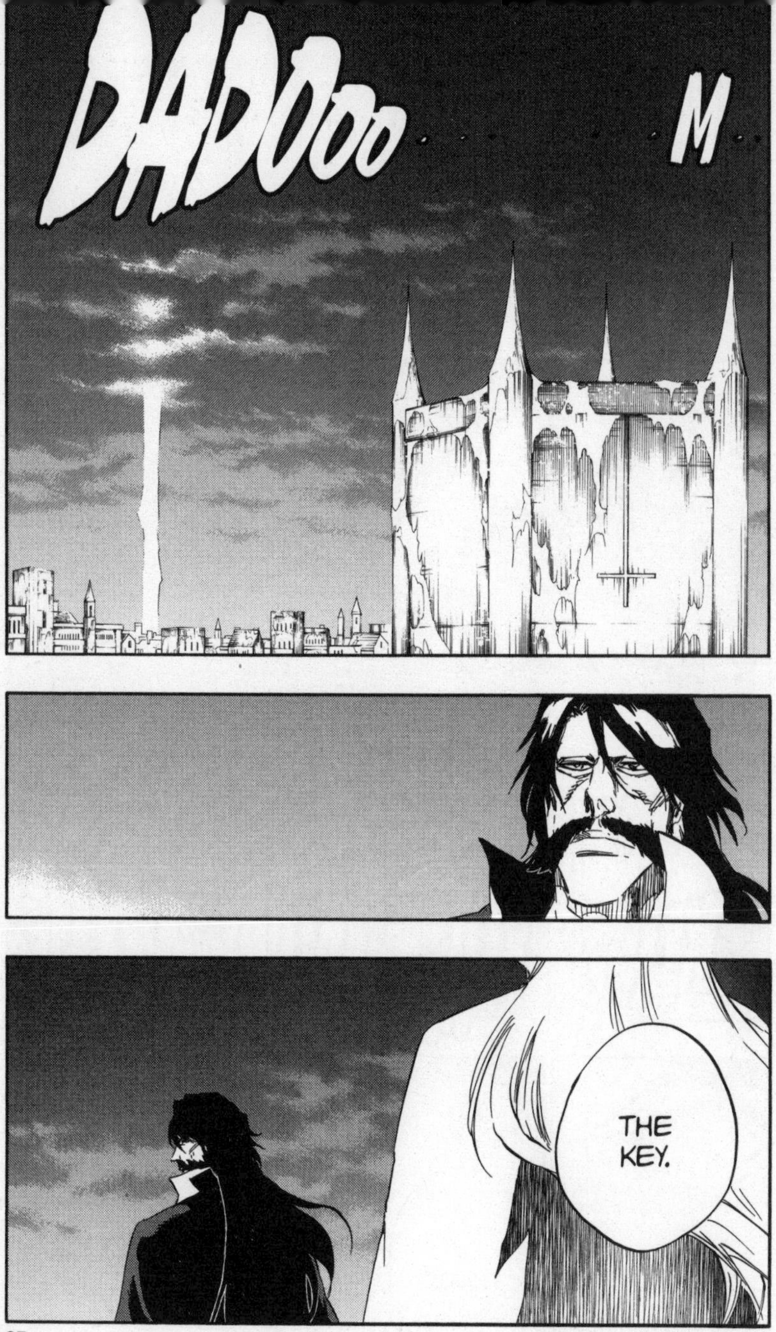
DADOOOO . . . . M . .
THE KEY.

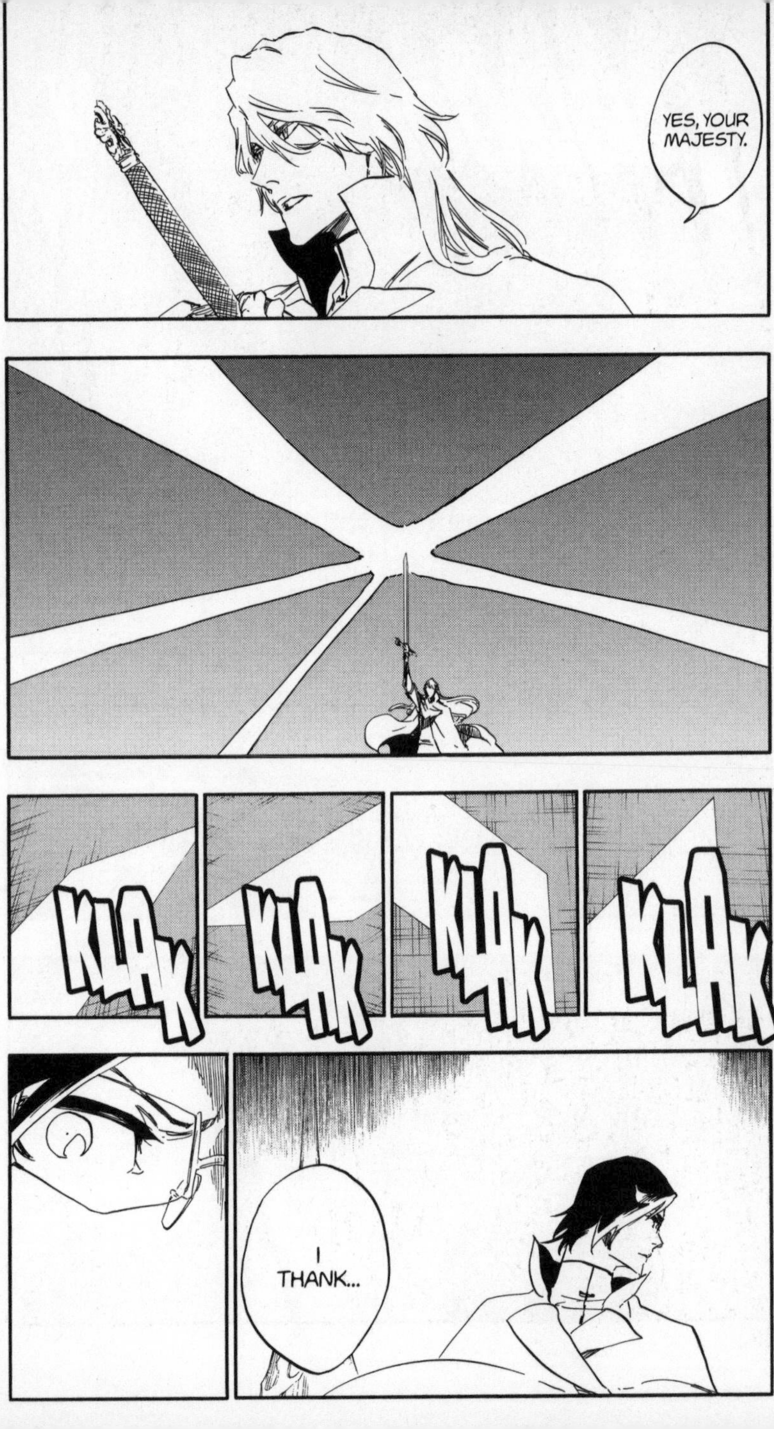
YES, YOUR MAJESTY.
KLAK
KLAK
KLAK
KLAK
I THANK...

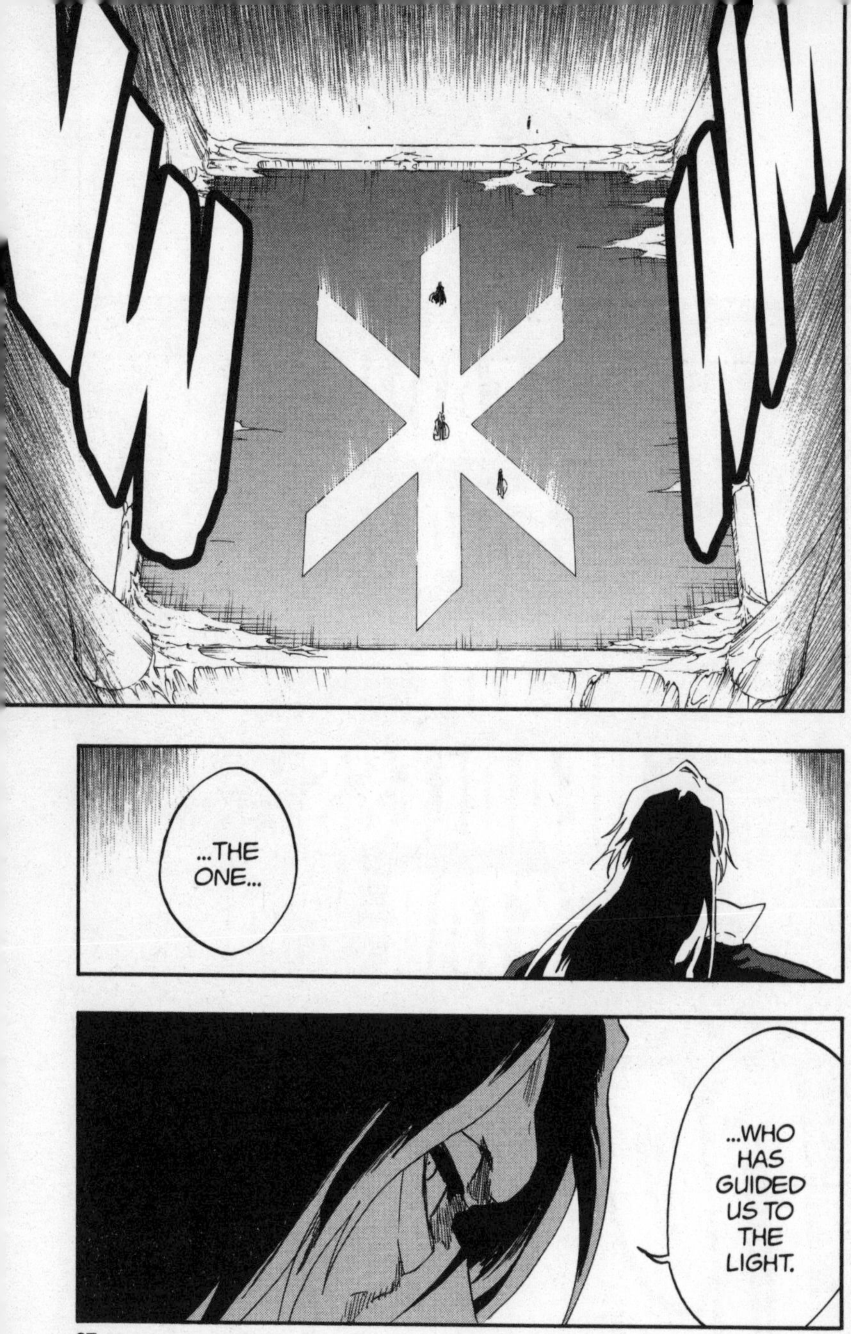
...THE ONE...
...WHO HAS GUIDED US TO THE LIGHT.

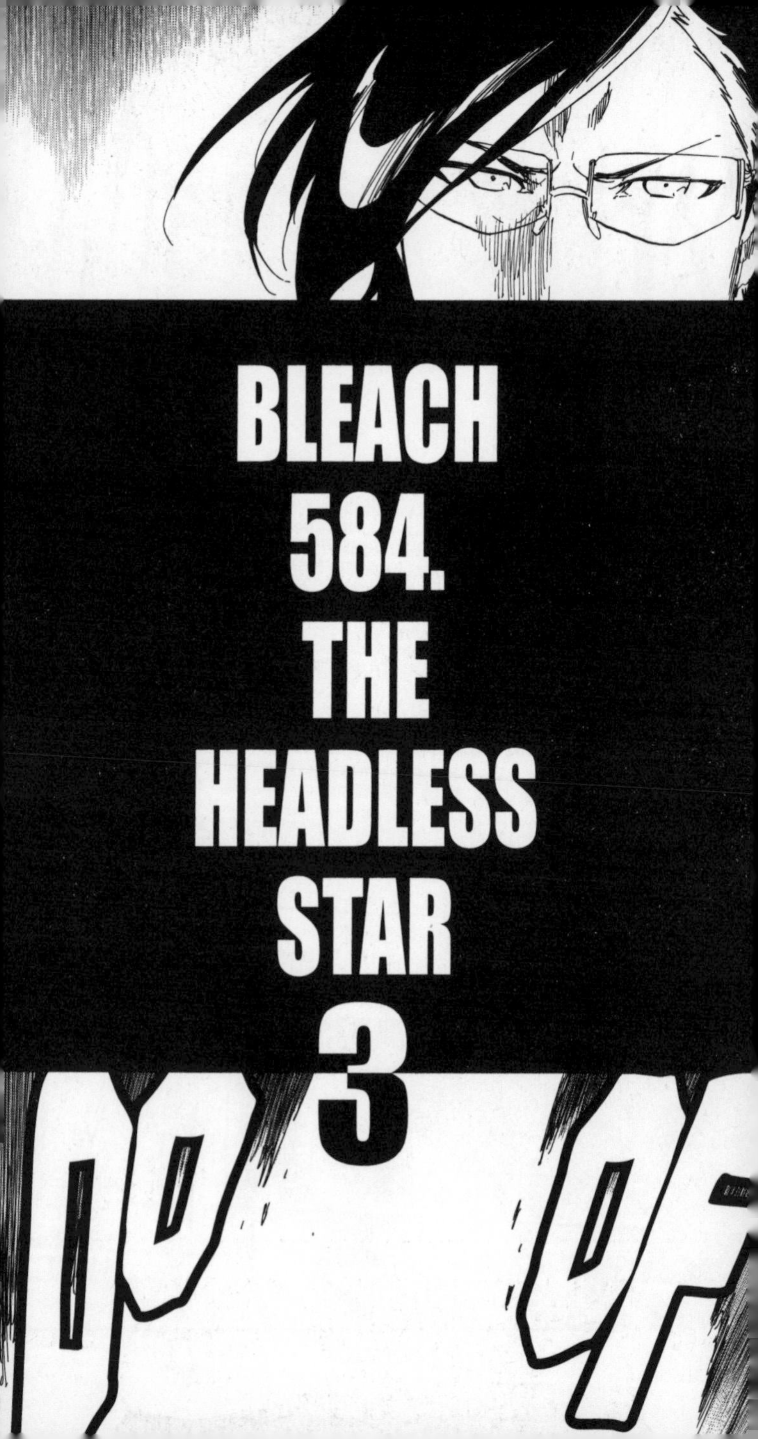
BLEACH
584.
THE HEADLESS STAR 3

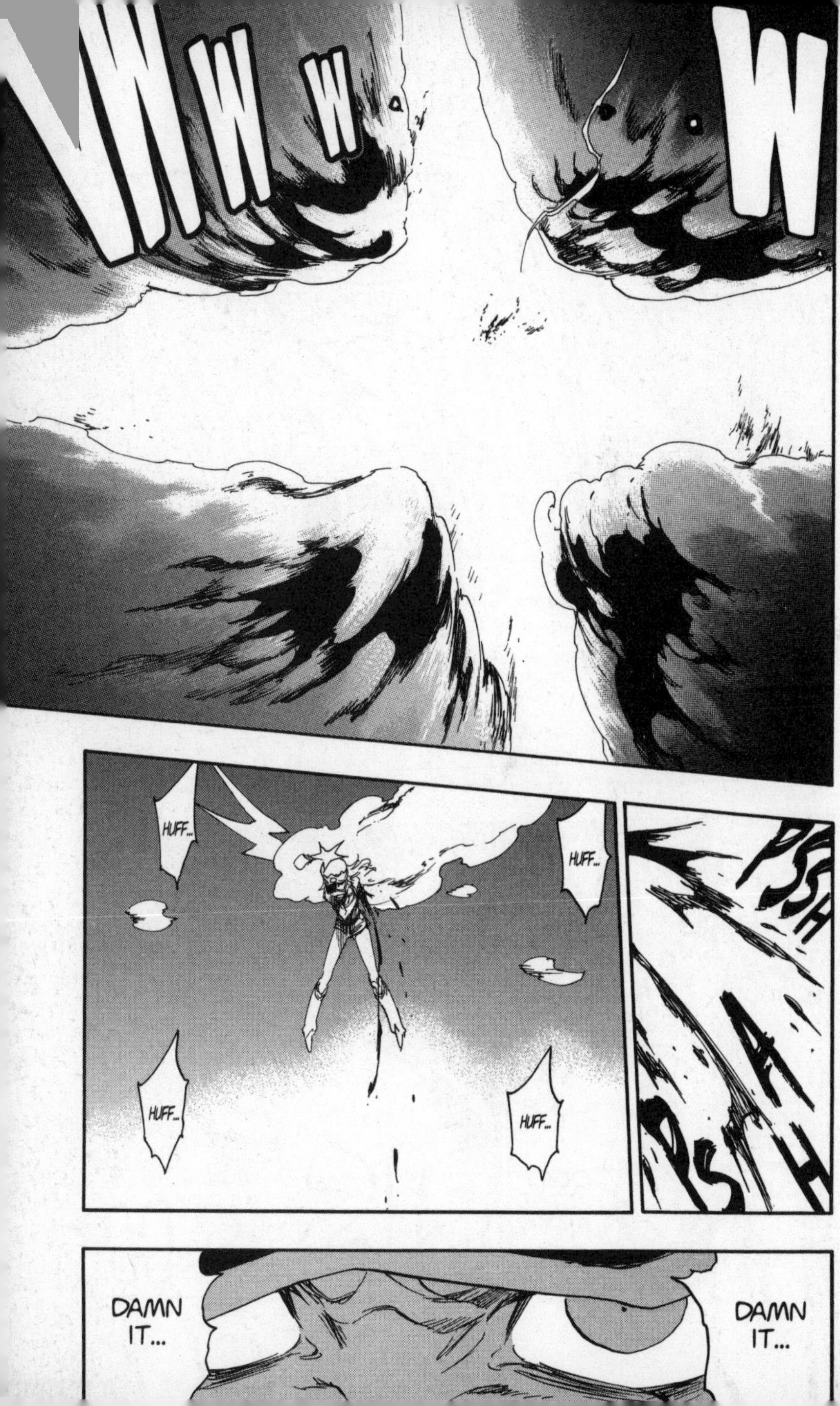
WWWW... W
PSH
PSH
HUFF...
HUFF...
HUFF...
HUFF...
DAMN IT...
DAMN IT...

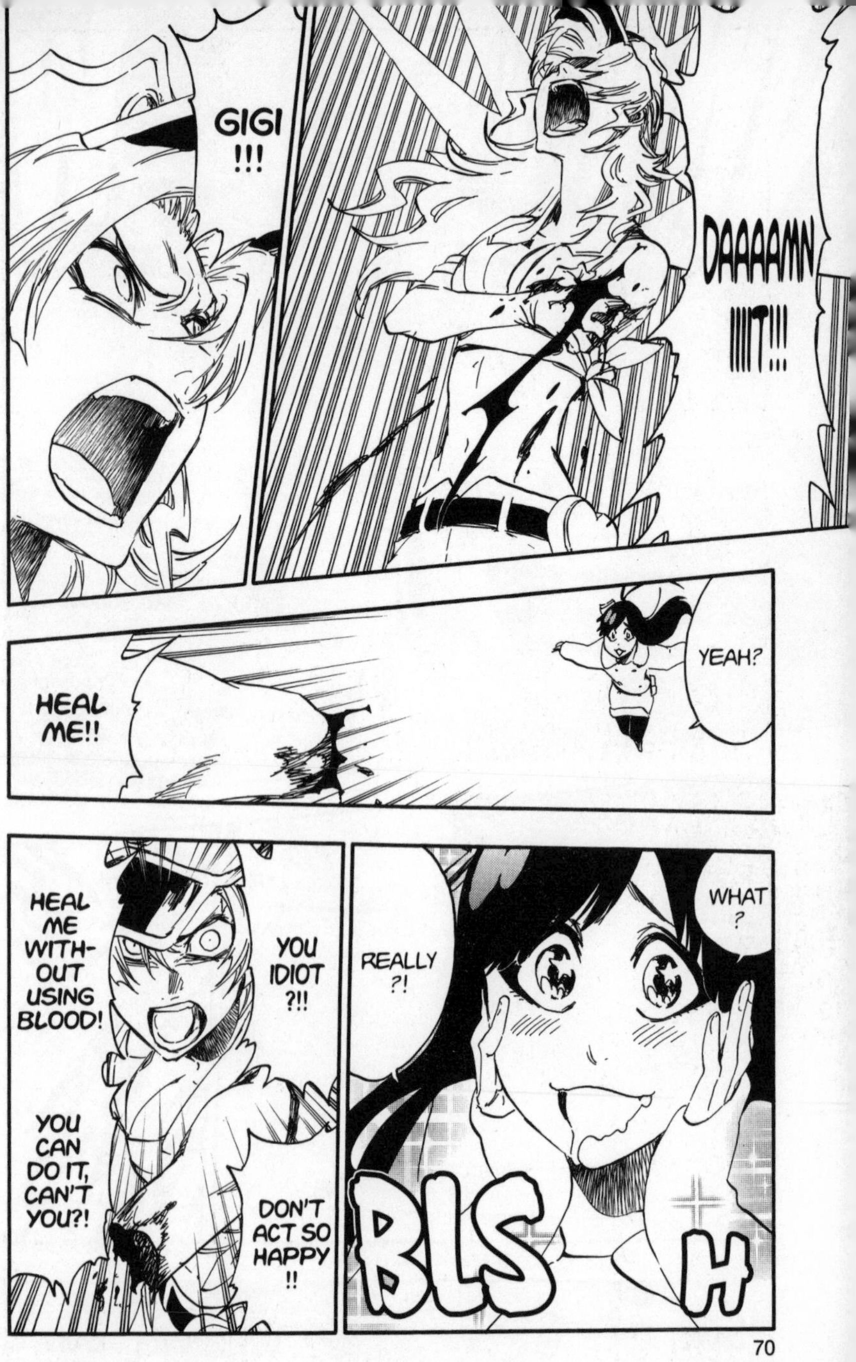

DAAAAMN IIIIT!!!
GIGI!!!
YEAH?
HEAL ME!!
WHAT?
REALLY?!
BLSH
YOU IDIOT?!!
HEAL ME WITH-OUT USING BLOOD!
DON'T ACT SO HAPPY!!
YOU CAN DO IT, CAN'T YOU?!

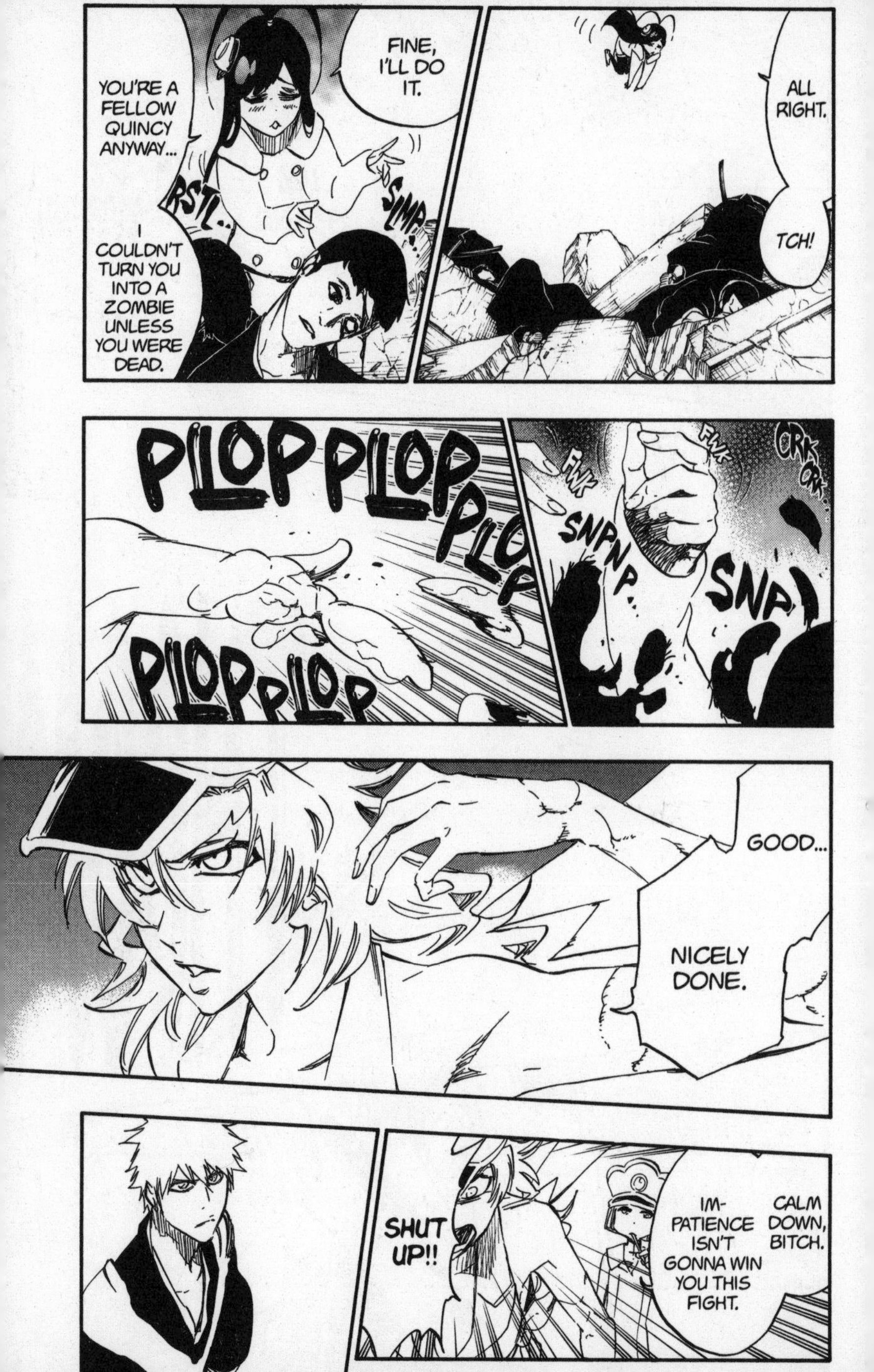
ALL RIGHT.
TCH!
FINE, I'LL DO IT.
YOU'RE A FELLOW QUINCY ANYWAY...
RSTL...
SLMP...
I COULDN'T TURN YOU INTO A ZOMBIE UNLESS YOU WERE DEAD.
CRK CRK
FWK
FWK
SNP
SNPNP...
PLOP PLOP PLOP PLOP
PLOP PLOP
GOOD...
NICELY DONE.
CALM DOWN, BITCH.
IM-PATIENCE ISN'T GONNA WIN YOU THIS FIGHT.
SHUT UP!!

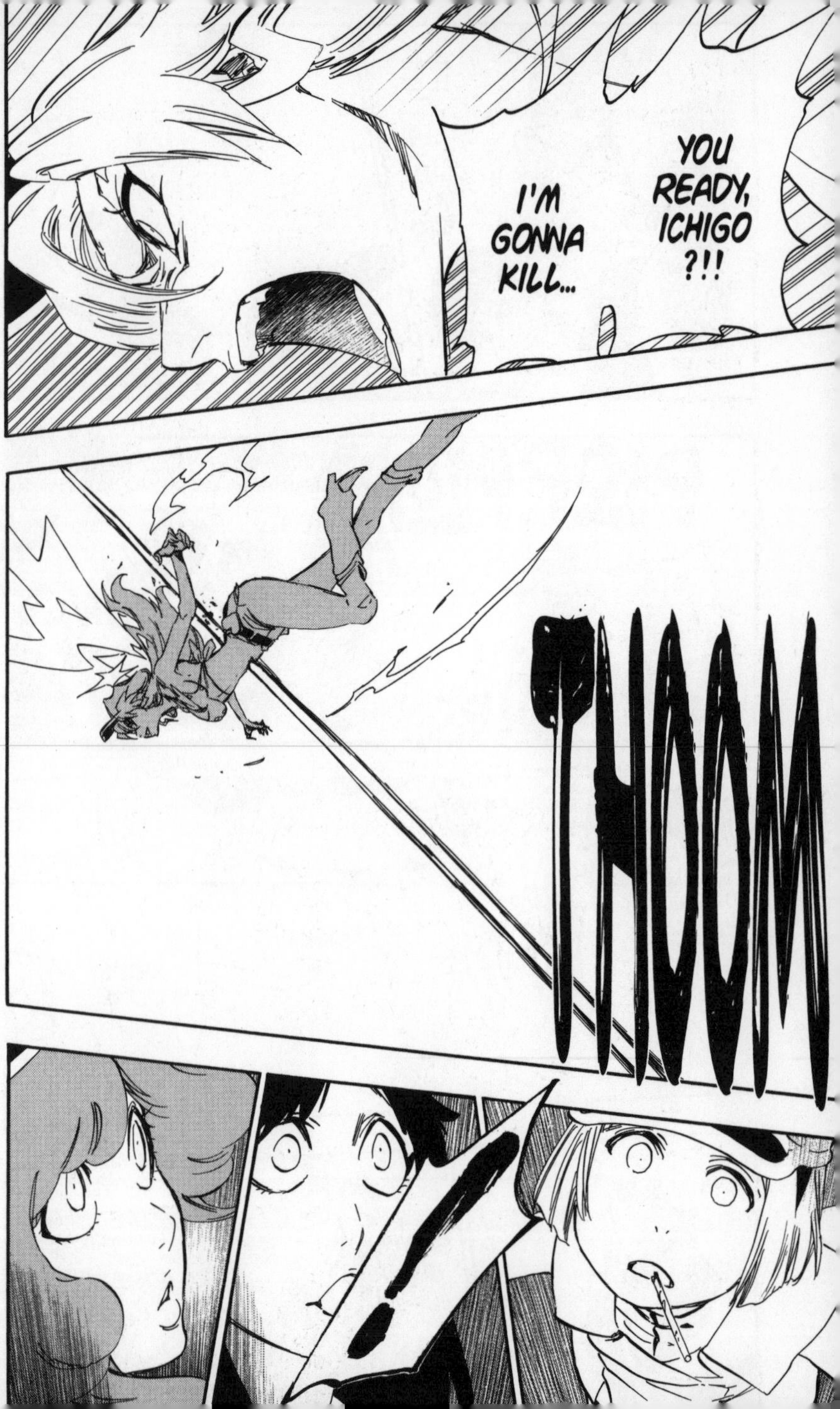
YOU READY, ICHIGO ?!!
I'M GONNA KILL...
THOOM

READ THIS WAY

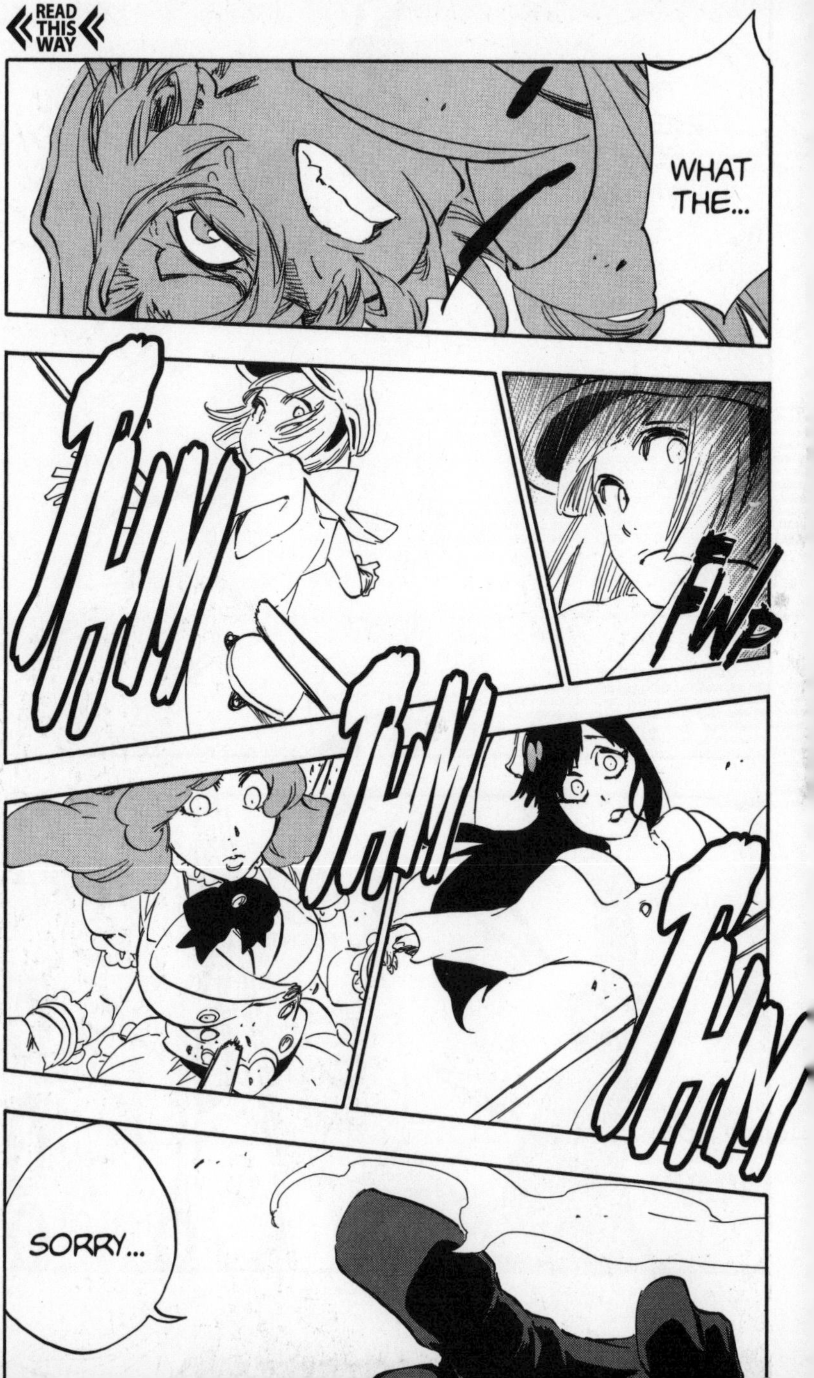
WHAT THE...
FWP
THM
THM
THM
SORRY...

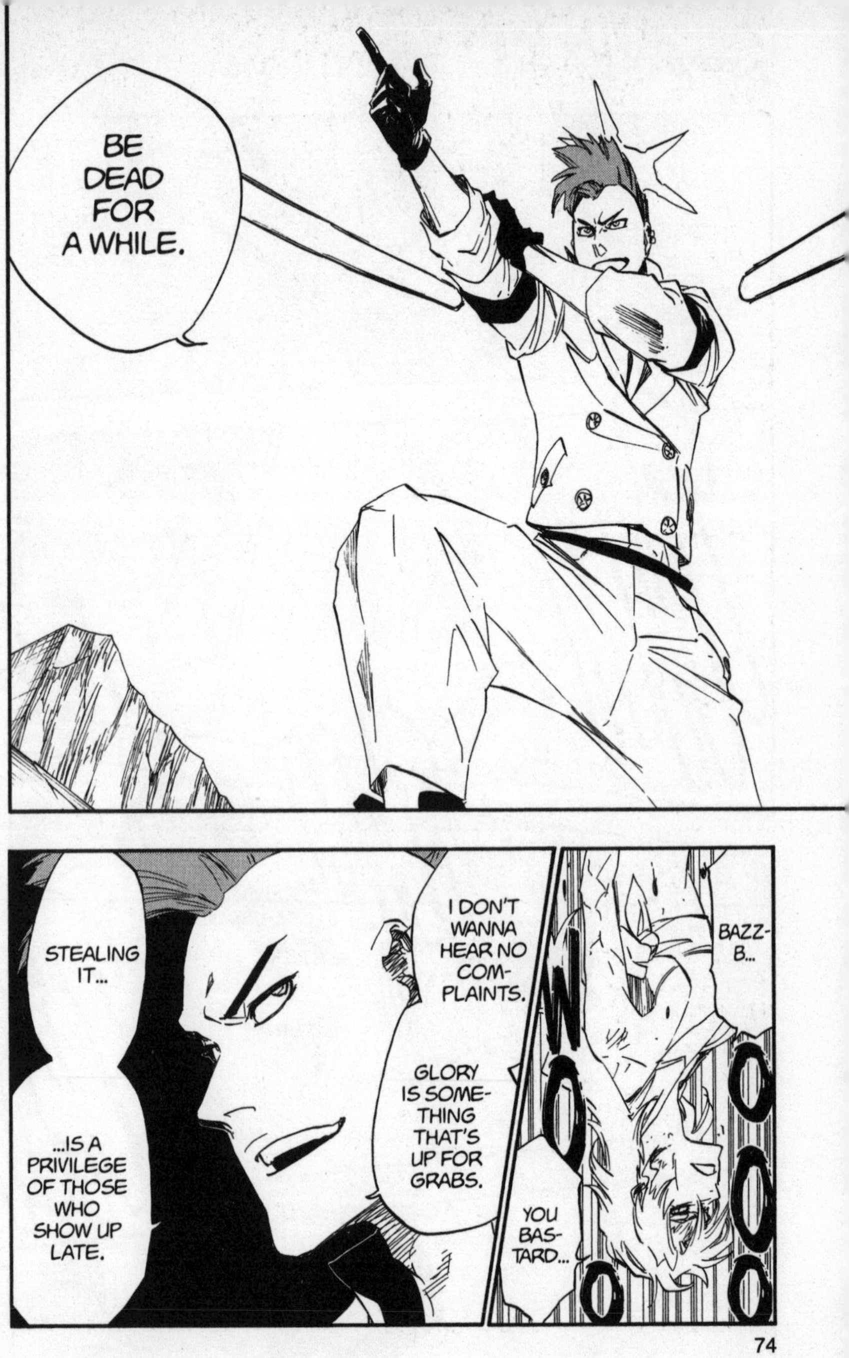
BE DEAD FOR A WHILE.
BAZZ-B...
YOU BAS-TARD...
I DON'T WANNA HEAR NO COM-PLAINTS.
GLORY IS SOME-THING THAT'S UP FOR GRABS.
STEALING IT...
...IS A PRIVILEGE OF THOSE WHO SHOW UP LATE.

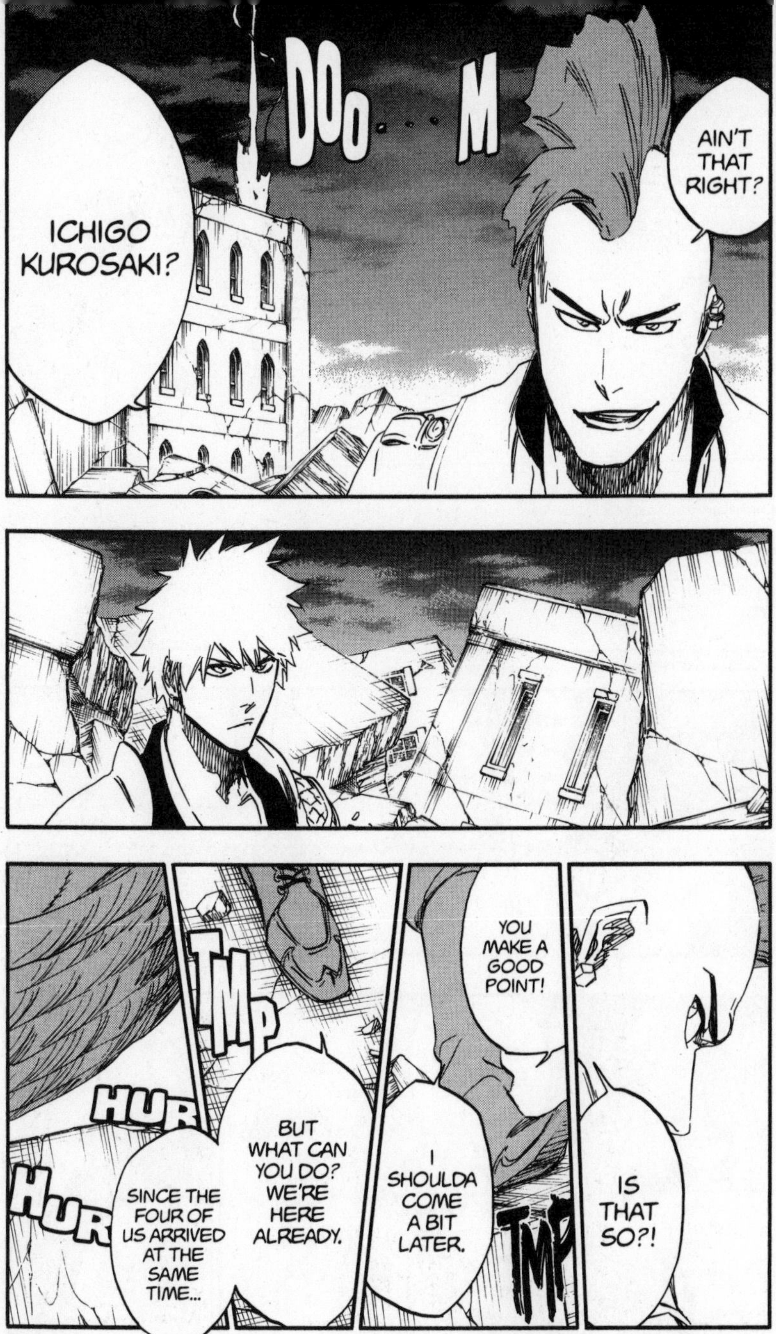
AIN'T THAT RIGHT?
DOO...M
ICHIGO KUROSAKI?
IS THAT SO?!
YOU MAKE A GOOD POINT!
I SHOULDA COME A BIT LATER.
TMP
TMP
BUT WHAT CAN YOU DO? WE'RE HERE ALREADY.
HUR
HUR
SINCE THE FOUR OF US ARRIVED AT THE SAME TIME...

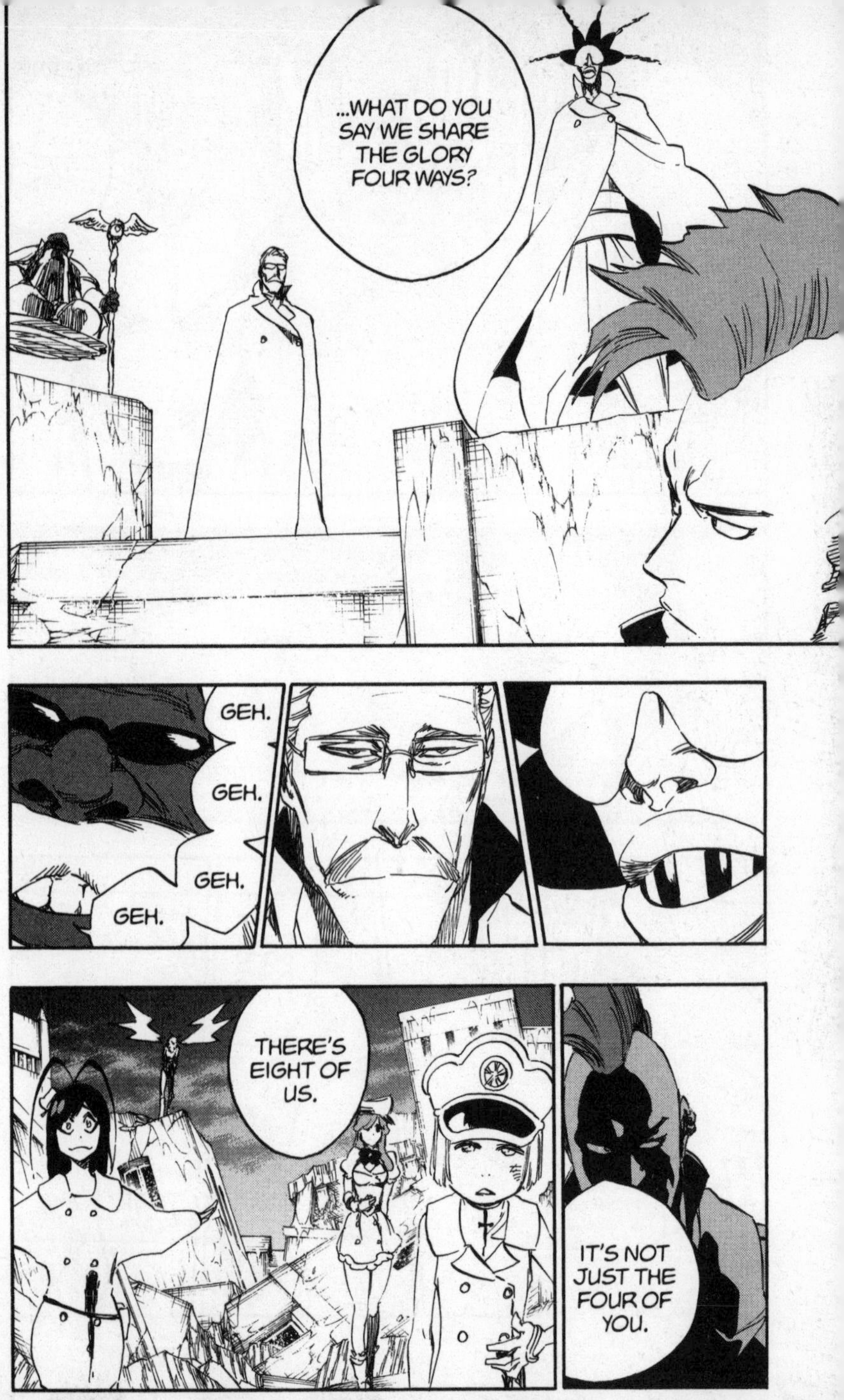
...WHAT DO YOU SAY WE SHARE THE GLORY FOUR WAYS?
GEH.
GEH.
GEH.
GEH.
IT'S NOT JUST THE FOUR OF YOU.
THERE'S EIGHT OF US.

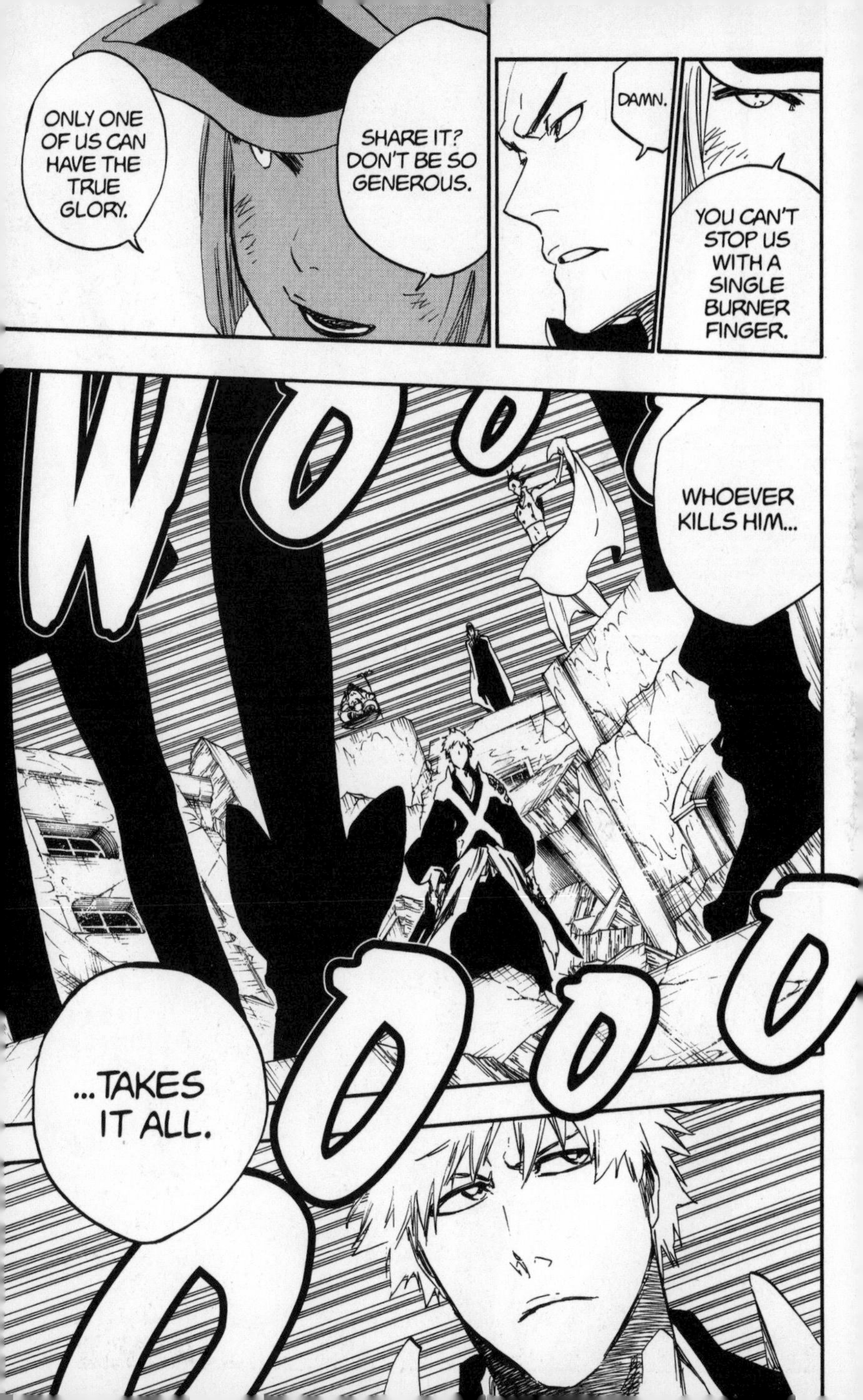
YOU CAN'T STOP US WITH A SINGLE BURNER FINGER.
DAMN.
SHARE IT? DON'T BE SO GENEROUS.
ONLY ONE OF US CAN HAVE THE TRUE GLORY.
WHOEVER KILLS HIM...
WOOOOOOO
...TAKES IT ALL.

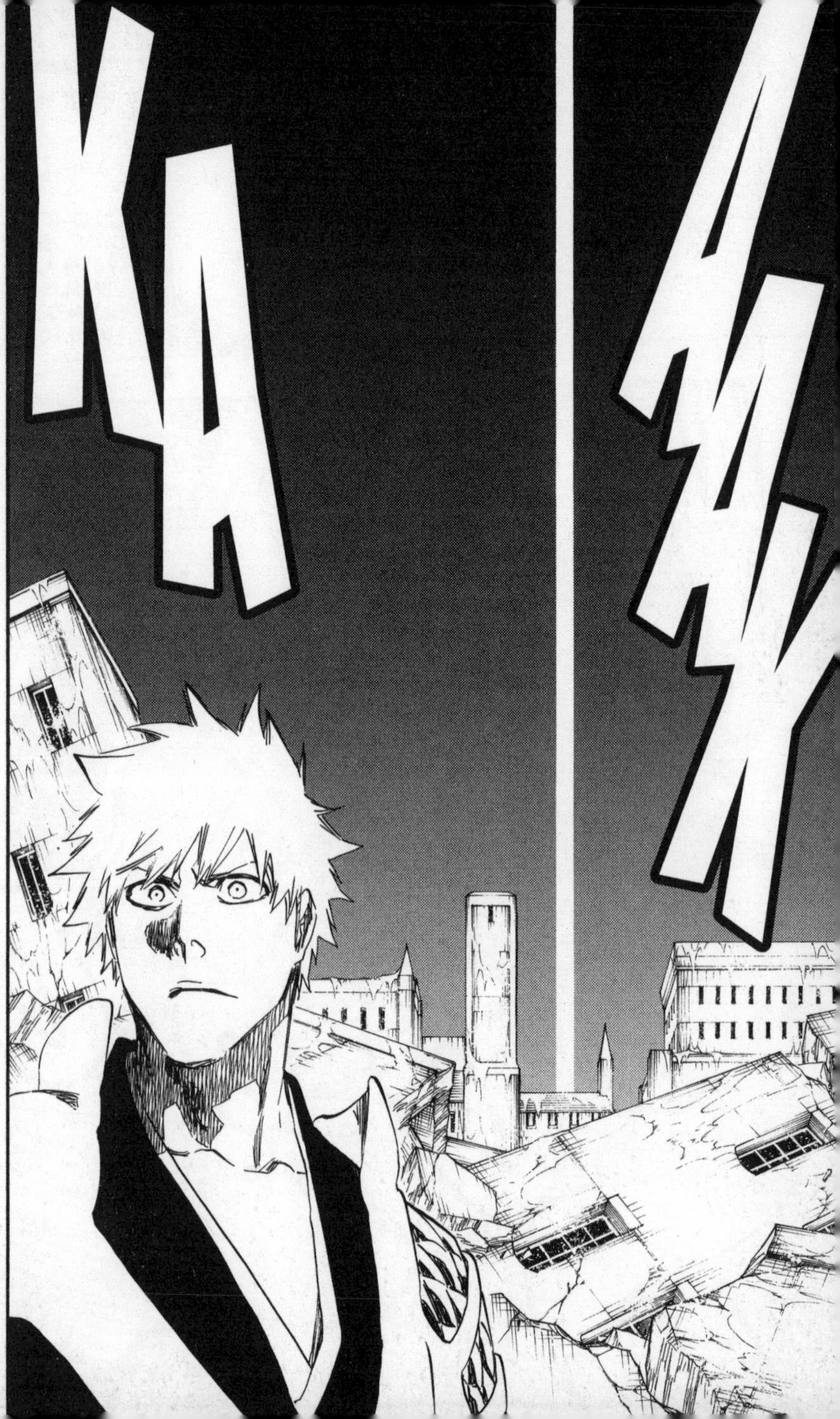
KA
AAK

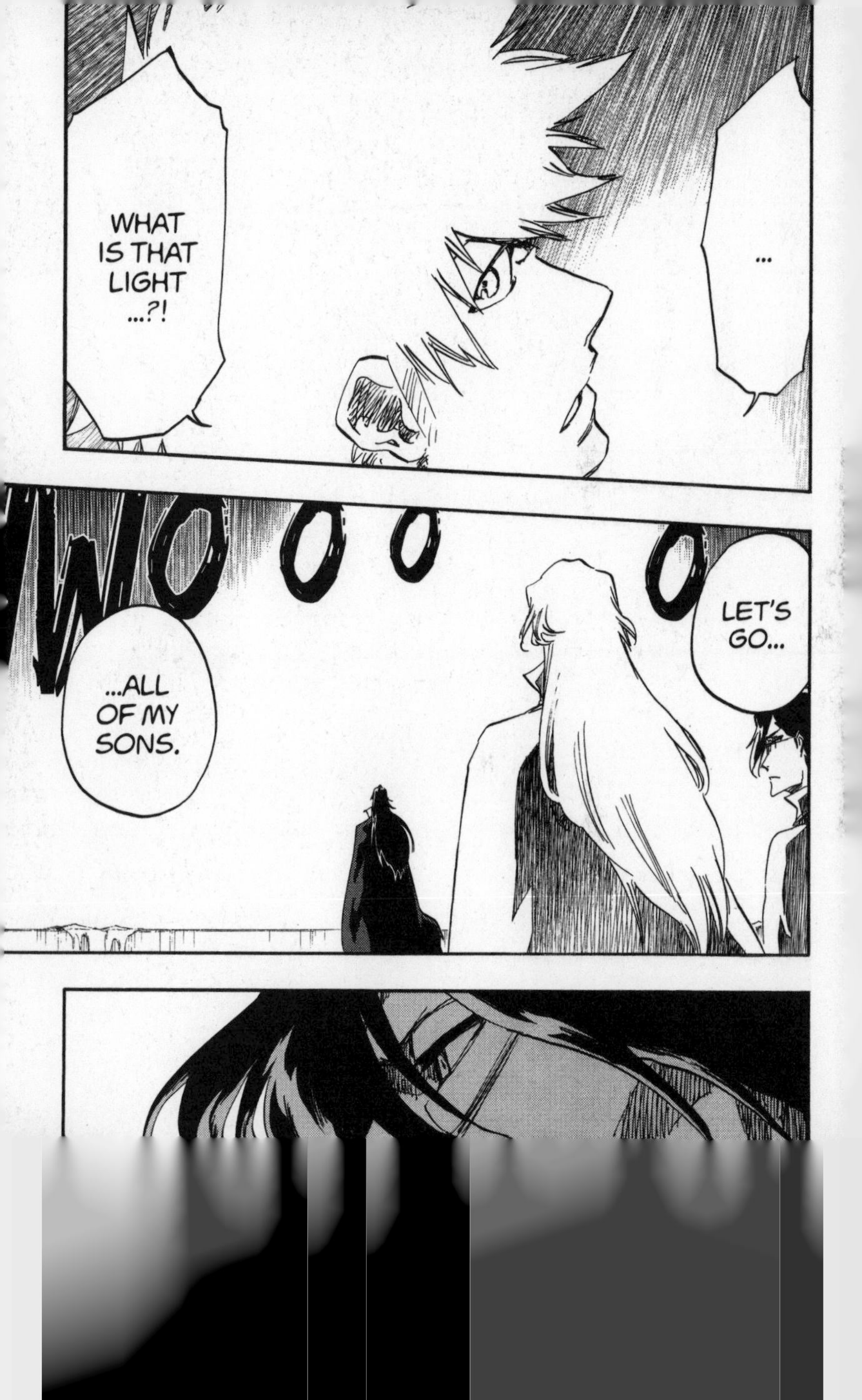
...
WHAT IS THAT LIGHT ...?!
WOOOO
LET'S GO...
...ALL OF MY SONS.

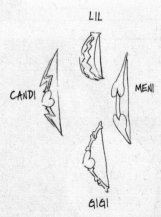

LIL

CANDI

MENI

GIGI

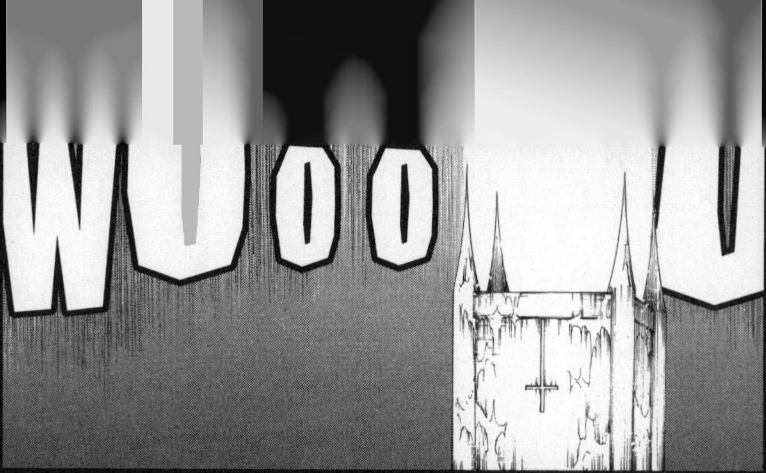

The Headless Star 4

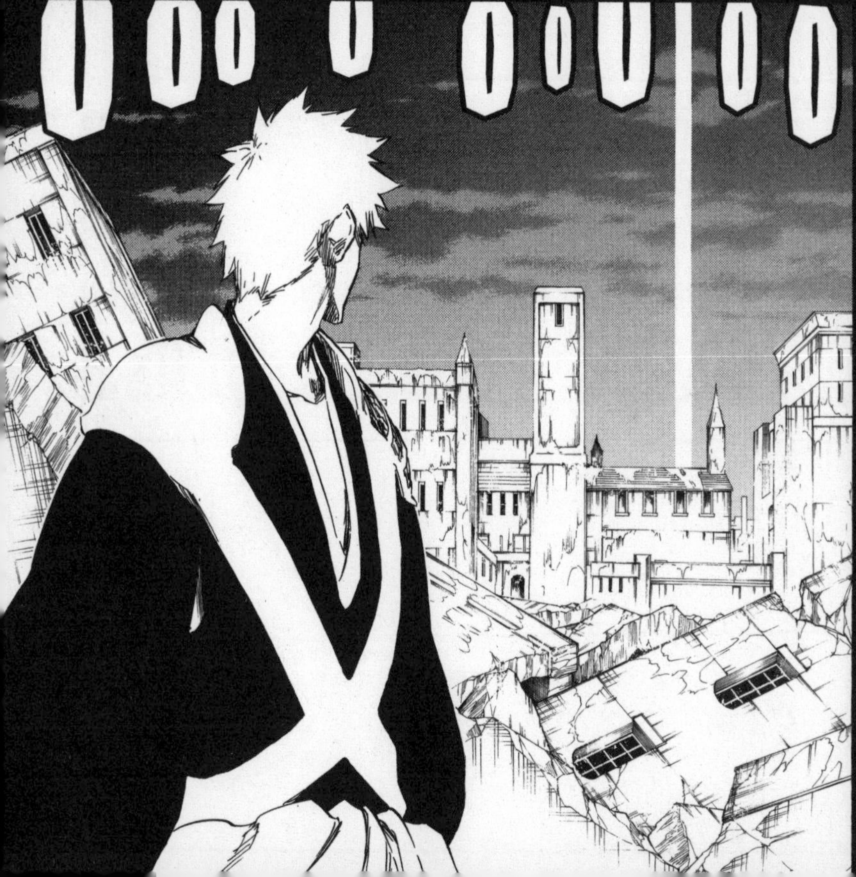

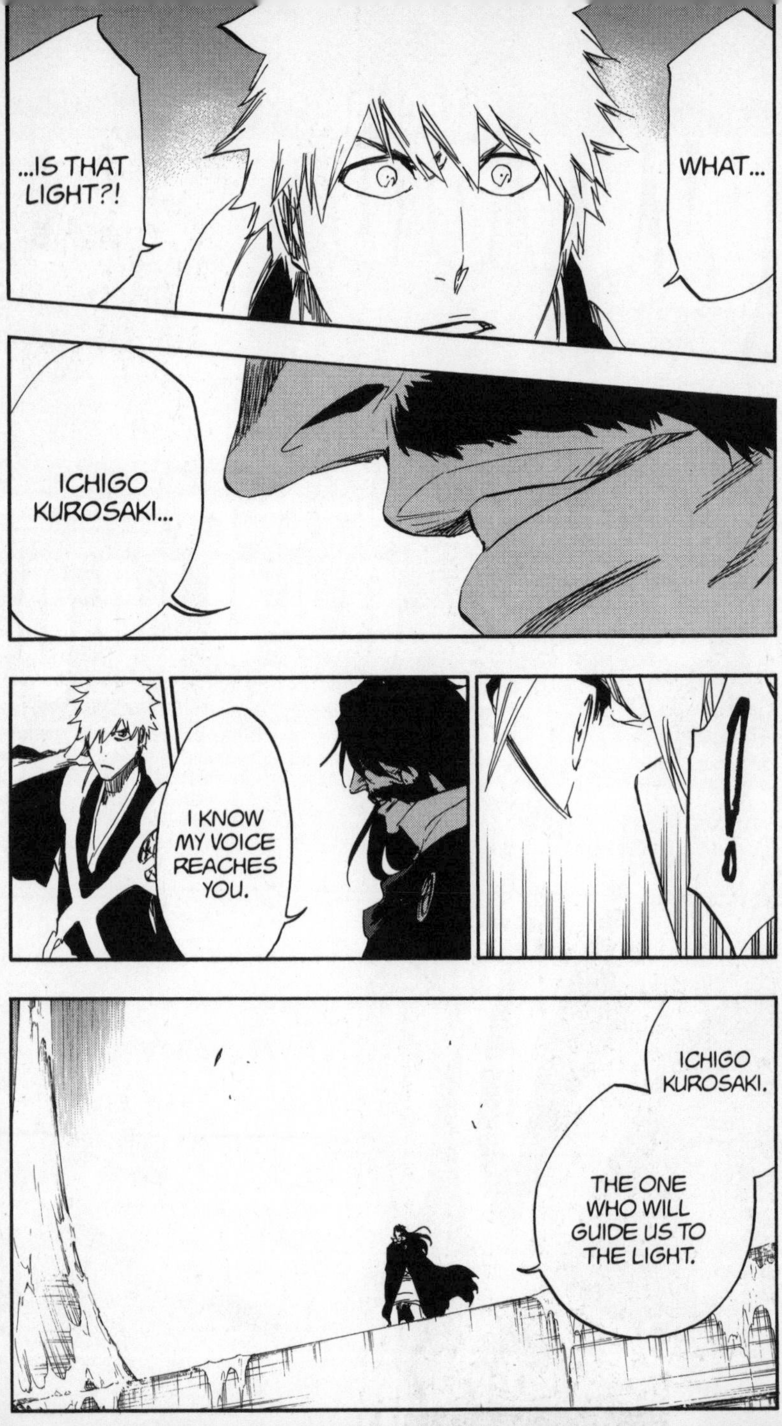
WHAT...
...IS THAT LIGHT?!
ICHIGO KUROSAKI...
!
I KNOW MY VOICE REACHES YOU.
ICHIGO KUROSAKI.
THE ONE WHO WILL GUIDE US TO THE LIGHT.

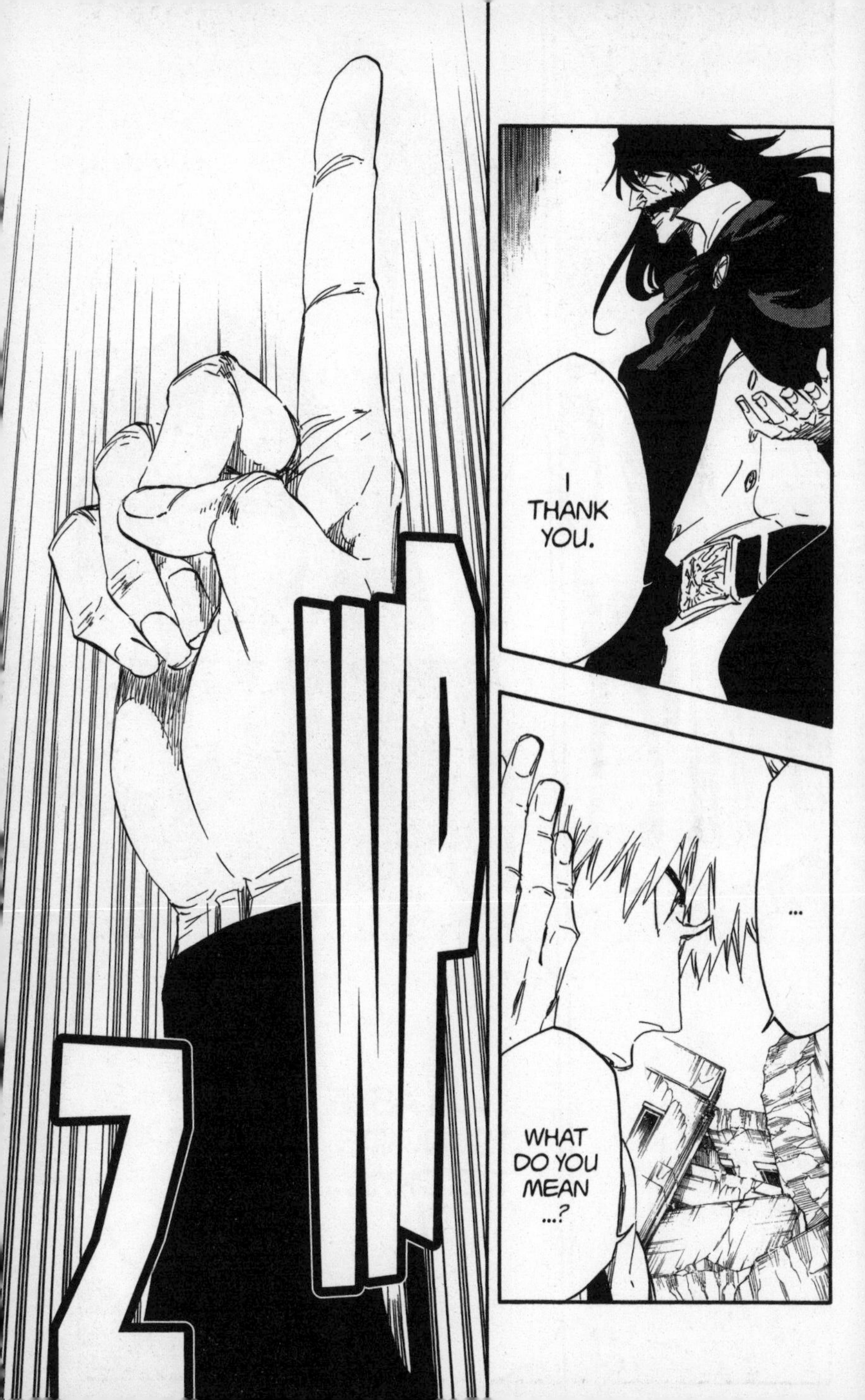
I THANK YOU.
...
WHAT DO YOU MEAN ...?

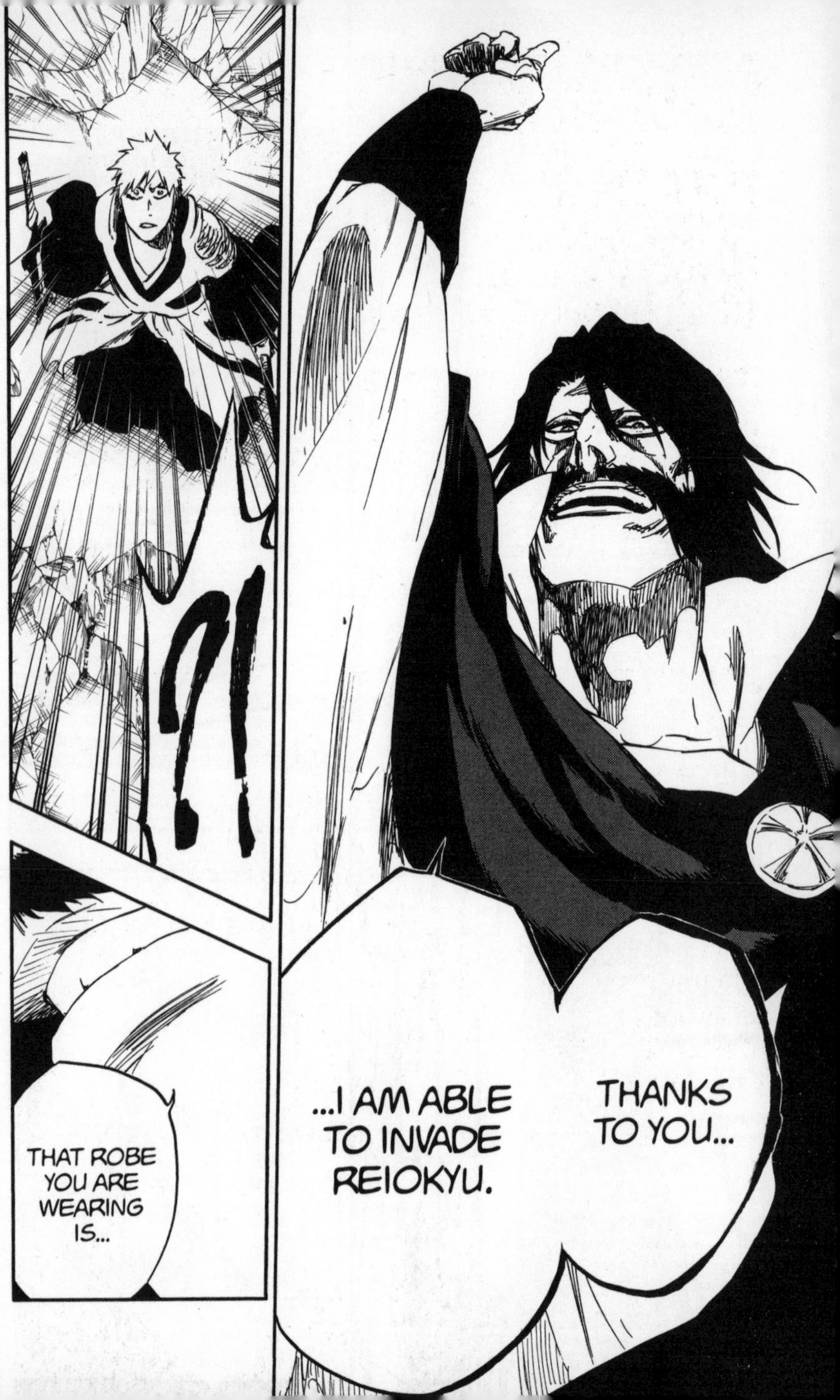
THANKS TO YOU...
...I AM ABLE TO INVADE REIOKYU.
?!
THAT ROBE YOU ARE WEARING IS...

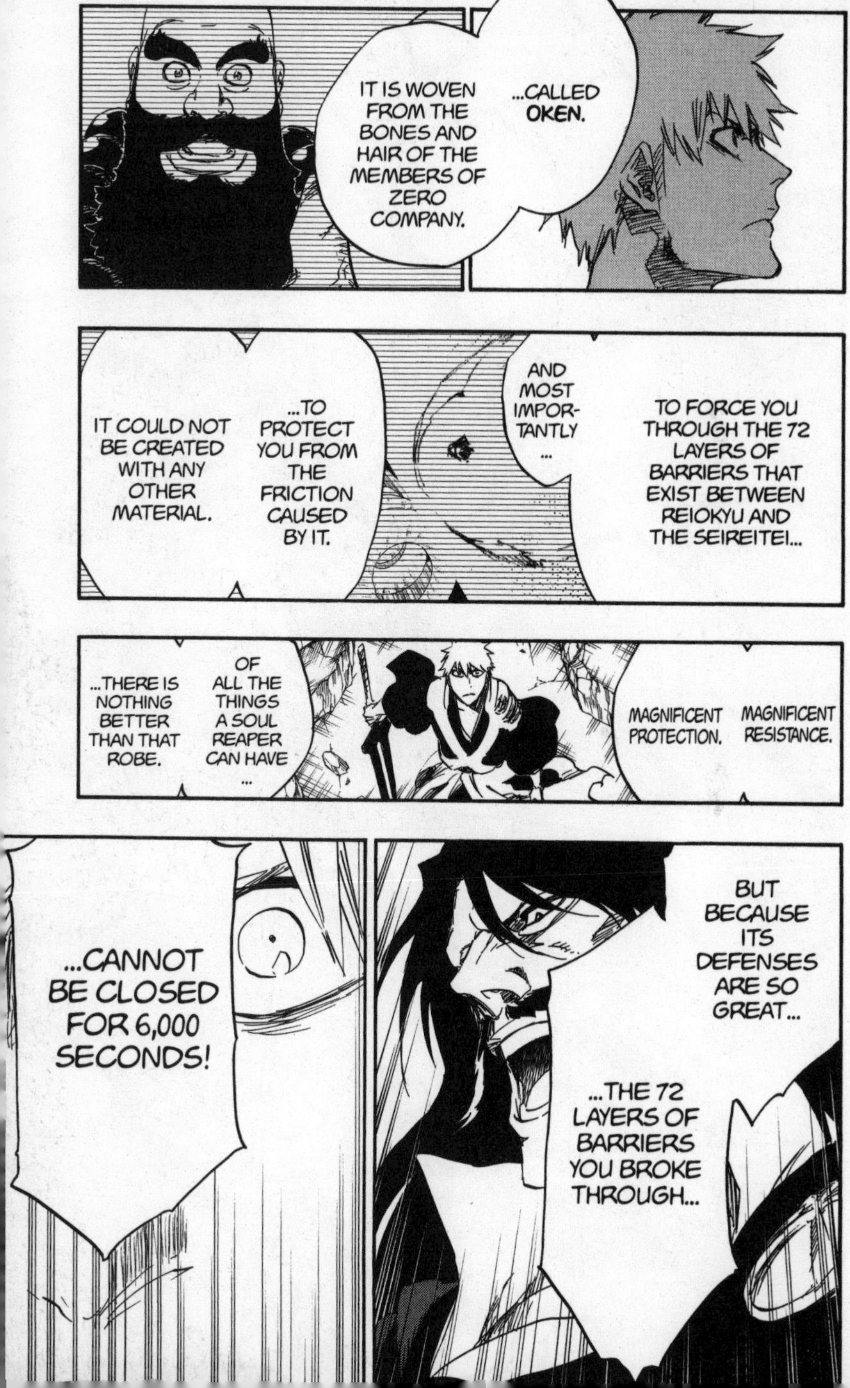
...CALLED OKEN.
IT IS WOVEN FROM THE BONES AND HAIR OF THE MEMBERS OF ZERO COMPANY.
TO FORCE YOU THROUGH THE 72 LAYERS OF BARRIERS THAT EXIST BETWEEN REIOKYU AND THE SEIREITEI...
AND MOST IMPOR-TANTLY...
...TO PROTECT YOU FROM THE FRICTION CAUSED BY IT.
IT COULD NOT BE CREATED WITH ANY OTHER MATERIAL.
MAGNIFICENT RESISTANCE.
MAGNIFICENT PROTECTION.
OF ALL THE THINGS A SOUL REAPER CAN HAVE...
...THERE IS NOTHING BETTER THAN THAT ROBE.
BUT BECAUSE ITS DEFENSES ARE SO GREAT...
...THE 72 LAYERS OF BARRIERS YOU BROKE THROUGH...
...CANNOT BE CLOSED FOR 6,000 SECONDS!

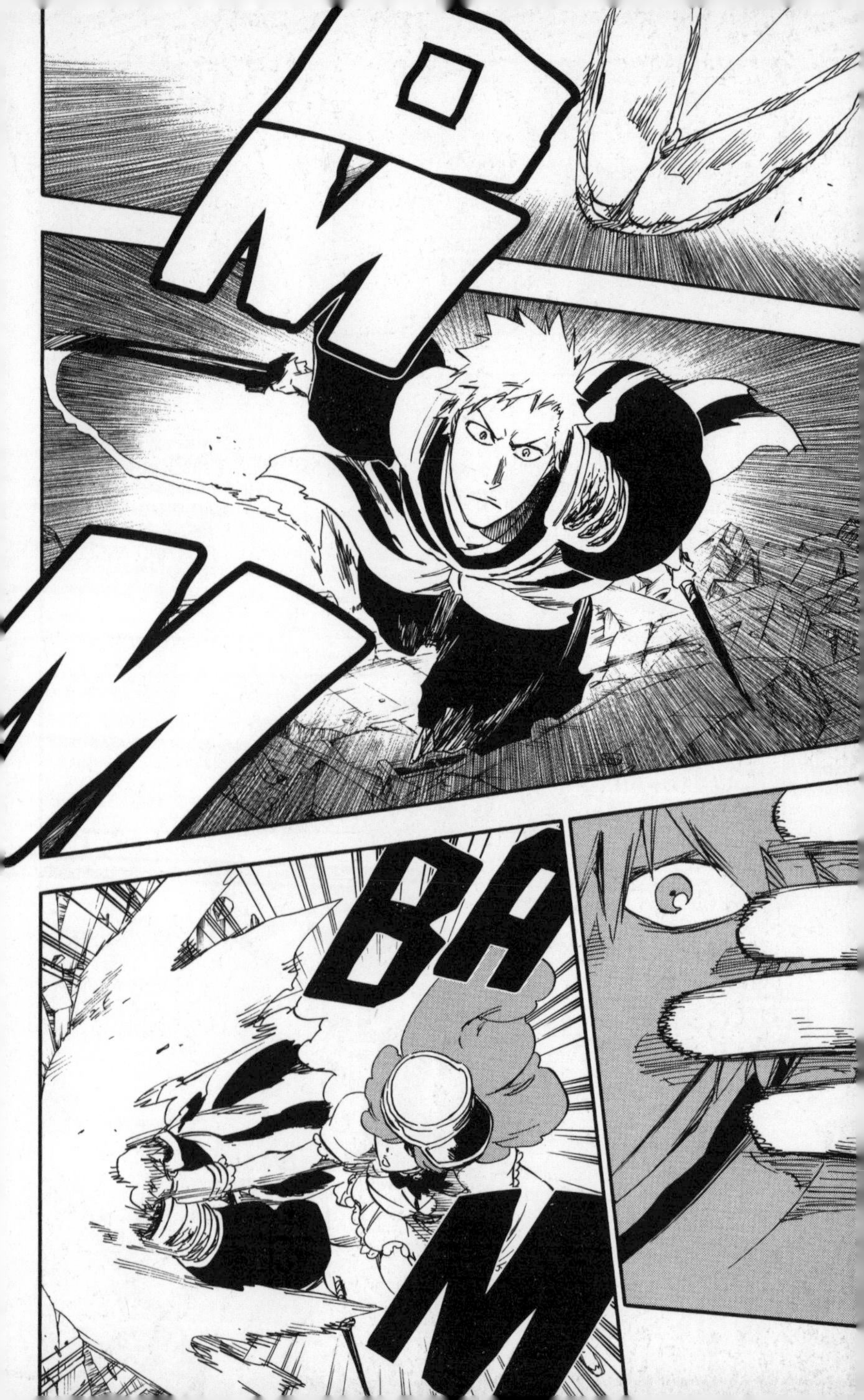
BAM

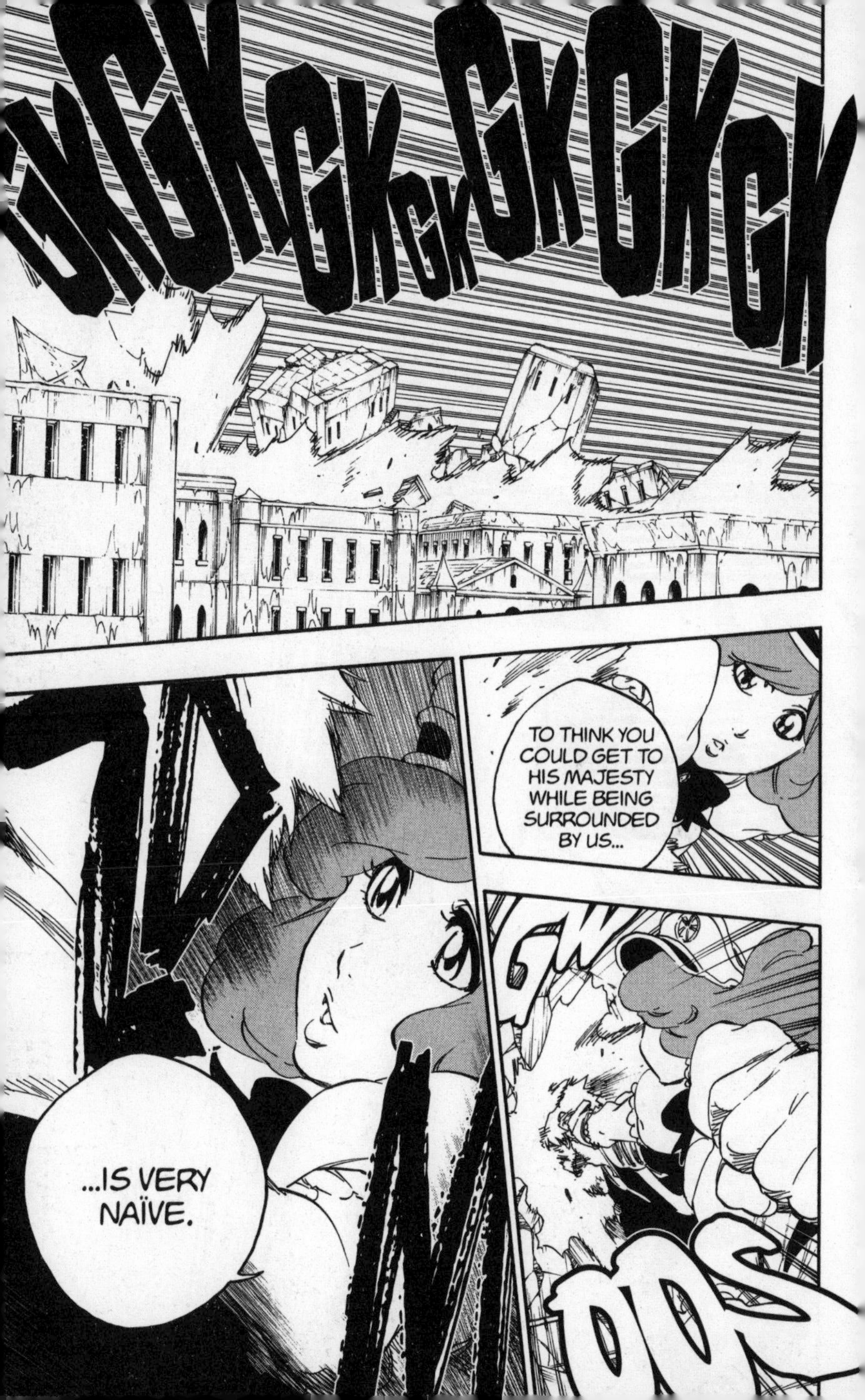
TO THINK YOU COULD GET TO HIS MAJESTY WHILE BEING SURROUNDED BY US...
...IS VERY NAÏVE.

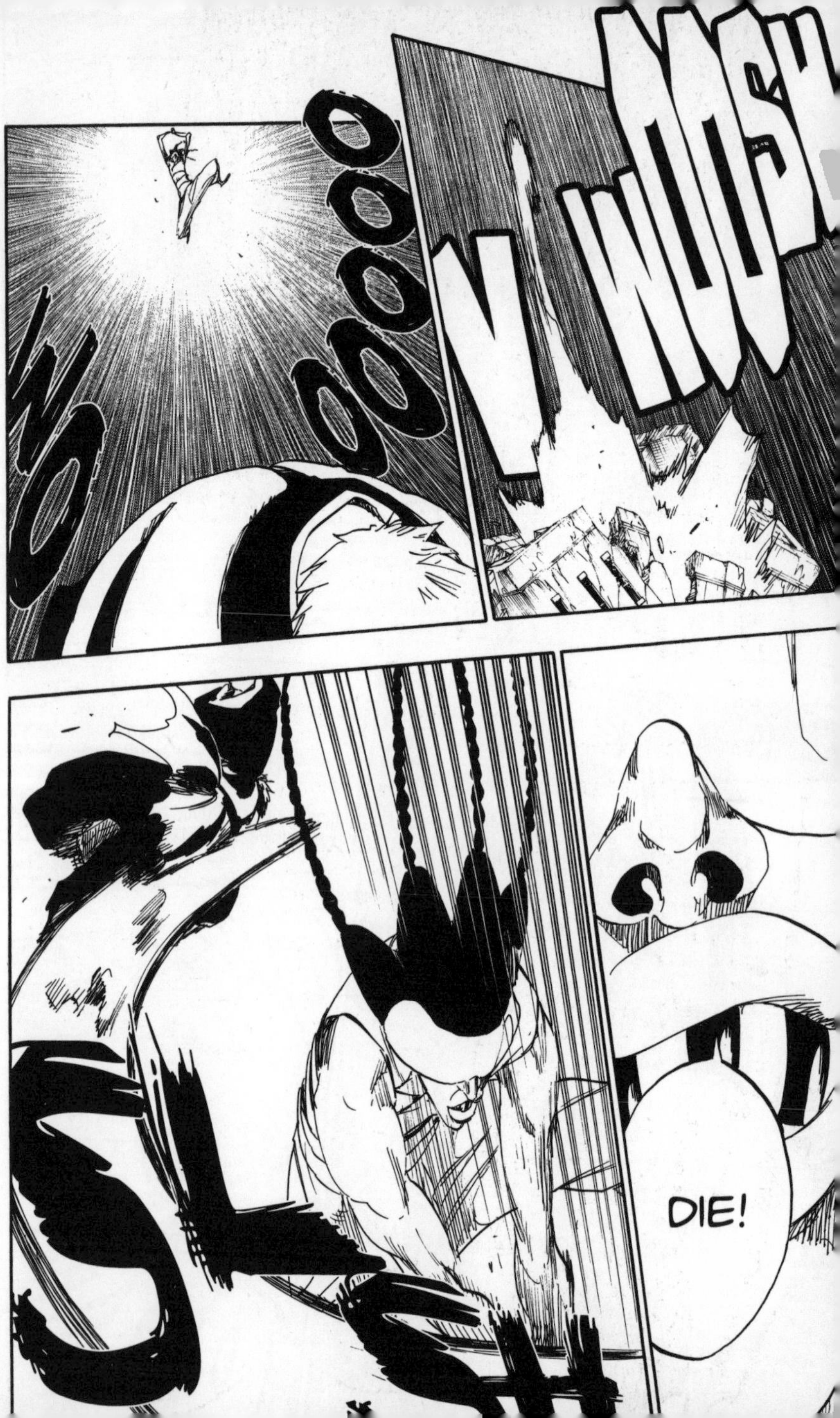
DIE!

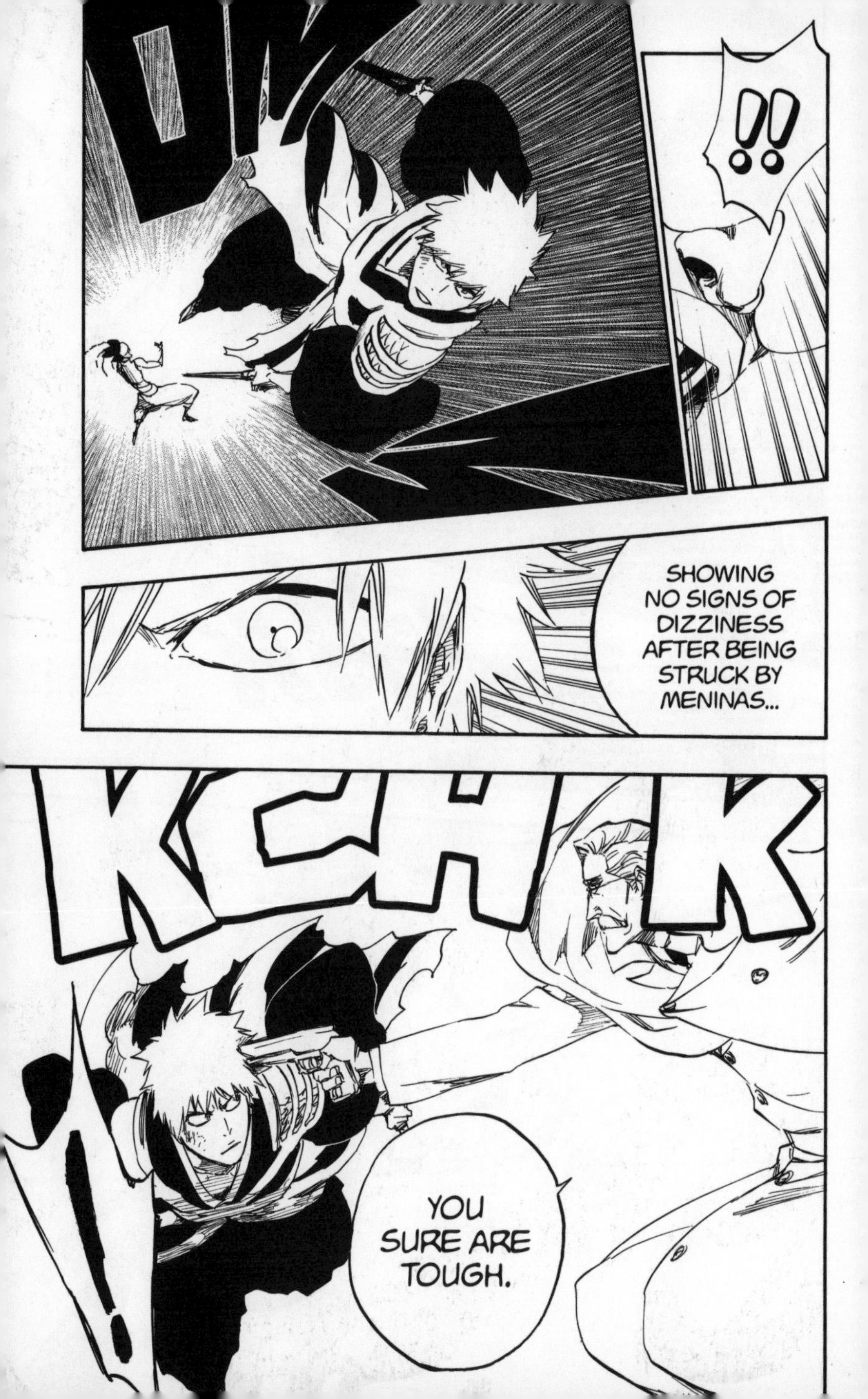
!!
SHOWING NO SIGNS OF DIZZINESS AFTER BEING STRUCK BY MENINAS...
YOU SURE ARE TOUGH.

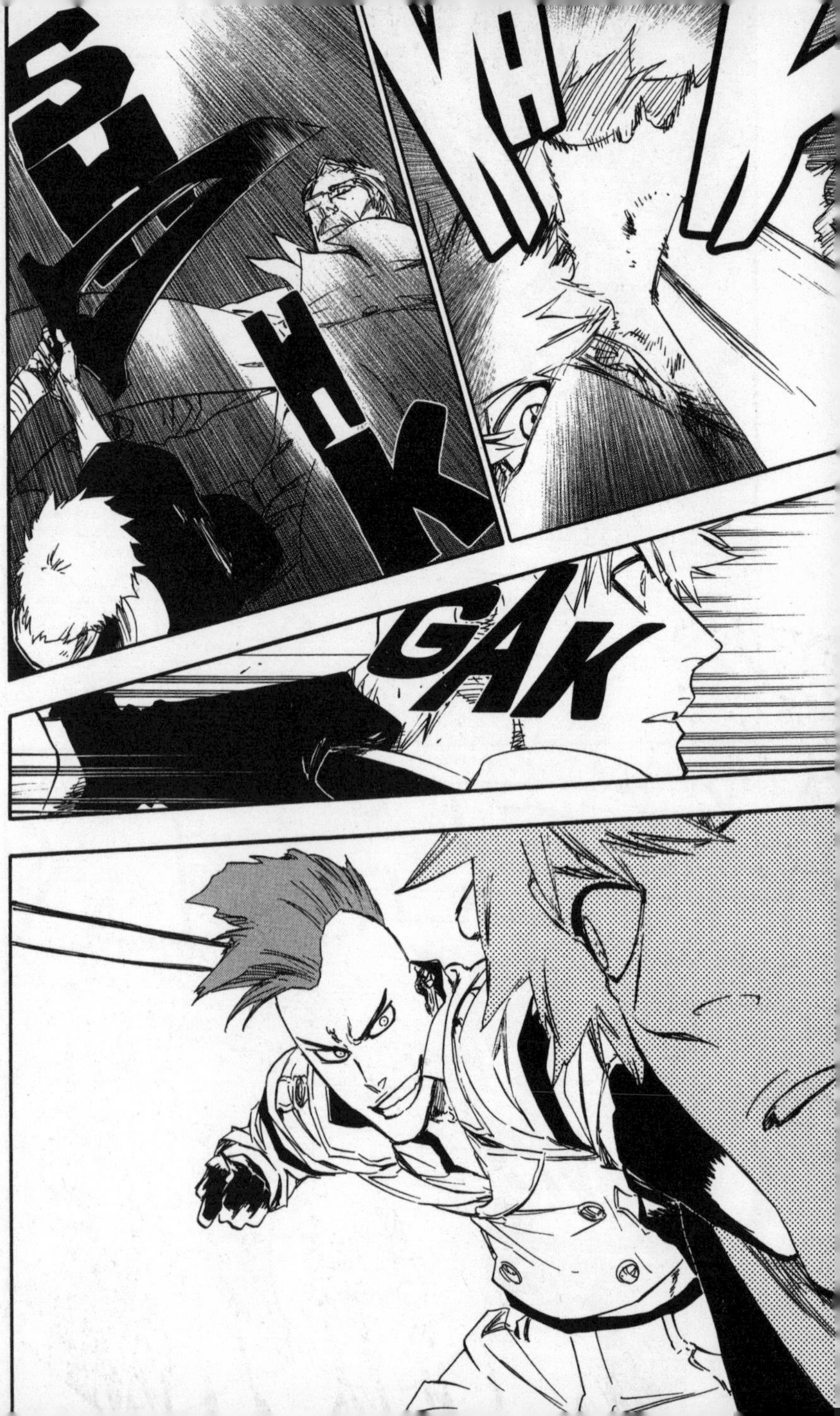
GAK

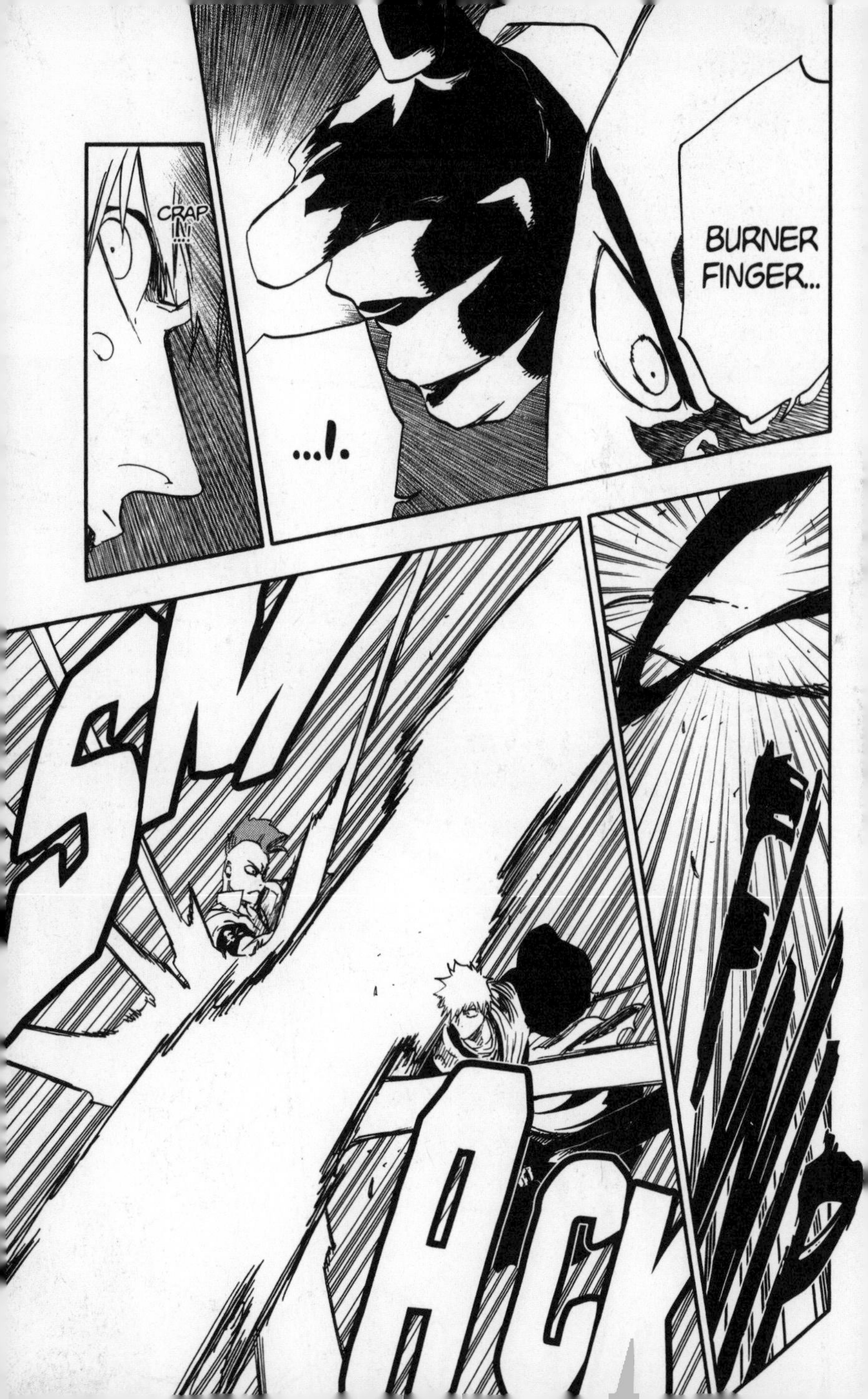
BURNER FINGER...
...I.
CRAP...
SMACK

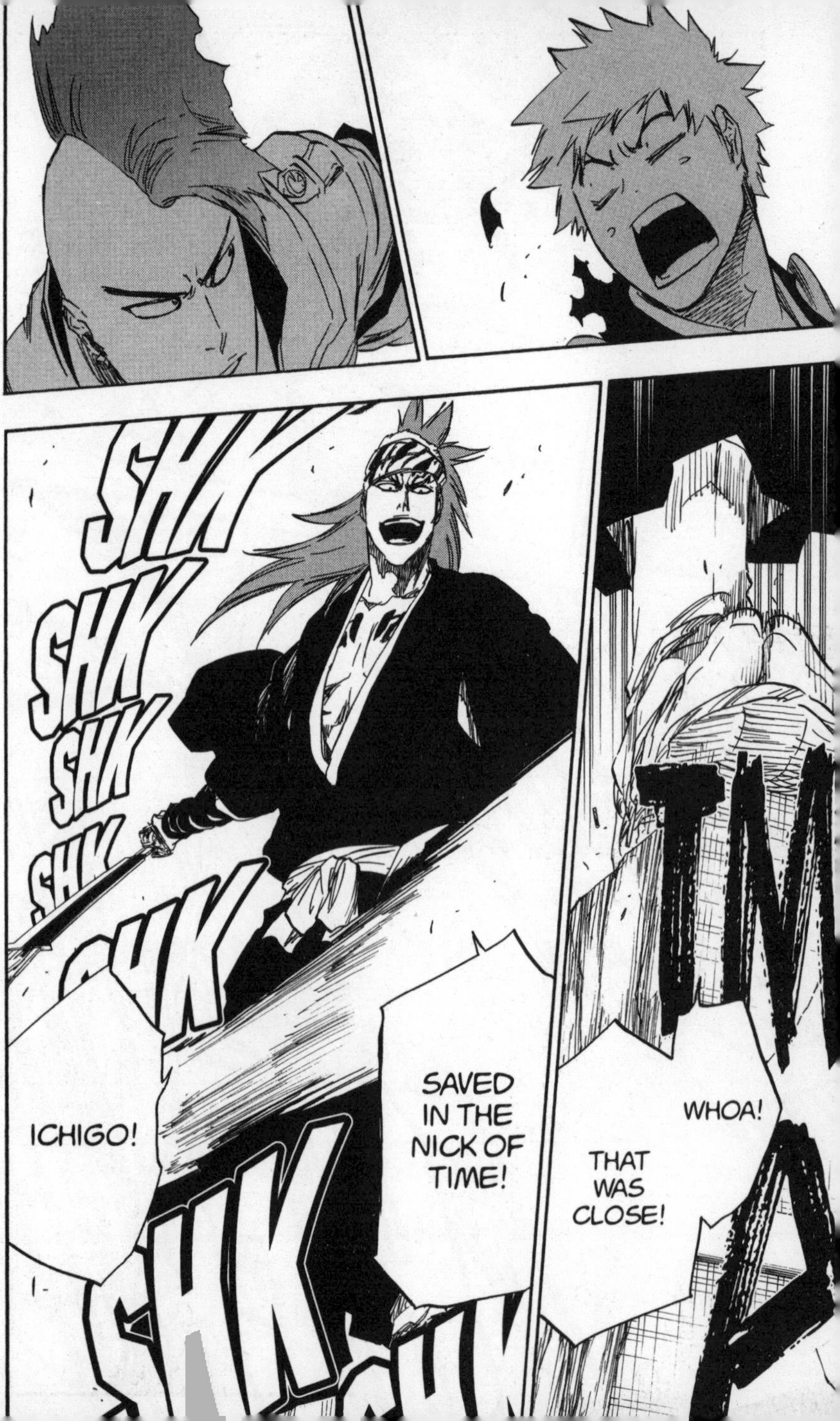
WHOA!
THAT WAS CLOSE!
SHK
SHK
SHK
SHK
SAVED IN THE NICK OF TIME!
ICHIGO!

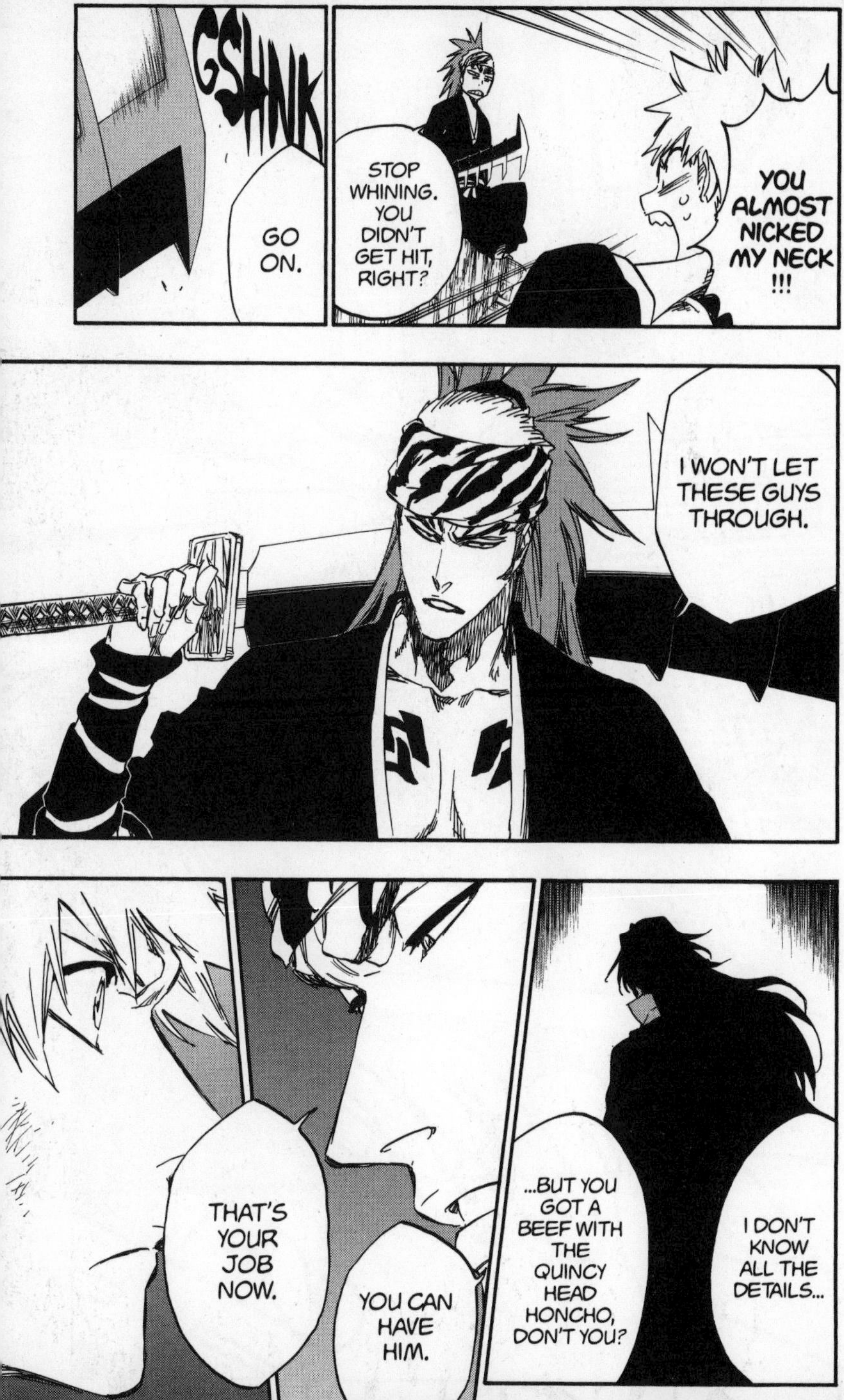
YOU ALMOST NICKED MY NECK!!!
STOP WHINING. YOU DIDN'T GET HIT, RIGHT?
GSHNK
GO ON.
I WON'T LET THESE GUYS THROUGH.
I DON'T KNOW ALL THE DETAILS...
...BUT YOU GOT A BEEF WITH THE QUINCY HEAD HONCHO, DON'T YOU?
YOU CAN HAVE HIM.
THAT'S YOUR JOB NOW.

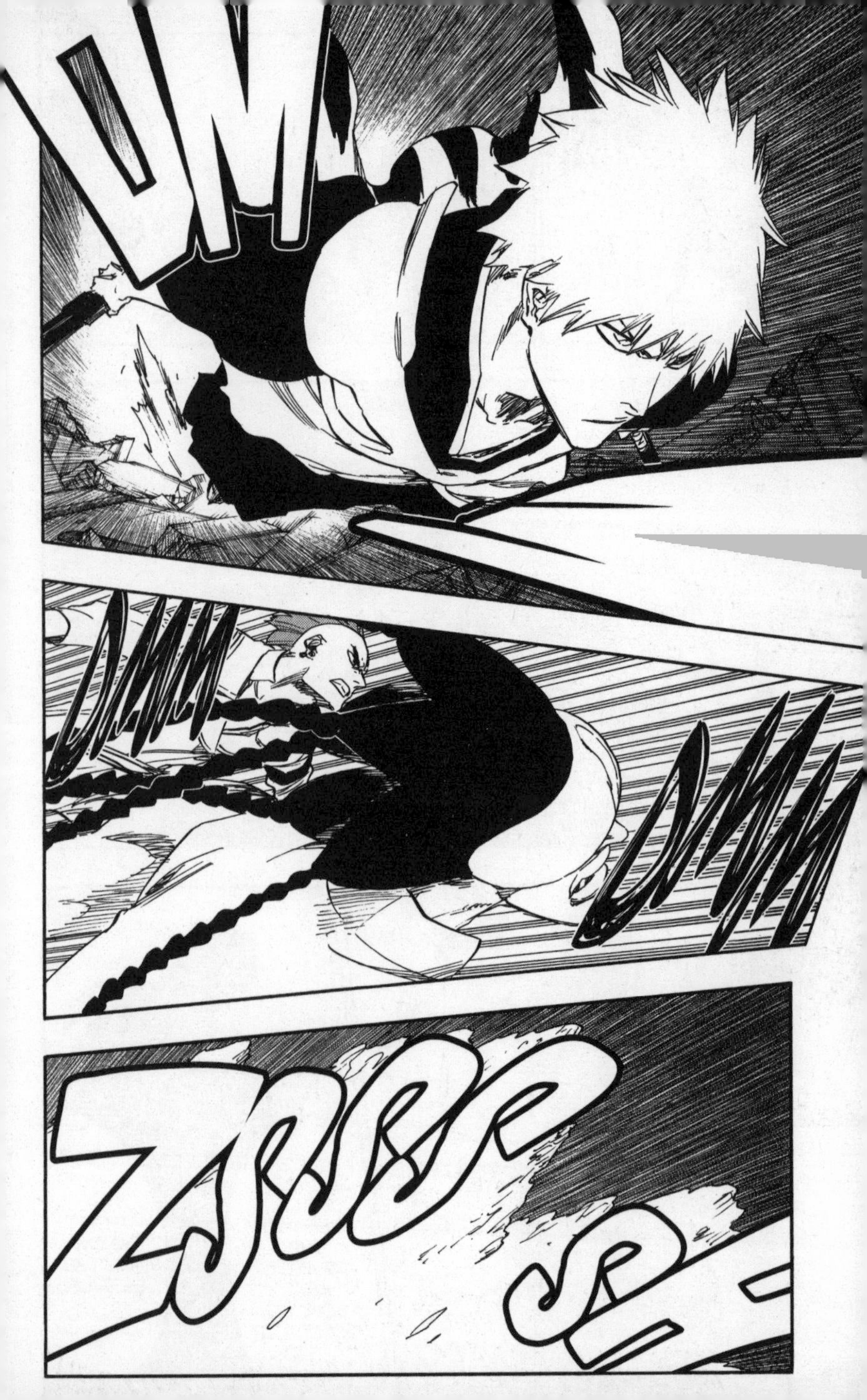

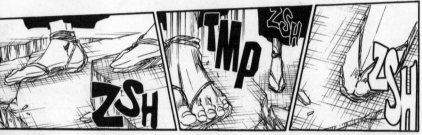

DON'T MAKE
ME REPEAT
MYSELF...

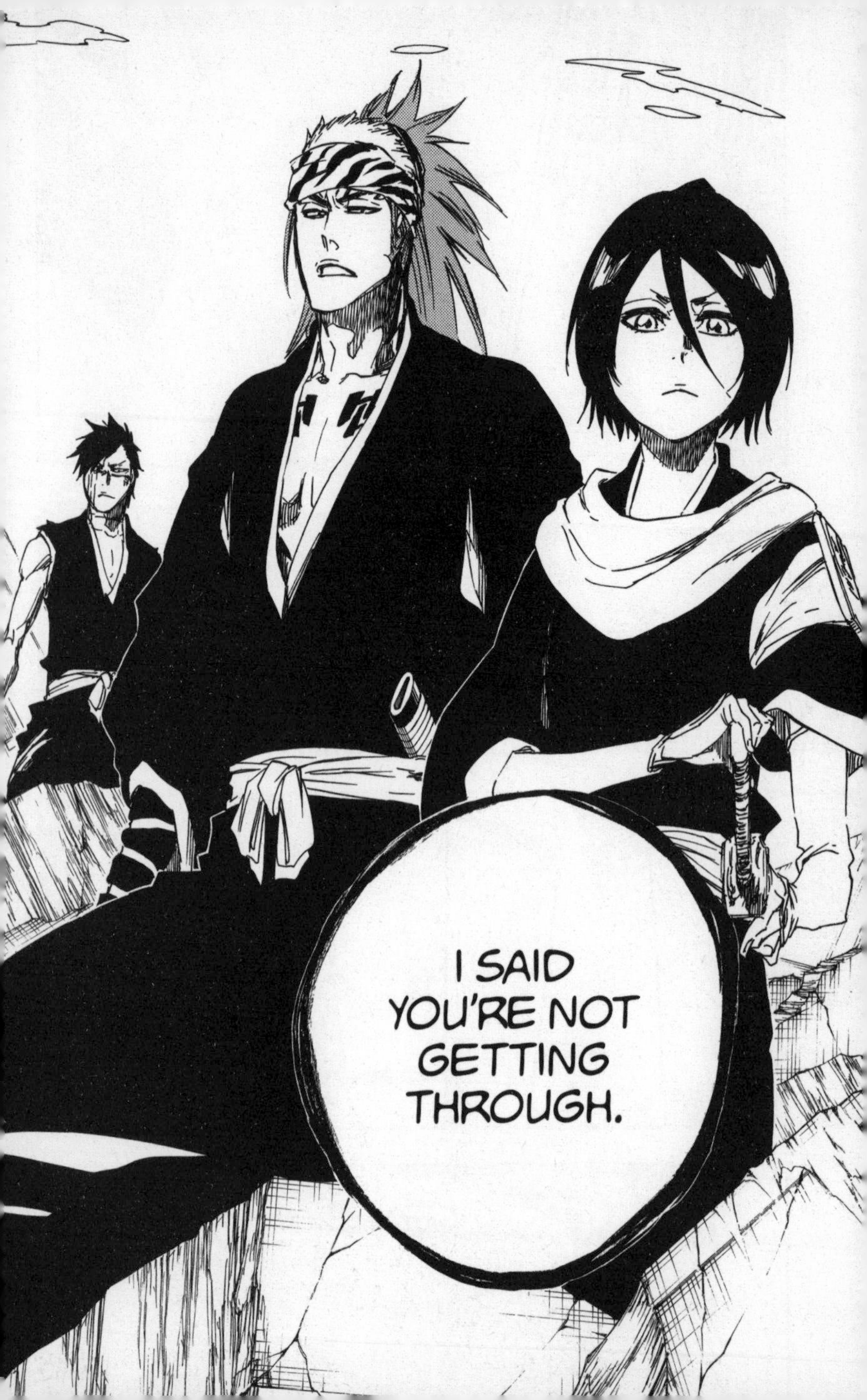
I SAID YOU'RE NOT GETTING THROUGH.

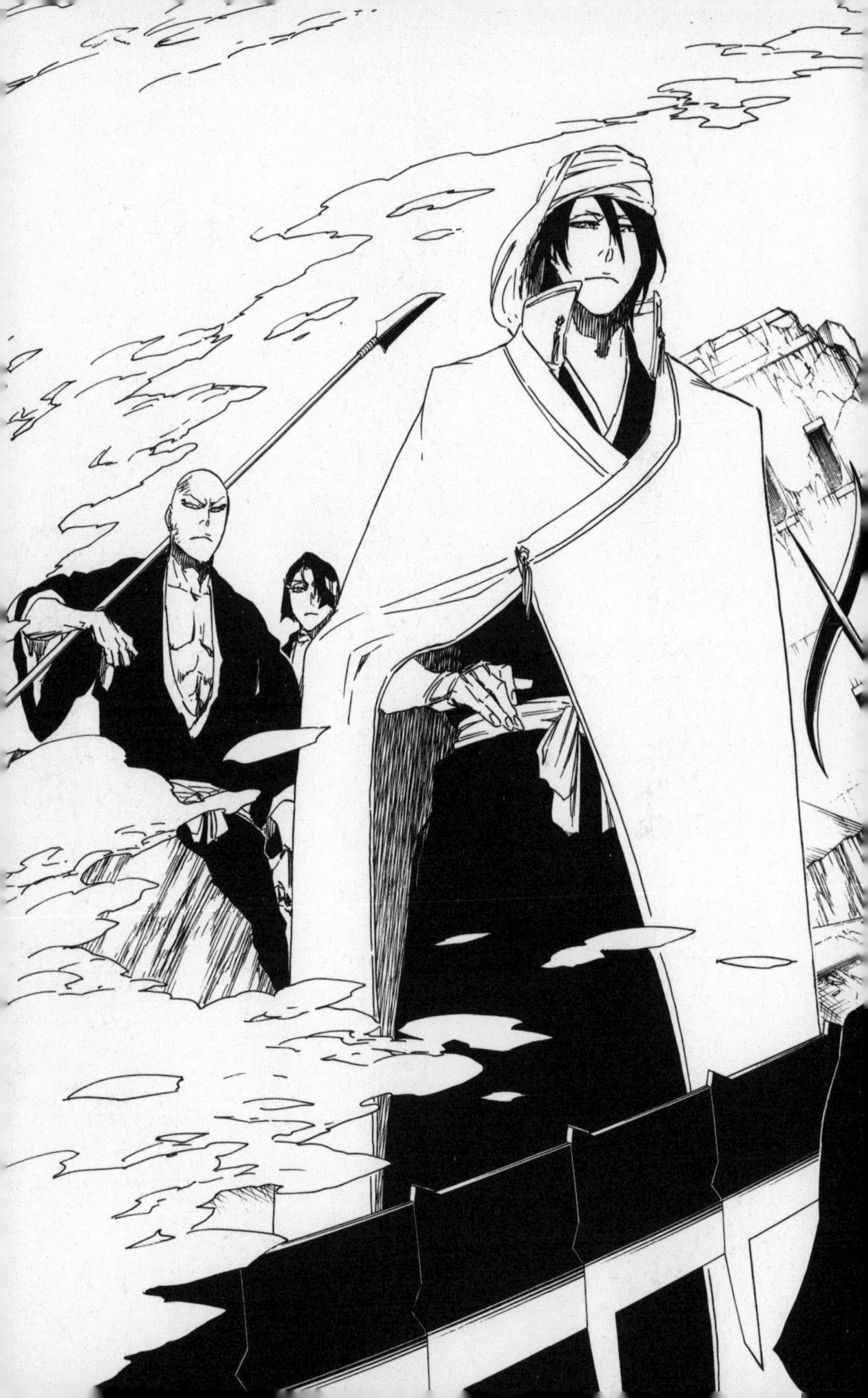

LIL
MENI
CANDI
GIGI

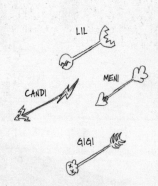

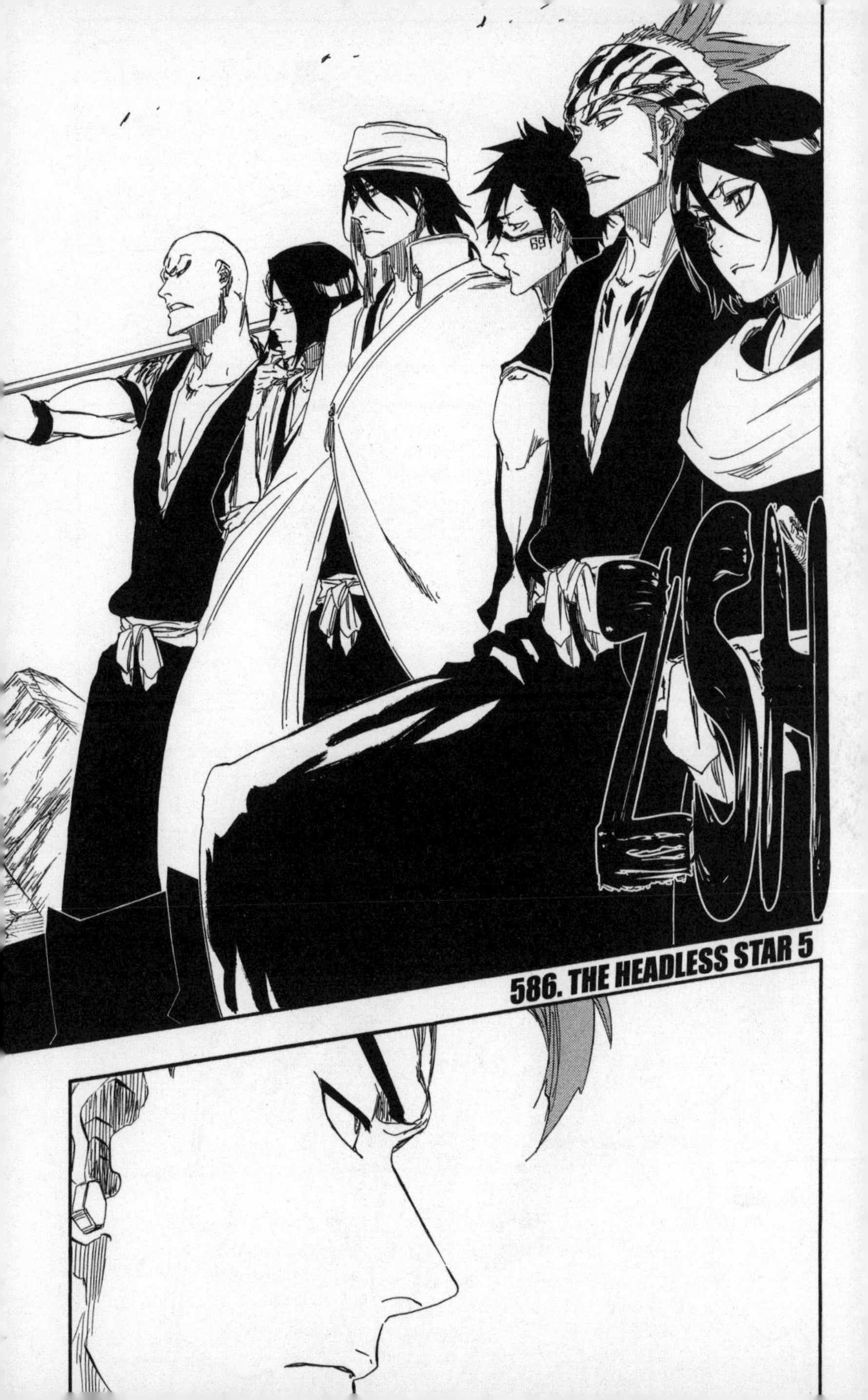
586. THE HEADLESS STAR 5

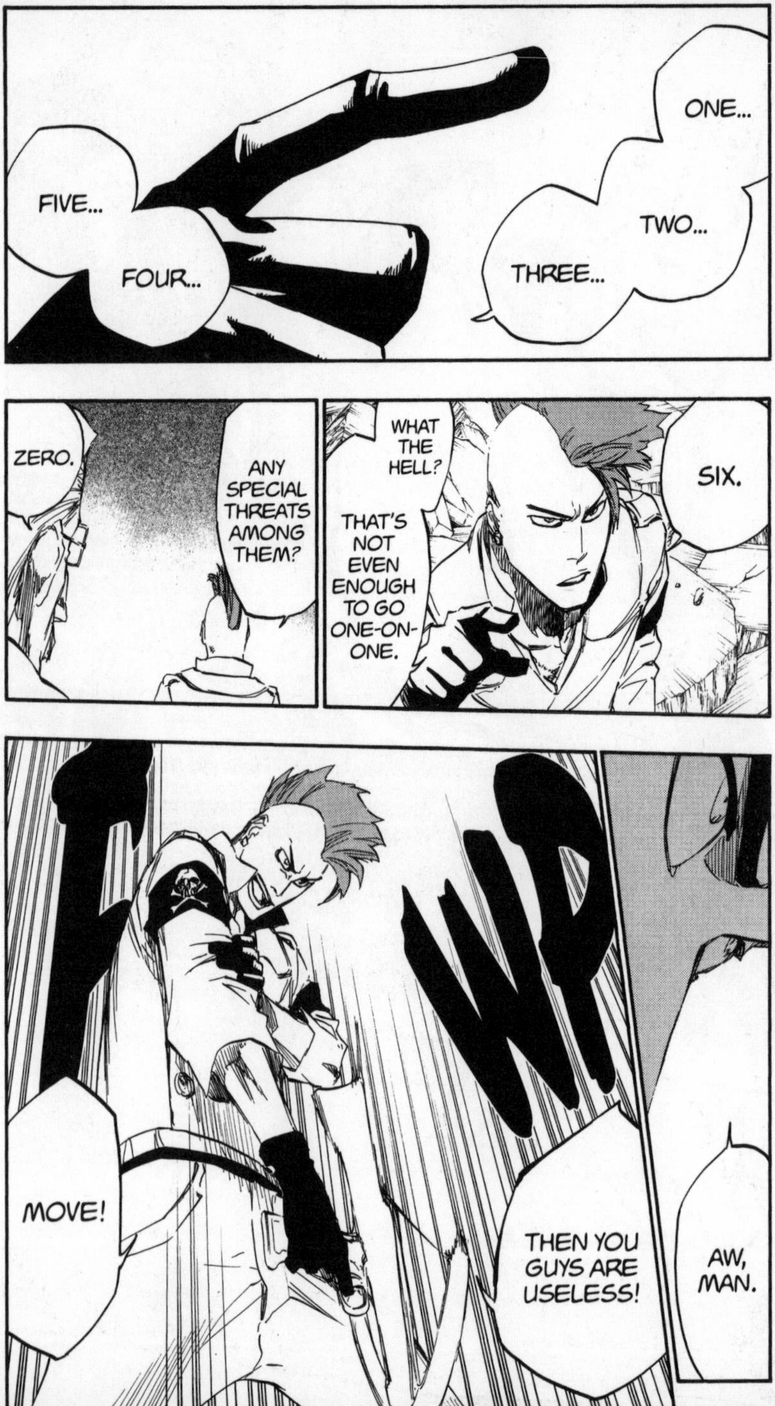
FIVE...
FOUR...
THREE...
TWO...
ONE...
SIX.
WHAT THE HELL?
THAT'S NOT EVEN ENOUGH TO GO ONE-ON-ONE.
ANY SPECIAL THREATS AMONG THEM?
ZERO.
THEN YOU GUYS ARE USELESS!
AW, MAN.
MOVE!

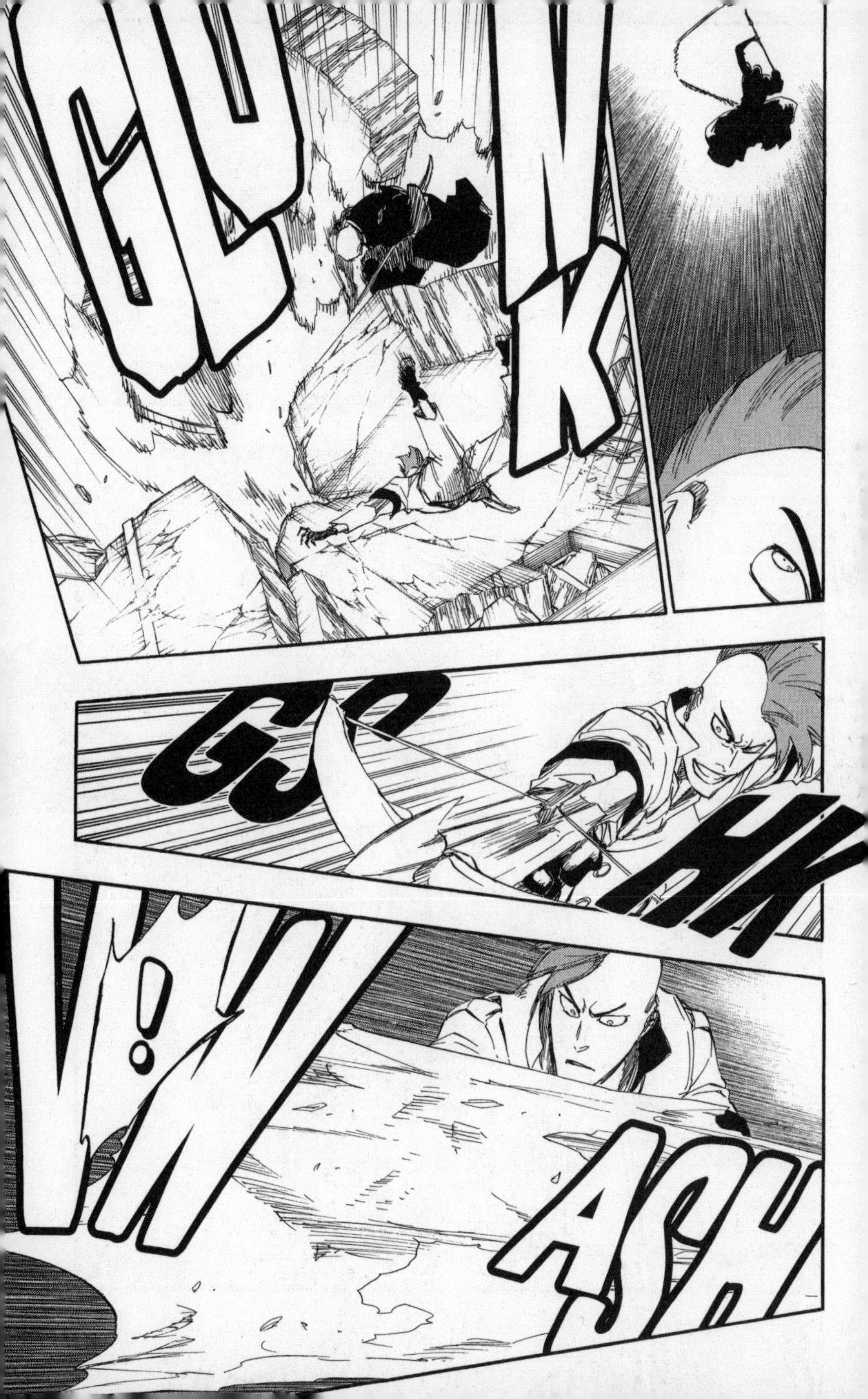
GUNK
GSHK
!
VWASH

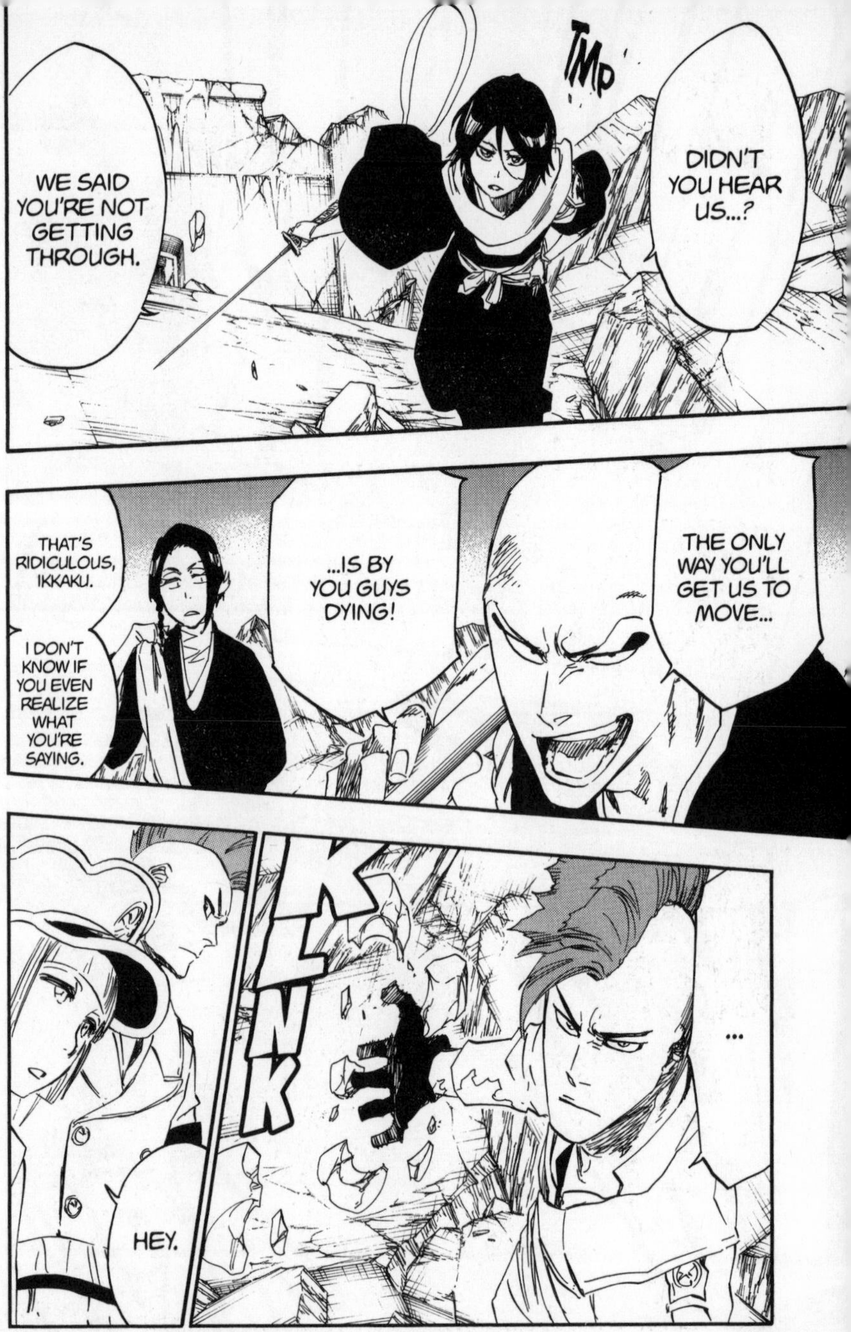
TMP
DIDN'T YOU HEAR US...?
WE SAID YOU'RE NOT GETTING THROUGH.
THE ONLY WAY YOU'LL GET US TO MOVE...
...IS BY YOU GUYS DYING!
THAT'S RIDICULOUS, IKKAKU.
I DON'T KNOW IF YOU EVEN REALIZE WHAT YOU'RE SAYING.
...
KLINK
HEY.

READ THIS WAY

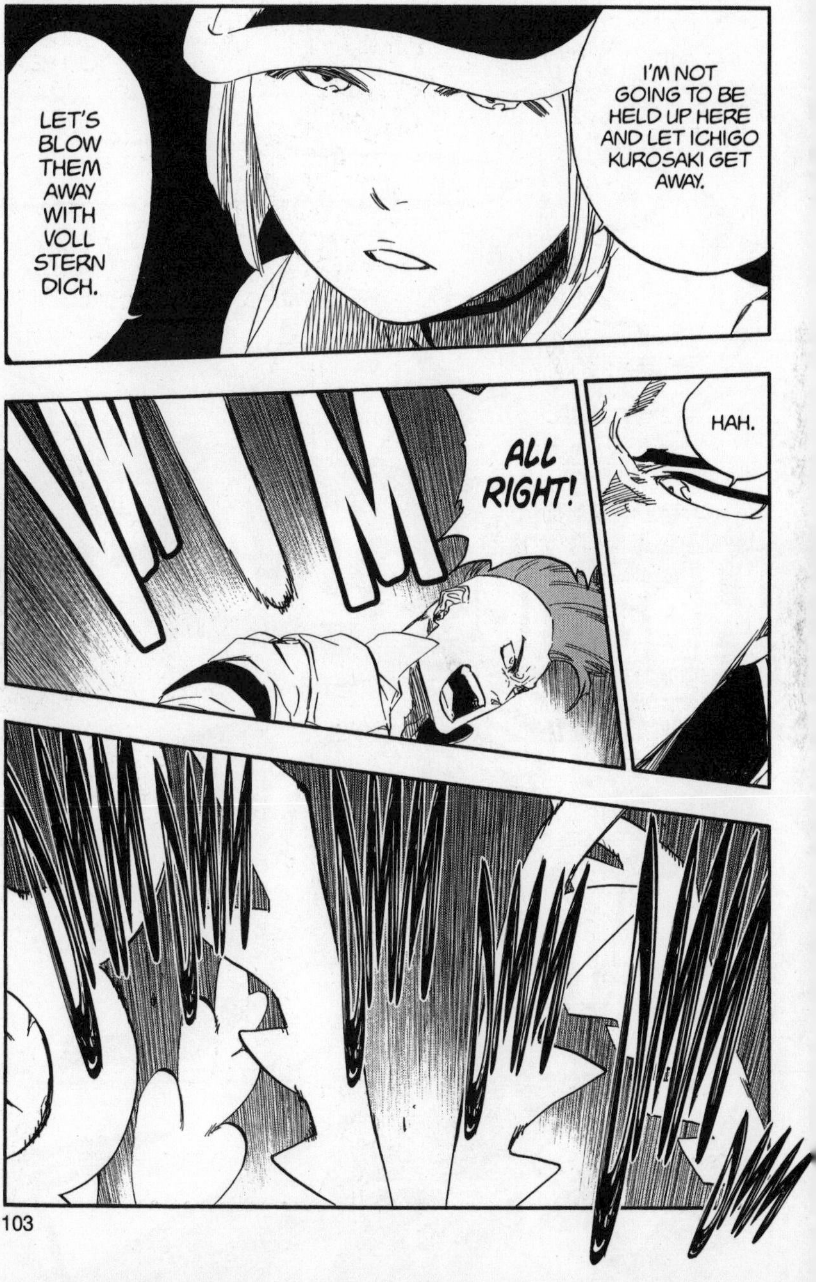

I'M NOT GOING TO BE HELD UP HERE AND LET ICHIGO KUROSAKI GET AWAY.
LET'S BLOW THEM AWAY WITH VOLL STERN DICH.
HAH.
ALL RIGHT!

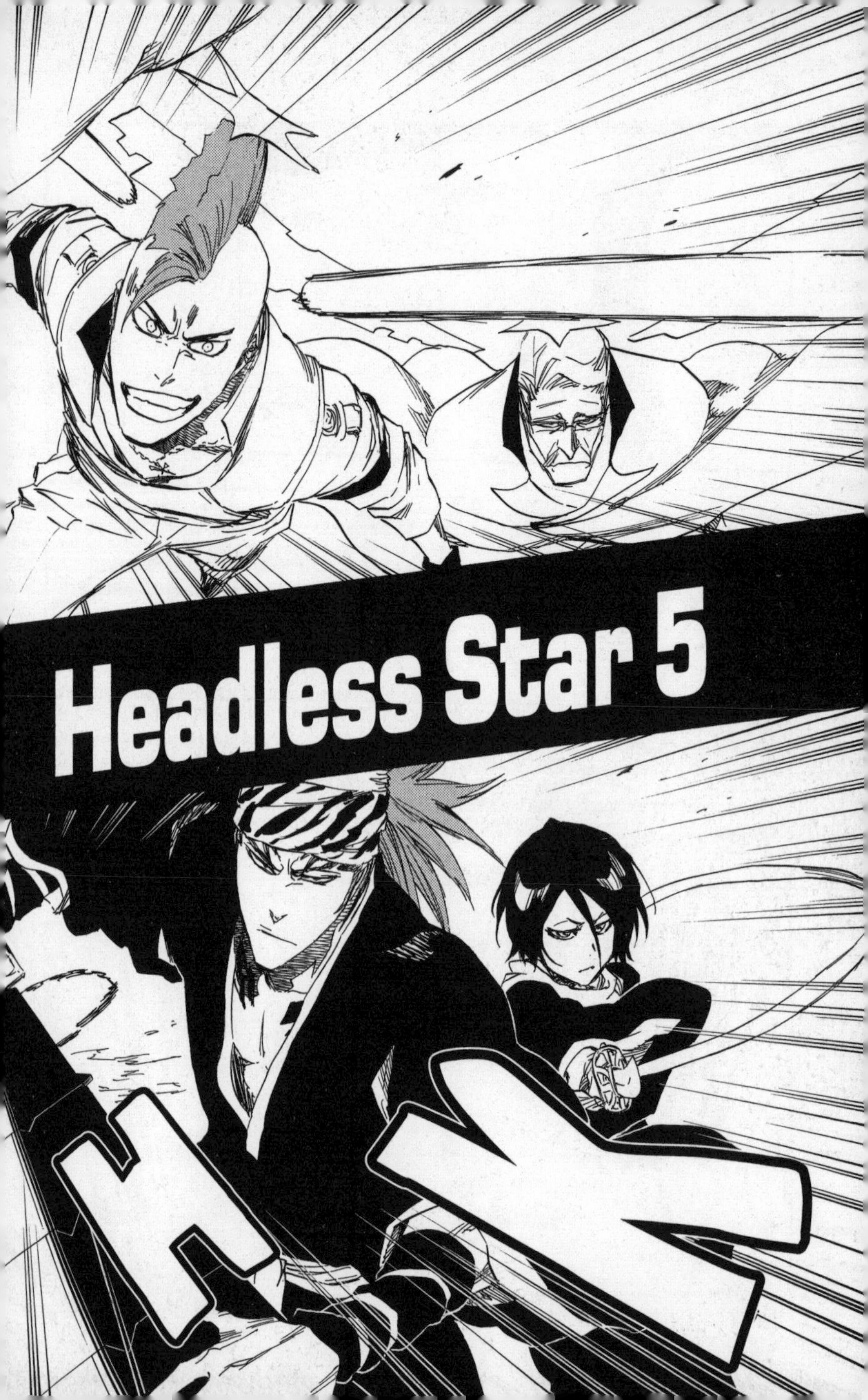
Headless Star 5

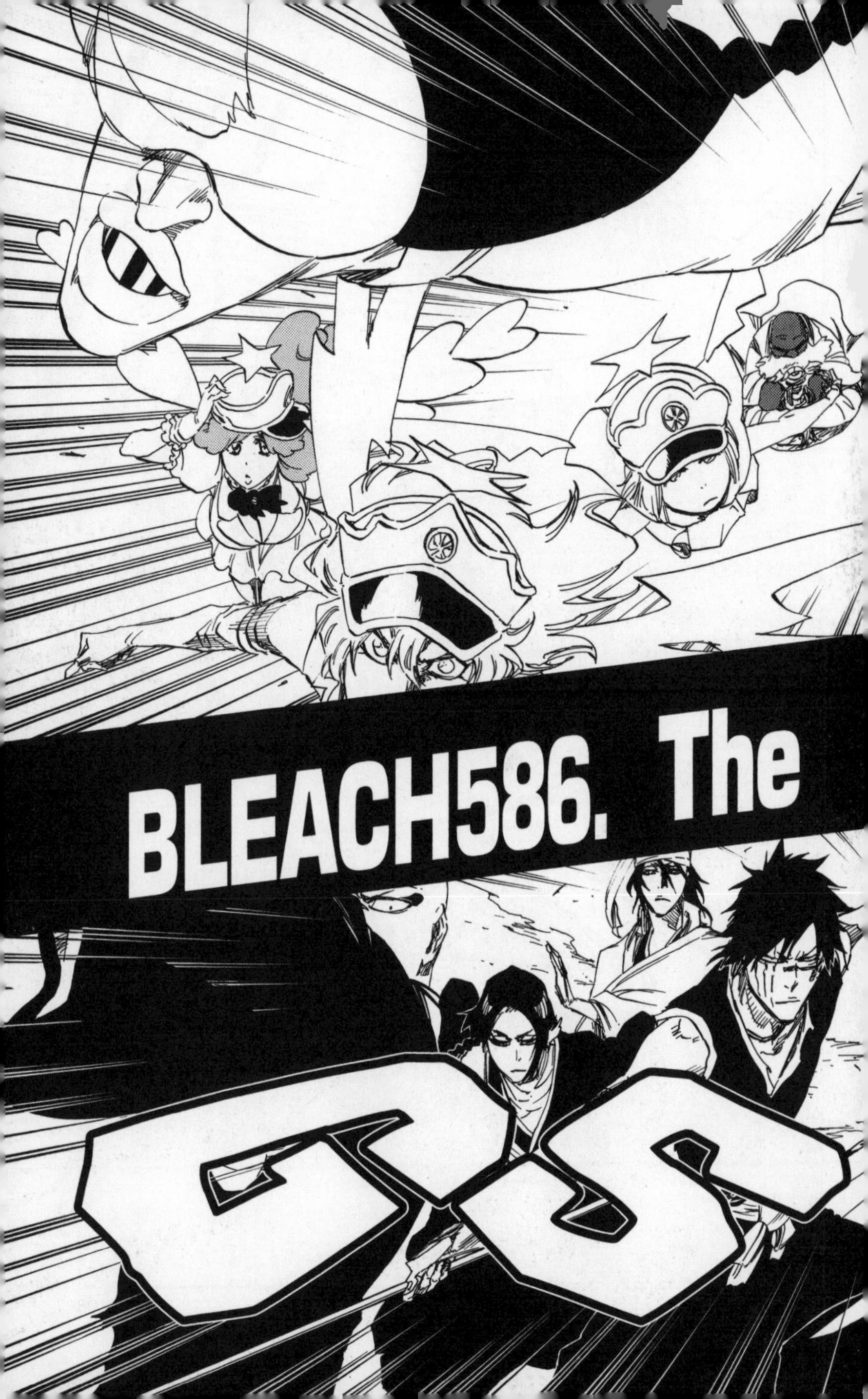
BLEACH586. The

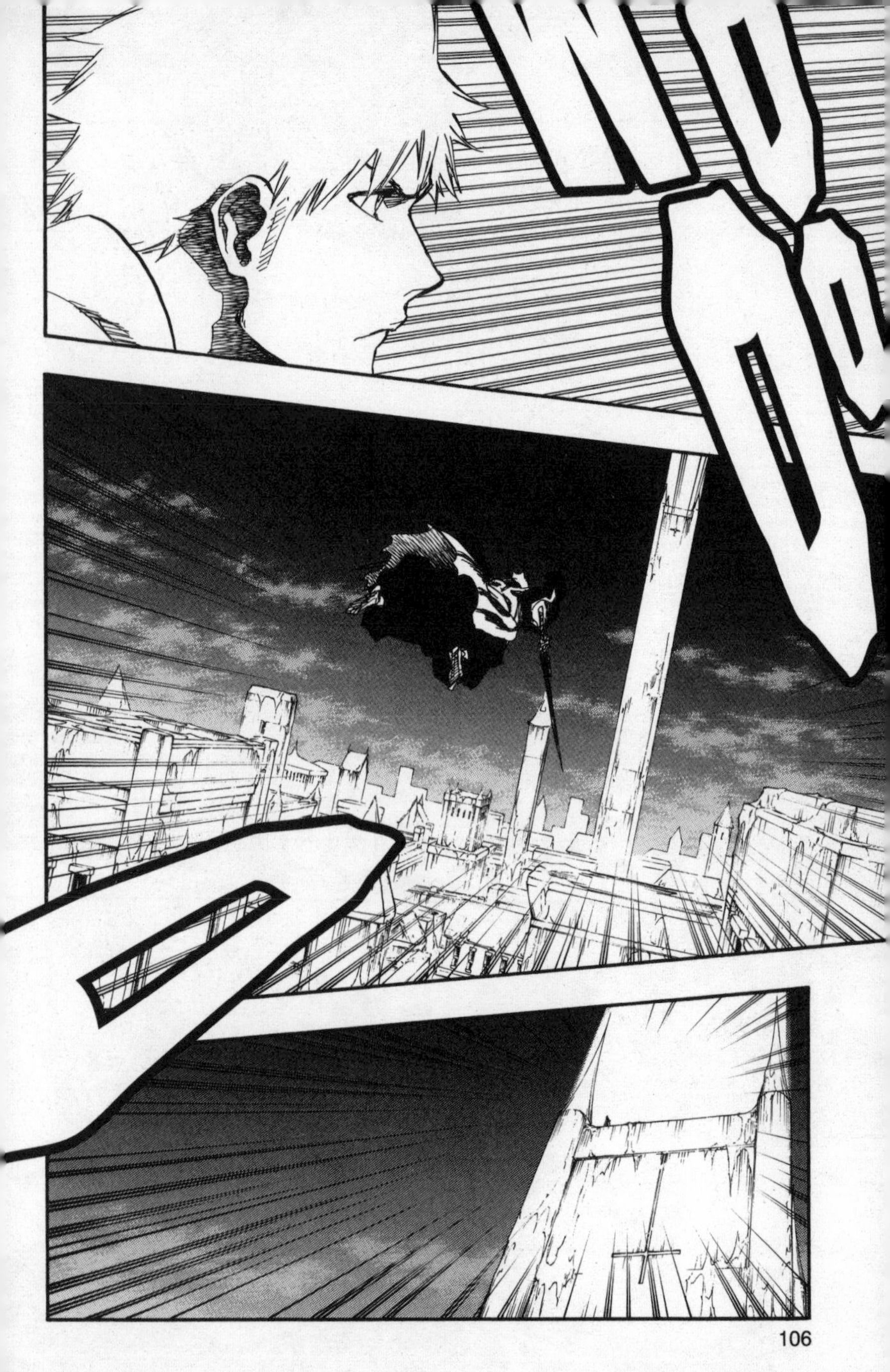

READ THIS WAY

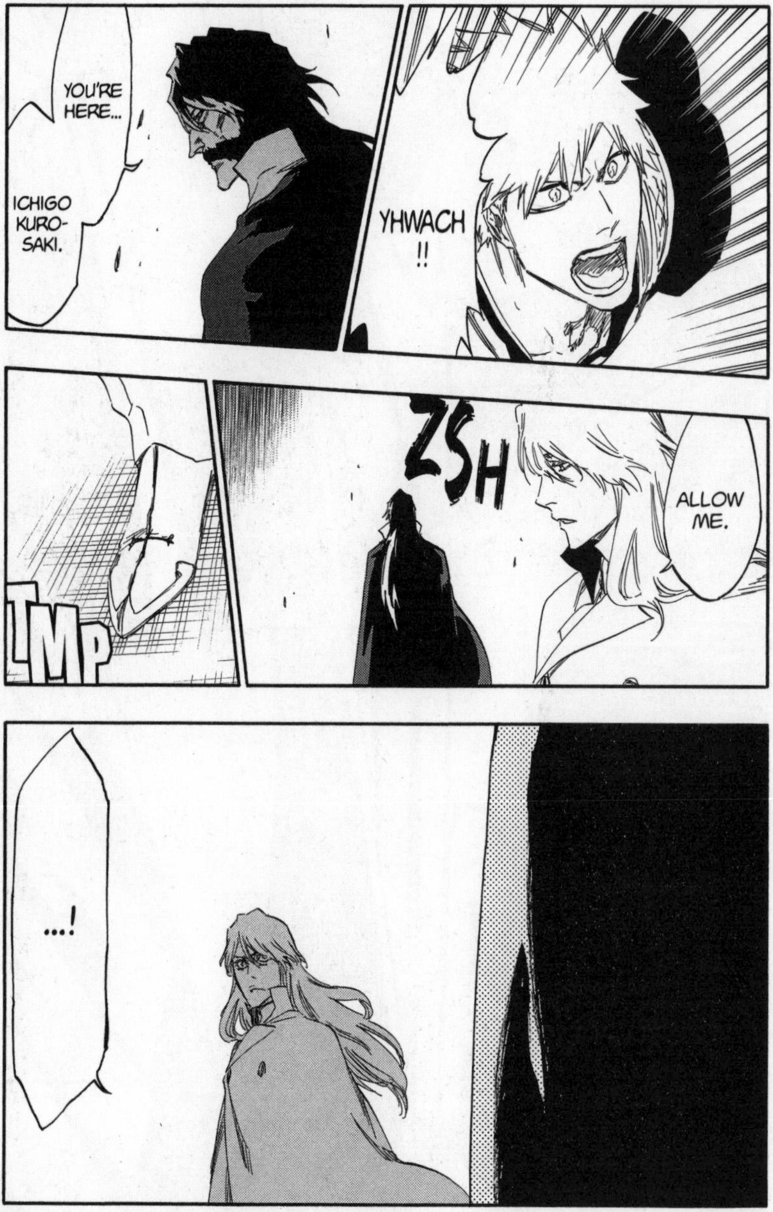

YHWACH !!
YOU'RE HERE...
ICHIGO KURO-SAKI.
ZSH
ALLOW ME.
TMP
...!

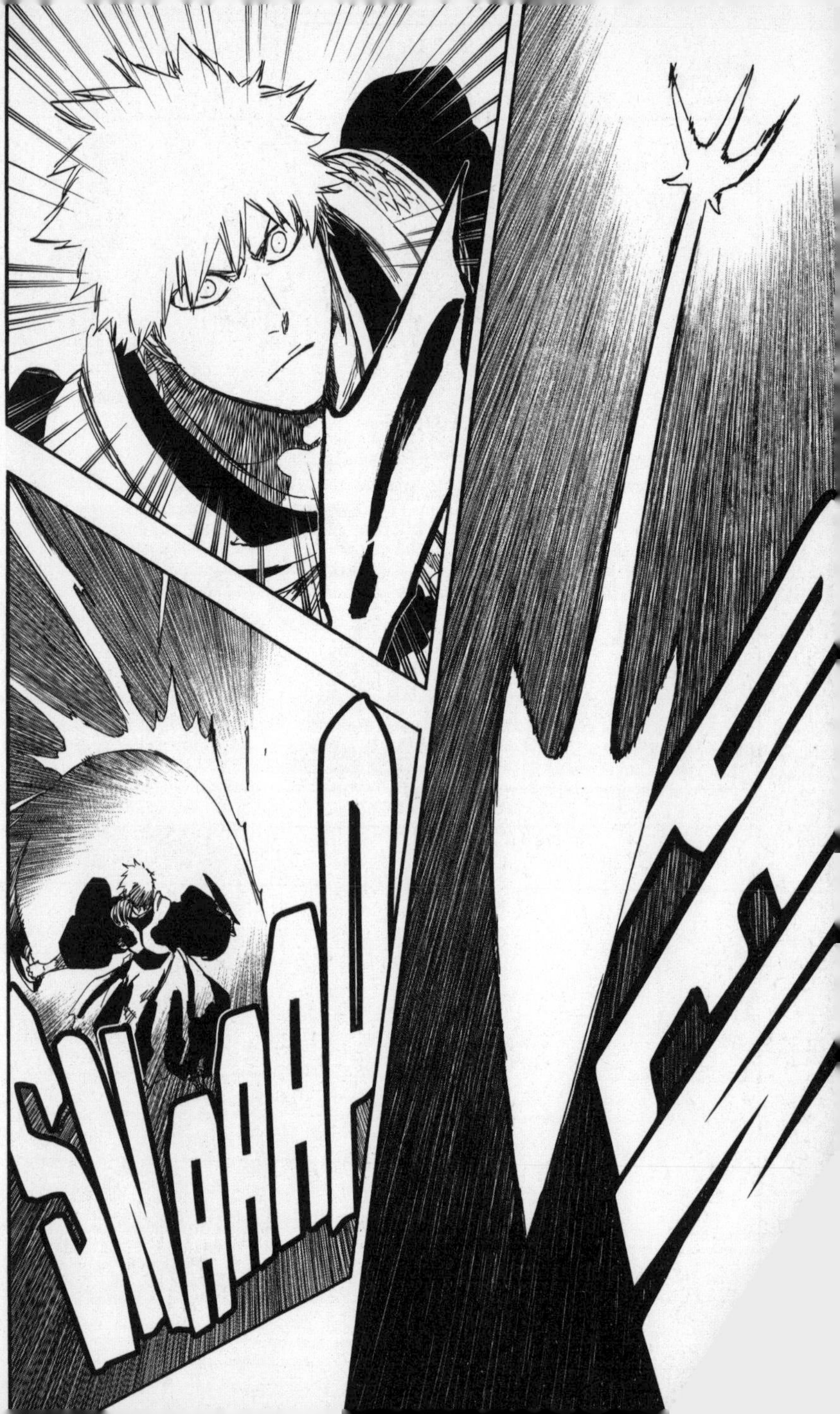
SNAAAP

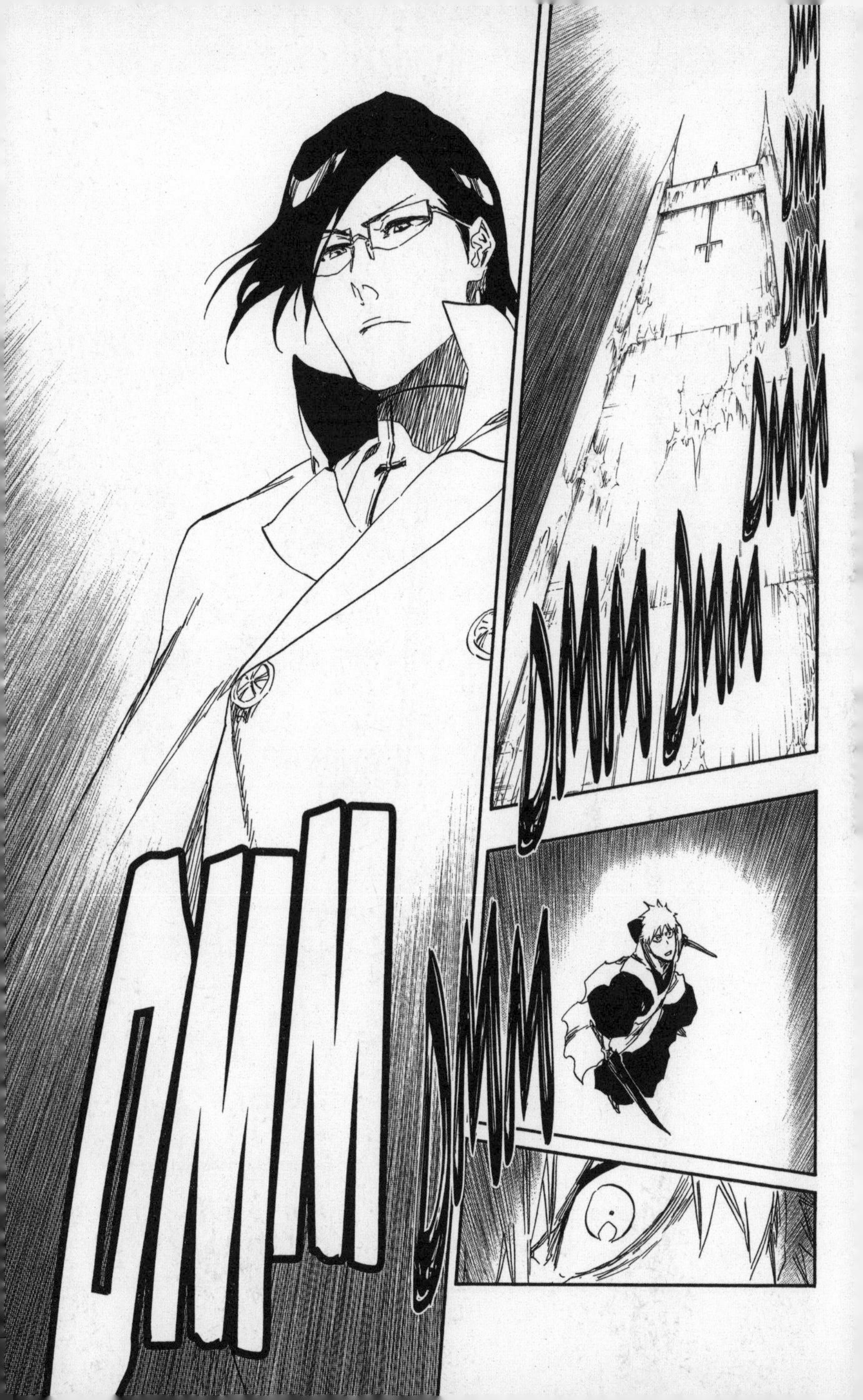

DMM
DMM
DMM
DMM
DMM
DMM DMM
DMM
DMM

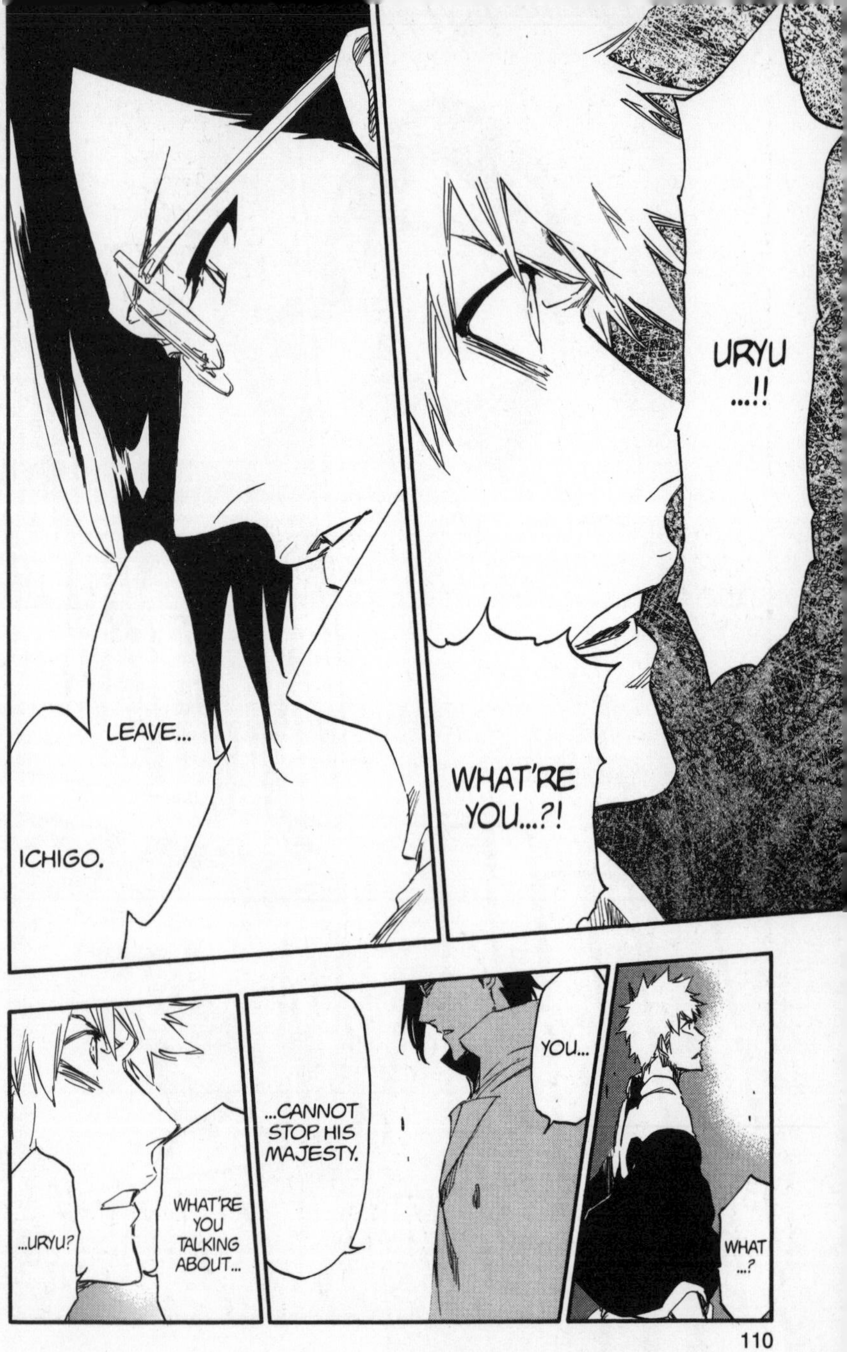
URYU ...!!
WHAT'RE YOU...?!
LEAVE...
ICHIGO.
WHAT ...?
YOU...
...CANNOT STOP HIS MAJESTY.
WHAT'RE YOU TALKING ABOUT...
...URYU?

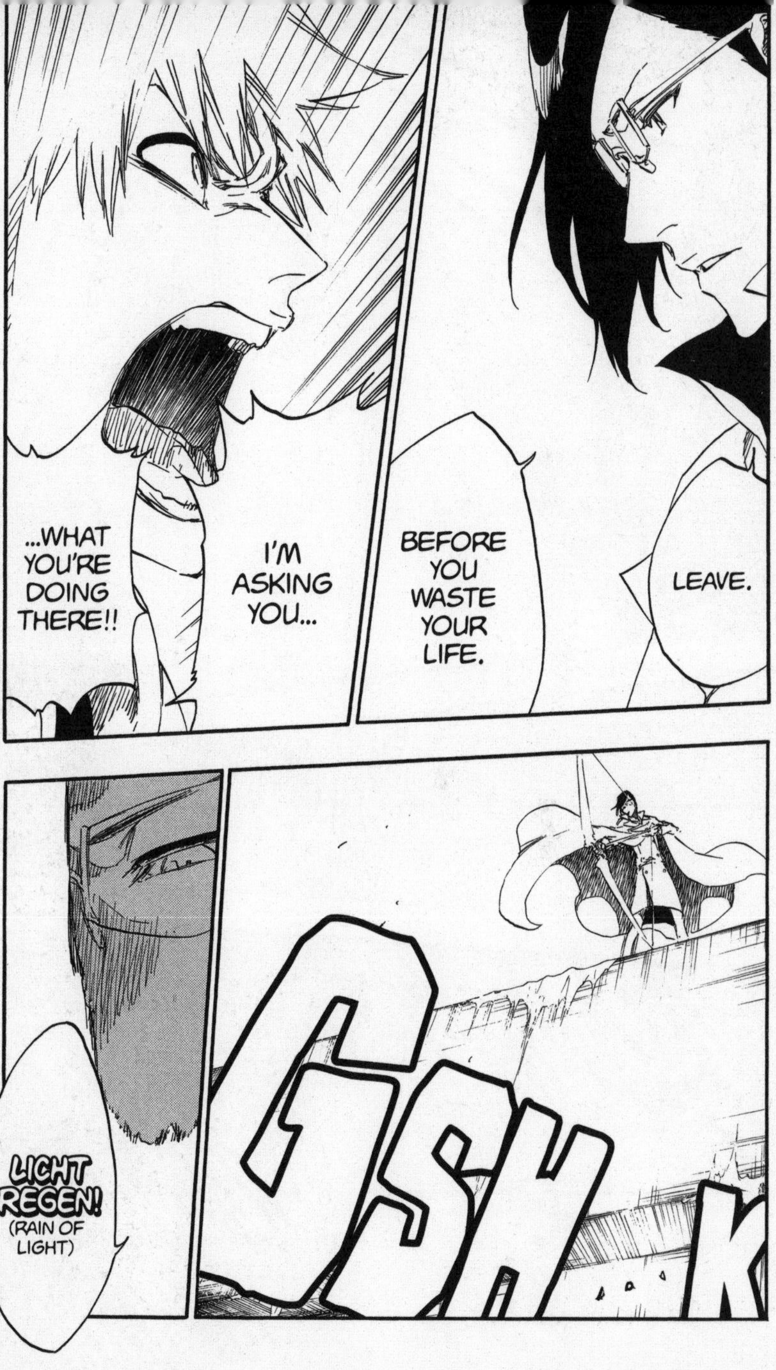
LEAVE.
BEFORE YOU WASTE YOUR LIFE.
I'M ASKING YOU...
...WHAT YOU'RE DOING THERE!!
GSH...K
LICHT REGEN!
(RAIN OF LIGHT)

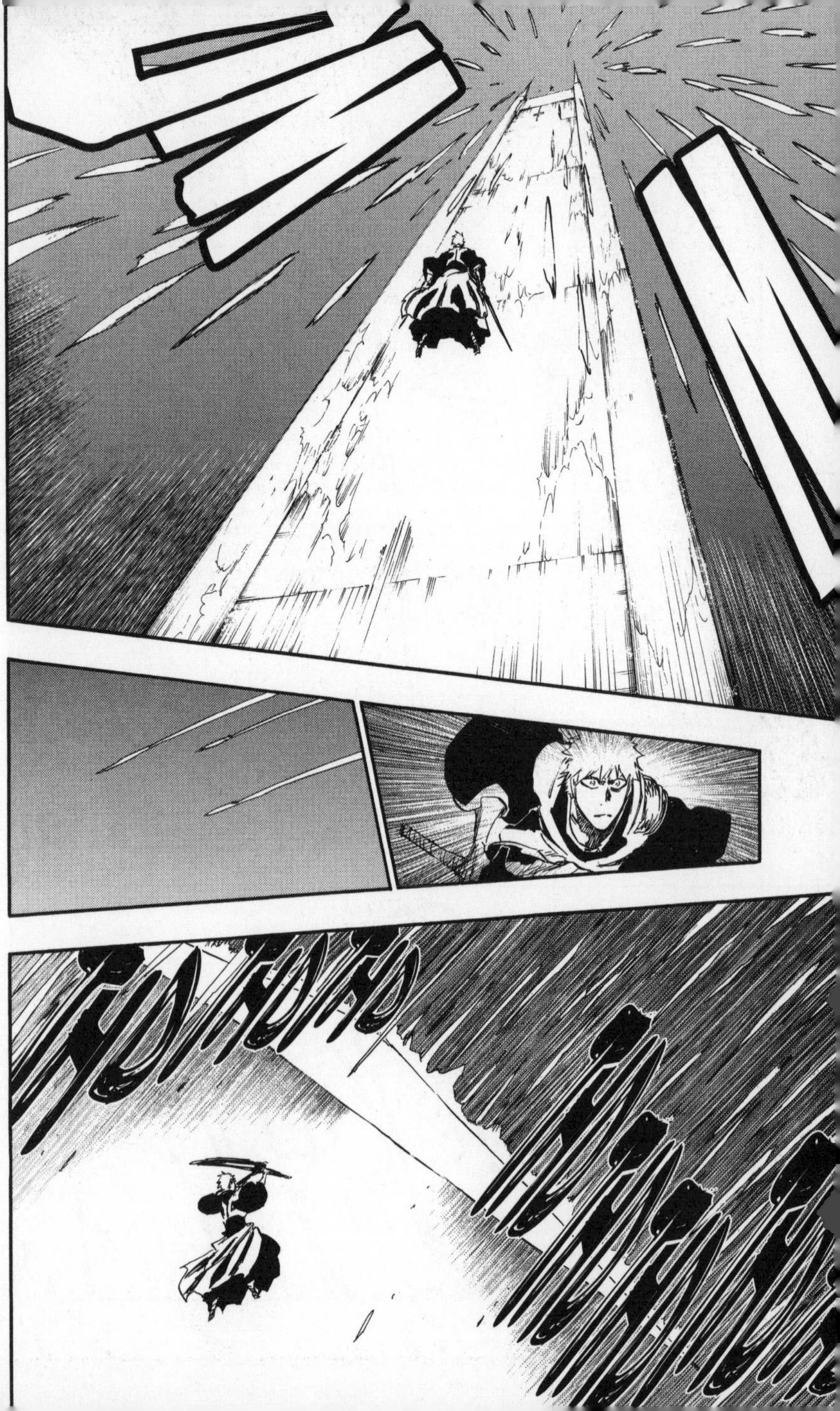

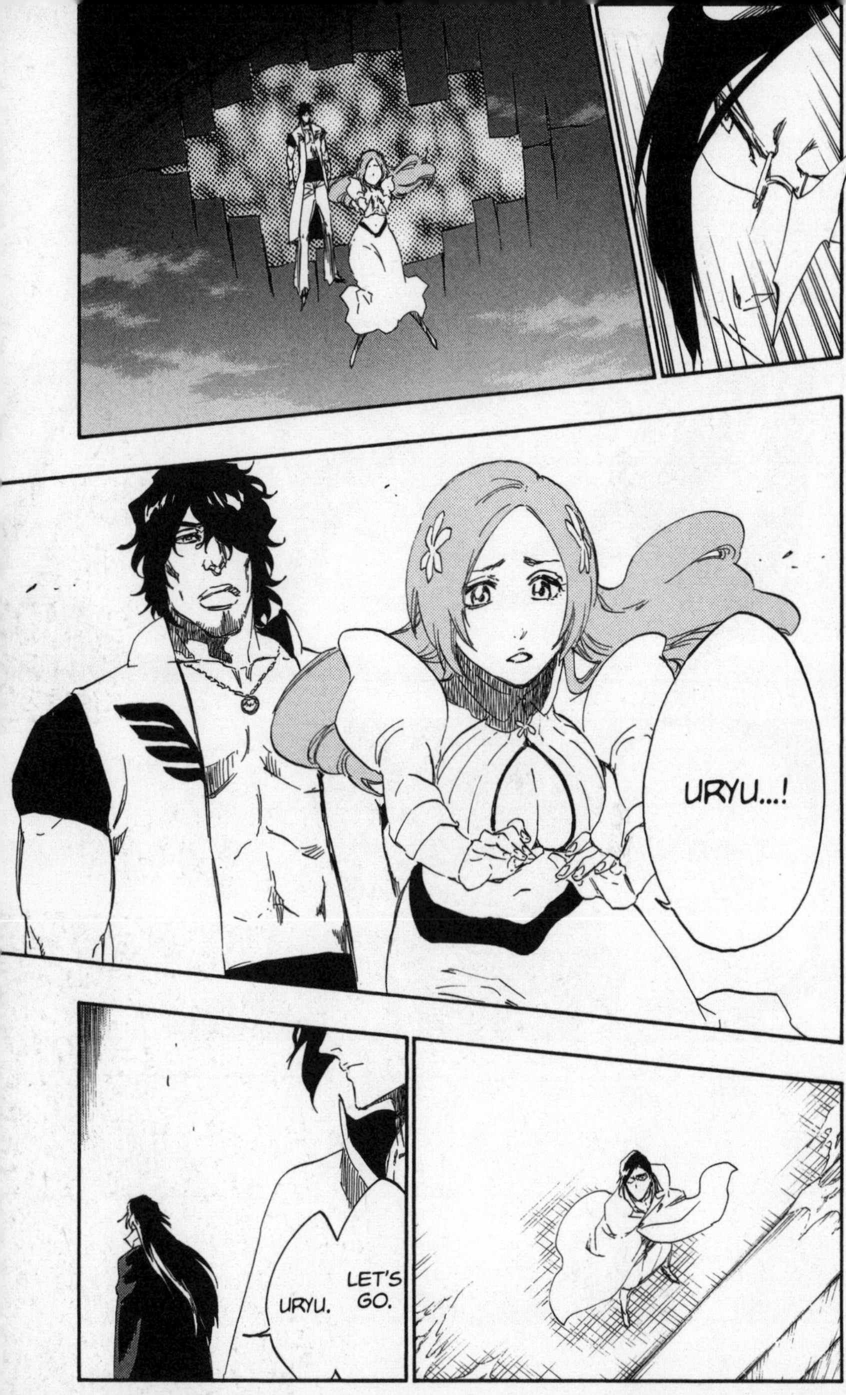
URYU...!
LET'S GO.
URYU.

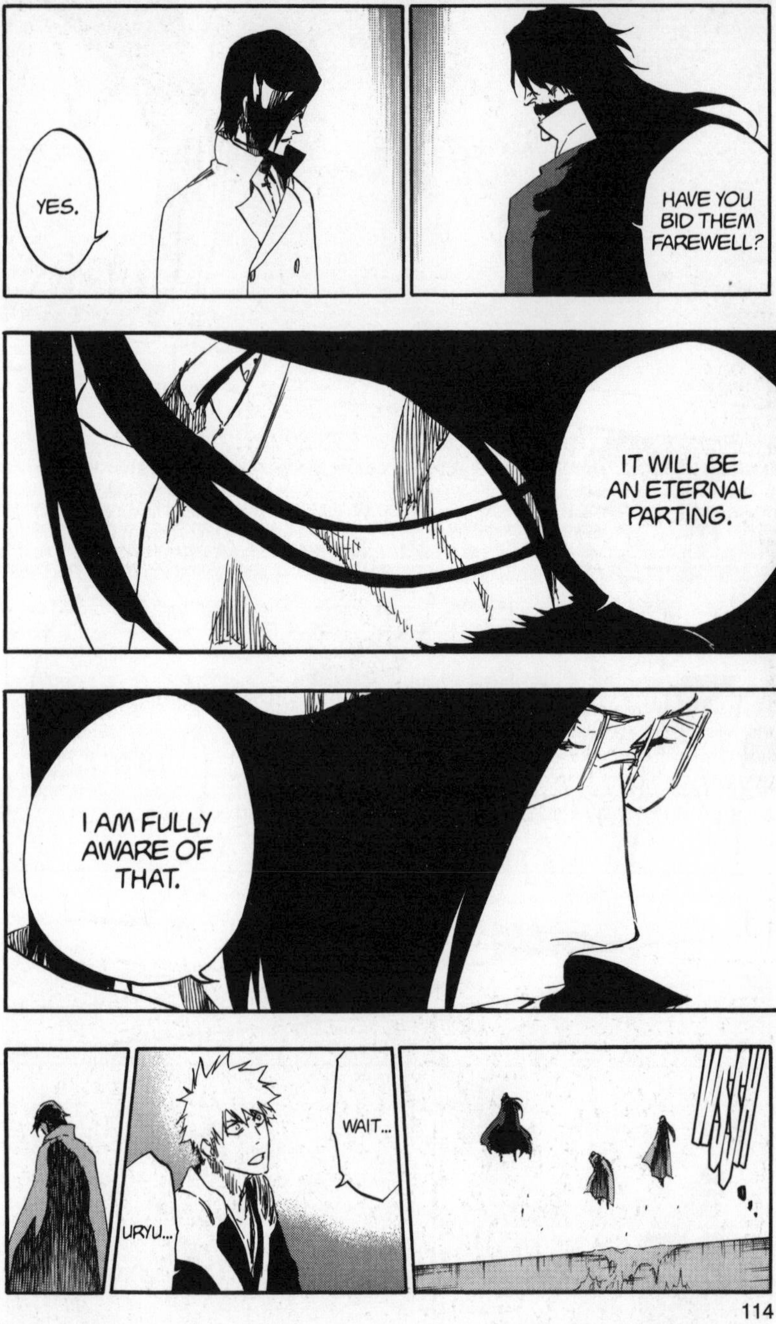
HAVE YOU BID THEM FAREWELL?
YES.
IT WILL BE AN ETERNAL PARTING.
I AM FULLY AWARE OF THAT.
WAIT...
URYU...

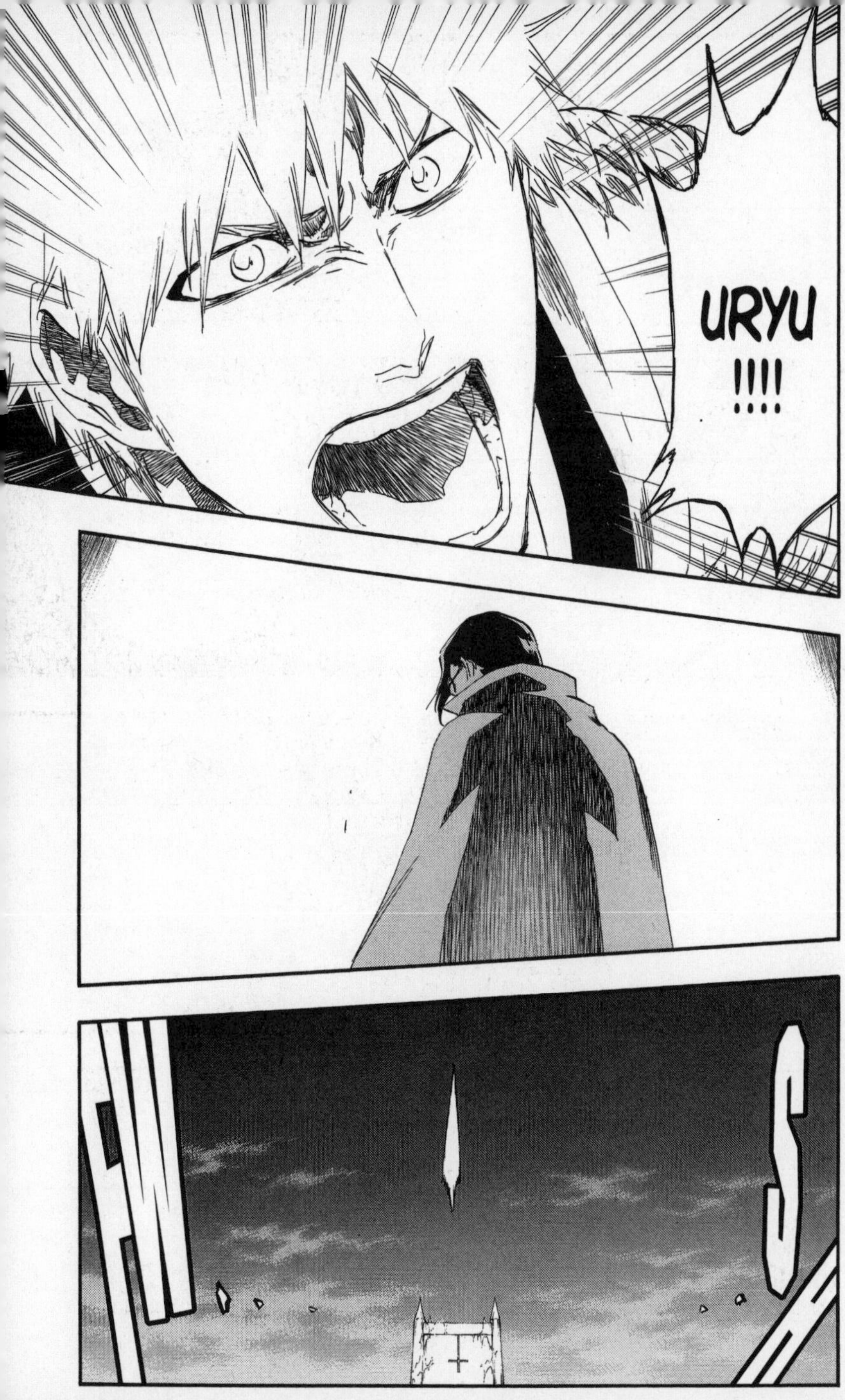
URYU
!!!!
FWSH

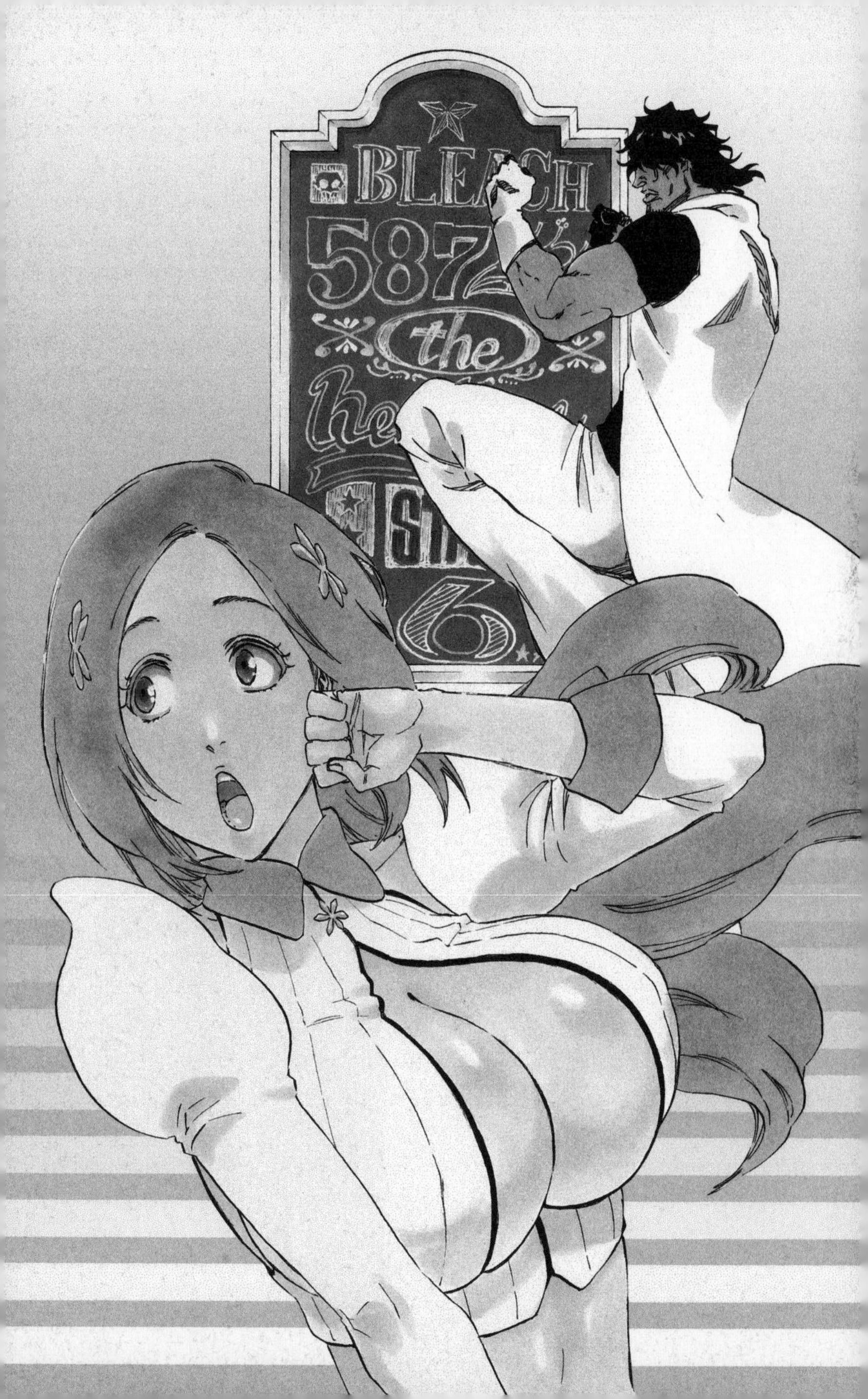
BLEACH
587
the
6

BLEACH
ブリーチ

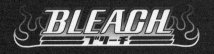

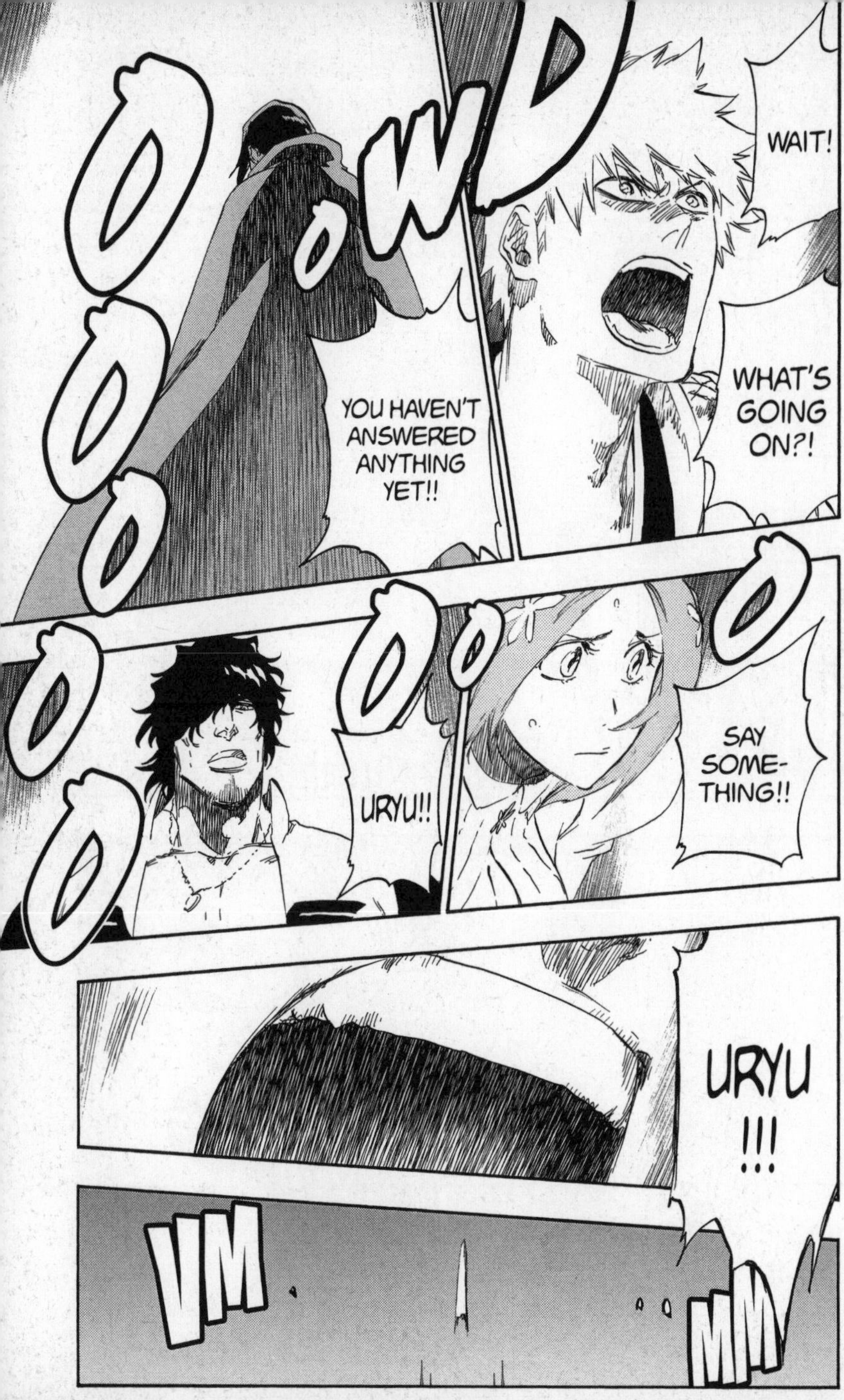
WAIT!
WHAT'S GOING ON?!
YOU HAVEN'T ANSWERED ANYTHING YET!!
SAY SOME-THING!!
URYU!!
URYU!!!
VM
MM

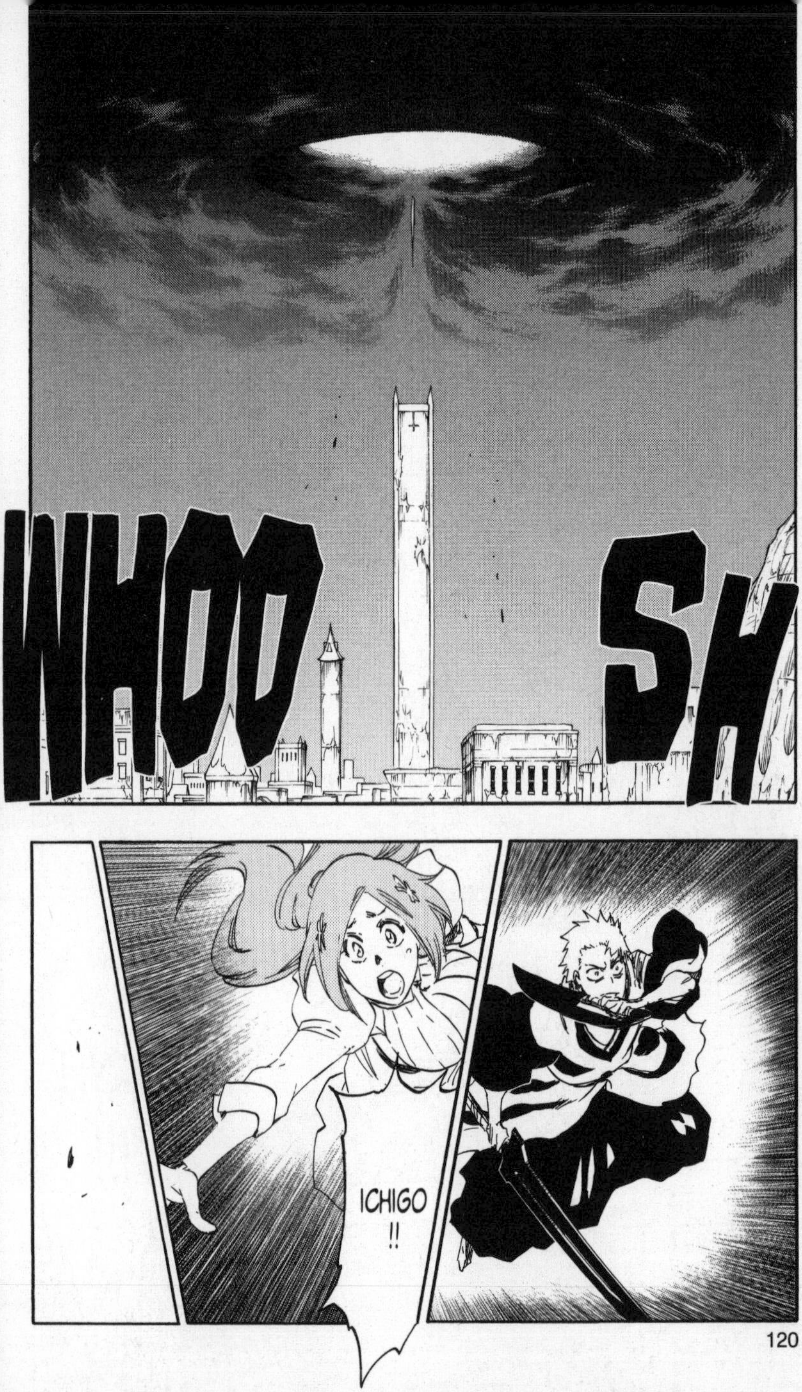
WHOOSH
ICHIGO!!

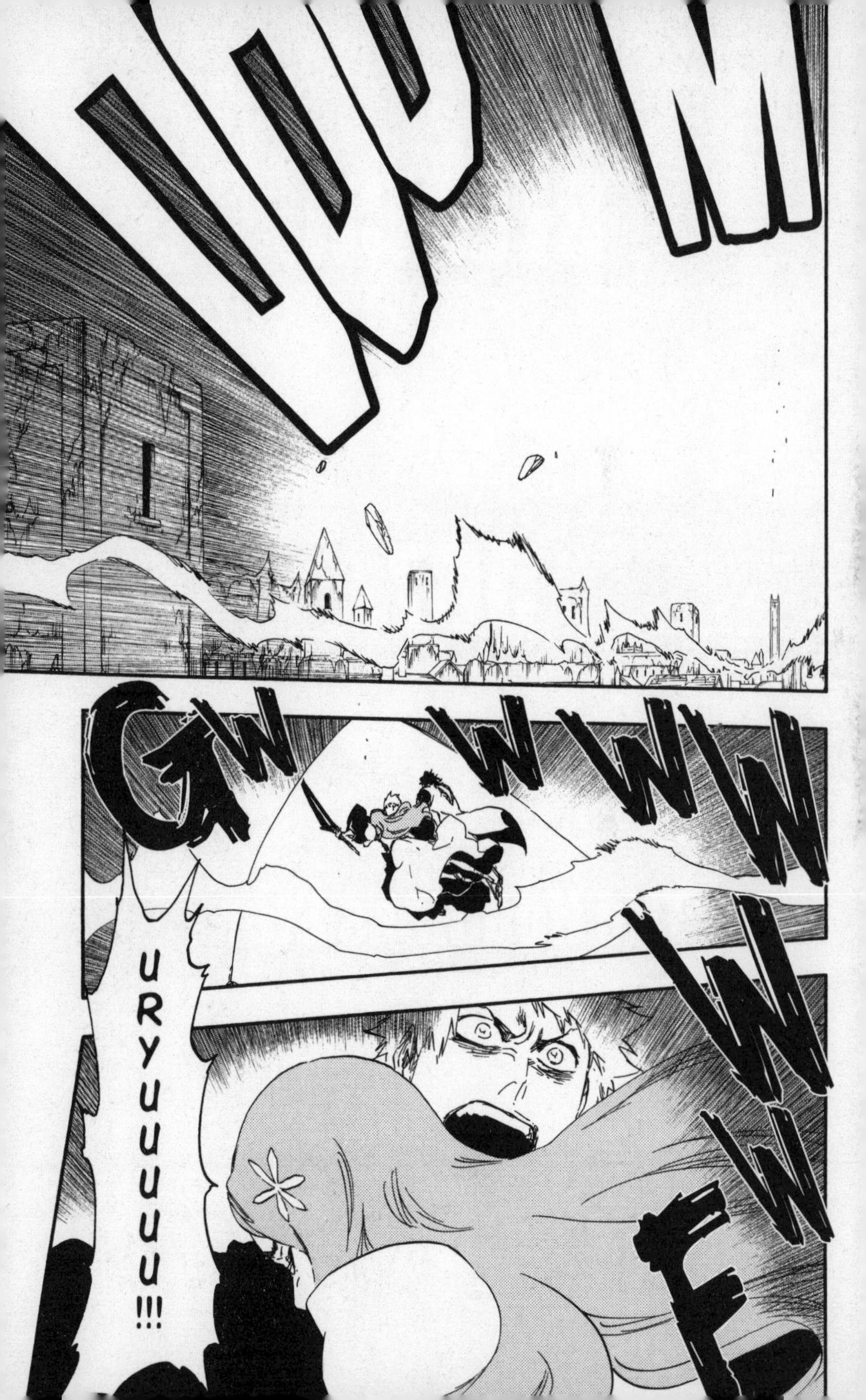
URYUUUUU!!!

BLEACH

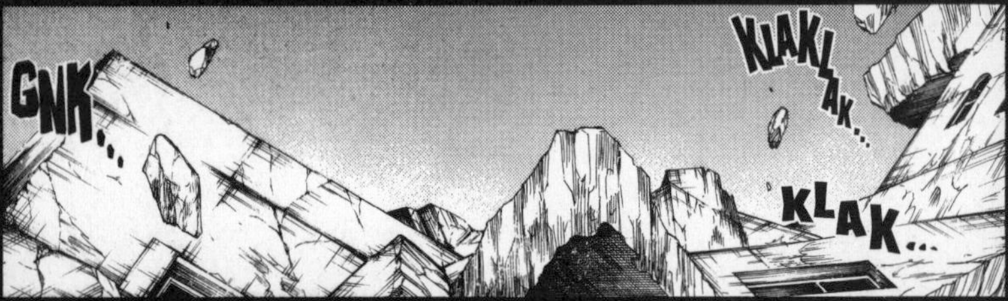
KLAKLAK...
KLAK...
GNK...

587.

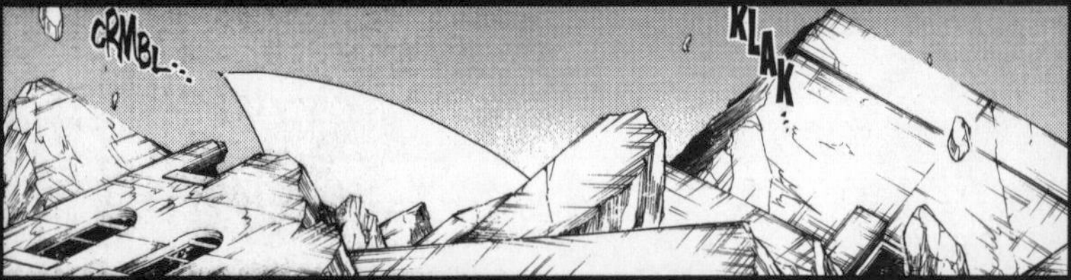
KLAK...
CRMBL...

The Headless Star

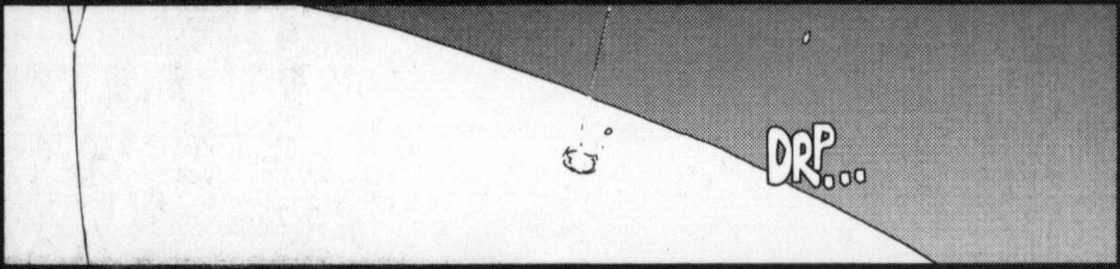
DRP...

6

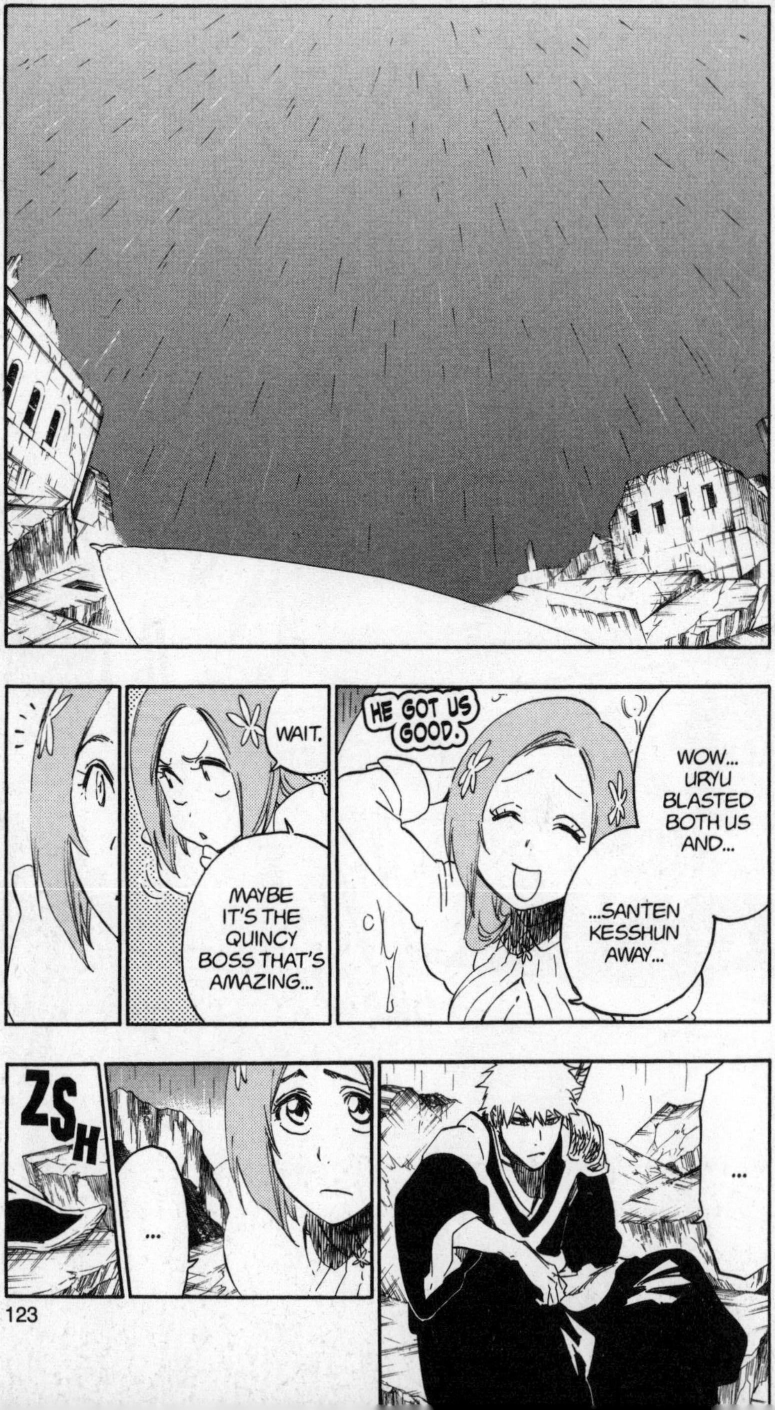
WOW... URYU BLASTED BOTH US AND...
...SANTEN KESSHUN AWAY...
HE GOT US GOOD.
WAIT.
MAYBE IT'S THE QUINCY BOSS THAT'S AMAZING...
...
...
ZSH

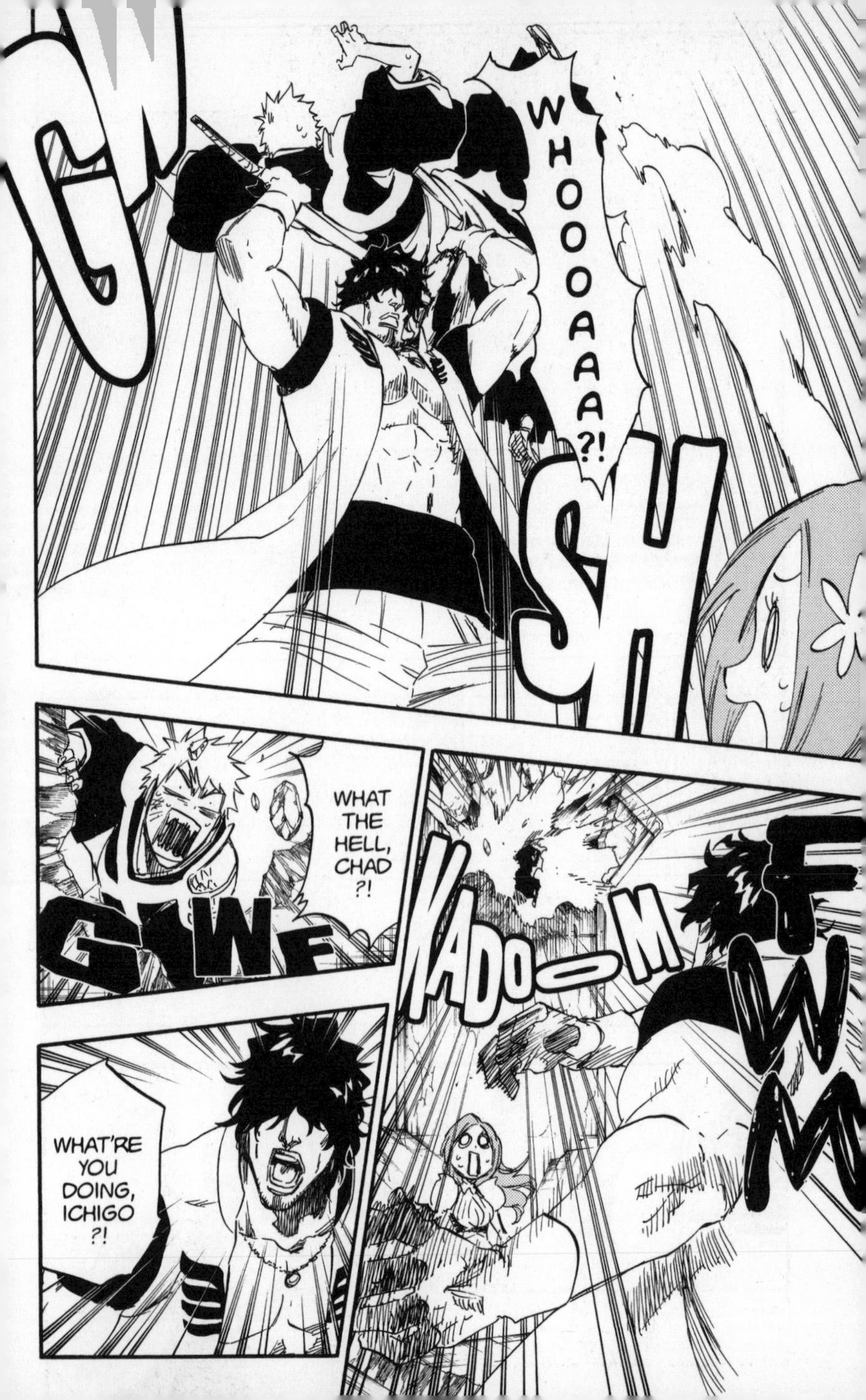

WHOOOAAAA?!
SH
GW
FWM
KADOOOM
WHAT THE HELL, CHAD?!
GWE
WHAT'RE YOU DOING, ICHIGO?!

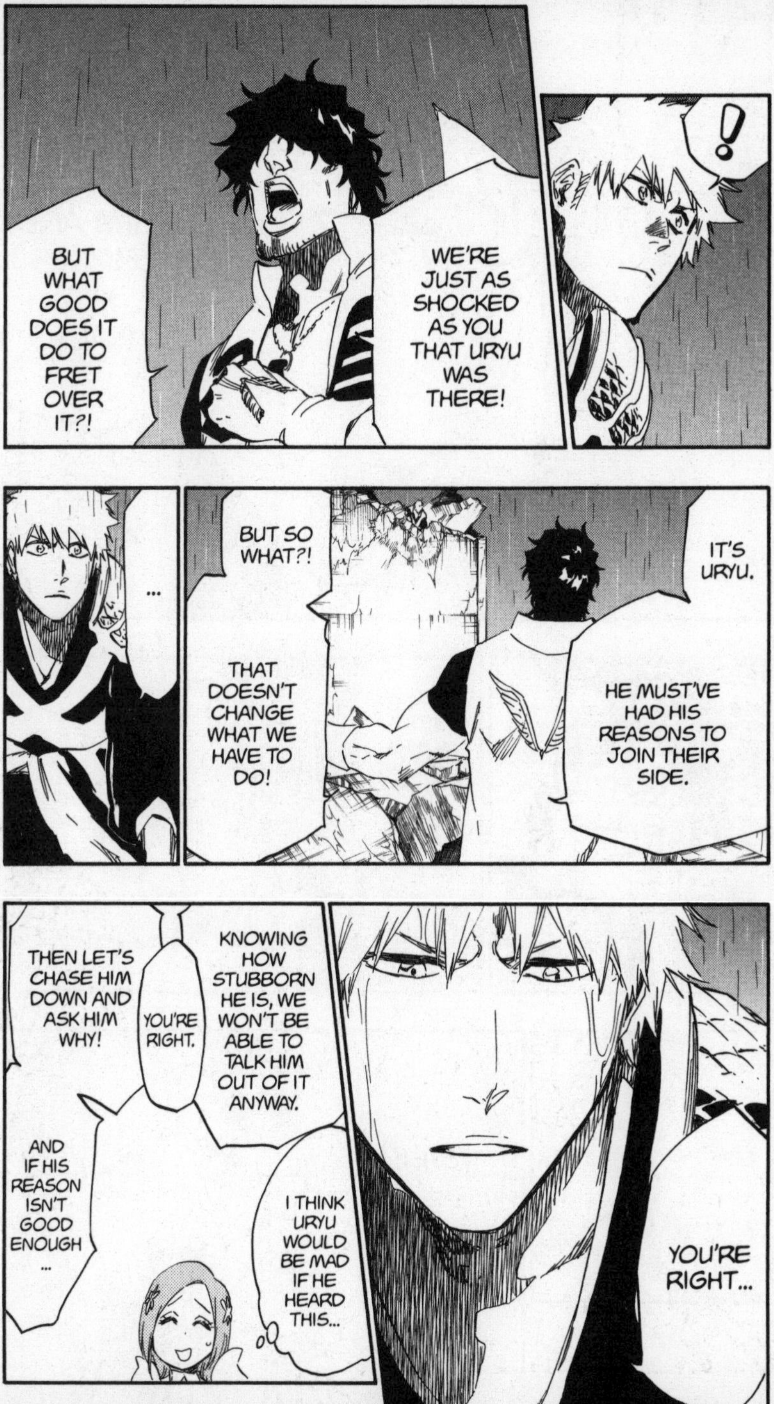
!
WE'RE JUST AS SHOCKED AS YOU THAT URYU WAS THERE!
BUT WHAT GOOD DOES IT DO TO FRET OVER IT?!
IT'S URYU.
HE MUST'VE HAD HIS REASONS TO JOIN THEIR SIDE.
BUT SO WHAT?!
THAT DOESN'T CHANGE WHAT WE HAVE TO DO!
...
YOU'RE RIGHT...
KNOWING HOW STUBBORN HE IS, WE WON'T BE ABLE TO TALK HIM OUT OF IT ANYWAY.
YOU'RE RIGHT.
THEN LET'S CHASE HIM DOWN AND ASK HIM WHY!
AND IF HIS REASON ISN'T GOOD ENOUGH...
I THINK URYU WOULD BE MAD IF HE HEARD THIS...

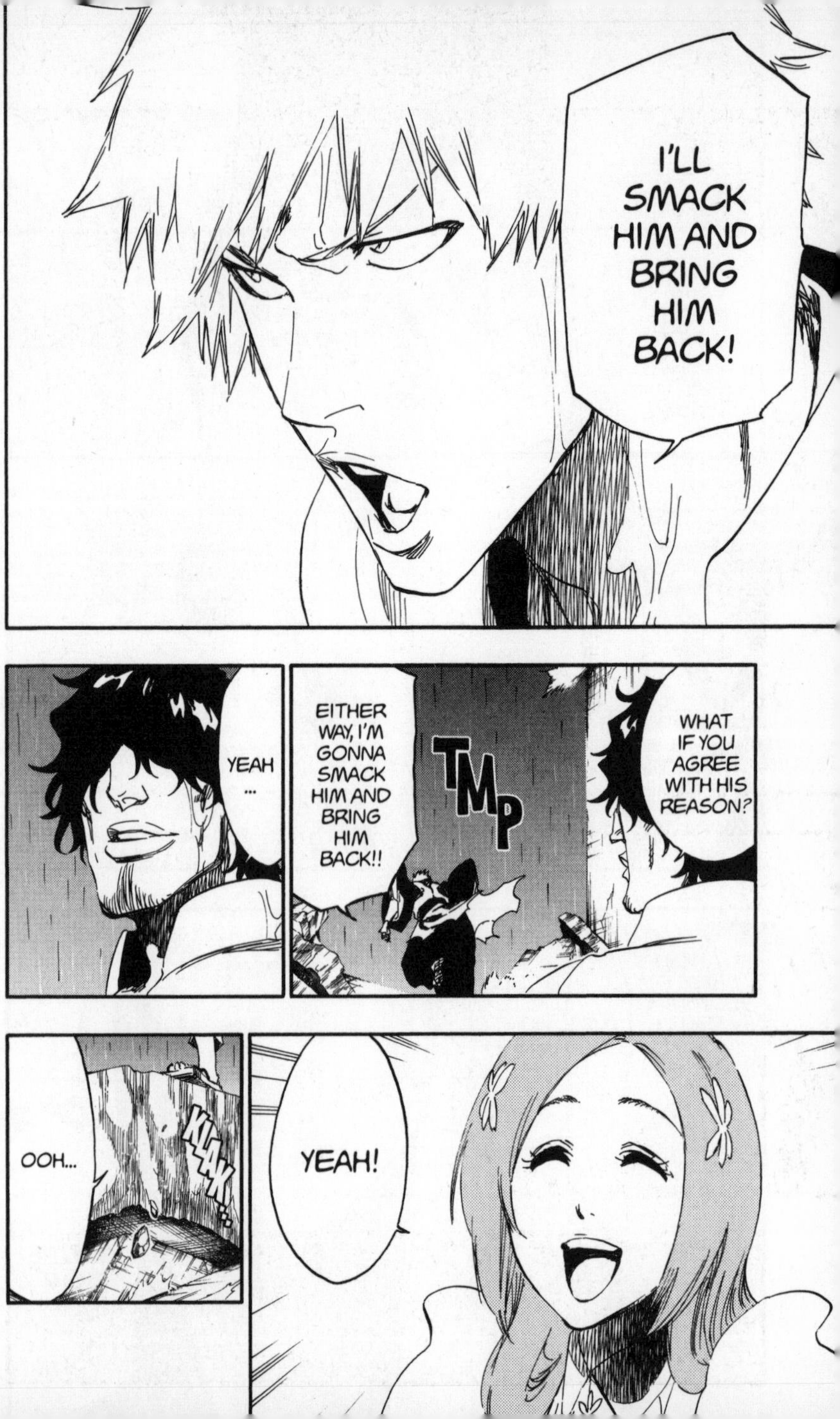
I'LL SMACK HIM AND BRING HIM BACK!
WHAT IF YOU AGREE WITH HIS REASON?
TMP
EITHER WAY, I'M GONNA SMACK HIM AND BRING HIM BACK!!
YEAH...
YEAH!
KLAK...
OOH...

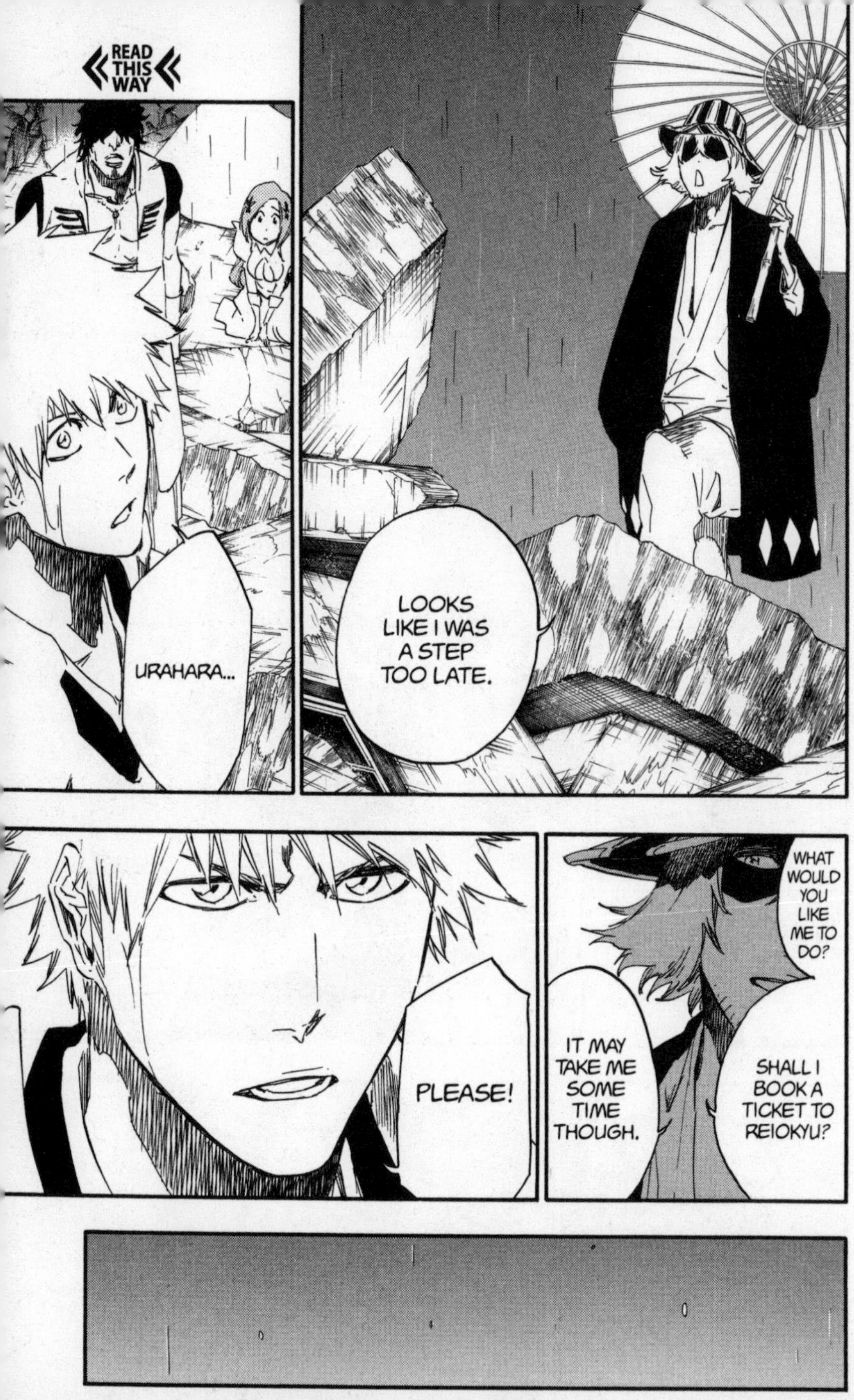
READ THIS WAY
LOOKS LIKE I WAS A STEP TOO LATE.
URAHARA...
WHAT WOULD YOU LIKE ME TO DO?
SHALL I BOOK A TICKET TO REIOKYU?
IT MAY TAKE ME SOME TIME THOUGH.
PLEASE!

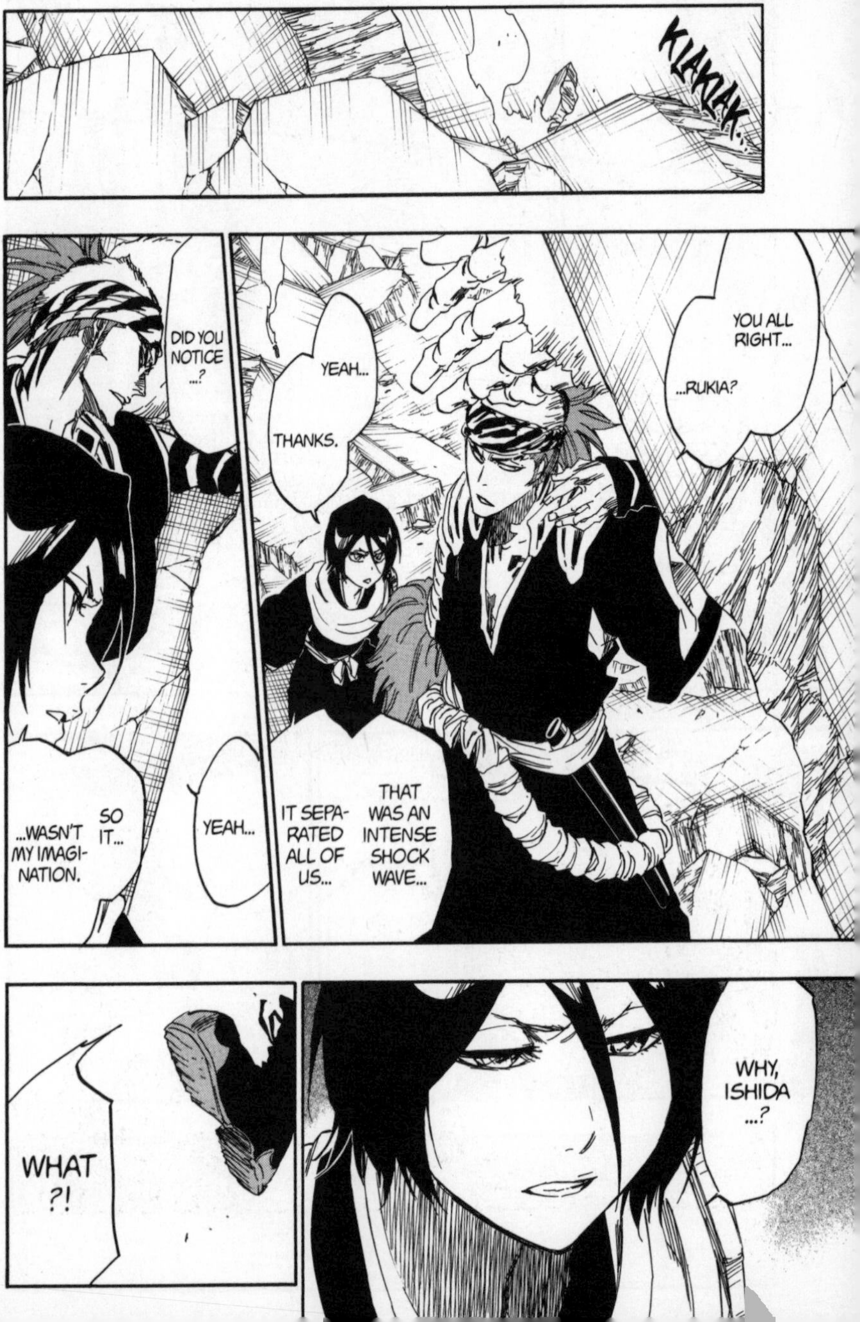
KLAKLAK...
YOU ALL RIGHT... ...RUKIA?
YEAH... THANKS.
THAT WAS AN INTENSE SHOCK WAVE...
IT SEPARATED ALL OF US...
DID YOU NOTICE ...?
YEAH...
SO IT... ...WASN'T MY IMAGINATION.
WHY, ISHIDA ...?
WHAT ?!

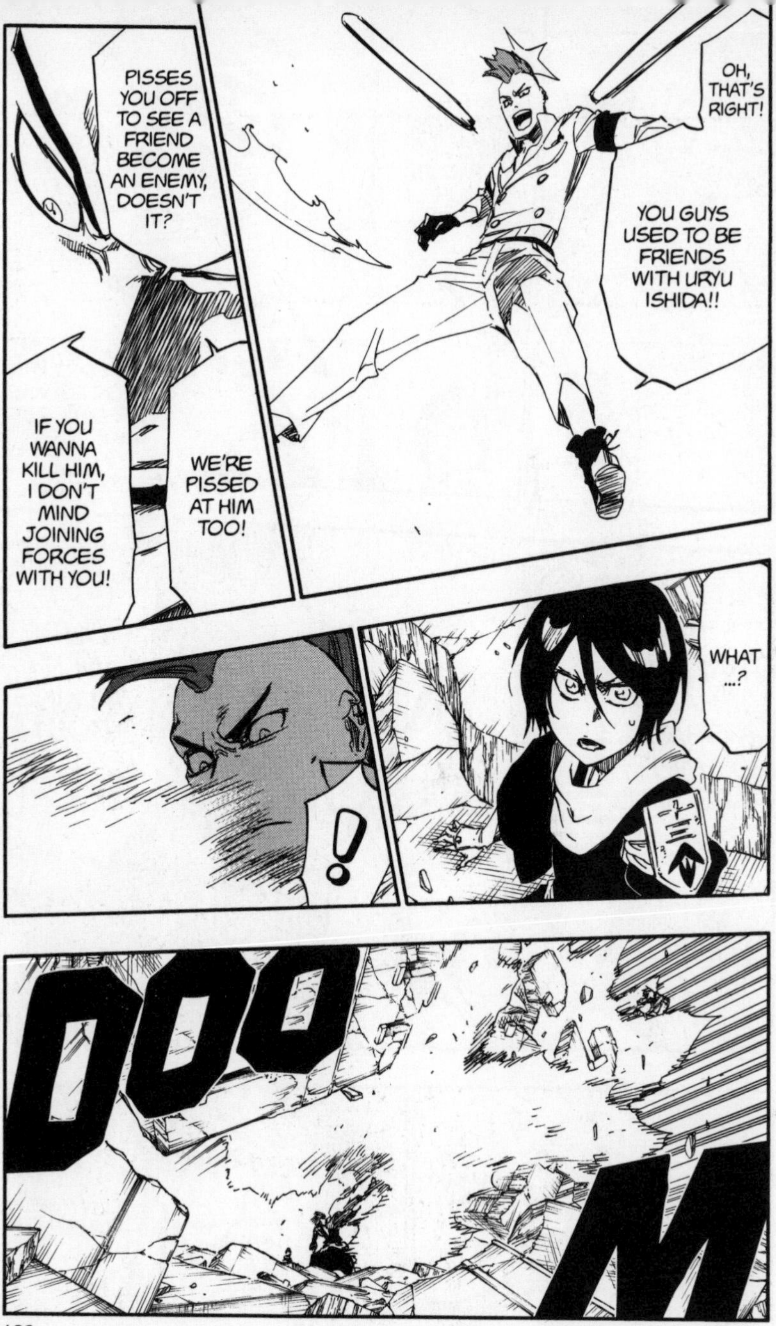

OH, THAT'S RIGHT!
YOU GUYS USED TO BE FRIENDS WITH URYU ISHIDA!!
PISSES YOU OFF TO SEE A FRIEND BECOME AN ENEMY, DOESN'T IT?
WE'RE PISSED AT HIM TOO!
IF YOU WANNA KILL HIM, I DON'T MIND JOINING FORCES WITH YOU!
WHAT ...?
!
DOOOM

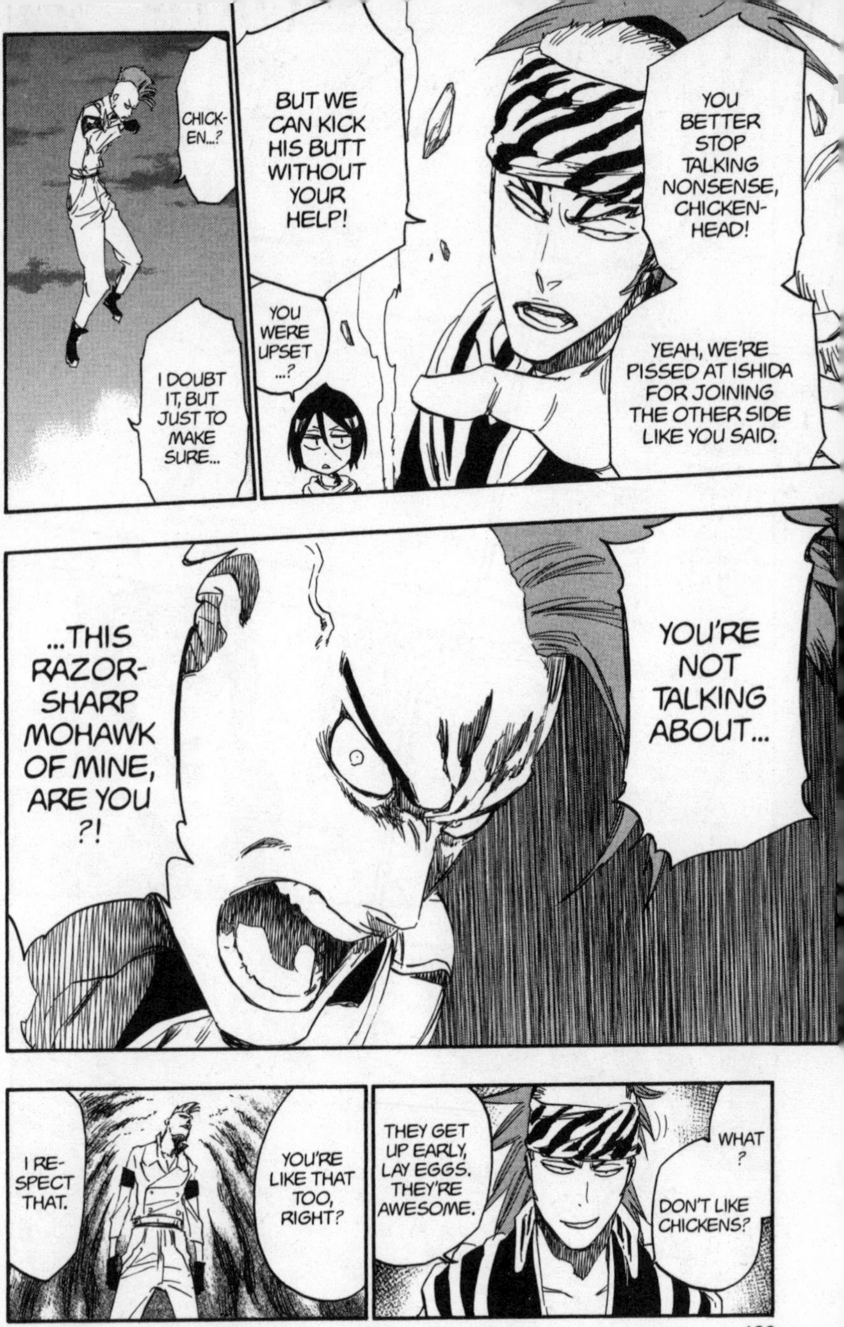
YOU BETTER STOP TALKING NONSENSE, CHICKEN-HEAD!
YEAH, WE'RE PISSED AT ISHIDA FOR JOINING THE OTHER SIDE LIKE YOU SAID.
BUT WE CAN KICK HIS BUTT WITHOUT YOUR HELP!
YOU WERE UPSET...?
CHICK-EN...?
I DOUBT IT, BUT JUST TO MAKE SURE...
YOU'RE NOT TALKING ABOUT...
...THIS RAZOR-SHARP MOHAWK OF MINE, ARE YOU?!
WHAT? DON'T LIKE CHICKENS?
THEY GET UP EARLY, LAY EGGS. THEY'RE AWESOME.
YOU'RE LIKE THAT TOO, RIGHT?
I RE-SPECT THAT.

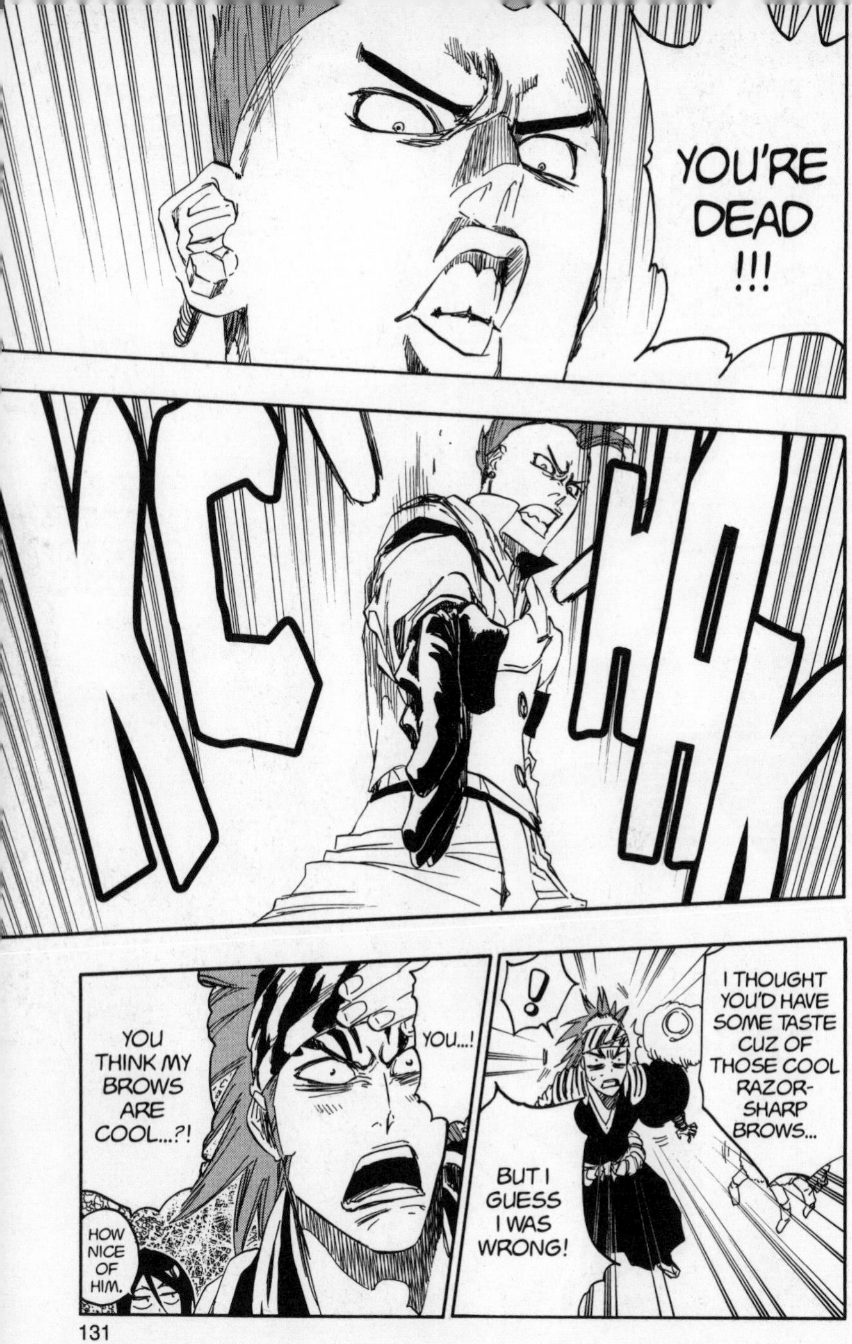
YOU'RE DEAD !!!
KCHAK
!
I THOUGHT YOU'D HAVE SOME TASTE CUZ OF THOSE COOL RAZOR-SHARP BROWS...
BUT I GUESS I WAS WRONG!
YOU...!
YOU THINK MY BROWS ARE COOL...?!
HOW NICE OF HIM.

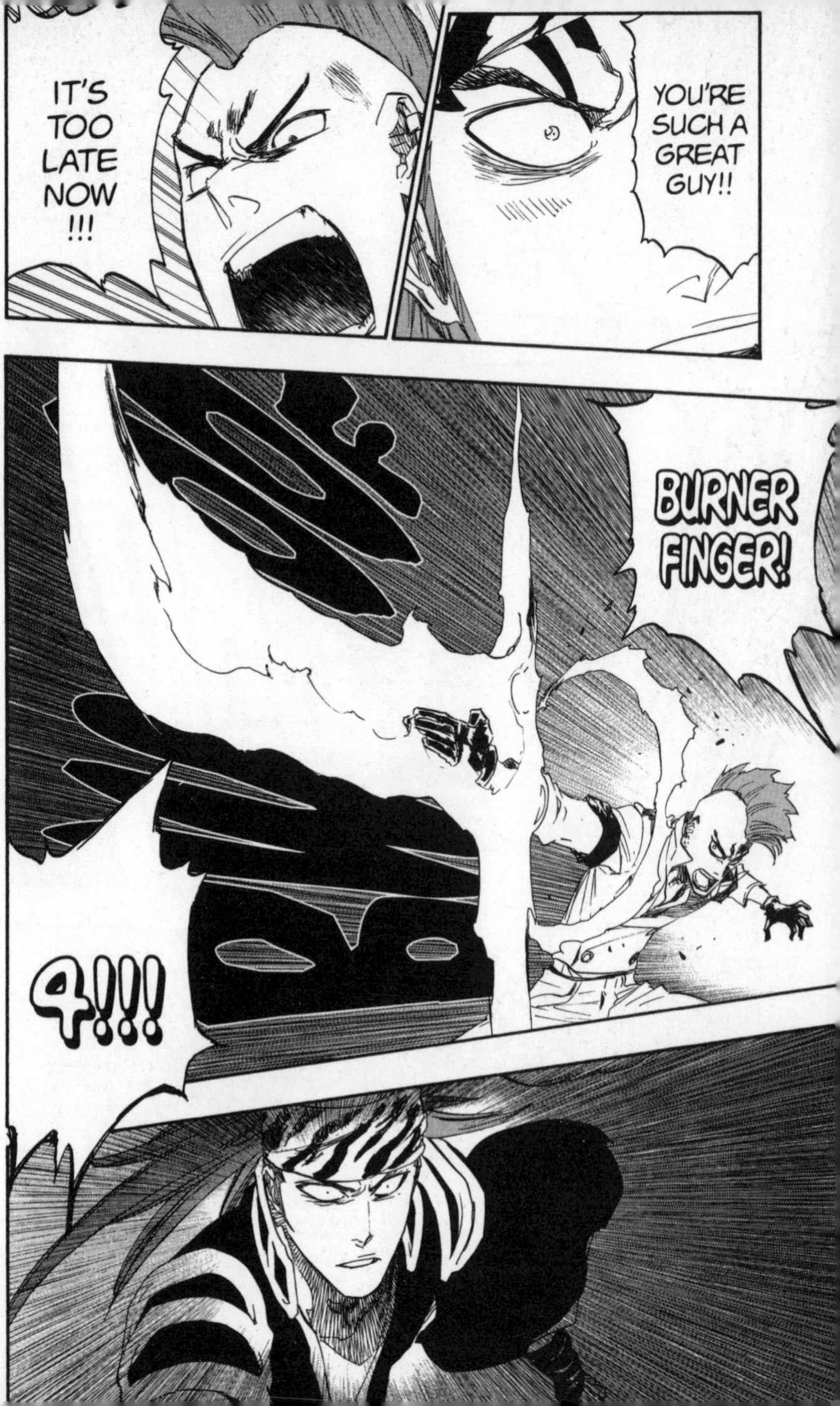
YOU'RE SUCH A GREAT GUY!!
IT'S TOO LATE NOW!!!
BURNER FINGER!
4!!!

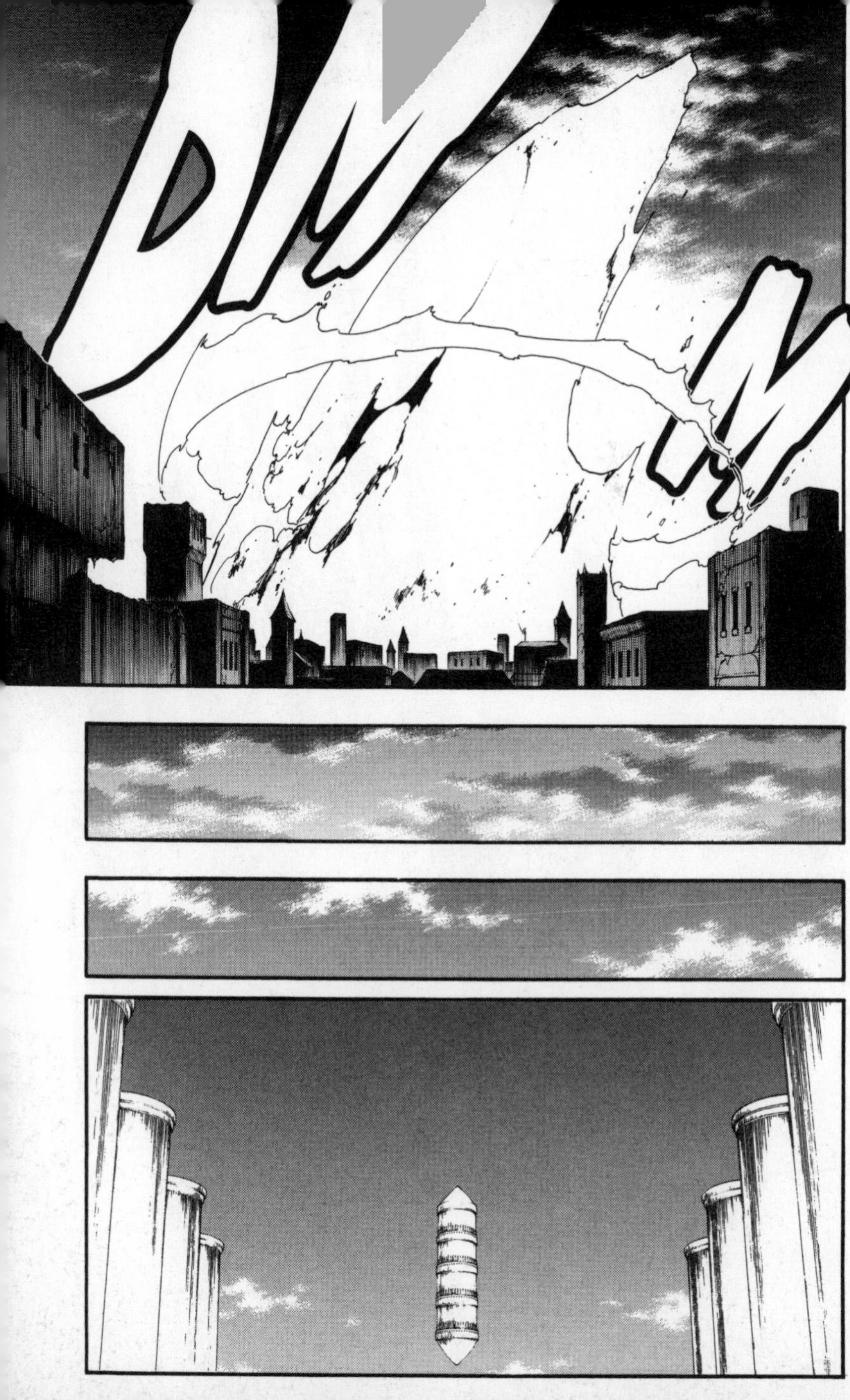
DMM

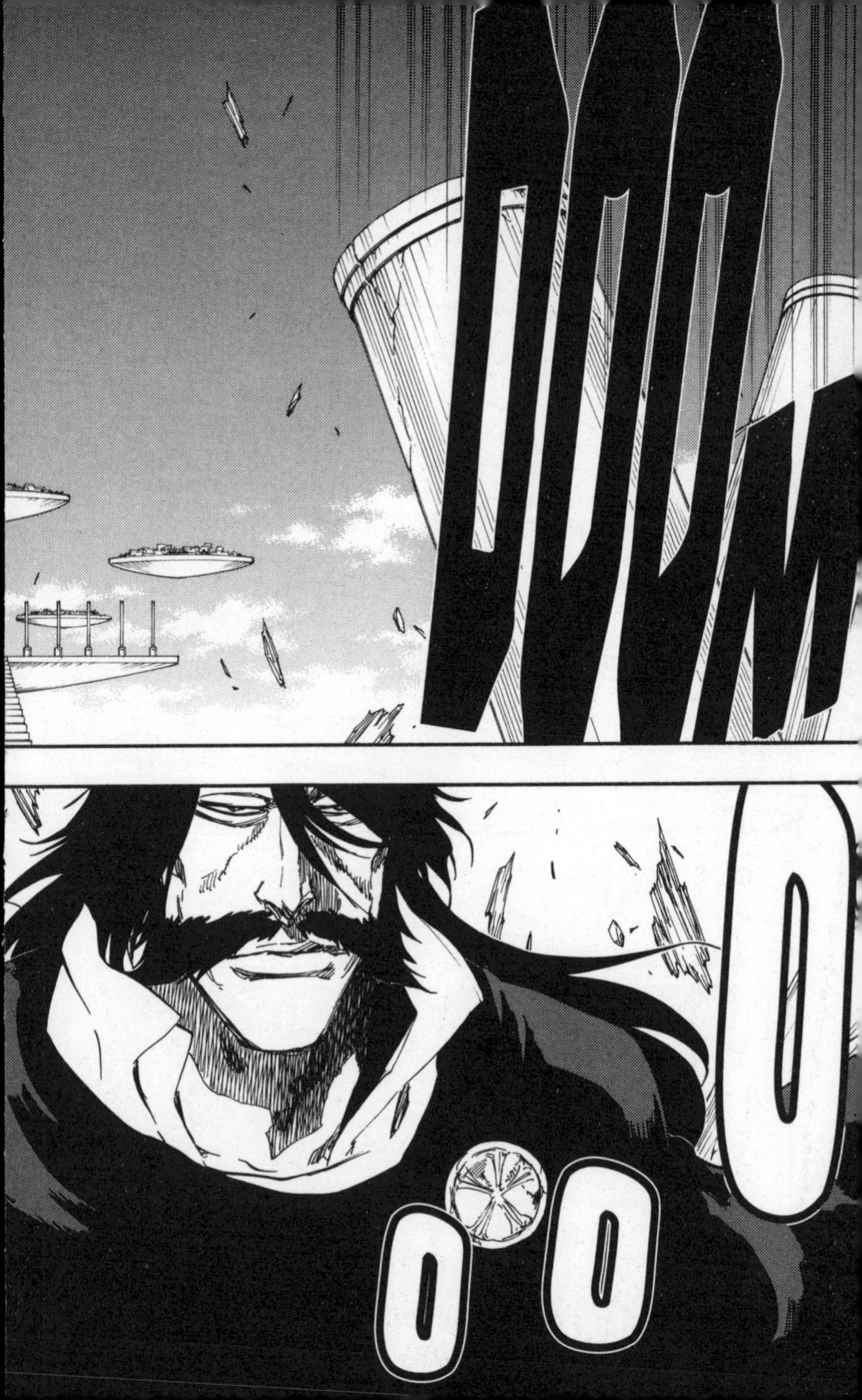
DOOM
OOO

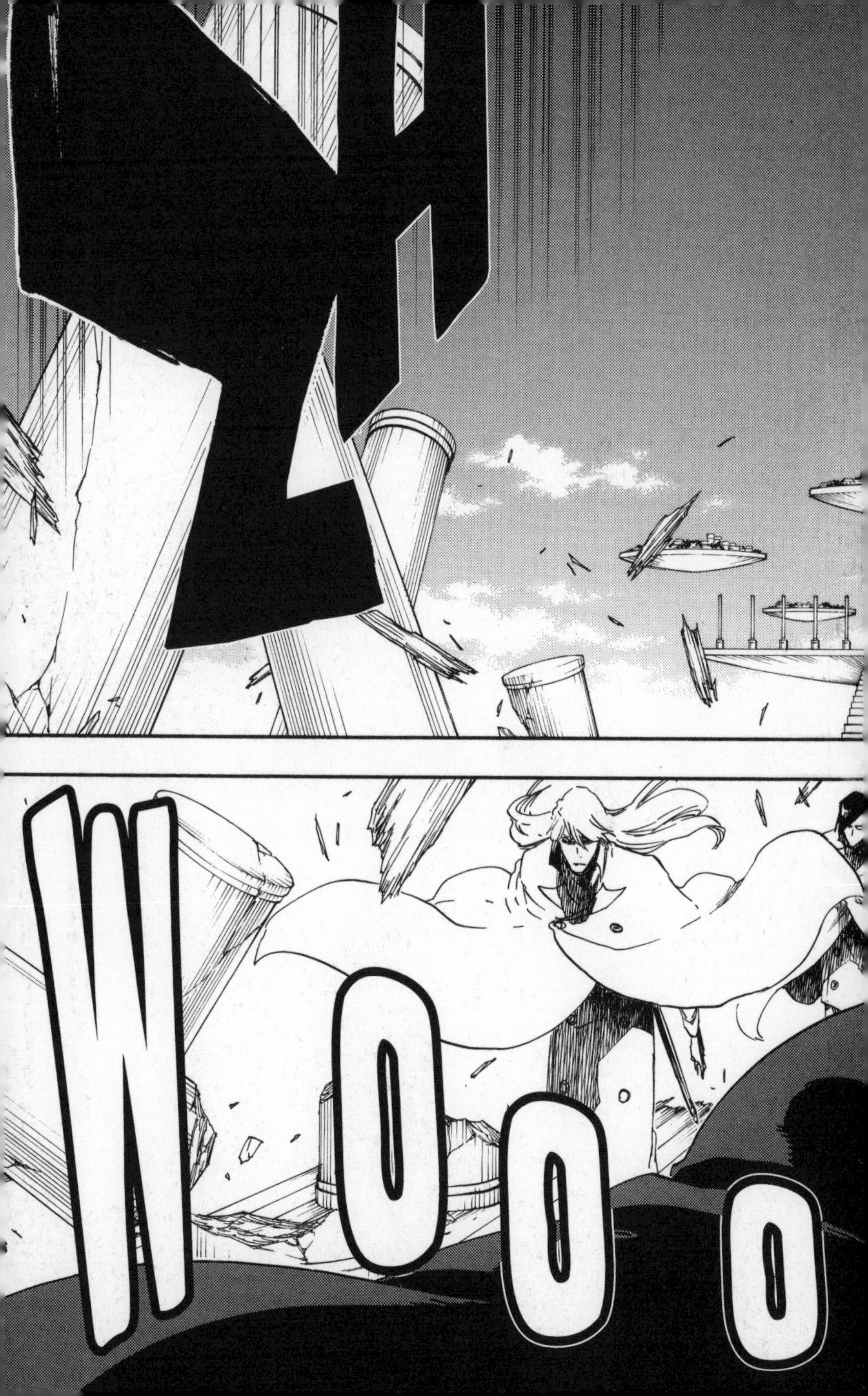
WOOO

VS

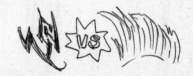

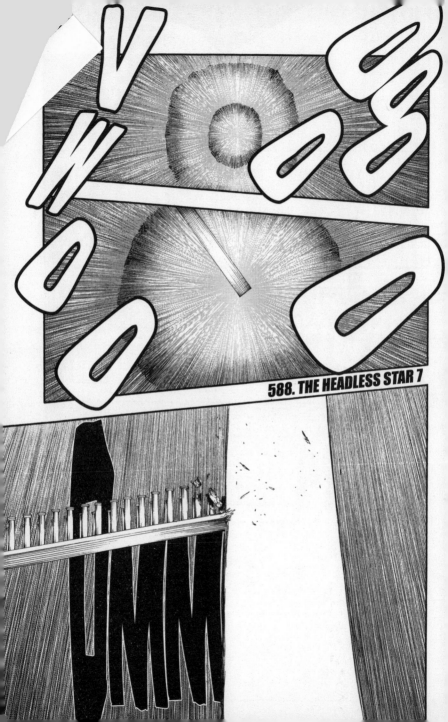

588. THE HEADLESS STAR 7

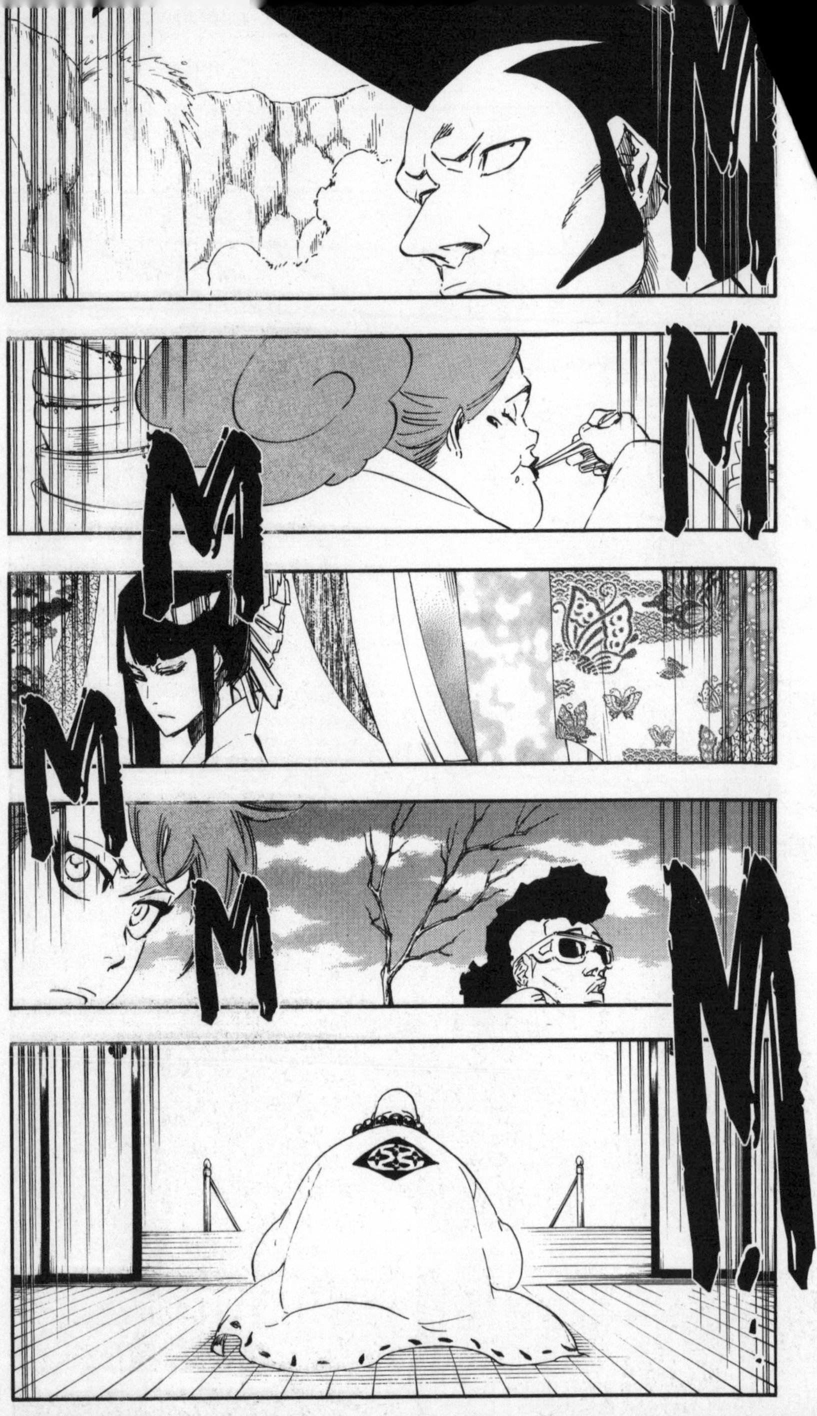
M
M
M
M
M
M...

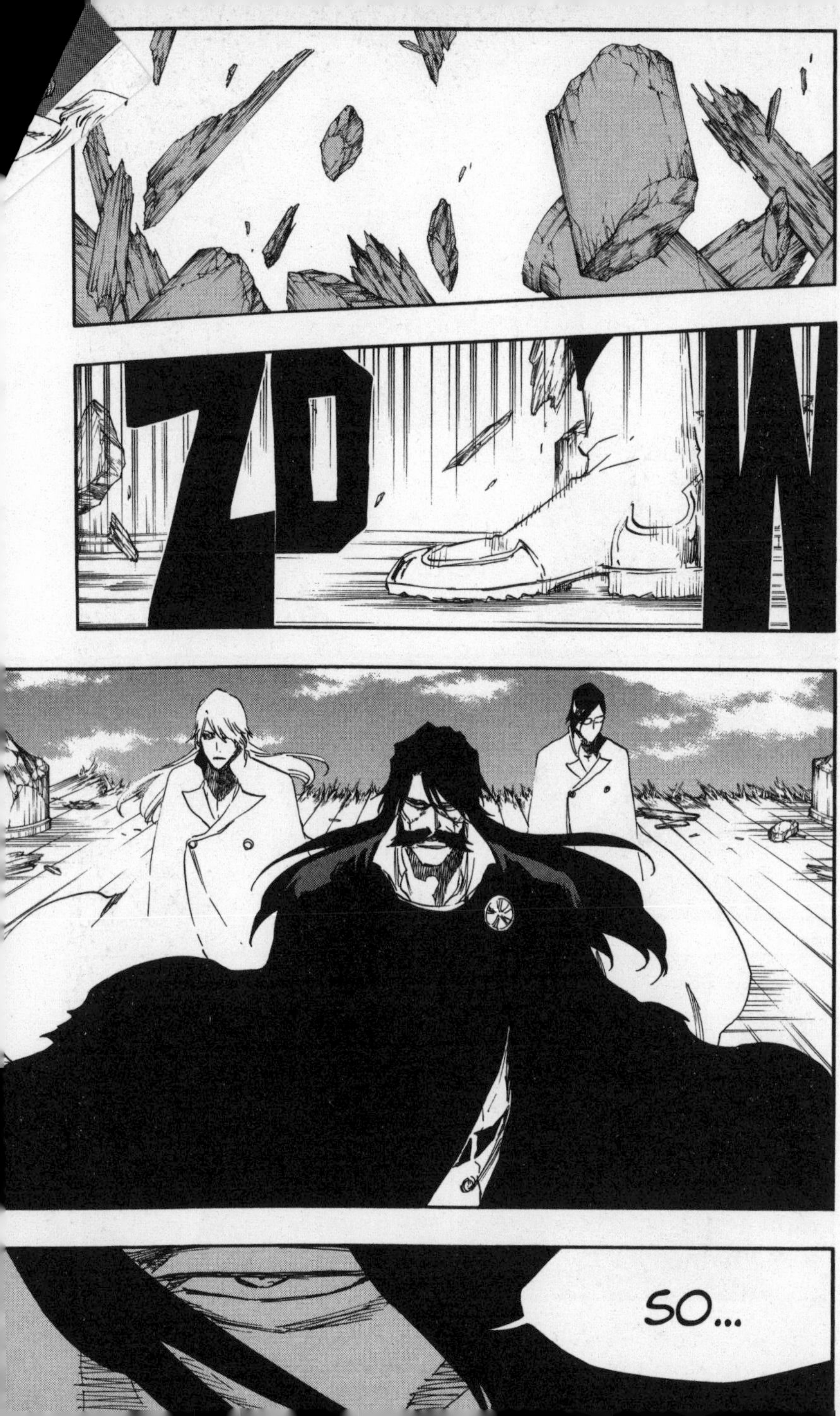
SO...

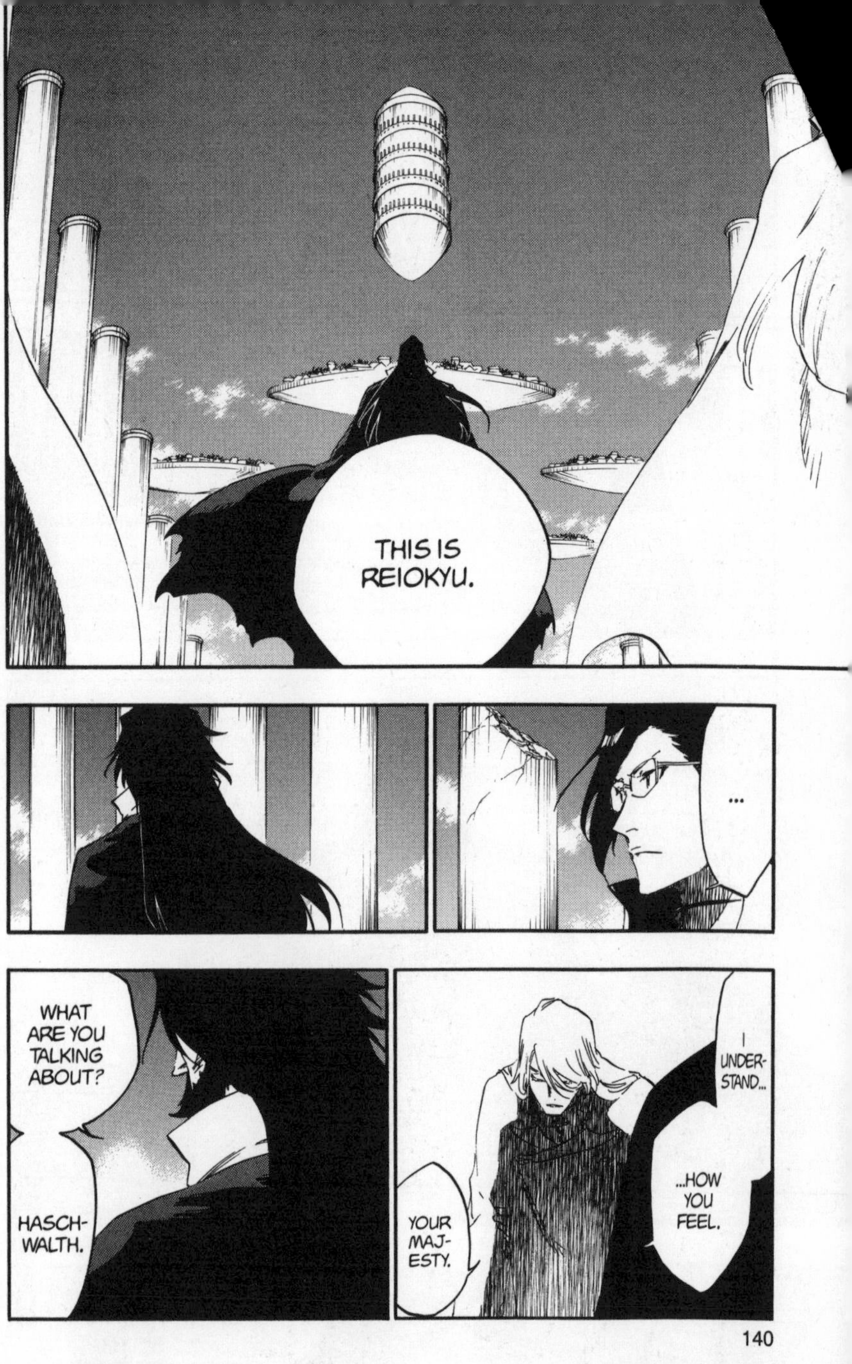
THIS IS REIOKYU.
...
I UNDERSTAND...
...HOW YOU FEEL.
YOUR MAJESTY.
WHAT ARE YOU TALKING ABOUT?
HASCHWALTH.

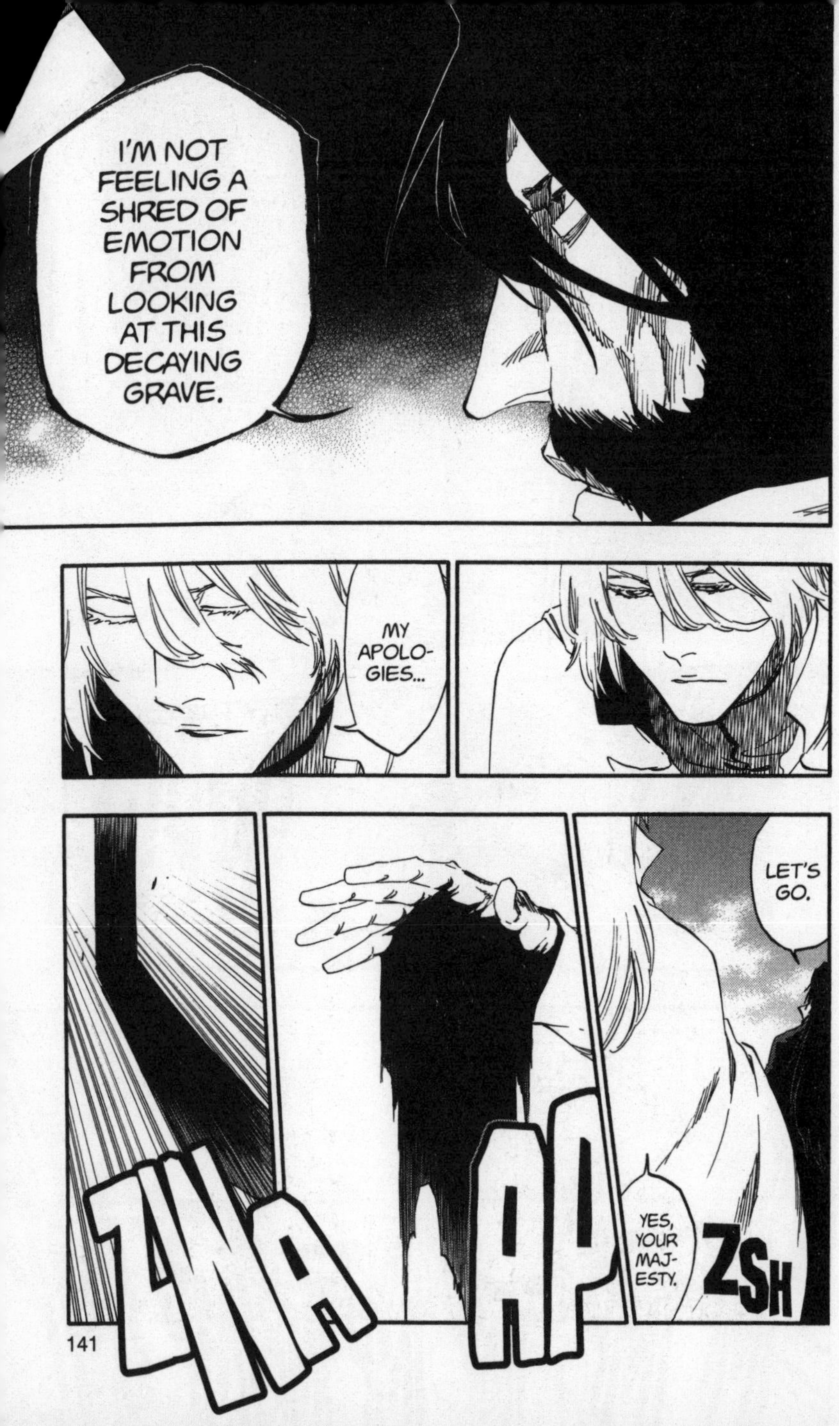
I'M NOT FEELING A SHRED OF EMOTION FROM LOOKING AT THIS DECAYING GRAVE.
MY APOLO-GIES...
LET'S GO.
YES, YOUR MAJ-ESTY.
ZSH
ZWA AP

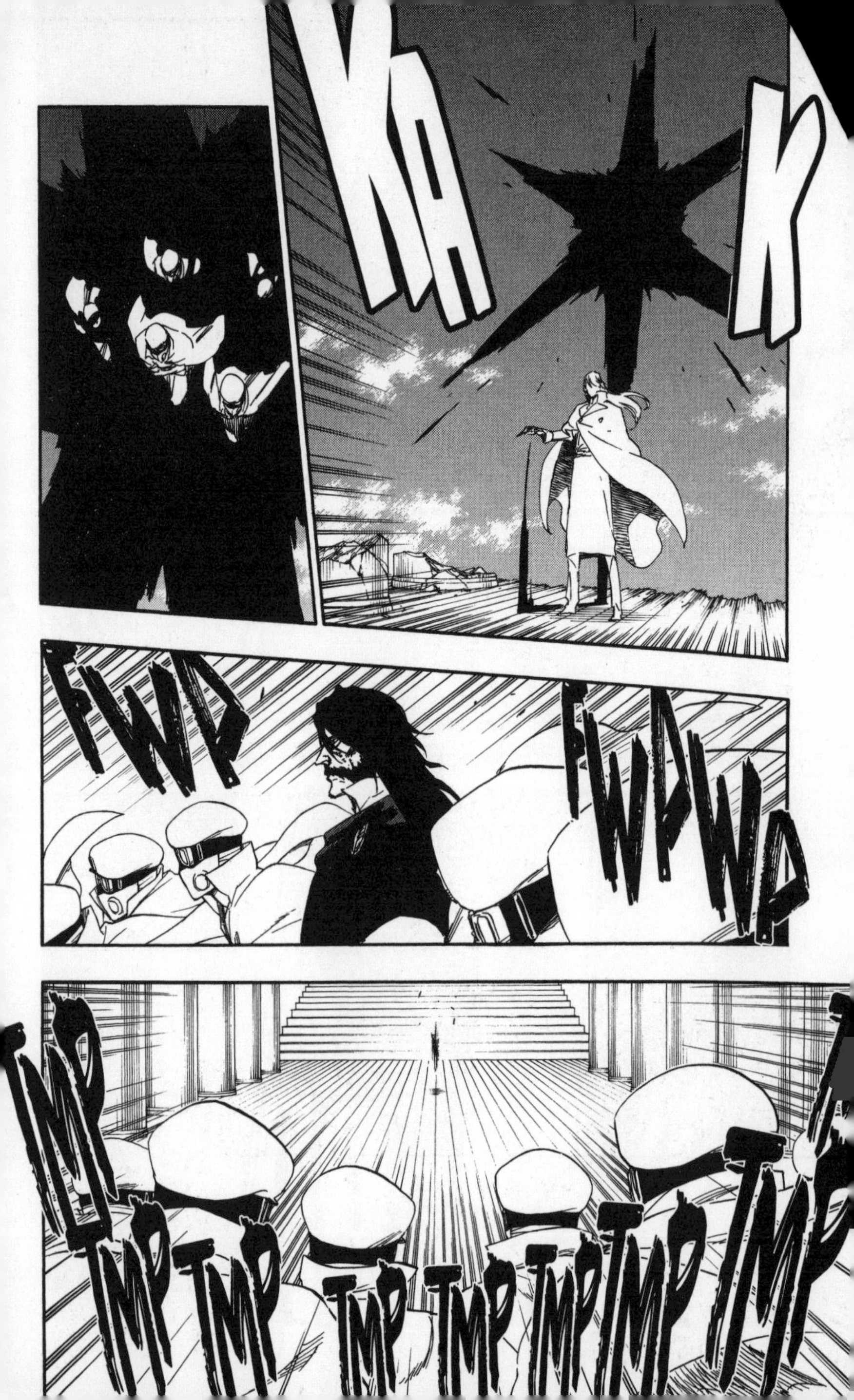
KRAK
FWPWP
FWP
TMP TMP TMP TMP TMP TMP TMP TMP TMP

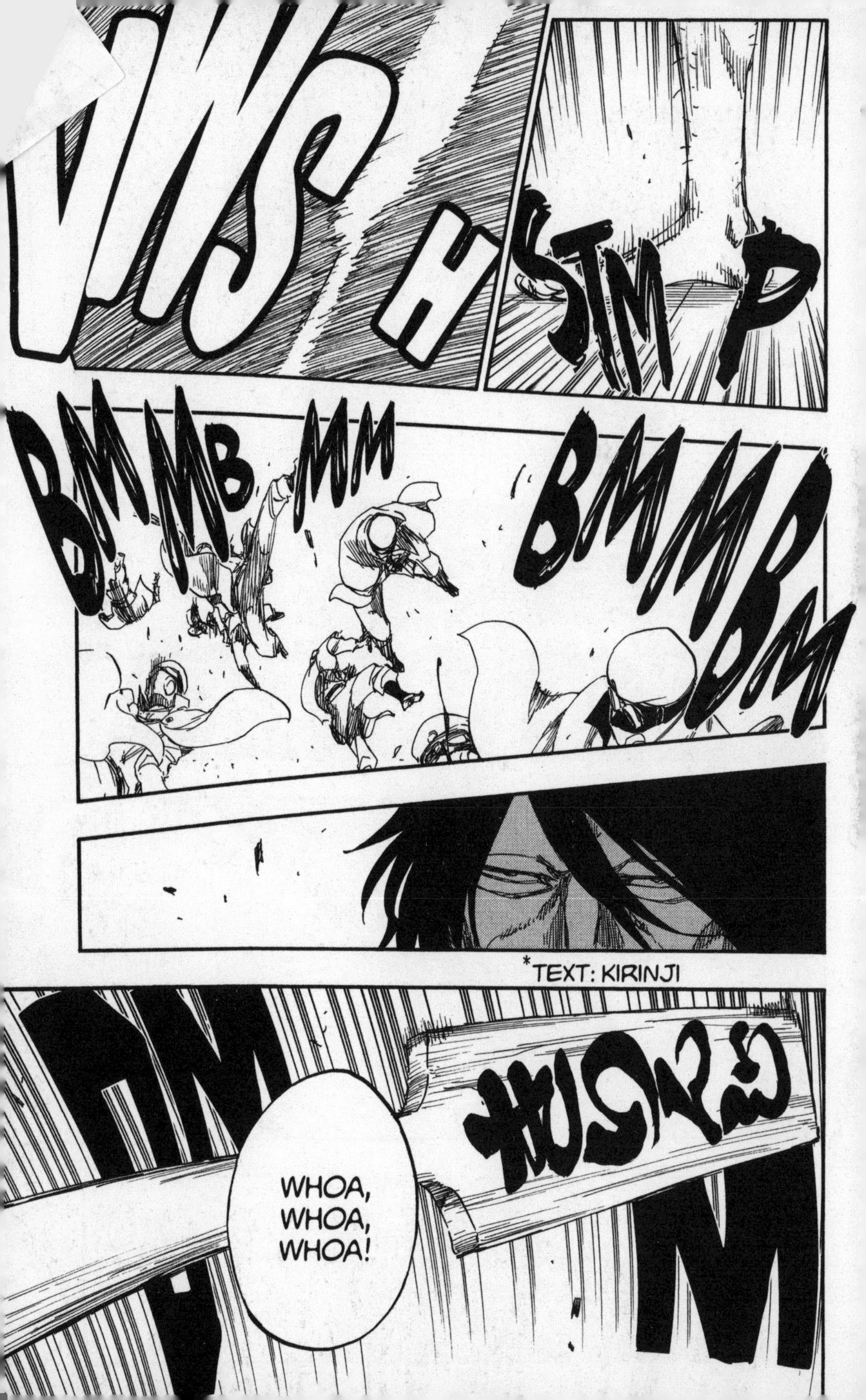
STMP
*TEXT: KIRINJI
WHOA, WHOA, WHOA!

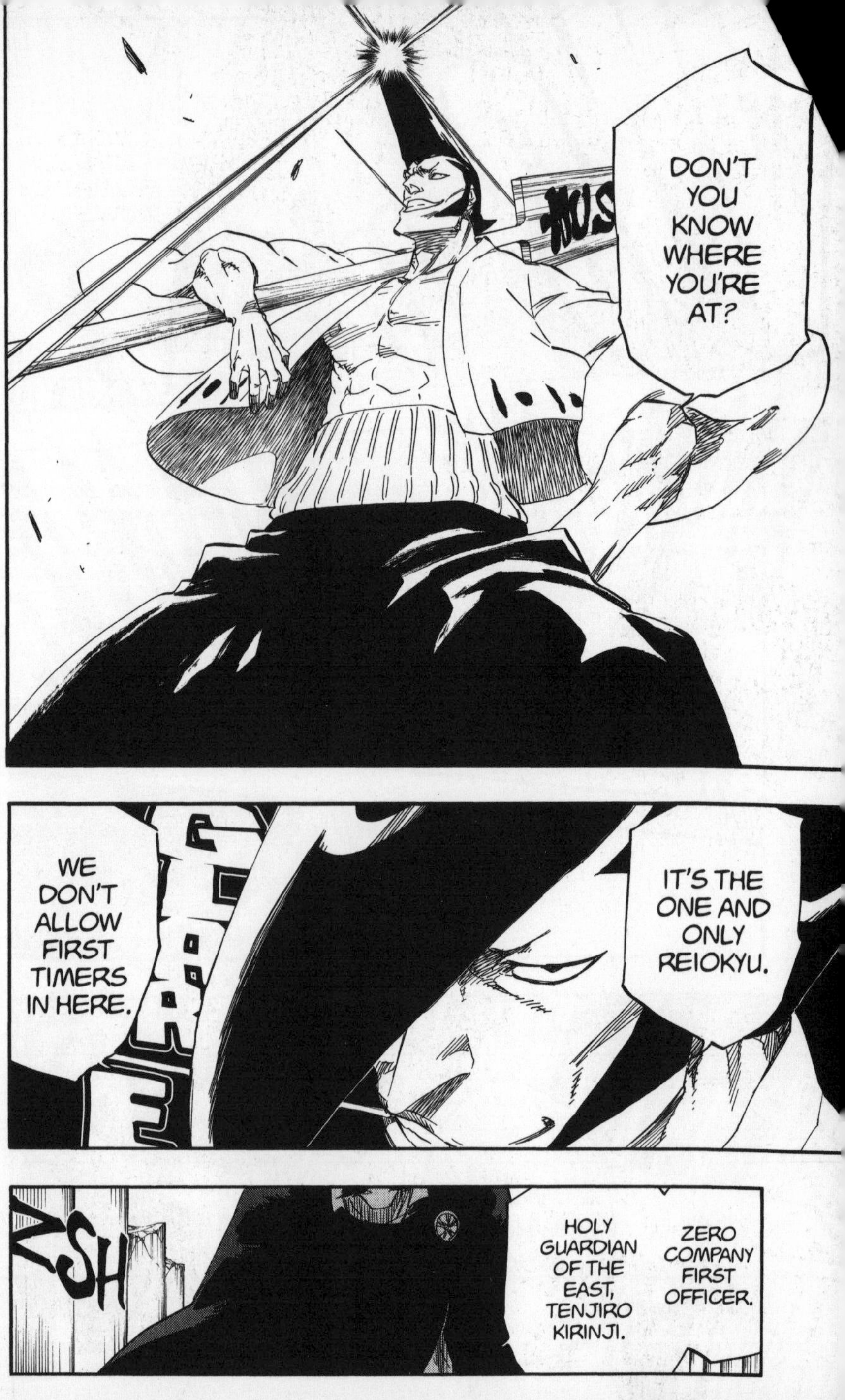
DON'T YOU KNOW WHERE YOU'RE AT?
IT'S THE ONE AND ONLY REIOKYU.
WE DON'T ALLOW FIRST TIMERS IN HERE.
ZERO COMPANY FIRST OFFICER.
HOLY GUARDIAN OF THE EAST, TENJIRO KIRINJI.
ZSH

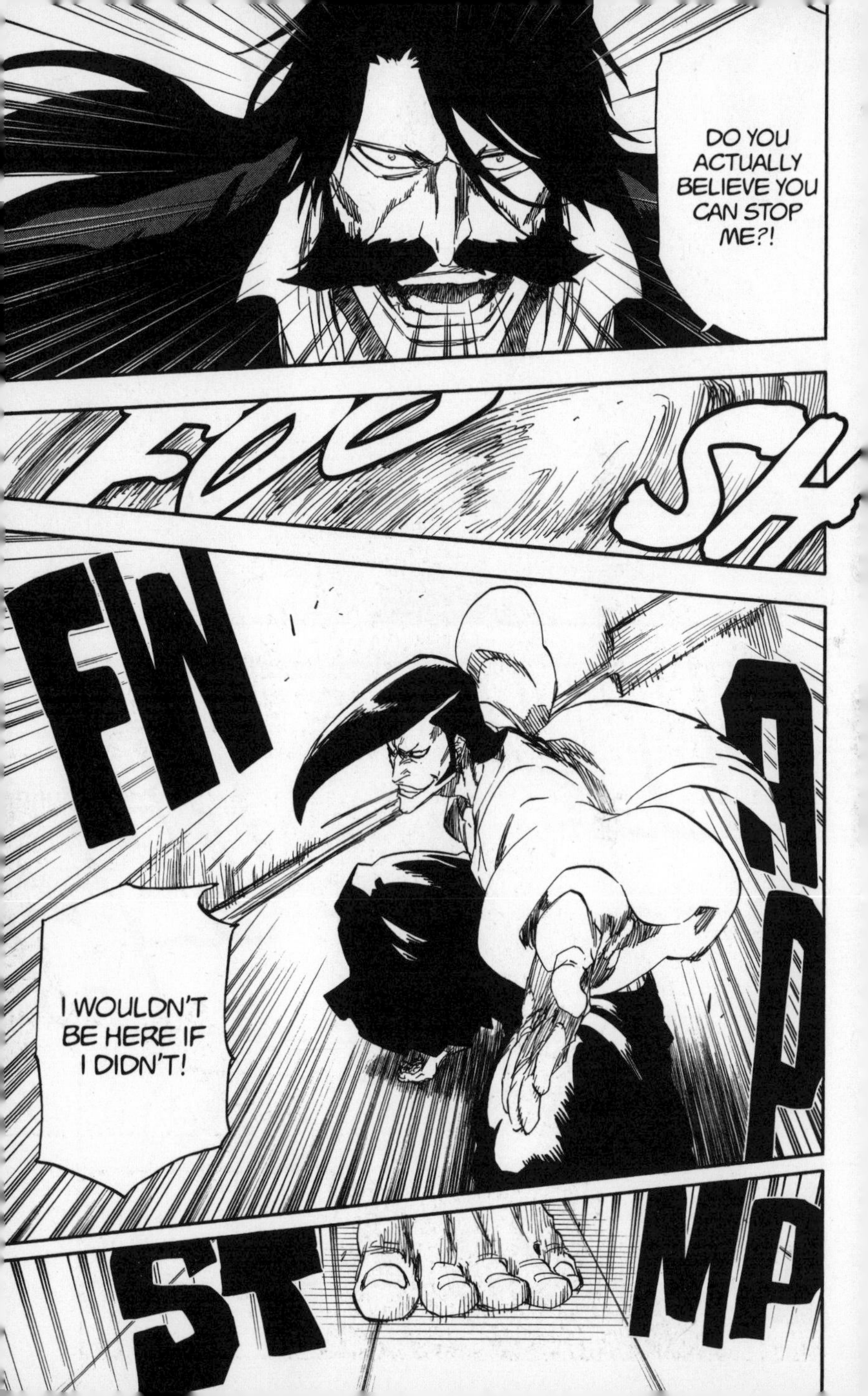
DO YOU ACTUALLY BELIEVE YOU CAN STOP ME?!
FWN
I WOULDN'T BE HERE IF I DIDN'T!

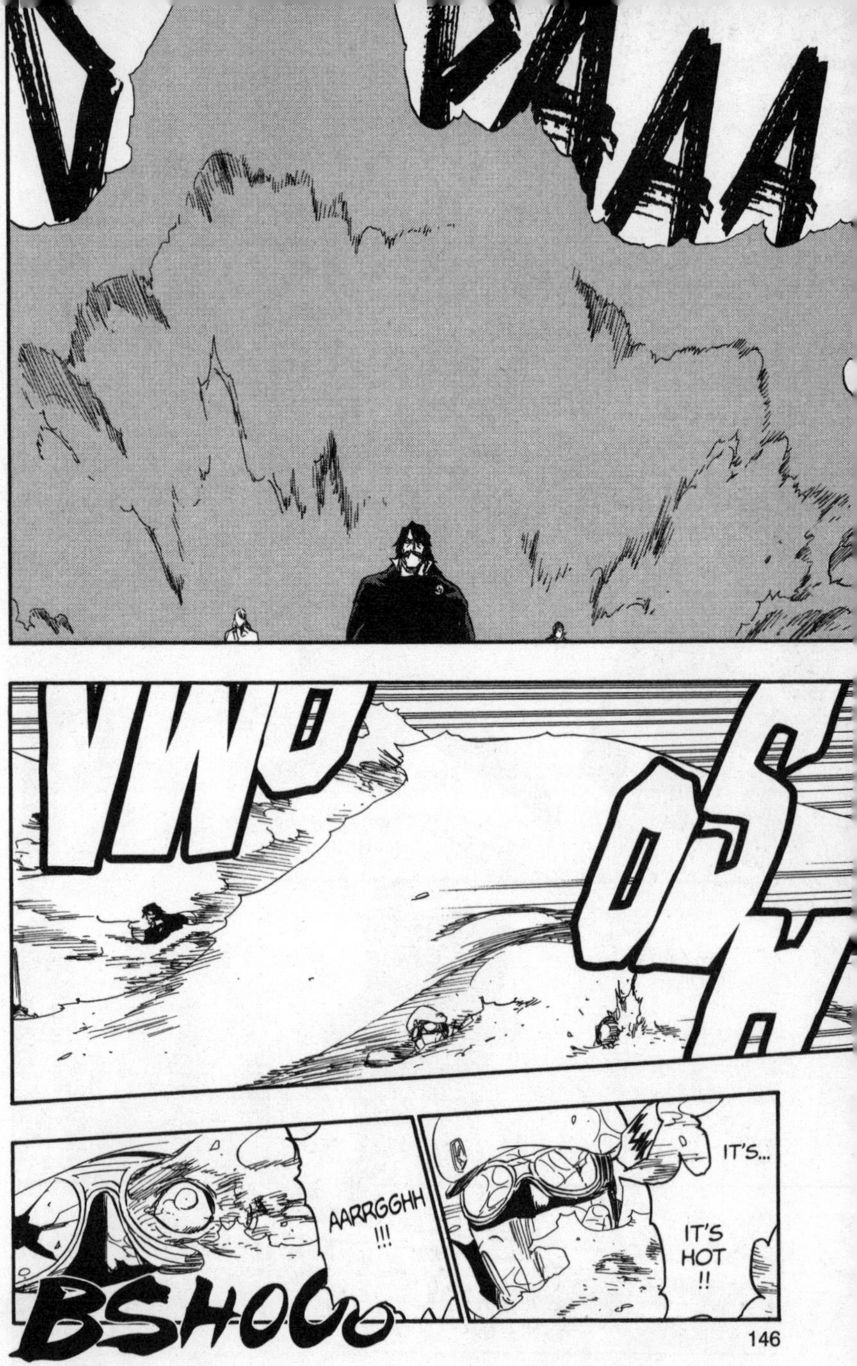
IT'S...
IT'S HOT !!
AARRGGHH !!!
BSHOOO

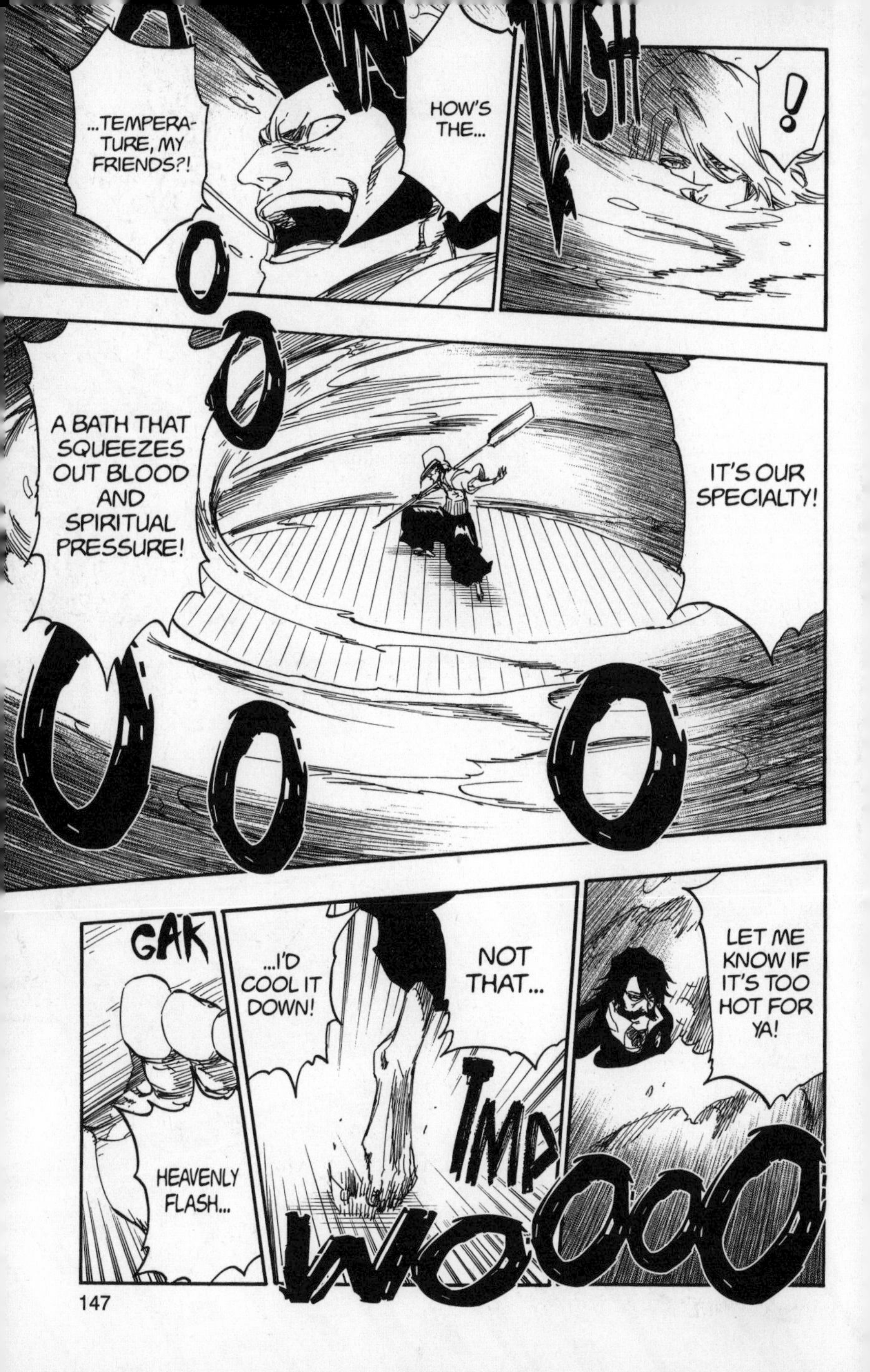
TWSH!!
!
HOW'S THE...
...TEMPERA-TURE, MY FRIENDS?!
IT'S OUR SPECIALTY!
A BATH THAT SQUEEZES OUT BLOOD AND SPIRITUAL PRESSURE!
LET ME KNOW IF IT'S TOO HOT FOR YA!
NOT THAT...
...I'D COOL IT DOWN!
TMP
GAK
HEAVENLY FLASH...
WOOOO

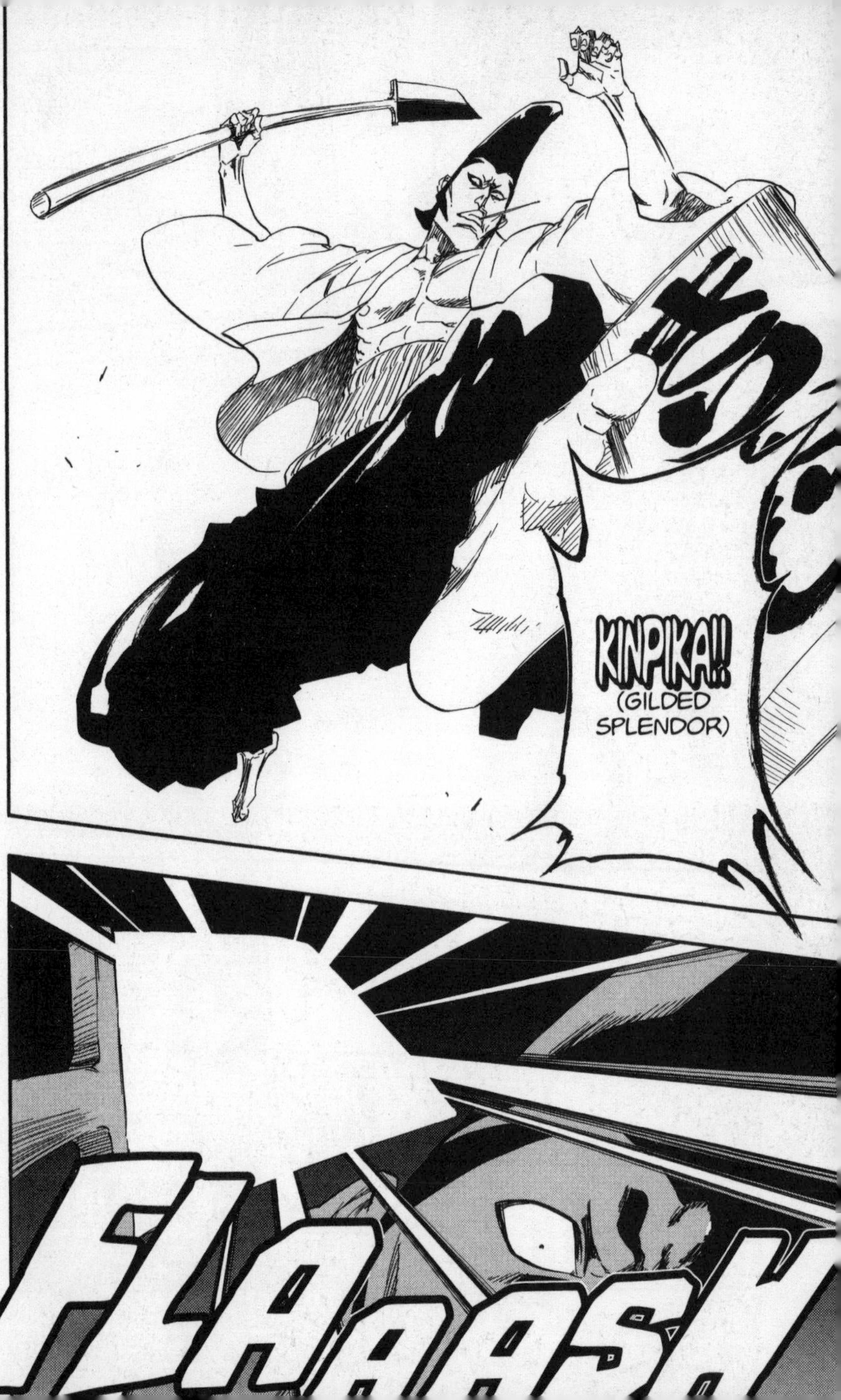
KINPIKA!!
(GILDED SPLENDOR)
FLAASH

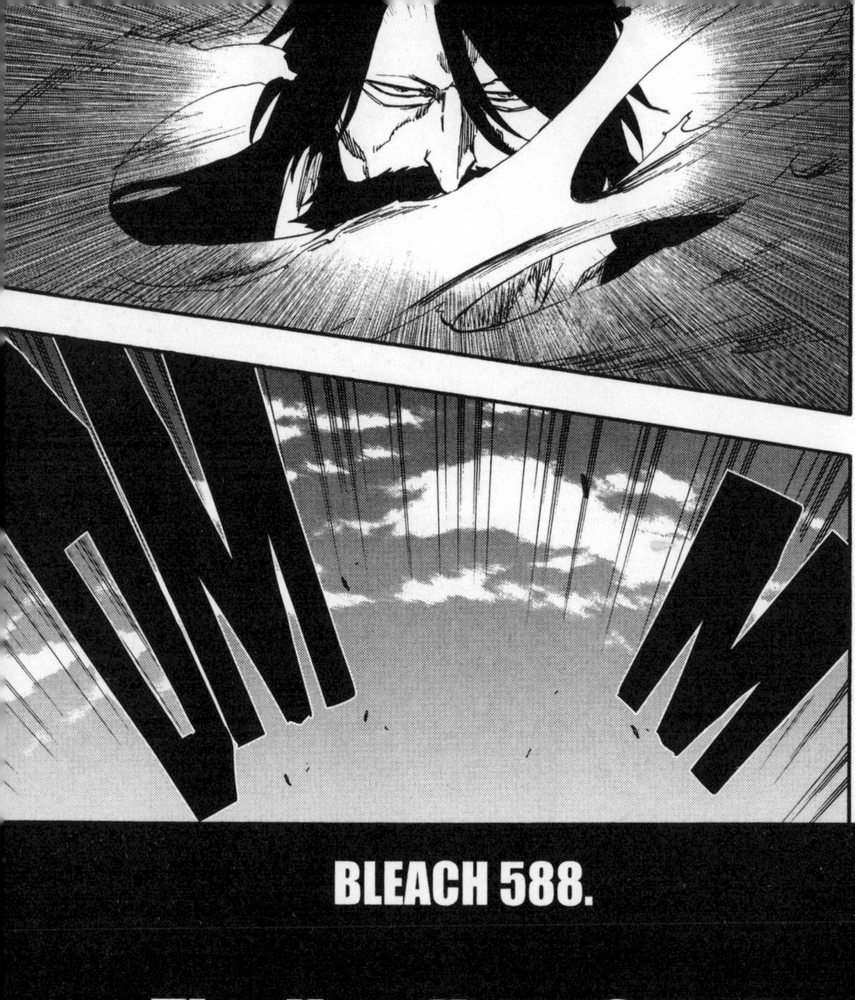

BLEACH 588.

The Headless Star 7

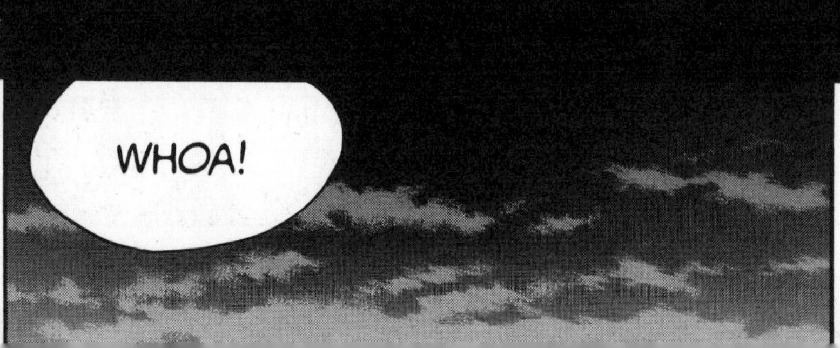
WHOA!

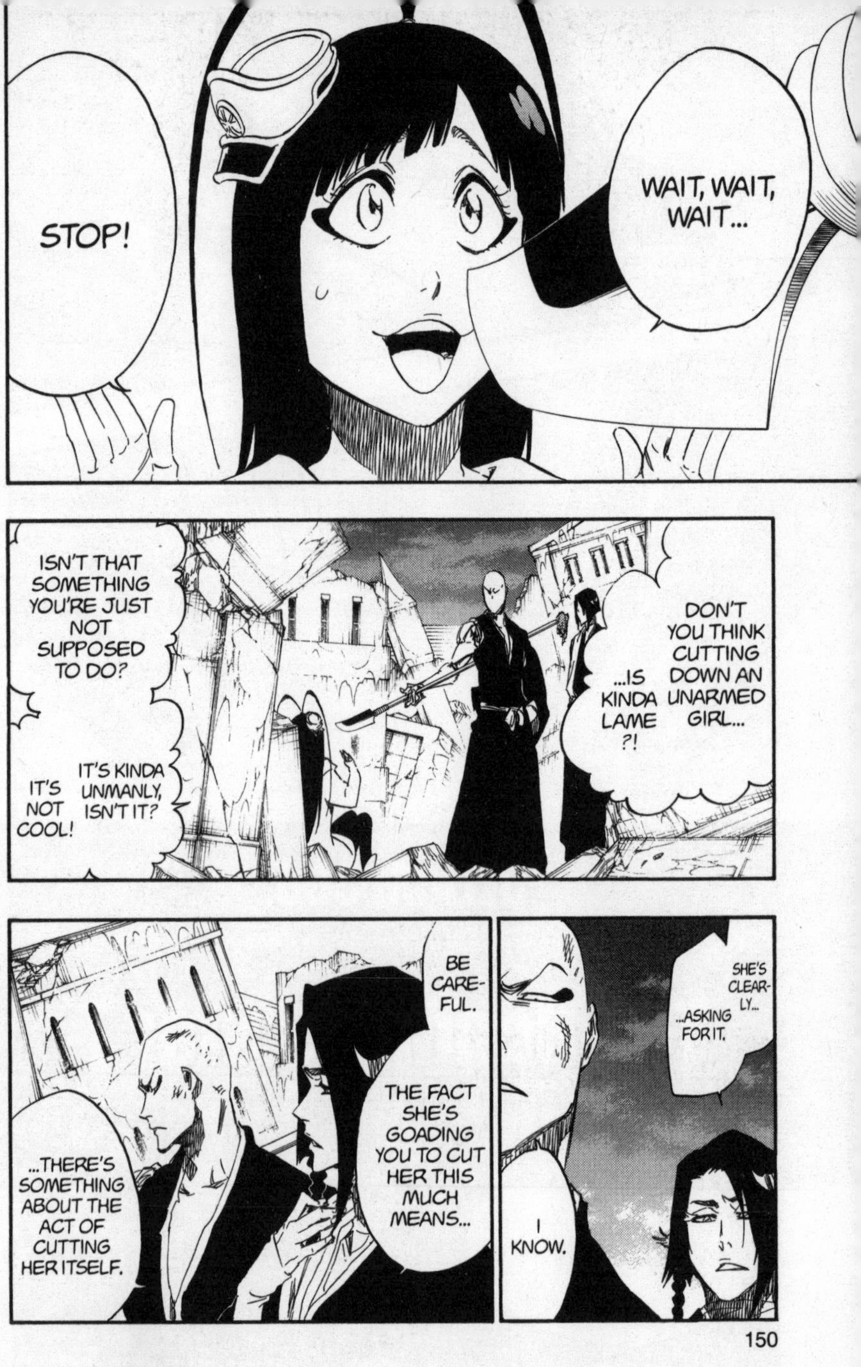
WAIT, WAIT, WAIT...
STOP!
DON'T YOU THINK CUTTING DOWN AN UNARMED GIRL...
...IS KINDA LAME ?!
ISN'T THAT SOMETHING YOU'RE JUST NOT SUPPOSED TO DO?
IT'S KINDA UNMANLY, ISN'T IT?
IT'S NOT COOL!
SHE'S CLEARLY...
...ASKING FOR IT.
I KNOW.
BE CAREFUL.
THE FACT SHE'S GOADING YOU TO CUT HER THIS MUCH MEANS...
...THERE'S SOMETHING ABOUT THE ACT OF CUTTING HER ITSELF.

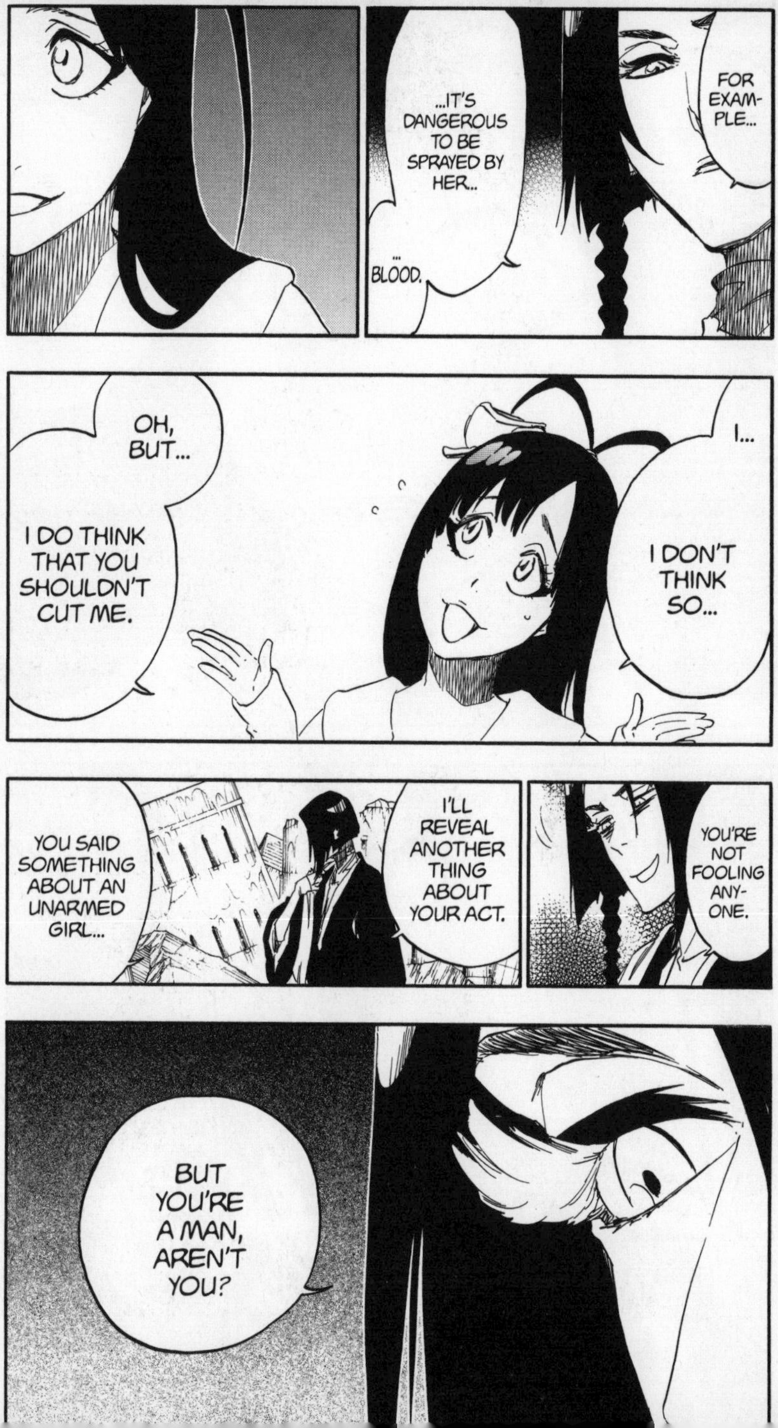
FOR EXAMPLE...
...IT'S DANGEROUS TO BE SPRAYED BY HER...
...BLOOD.
I...
I DON'T THINK SO...
OH, BUT...
I DO THINK THAT YOU SHOULDN'T CUT ME.
YOU'RE NOT FOOLING ANYONE.
I'LL REVEAL ANOTHER THING ABOUT YOUR ACT.
YOU SAID SOMETHING ABOUT AN UNARMED GIRL...
BUT YOU'RE A MAN, AREN'T YOU?

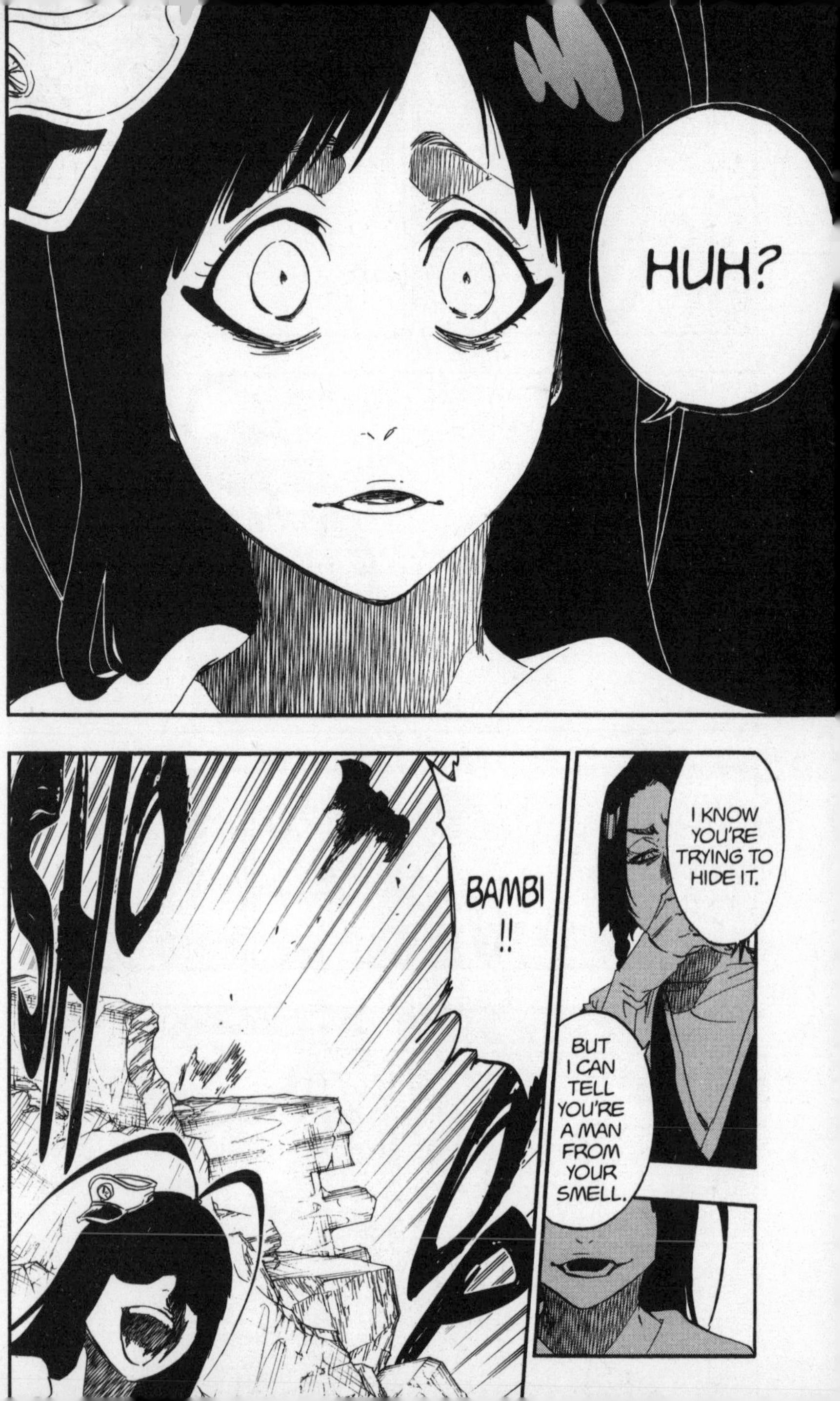
HUH?
I KNOW YOU'RE TRYING TO HIDE IT.
BUT I CAN TELL YOU'RE A MAN FROM YOUR SMELL.
BAMBI !!

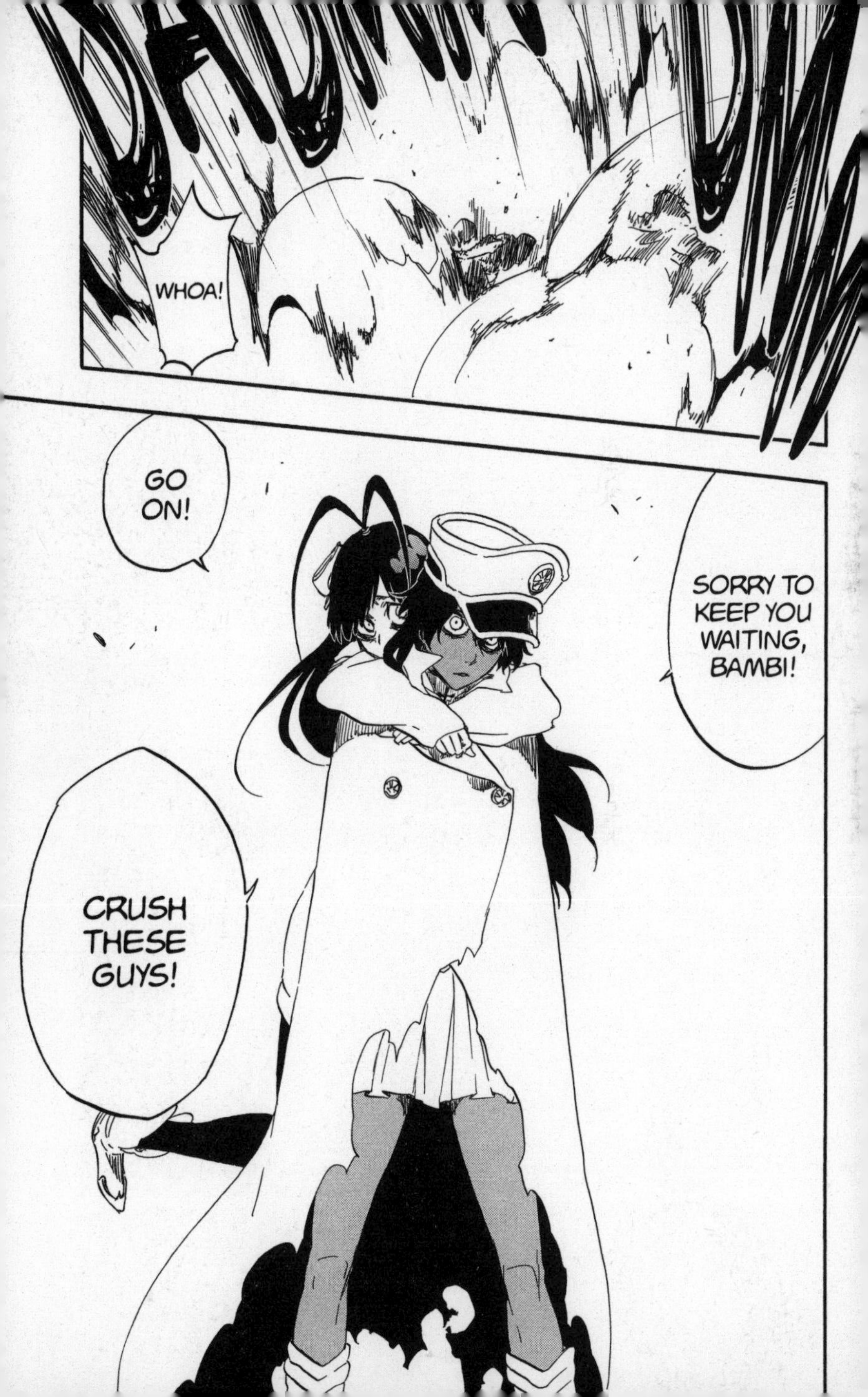
WHOA!
SORRY TO KEEP YOU WAITING, BAMBI!
GO ON!
CRUSH THESE GUYS!

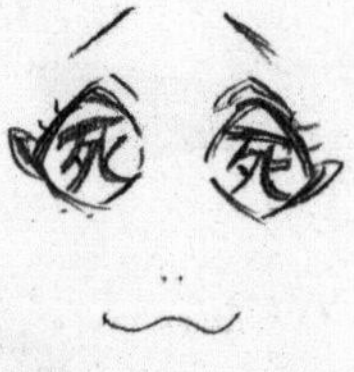
死
死

*NOTE: KANJI FOR "DEATH"

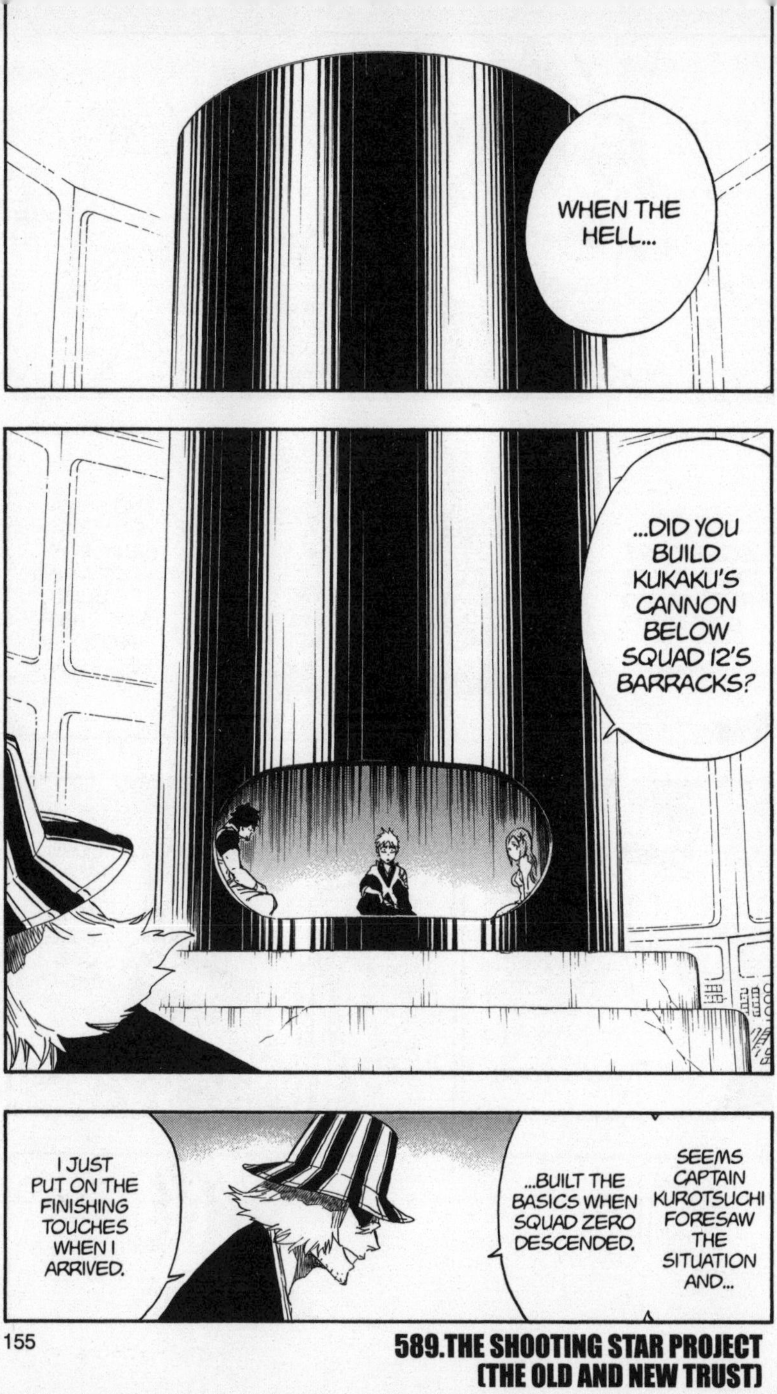
WHEN THE HELL...
...DID YOU BUILD KUKAKU'S CANNON BELOW SQUAD 12'S BARRACKS?
SEEMS CAPTAIN KUROTSUCHI FORESAW THE SITUATION AND...
...BUILT THE BASICS WHEN SQUAD ZERO DESCENDED.
I JUST PUT ON THE FINISHING TOUCHES WHEN I ARRIVED.

589. THE SHOOTING STAR PROJECT (THE OLD AND NEW TRUST)

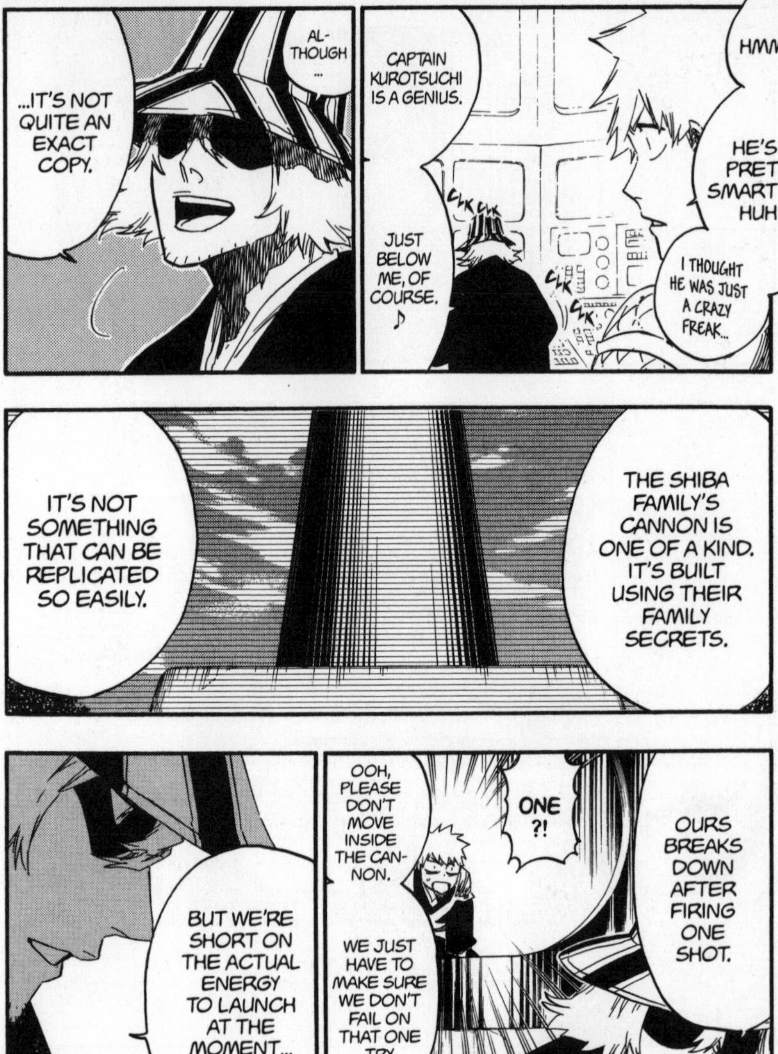
HMM...
HE'S A PRETTY SMART GUY, HUH?
I THOUGHT HE WAS JUST A CRAZY FREAK...
CAPTAIN KUROTSUCHI IS A GENIUS.
CLK CLK
JUST BELOW ME, OF COURSE. ♪
CLK
CLK
AL-THOUGH...
...IT'S NOT QUITE AN EXACT COPY.
THE SHIBA FAMILY'S CANNON IS ONE OF A KIND. IT'S BUILT USING THEIR FAMILY SECRETS.
IT'S NOT SOMETHING THAT CAN BE REPLICATED SO EASILY.
OURS BREAKS DOWN AFTER FIRING ONE SHOT.
ONE ?!
OOH, PLEASE DON'T MOVE INSIDE THE CAN-NON.
WE JUST HAVE TO MAKE SURE WE DON'T FAIL ON THAT ONE TRY.
BUT WE'RE SHORT ON THE ACTUAL ENERGY TO LAUNCH AT THE MOMENT...
BEEP BEEP

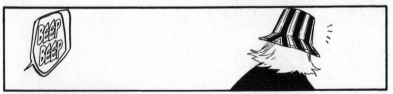

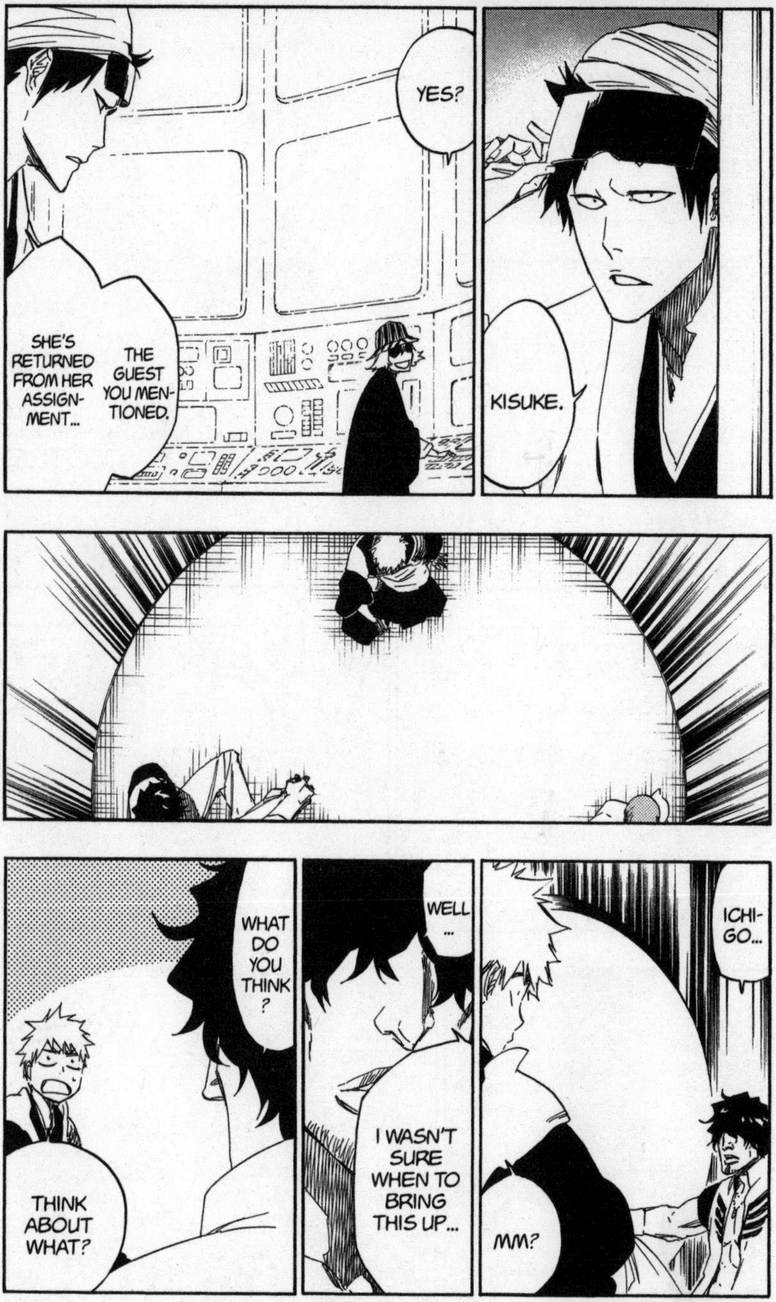
KISUKE.
YES?
THE GUEST YOU MENTIONED.
SHE'S RETURNED FROM HER ASSIGNMENT...
ICHIGO...
MM?
WELL...
I WASN'T SURE WHEN TO BRING THIS UP...
WHAT DO YOU THINK?
THINK ABOUT WHAT?

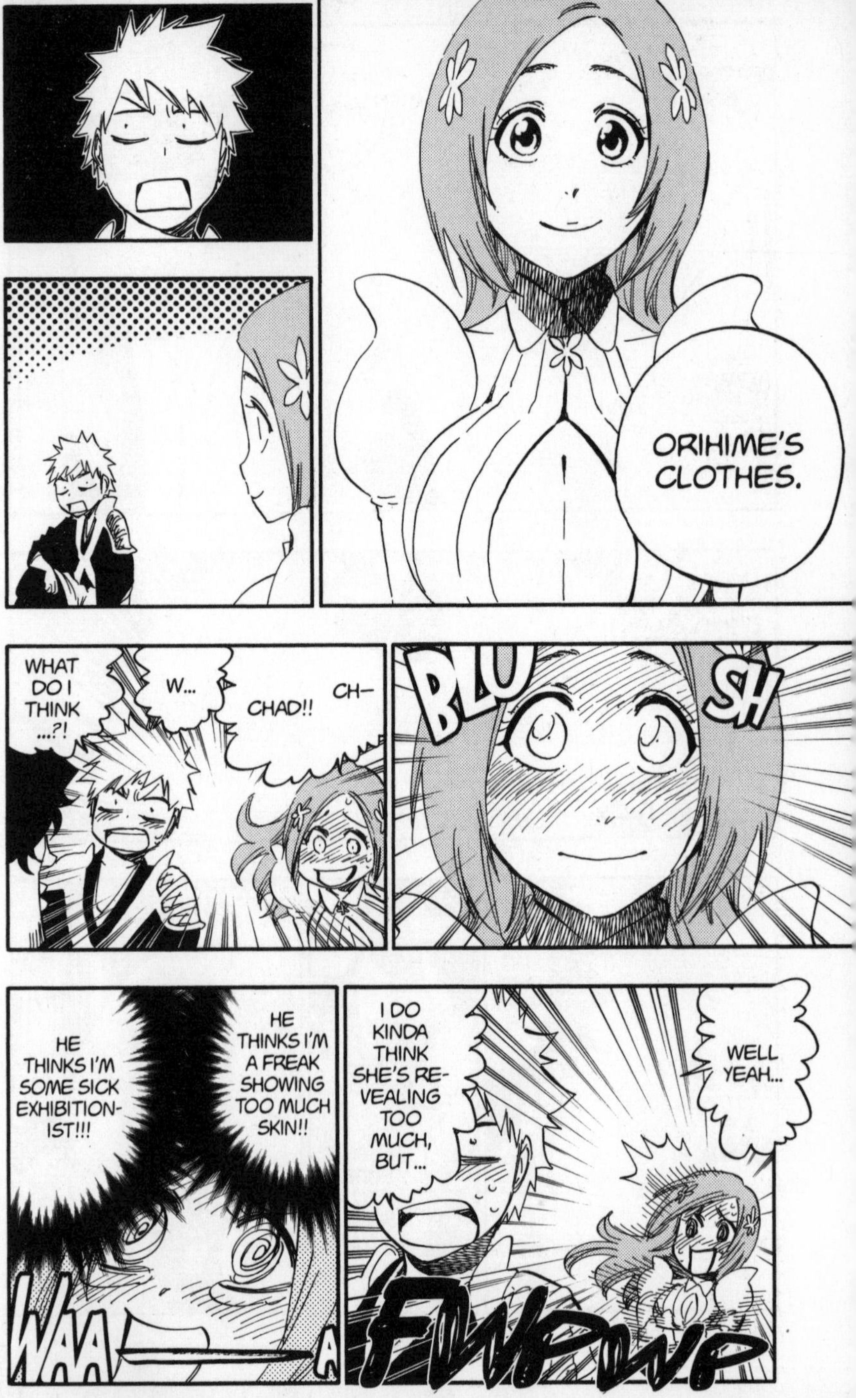
ORIHIME'S CLOTHES.
BLUSH
CH-
CHAD!!
W...
WHAT DO I THINK ...?!
WELL YEAH...
I DO KINDA THINK SHE'S RE-VEALING TOO MUCH, BUT...
FWPWP
HE THINKS I'M A FREAK SHOWING TOO MUCH SKIN!!
HE THINKS I'M SOME SICK EXHIBITION-IST!!!
WAA—A

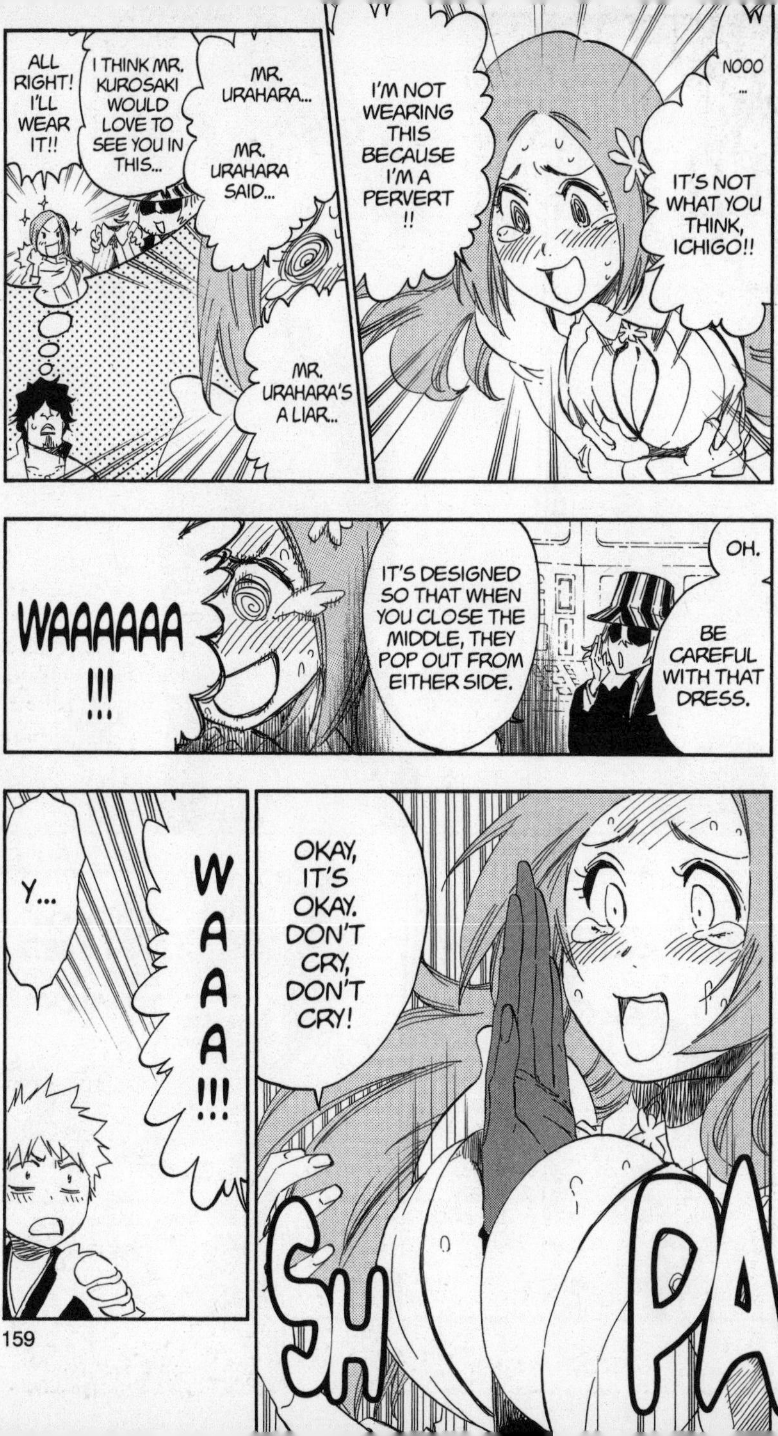

NOOO ...
IT'S NOT WHAT YOU THINK, ICHIGO!!
I'M NOT WEARING THIS BECAUSE I'M A PERVERT !!
MR. URAHARA...
MR. URAHARA SAID...
I THINK MR. KUROSAKI WOULD LOVE TO SEE YOU IN THIS...
ALL RIGHT! I'LL WEAR IT!!
MR. URAHARA'S A LIAR...
OH.
BE CAREFUL WITH THAT DRESS.
IT'S DESIGNED SO THAT WHEN YOU CLOSE THE MIDDLE, THEY POP OUT FROM EITHER SIDE.
WAAAAAA !!!
OKAY, IT'S OKAY. DON'T CRY, DON'T CRY!
SH PA
WAAAA!!!
Y...

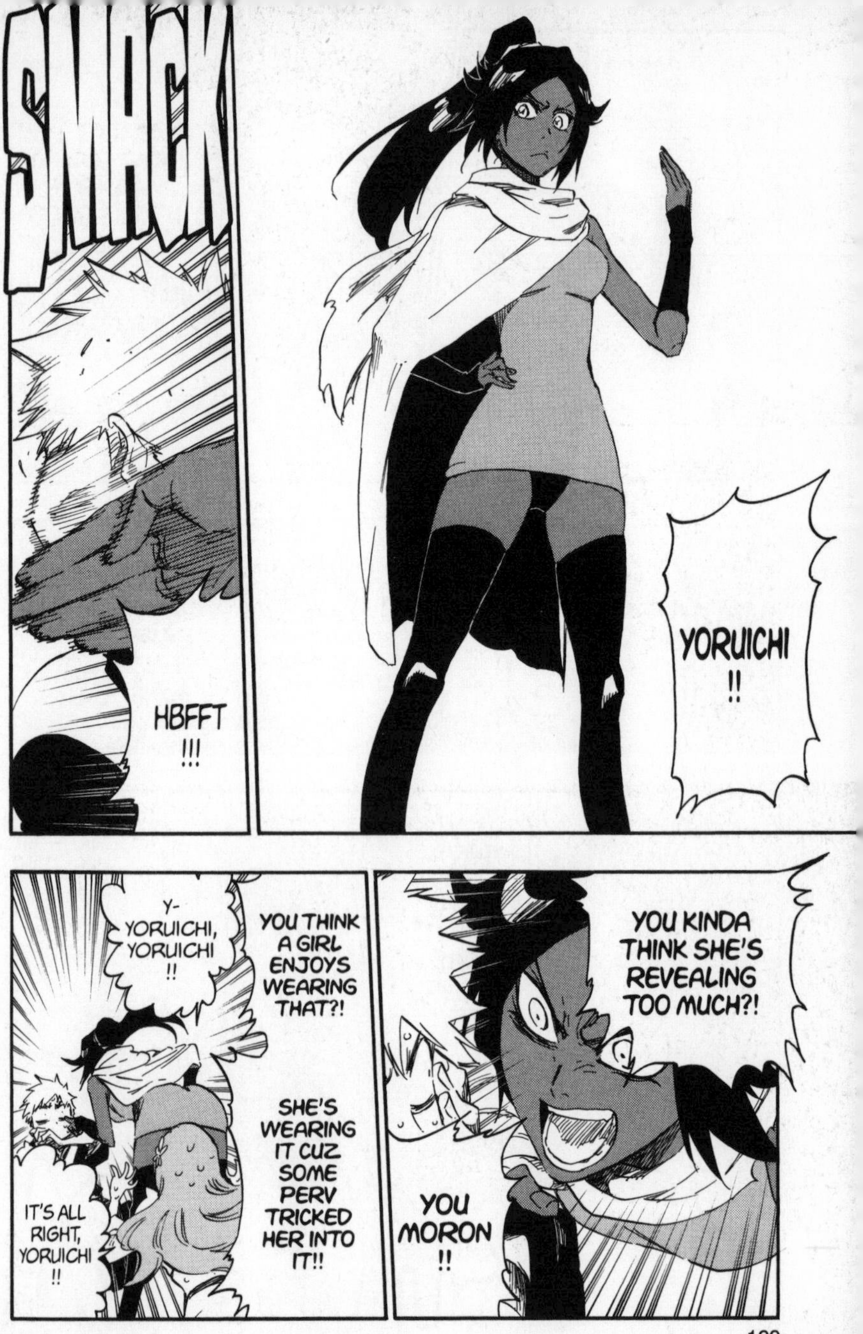
YORUICHI !!
SMACK
HBFFT !!!
YOU KINDA THINK SHE'S REVEALING TOO MUCH?!
YOU MORON !!
YOU THINK A GIRL ENJOYS WEARING THAT?!
Y- YORUICHI, YORUICHI !!
SHE'S WEARING IT CUZ SOME PERV TRICKED HER INTO IT!!
IT'S ALL RIGHT, YORUICHI !!

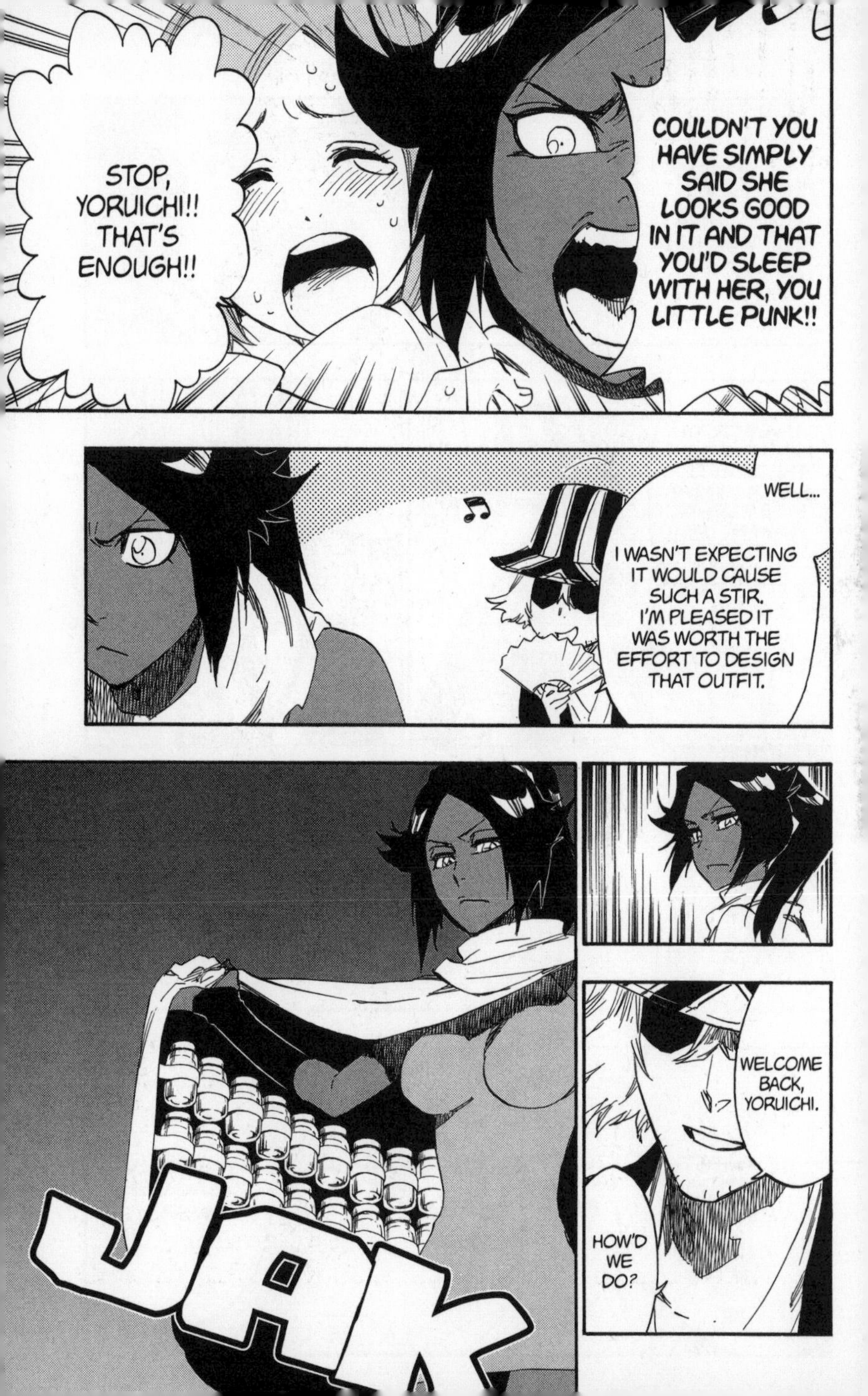
COULDN'T YOU HAVE SIMPLY SAID SHE LOOKS GOOD IN IT AND THAT YOU'D SLEEP WITH HER, YOU LITTLE PUNK!!
STOP, YORUICHI!! THAT'S ENOUGH!!
WELL...
I WASN'T EXPECTING IT WOULD CAUSE SUCH A STIR. I'M PLEASED IT WAS WORTH THE EFFORT TO DESIGN THAT OUTFIT.
WELCOME BACK, YORUICHI.
HOW'D WE DO?
JAK

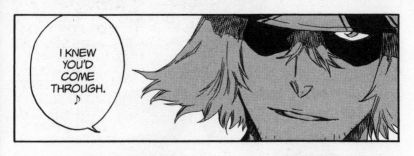

I KNEW YOU'D COME THROUGH. ♪
...
WHAT ARE THOSE ...?
I ASKED YORUICHI...
...TO INVESTIGATE THE DISTORTION THE QUINCIES WERE CAUSING AT THE BOUNDARY BETWEEN THE WORLD OF THE LIVING AND THE SOUL SOCIETY.
THAT DISTORTION...
...I BELIEVE, WAS GENERATED TO CAUSE CONFUSION IN THE SOUL SOCIETY AND SPLIT UP OUR FORCES.
THROUGH YORUICHI'S INVESTIGATION...
...WE DISCOVERED THAT A LARGE AMOUNT OF ENERGY IS CREATED THE MOMENT THE DISTORTION APPEARS AND DISAPPEARS.
A MASSIVE ENOUGH ENERGY...
...TO CONNECT THE TWO WORLDS.

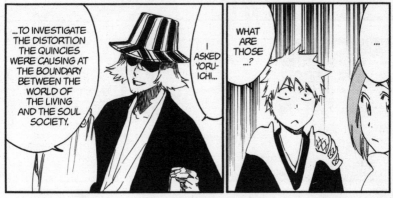

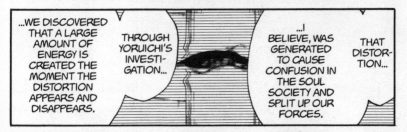

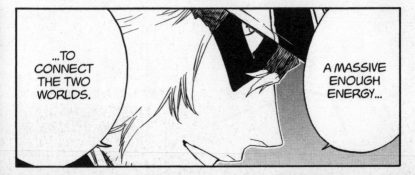

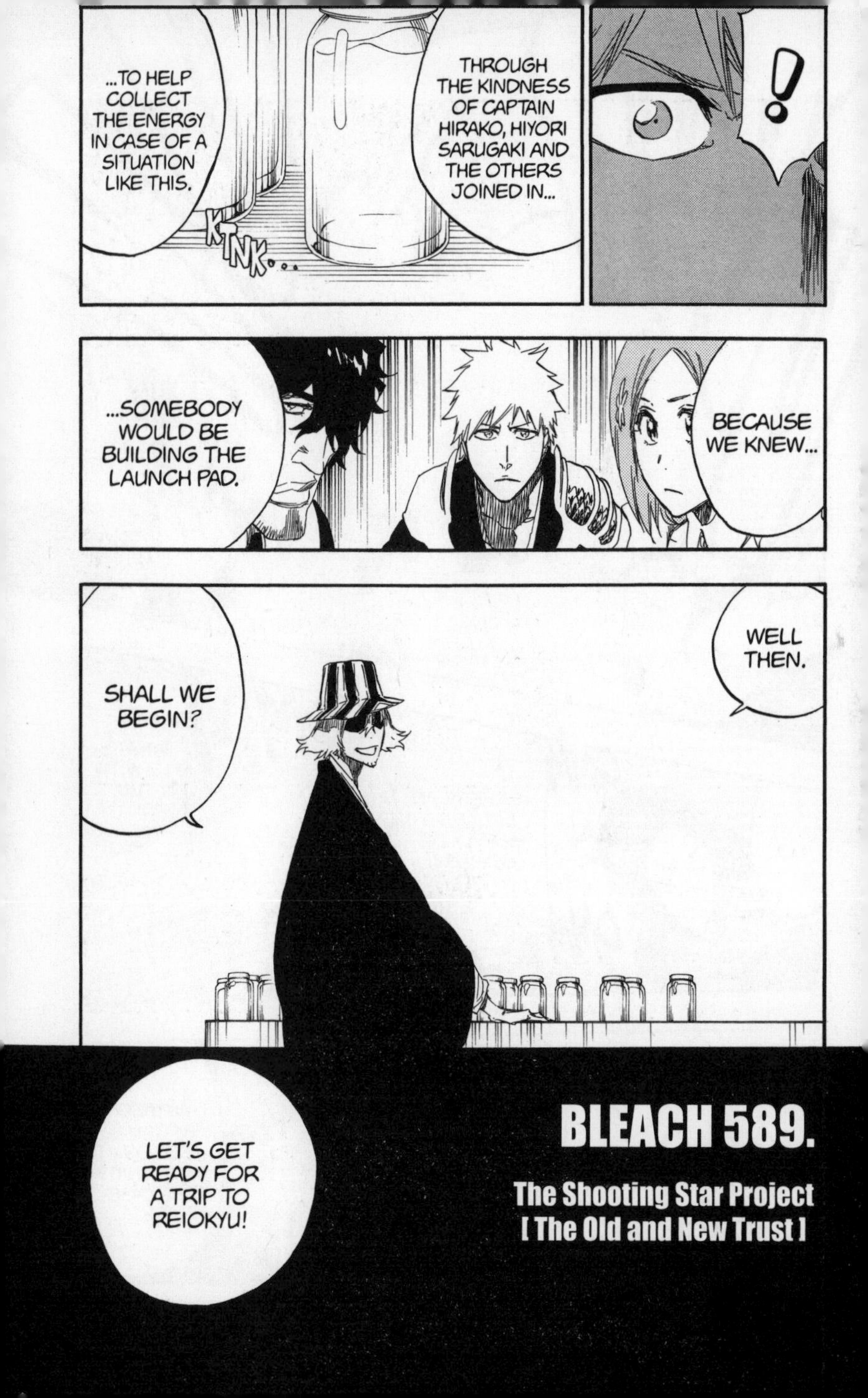
!
THROUGH THE KINDNESS OF CAPTAIN HIRAKO, HIYORI SARUGAKI AND THE OTHERS JOINED IN...
...TO HELP COLLECT THE ENERGY IN CASE OF A SITUATION LIKE THIS.
KTNK...
BECAUSE WE KNEW...
...SOMEBODY WOULD BE BUILDING THE LAUNCH PAD.
WELL THEN.
SHALL WE BEGIN?
BLEACH 589.
The Shooting Star Project
[The Old and New Trust]
LET'S GET READY FOR A TRIP TO REIOKYU!

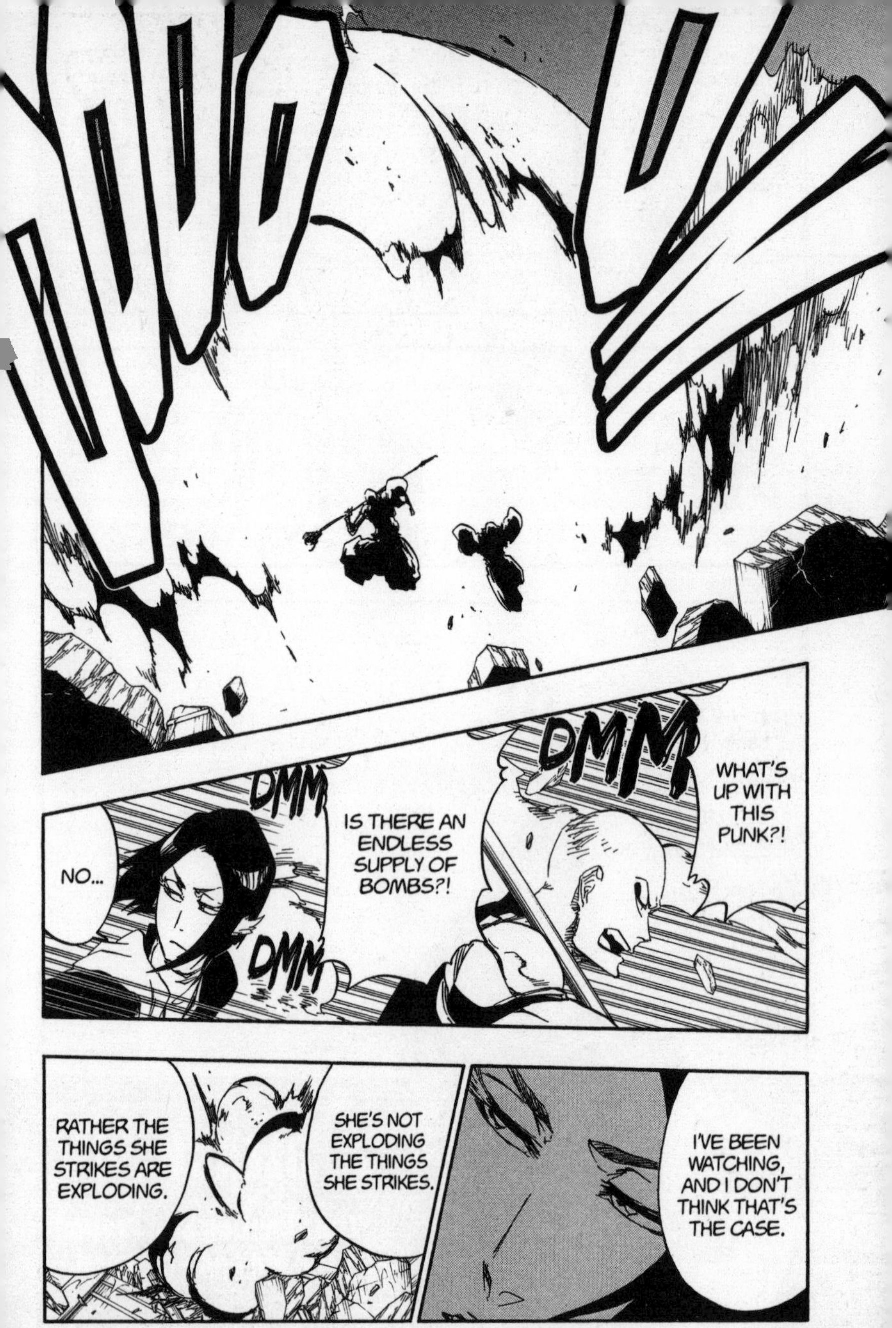
DMM
WHAT'S UP WITH THIS PUNK?!
IS THERE AN ENDLESS SUPPLY OF BOMBS?!
DMM
NO...
DMM
I'VE BEEN WATCHING, AND I DON'T THINK THAT'S THE CASE.
SHE'S NOT EXPLODING THE THINGS SHE STRIKES.
RATHER THE THINGS SHE STRIKES ARE EXPLODING.

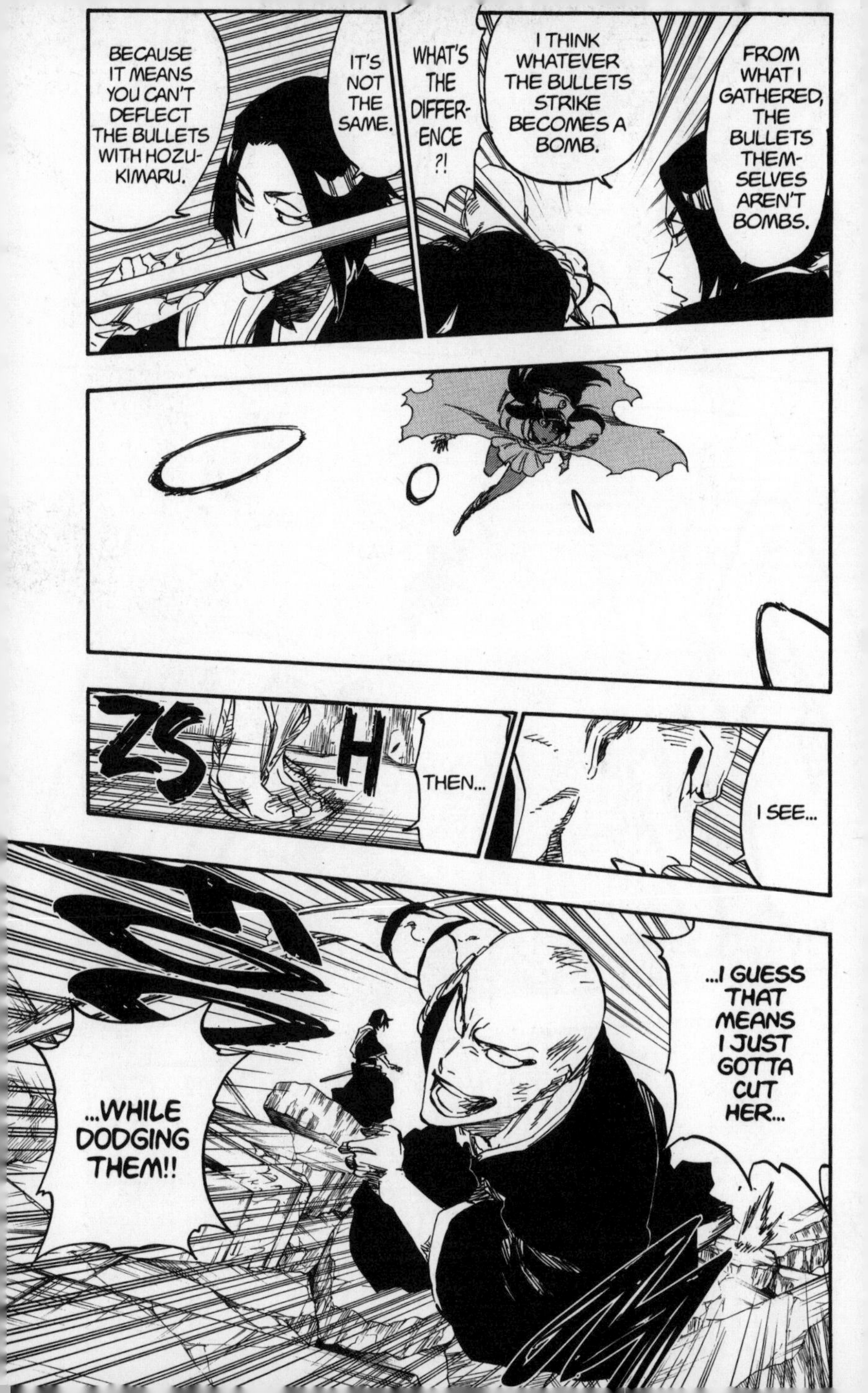
FROM WHAT I GATHERED, THE BULLETS THEMSELVES AREN'T BOMBS.
I THINK WHATEVER THE BULLETS STRIKE BECOMES A BOMB.
WHAT'S THE DIFFERENCE?!
IT'S NOT THE SAME.
BECAUSE IT MEANS YOU CAN'T DEFLECT THE BULLETS WITH HOZUKIMARU.
I SEE...
ZSH
THEN...
...I GUESS THAT MEANS I JUST GOTTA CUT HER...
...WHILE DODGING THEM!!

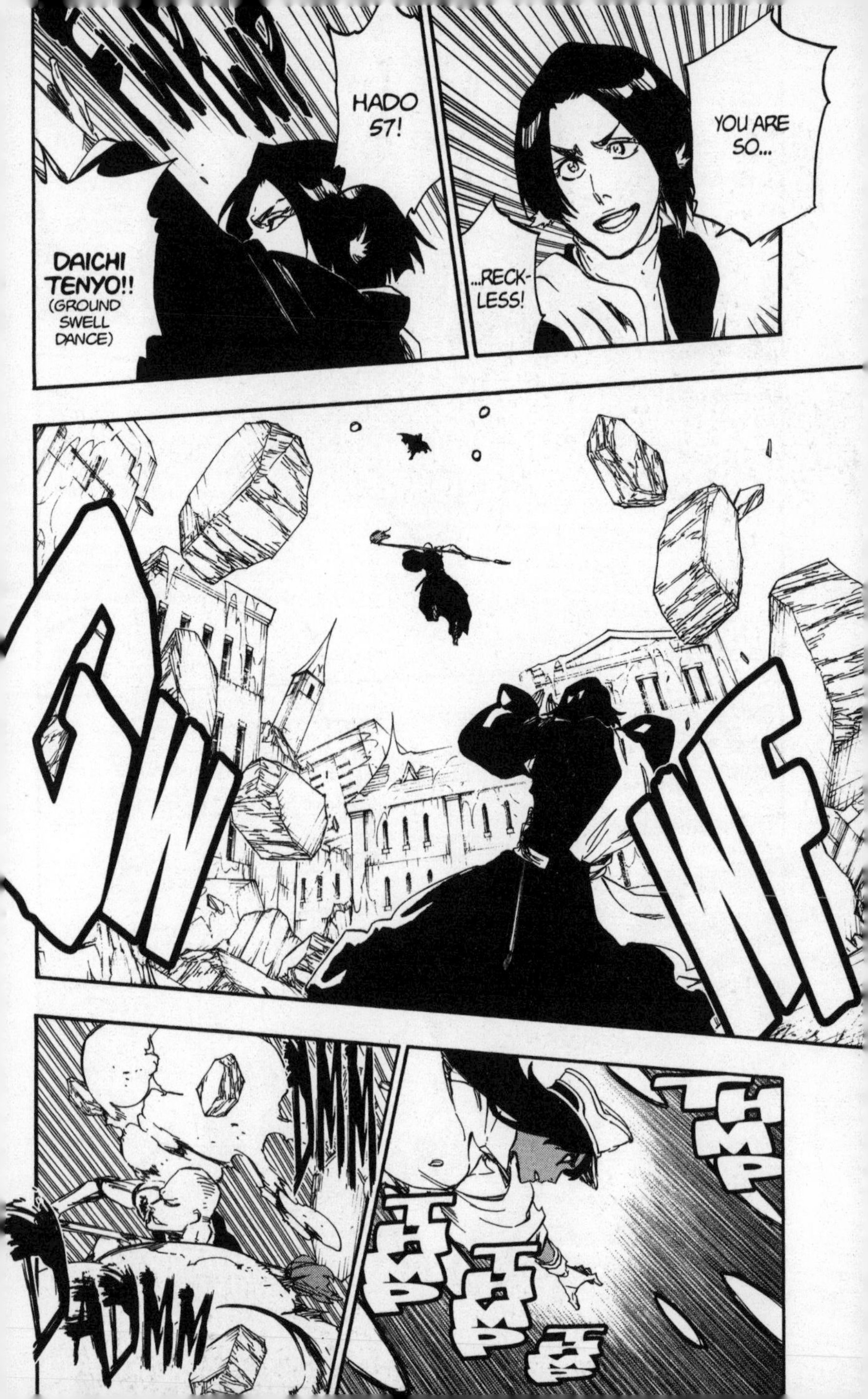
YOU ARE SO...
...RECK-LESS!
HADO 57!
DAICHI TENYO!!
(GROUND SWELL DANCE)
THMP
THMP
THMP
THMP
DMM
DADMM

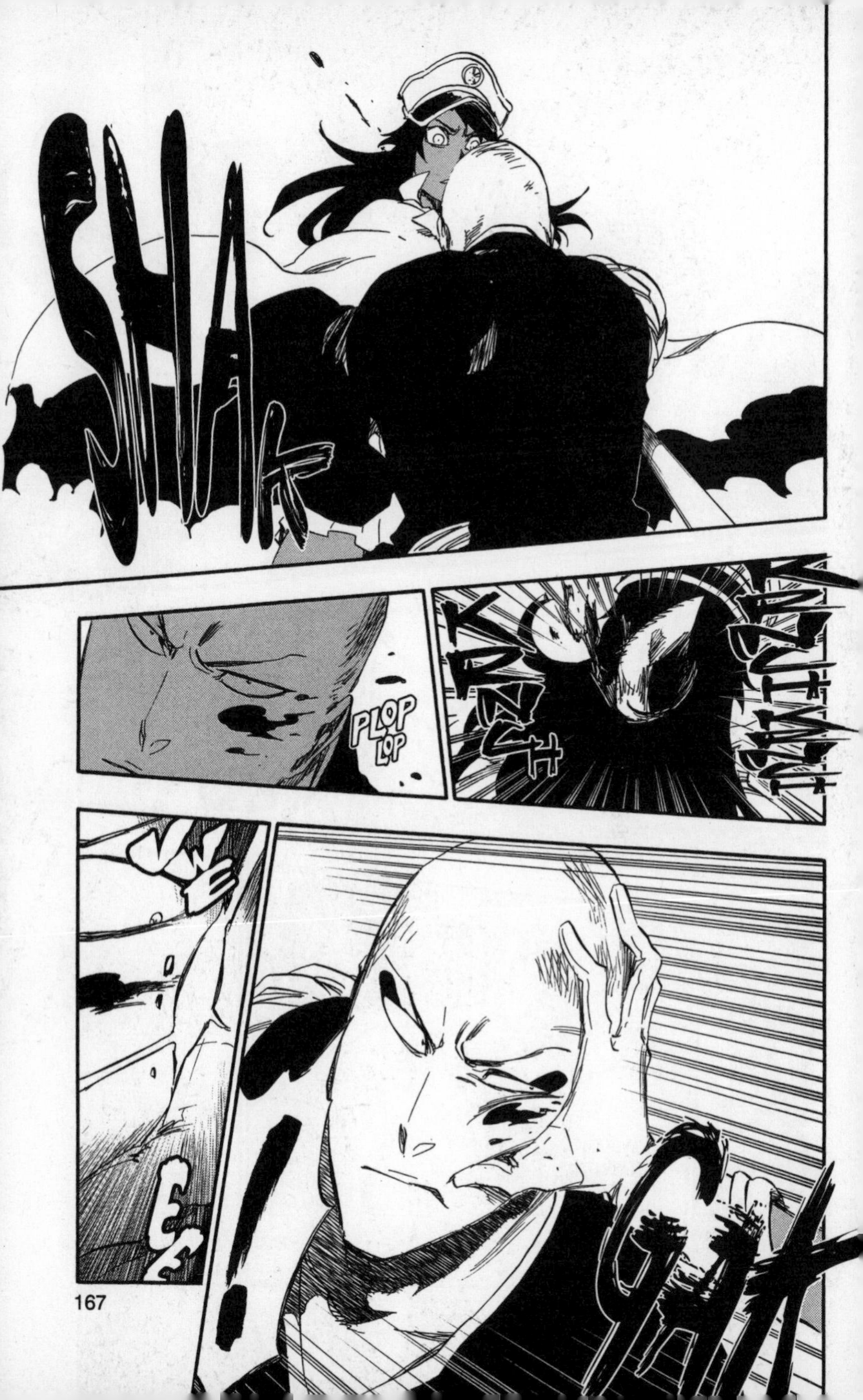
KRUNCH
PLOP
LOP

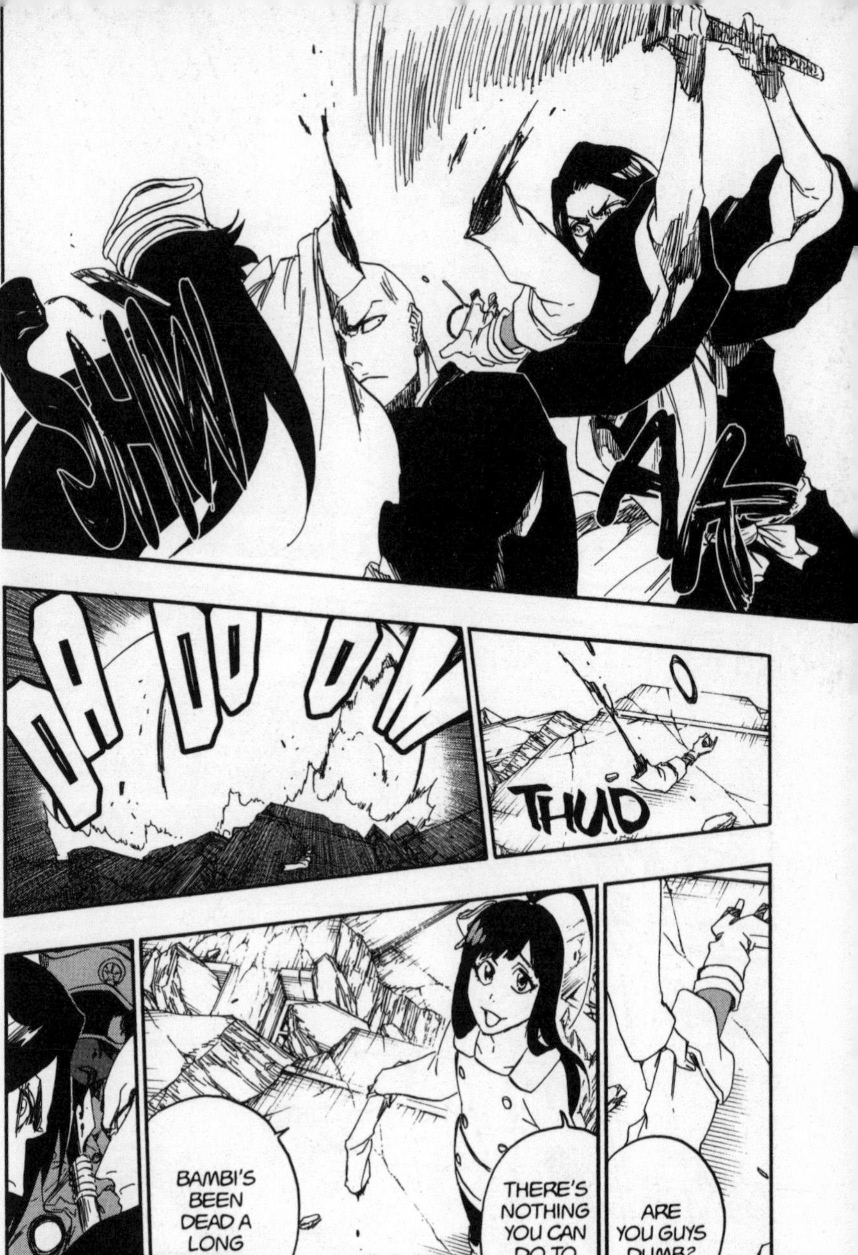
THUD
ARE YOU GUYS DUMB?
THERE'S NOTHING YOU CAN DO TO KILL HER.
BAMBI'S BEEN DEAD A LONG TIME.

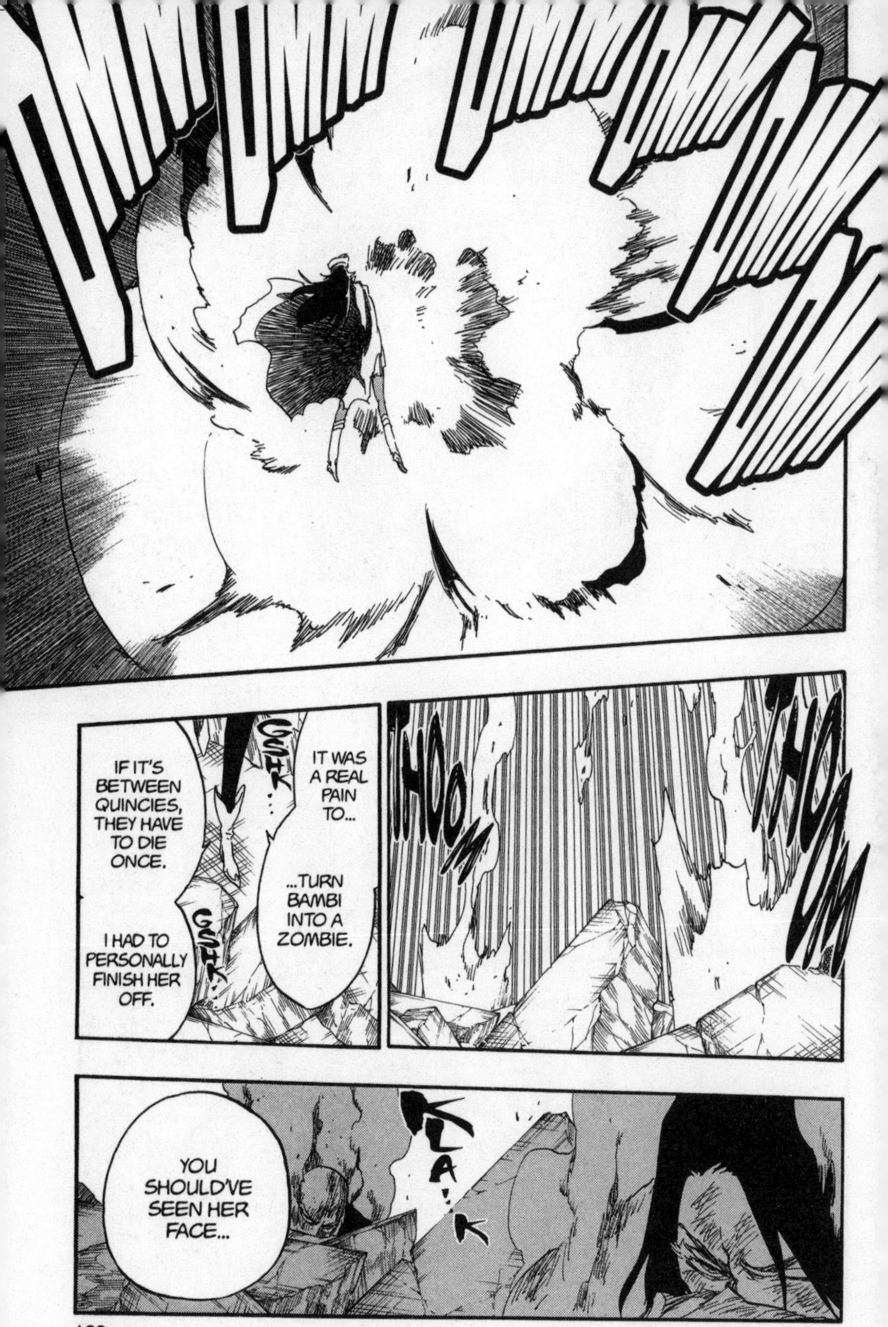
THOOM
THOOM
IT WAS A REAL PAIN TO...
...TURN BAMBI INTO A ZOMBIE.
GSHK...
IF IT'S BETWEEN QUINCIES, THEY HAVE TO DIE ONCE.
GSHK..
I HAD TO PERSONALLY FINISH HER OFF.
KLAK
YOU SHOULD'VE SEEN HER FACE...

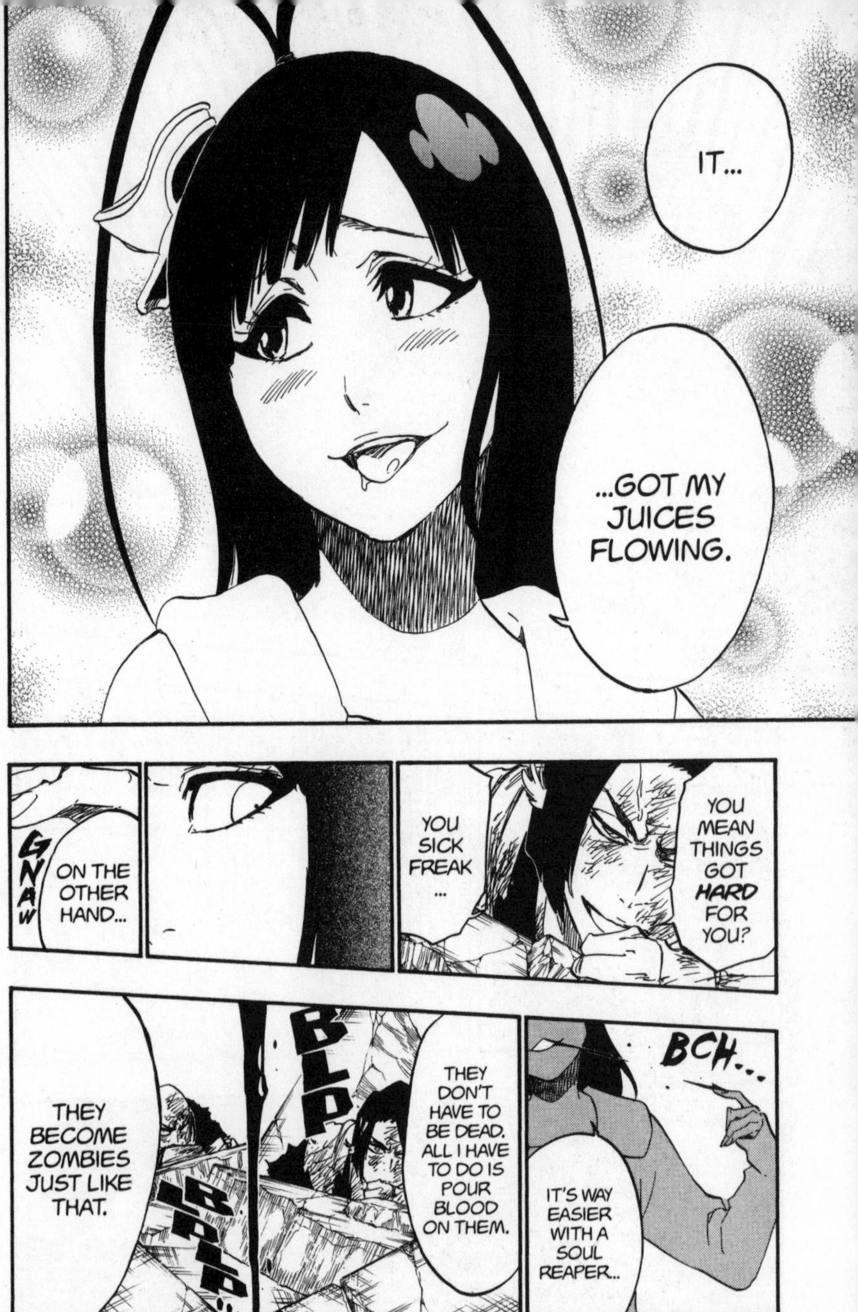
IT...
...GOT MY JUICES FLOWING.
YOU MEAN THINGS GOT HARD FOR YOU?
YOU SICK FREAK ...
GNAW
ON THE OTHER HAND...
BCH...
IT'S WAY EASIER WITH A SOUL REAPER...
BLD
THEY DON'T HAVE TO BE DEAD. ALL I HAVE TO DO IS POUR BLOOD ON THEM.
THEY BECOME ZOMBIES JUST LIKE THAT.

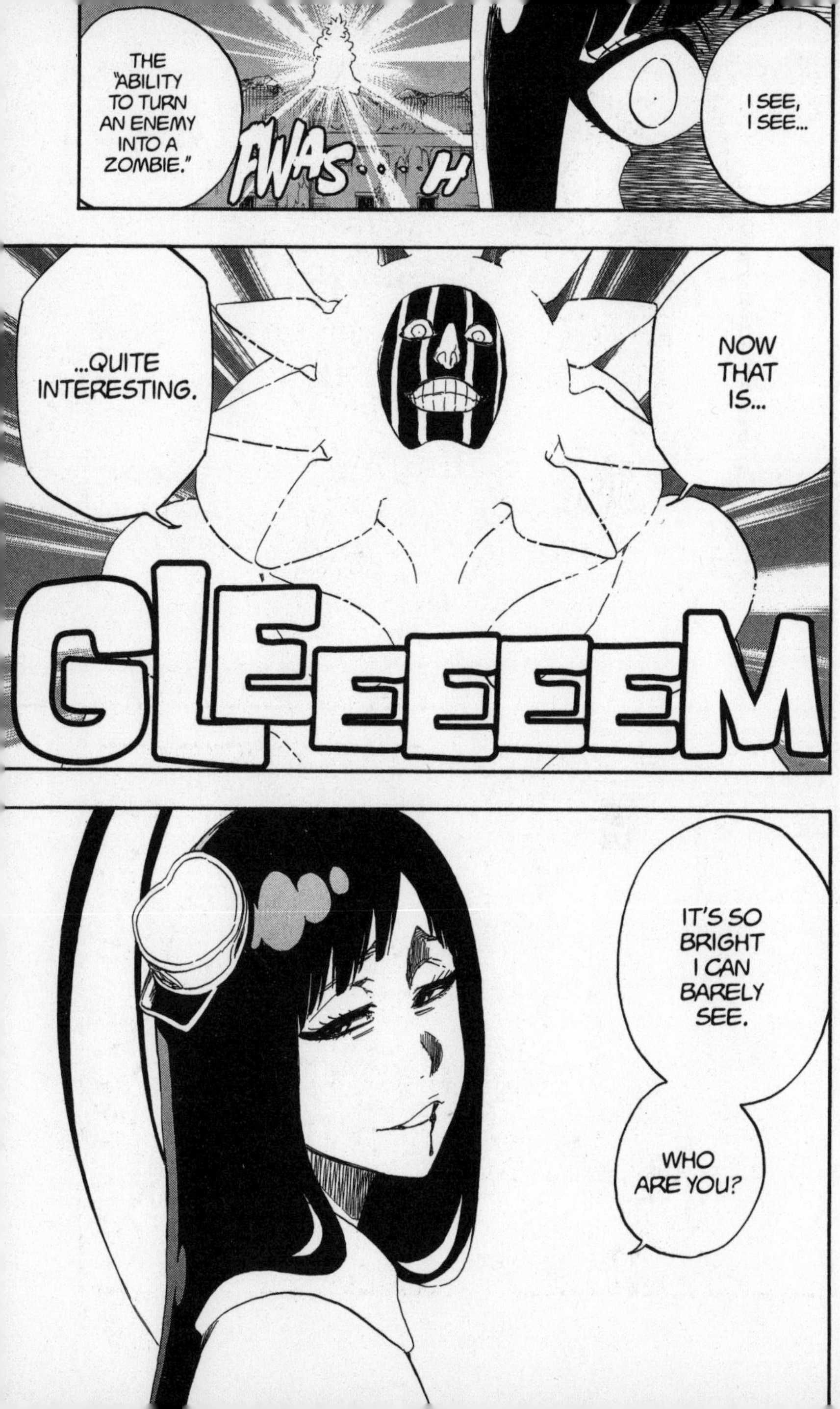
I SEE, I SEE...
THE "ABILITY TO TURN AN ENEMY INTO A ZOMBIE."
FWAS...H
NOW THAT IS...
...QUITE INTERESTING.
GLEEEEEM
IT'S SO BRIGHT I CAN BARELY SEE.
WHO ARE YOU?

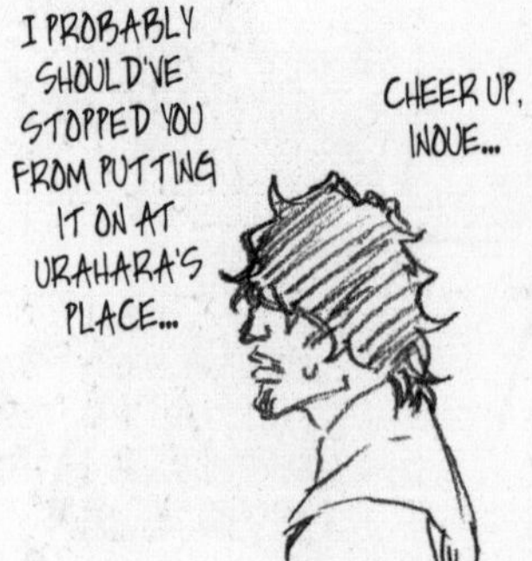
CHEER UP, INOUE...
I PROBABLY SHOULD'VE STOPPED YOU FROM PUTTING IT ON AT URAHARA'S PLACE...

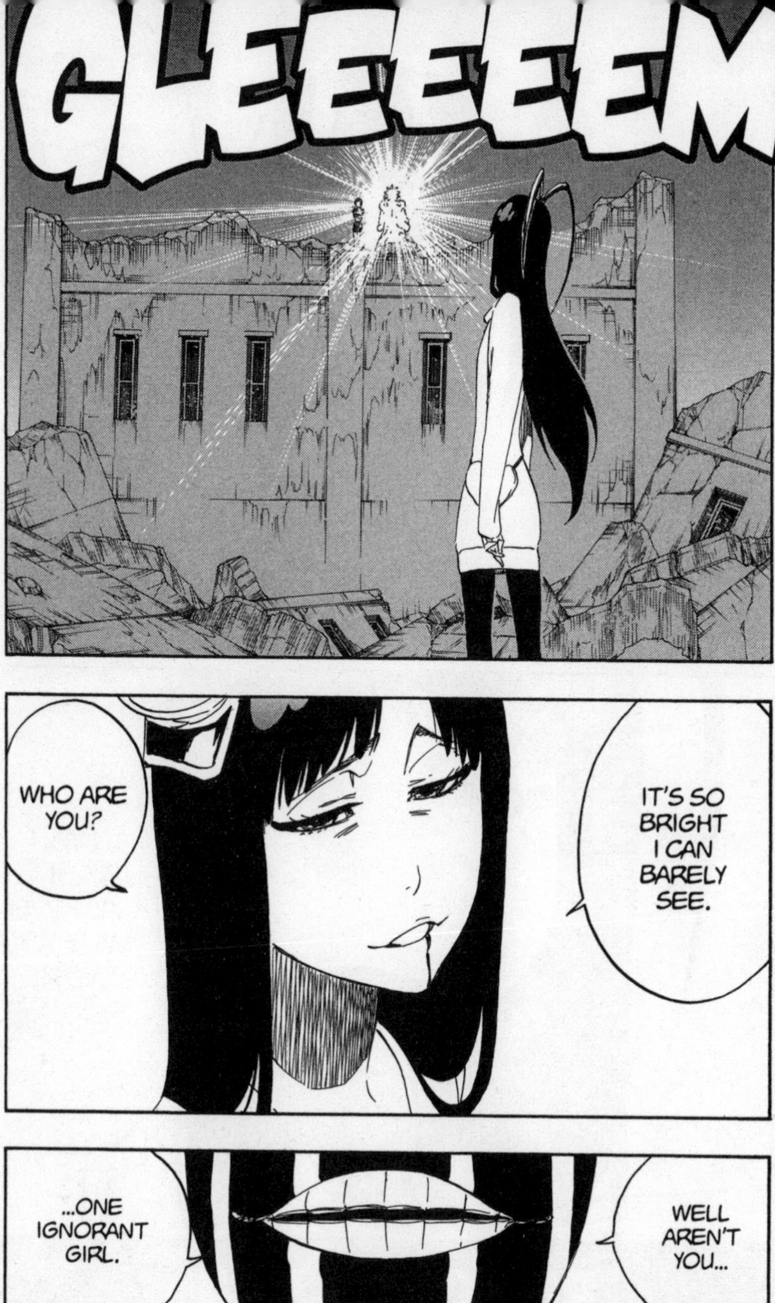
GLEEEEEM
IT'S SO BRIGHT I CAN BARELY SEE.
WHO ARE YOU?
WELL AREN'T YOU...
...ONE IGNORANT GIRL.

590. MARCHING OUT THE ZOMBIES

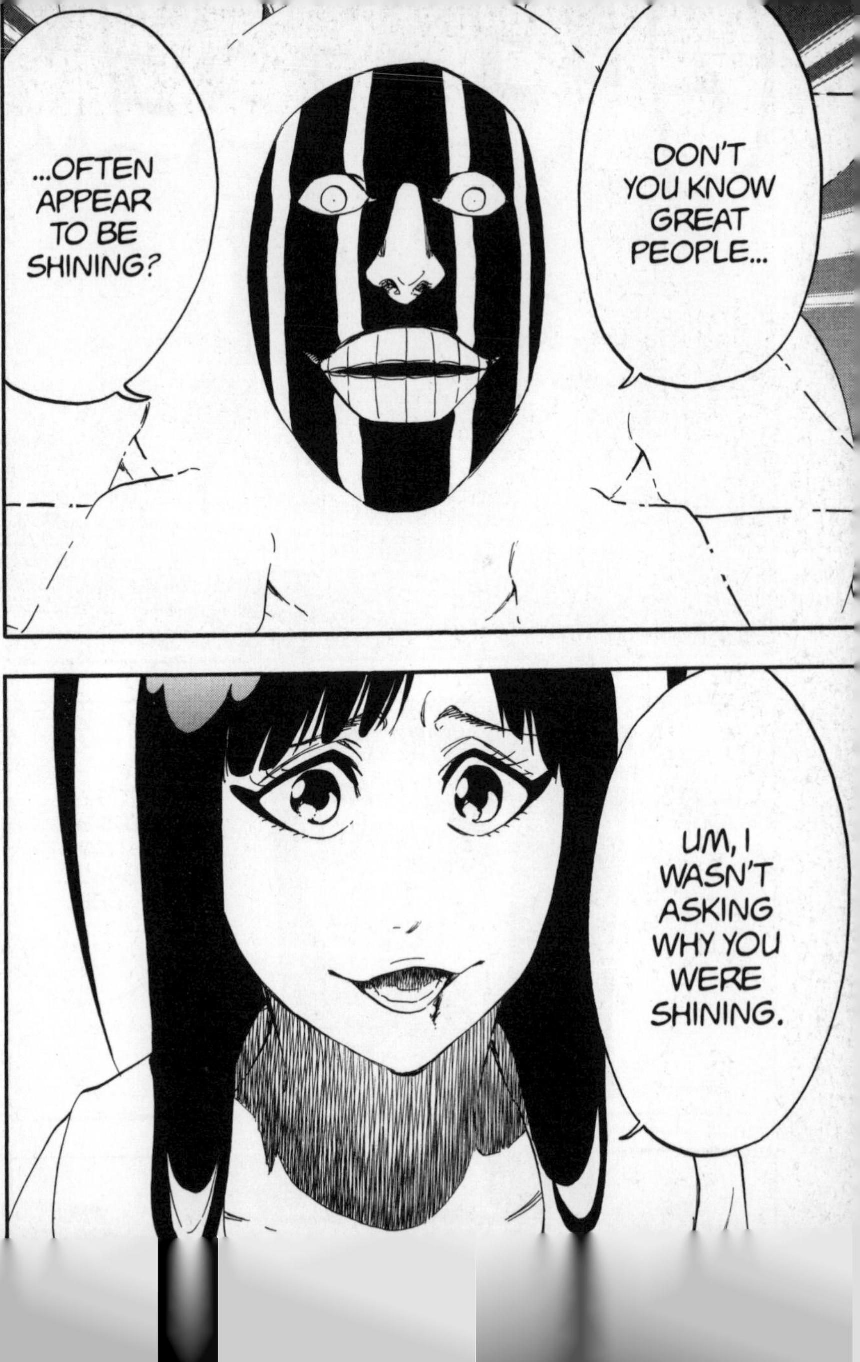
DON'T YOU KNOW GREAT PEOPLE...
...OFTEN APPEAR TO BE SHINING?
UM, I WASN'T ASKING WHY YOU WERE SHINING.

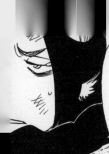

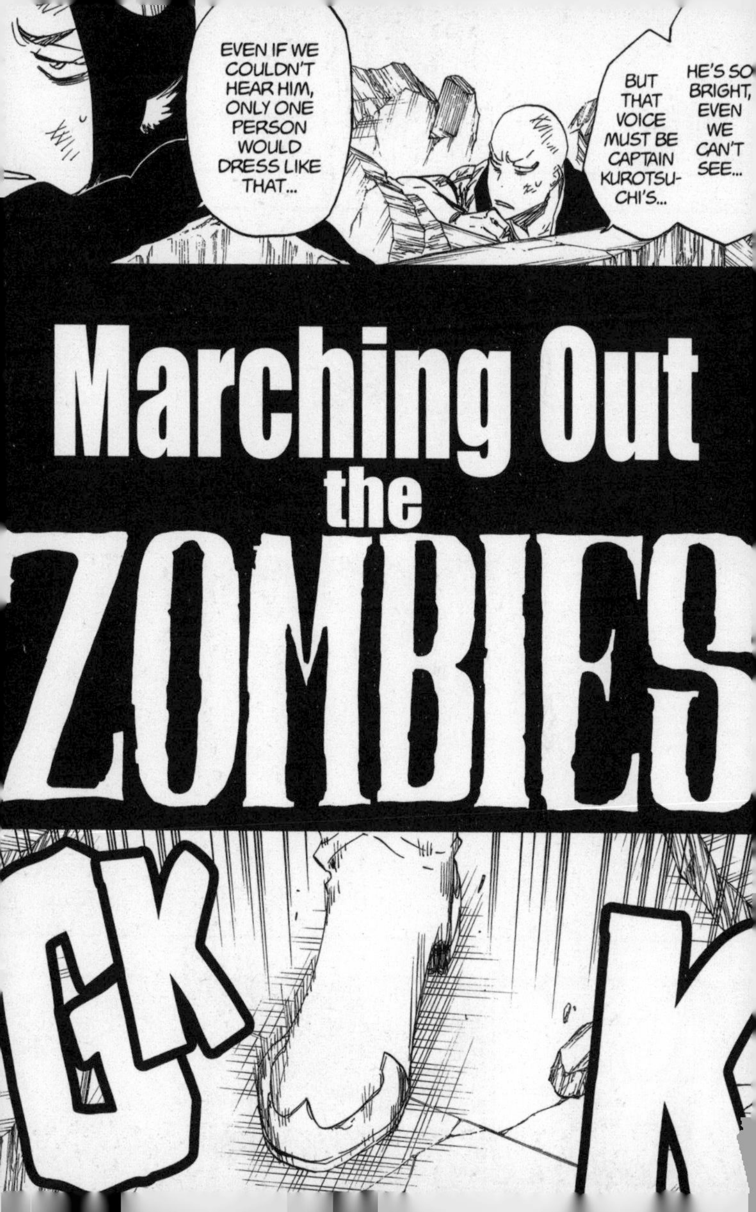
HE'S SO BRIGHT, EVEN WE CAN'T SEE...
BUT THAT VOICE MUST BE CAPTAIN KUROTSU-CHI'S...
EVEN IF WE COULDN'T HEAR HIM, ONLY ONE PERSON WOULD DRESS LIKE THAT...
Marching Out the ZOMBIES
K
CK

DID YOU JUST SAY YOU'LL PROTECT ME, BAMBI?

WHAT?

THANKS! ♥

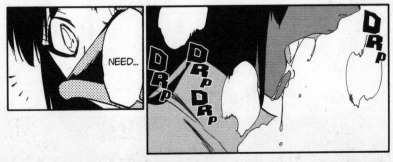

NEED...

DRP
DRP
DRP
DRP
DRP

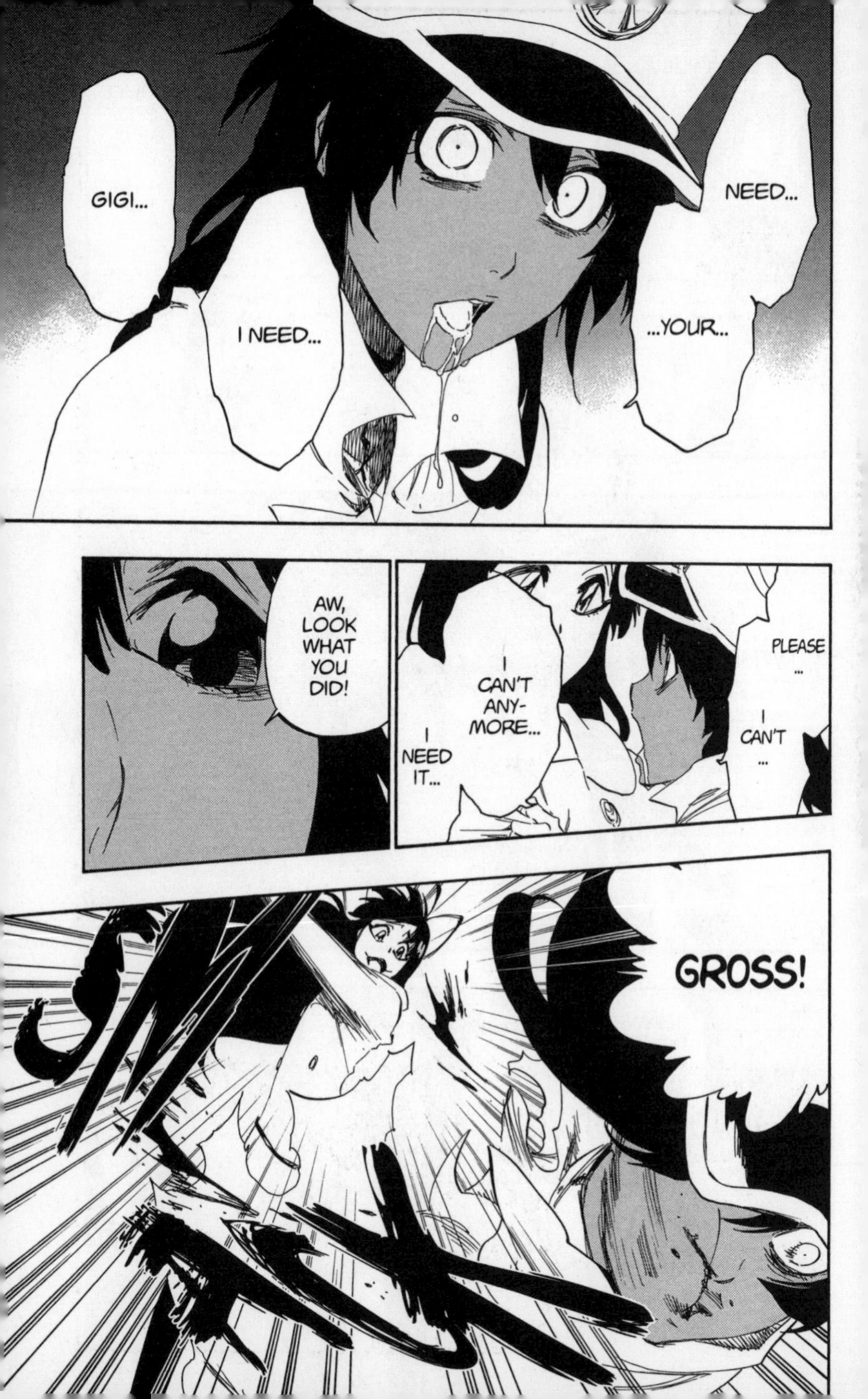

NEED...
GIGI...
...YOUR...
I NEED...
PLEASE ...
I CAN'T ...
I CAN'T ANYMORE...
I NEED IT...
AW, LOOK WHAT YOU DID!
GROSS!

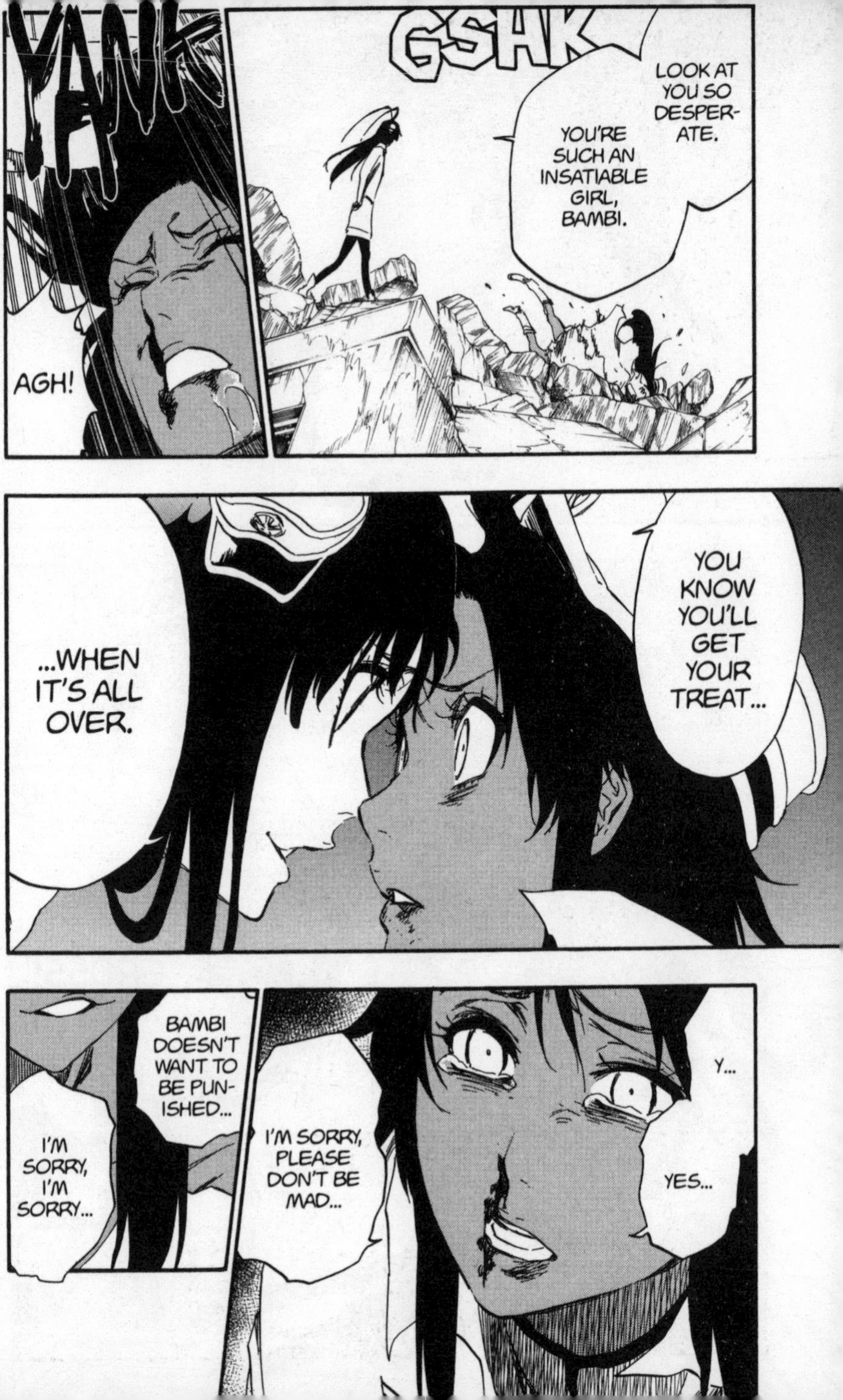
GSAK
LOOK AT YOU SO DESPERATE.
YOU'RE SUCH AN INSATIABLE GIRL, BAMBI.
YANK
AGH!
YOU KNOW YOU'LL GET YOUR TREAT...
...WHEN IT'S ALL OVER.
Y...
YES...
I'M SORRY, PLEASE DON'T BE MAD...
BAMBI DOESN'T WANT TO BE PUNISHED...
I'M SORRY, I'M SORRY...

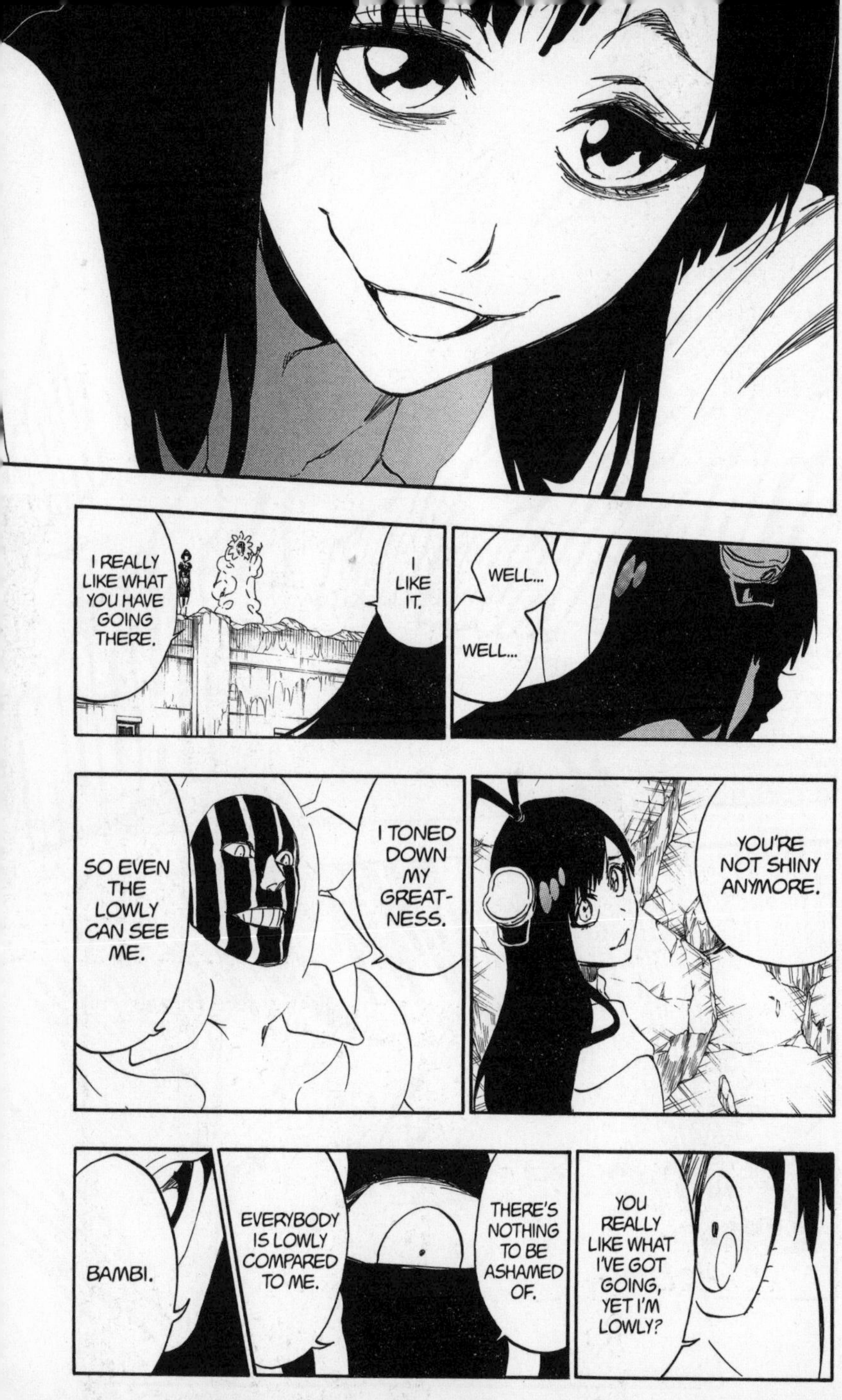
WELL...
WELL...
I LIKE IT.
I REALLY LIKE WHAT YOU HAVE GOING THERE.
YOU'RE NOT SHINY ANYMORE.
I TONED DOWN MY GREATNESS.
SO EVEN THE LOWLY CAN SEE ME.
YOU REALLY LIKE WHAT I'VE GOT GOING, YET I'M LOWLY?
THERE'S NOTHING TO BE ASHAMED OF.
EVERYBODY IS LOWLY COMPARED TO ME.
BAMBI.

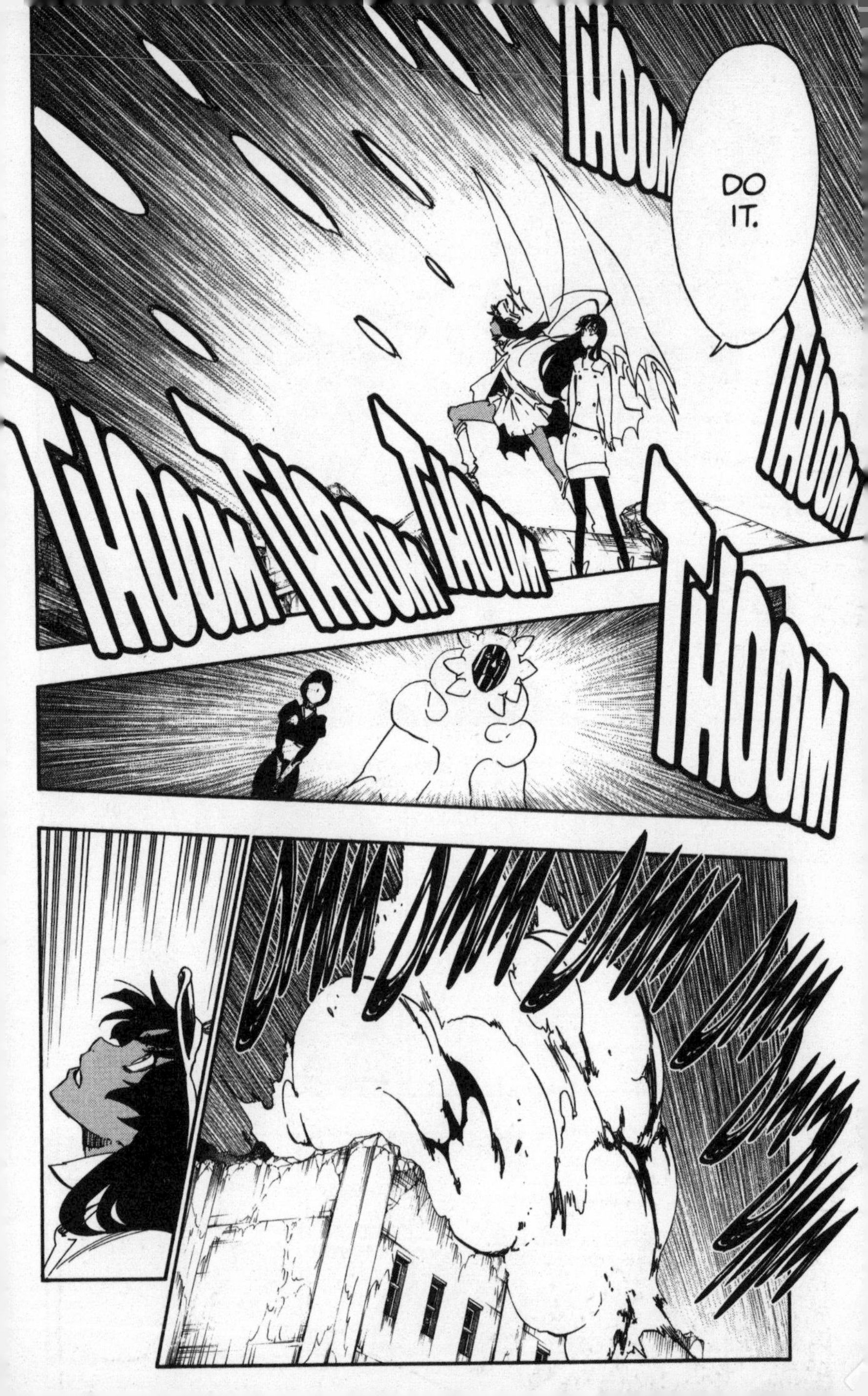
THOOM
DO IT.
THOOM
THOOM
THOOM
THOOM
THOOM

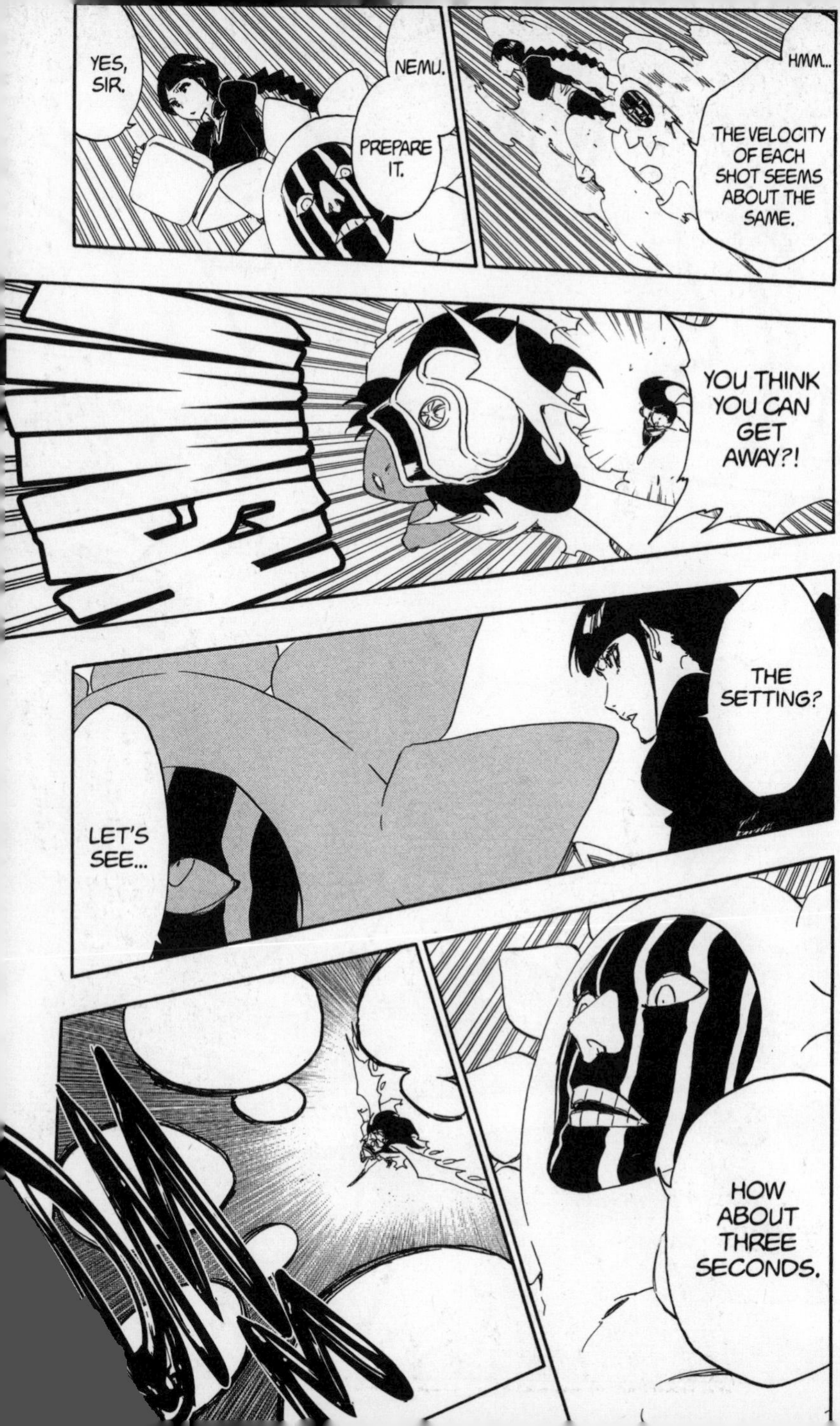
HMM...
THE VELOCITY OF EACH SHOT SEEMS ABOUT THE SAME.
NEMU.
PREPARE IT.
YES, SIR.
YOU THINK YOU CAN GET AWAY?!
THE SETTING?
LET'S SEE...
HOW ABOUT THREE SECONDS.

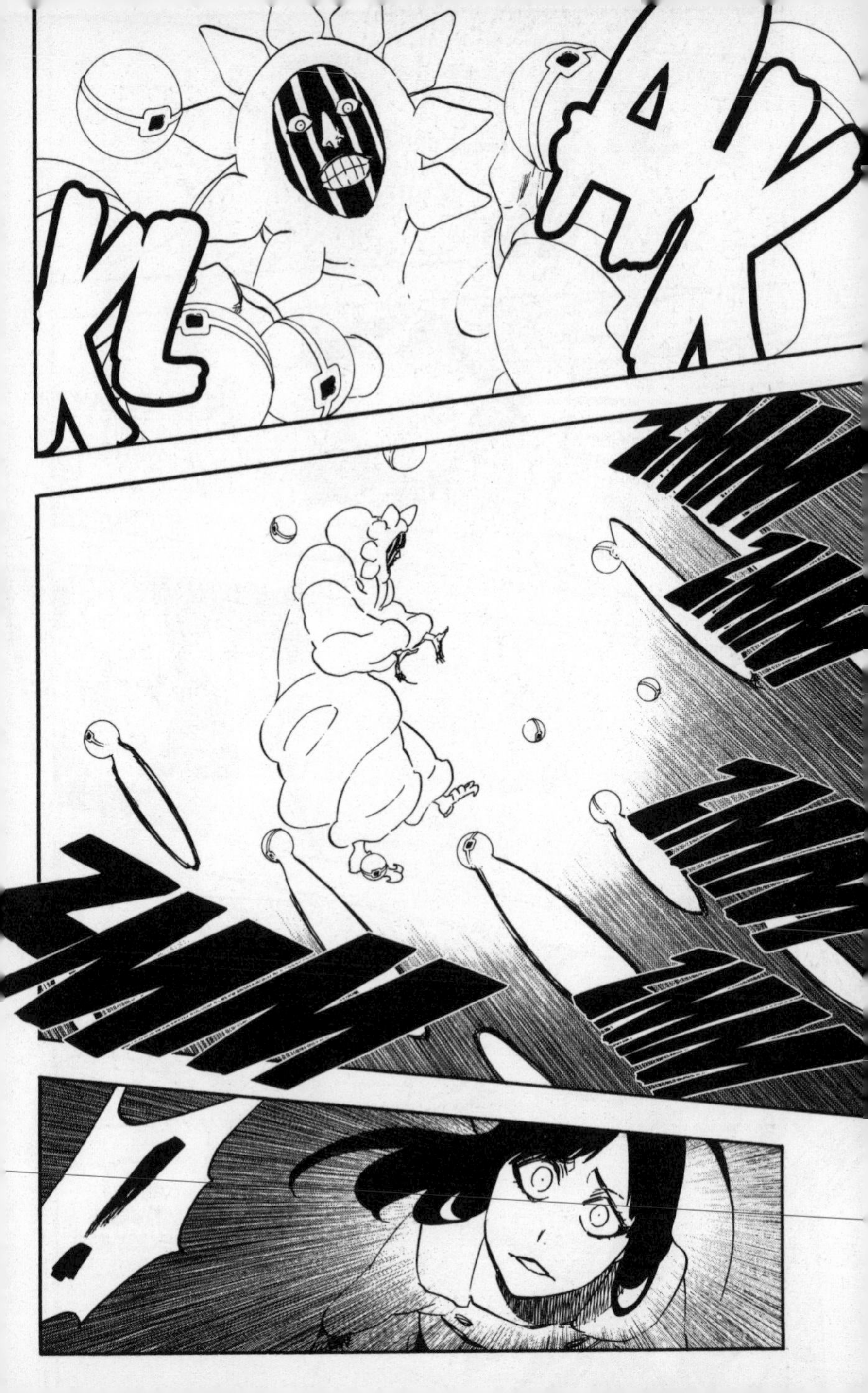
!

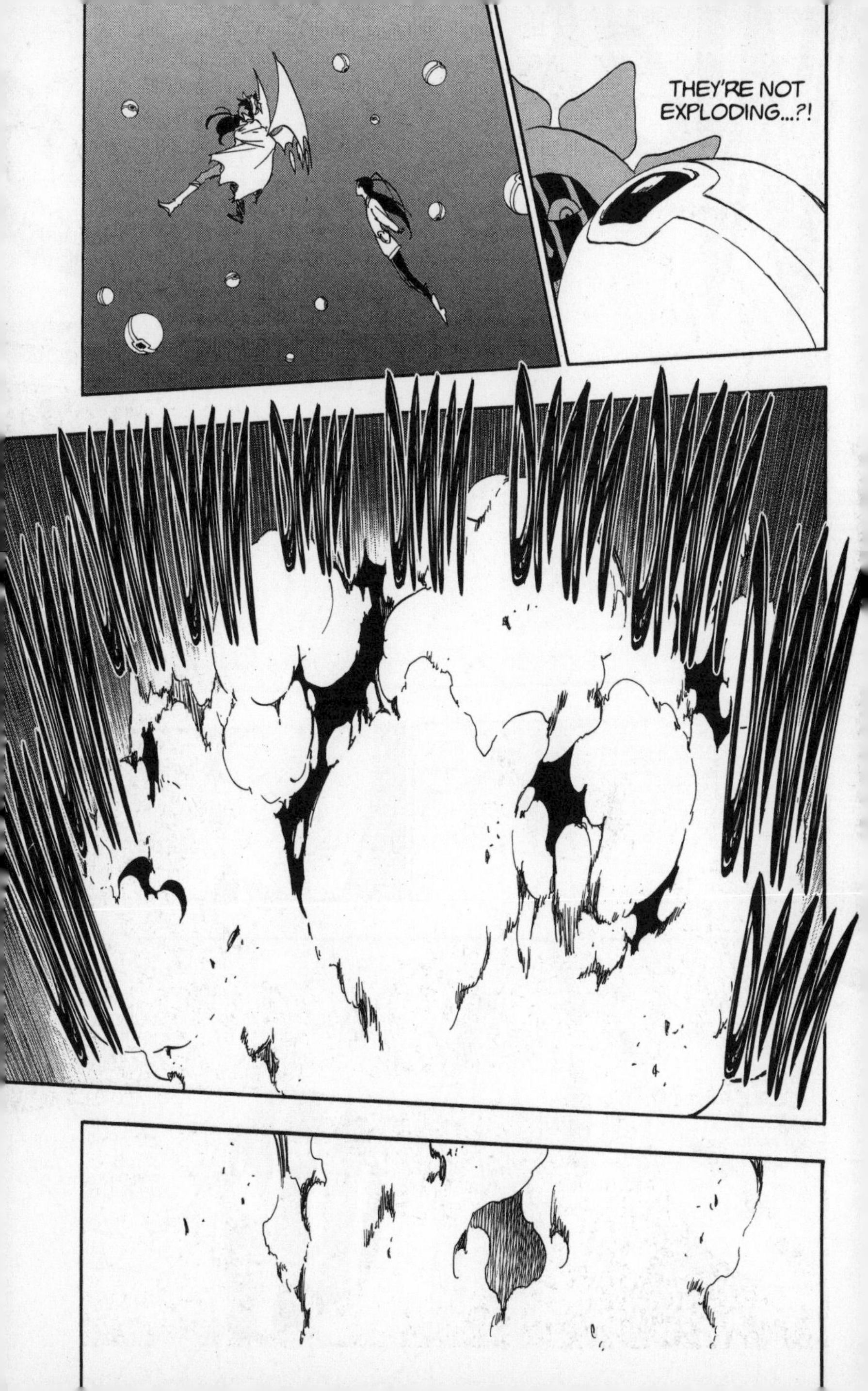
THEY'RE NOT EXPLODING...?!

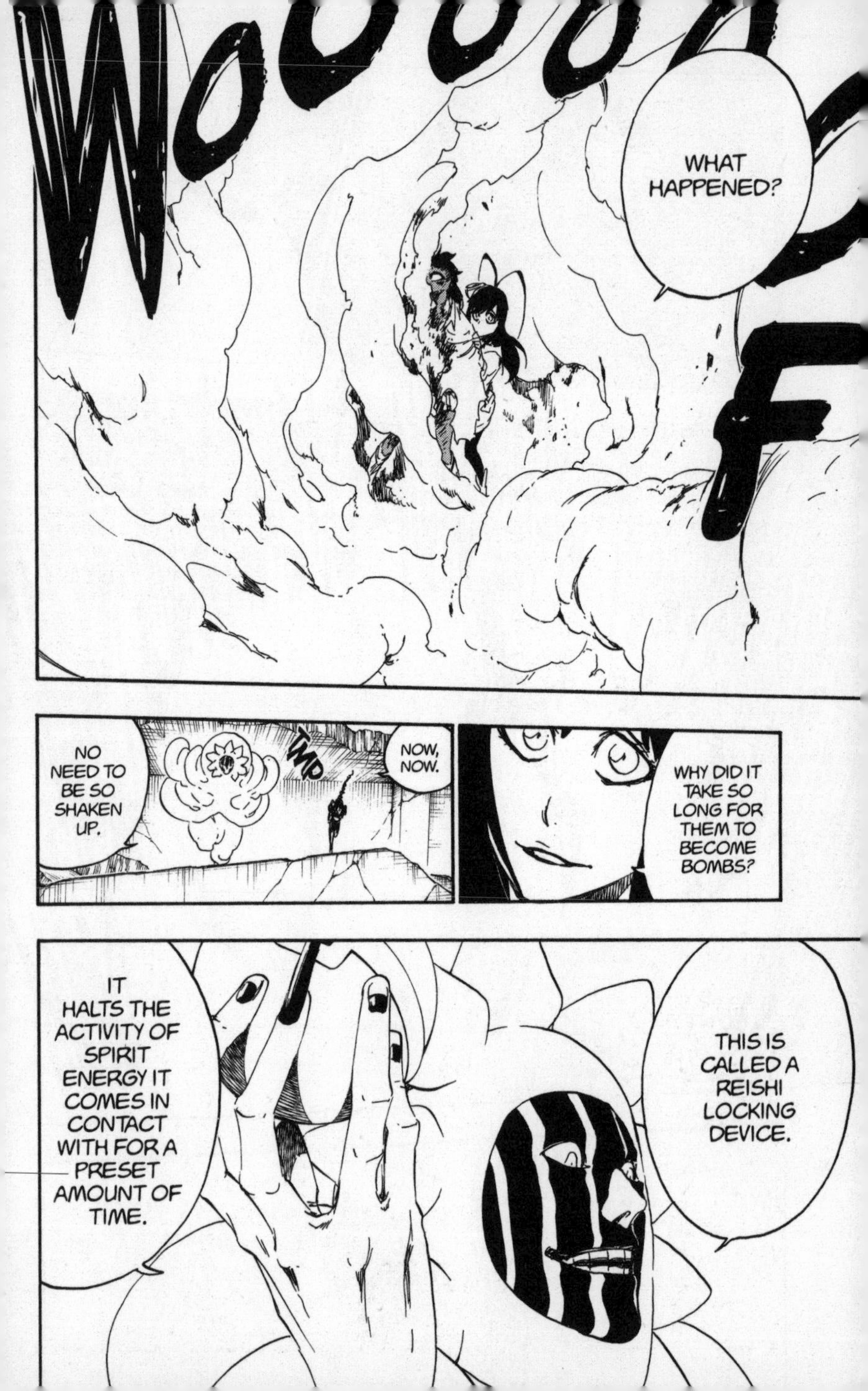
WHAT HAPPENED?
WHY DID IT TAKE SO LONG FOR THEM TO BECOME BOMBS?
NOW, NOW.
TMP
NO NEED TO BE SO SHAKEN UP.
THIS IS CALLED A REISHI LOCKING DEVICE.
IT HALTS THE ACTIVITY OF SPIRIT ENERGY IT COMES IN CONTACT WITH FOR A PRESET AMOUNT OF TIME.

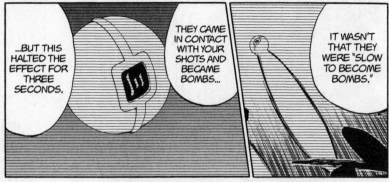

READ THIS WAY

IT WASN'T THAT THEY WERE "SLOW TO BECOME BOMBS."
THEY CAME IN CONTACT WITH YOUR SHOTS AND BECAME BOMBS...
...BUT THIS HALTED THE EFFECT FOR THREE SECONDS.
IT IS...
...AN EXTREMELY SIMPLE MECHANISM.
TMP
AND WITH THIS SIMPLE MECHANISM...
...I COMPLETELY SUBDUED THAT ZOMBIE GIRL'S POWER.
ALL THAT'S LEFT...
...IS FOR YOU TWO TO BECOME MY LOVELY RESEARCH SUBJECTS.
HEH HEH...
BY "YOU TWO" ...
EXACTLY ...
ZSH
ZSH
ZSH

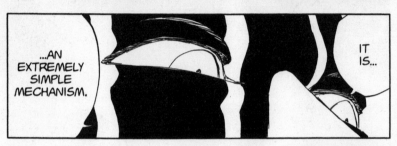

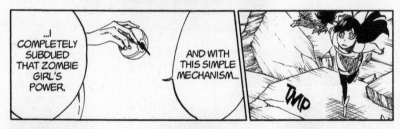

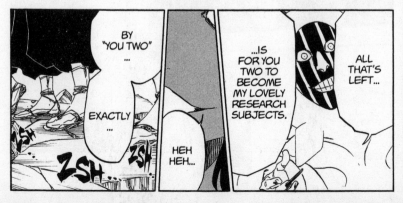

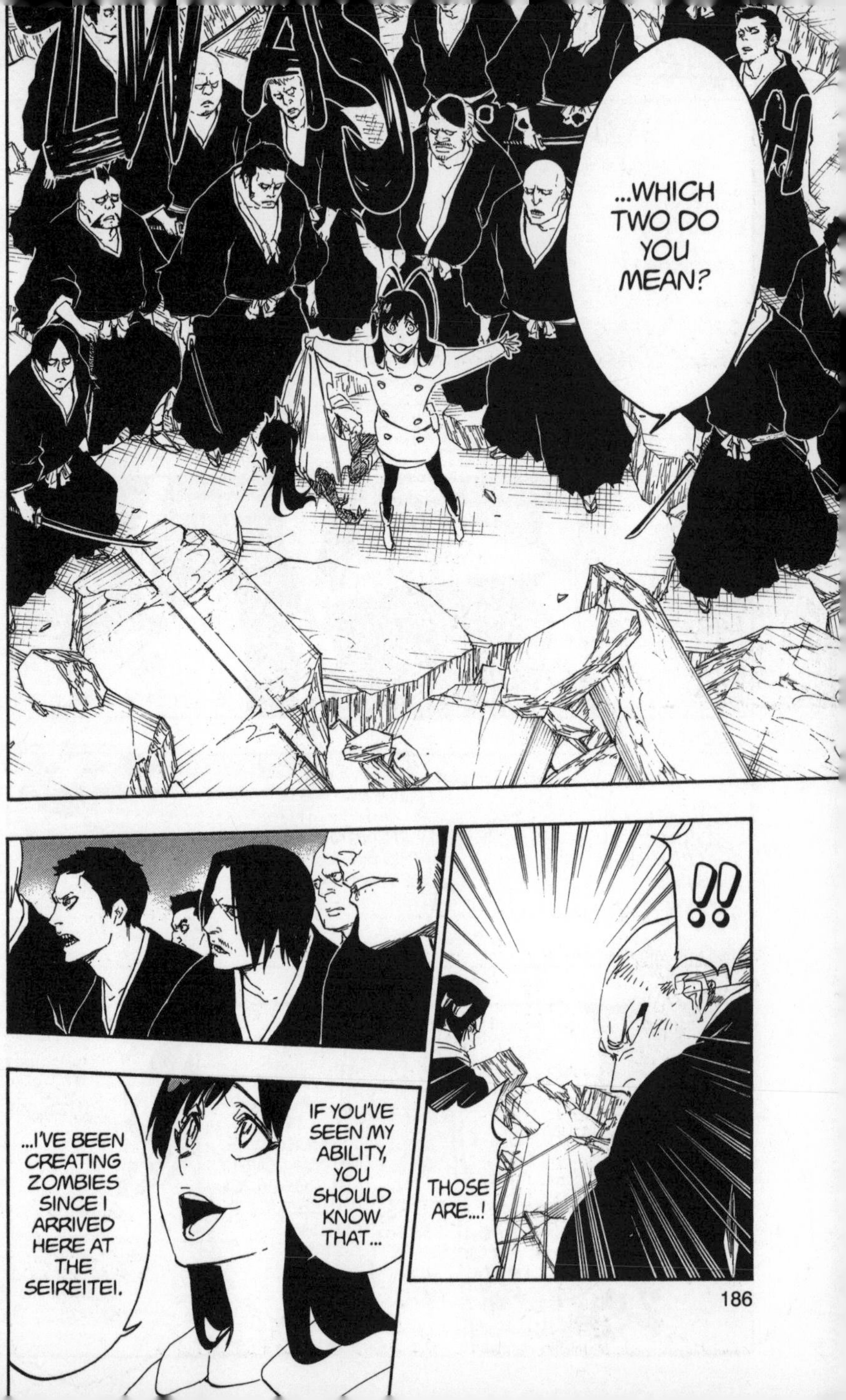
...WHICH TWO DO YOU MEAN?
!!
THOSE ARE...!
IF YOU'VE SEEN MY ABILITY, YOU SHOULD KNOW THAT...
...I'VE BEEN CREATING ZOMBIES SINCE I ARRIVED HERE AT THE SEIREITEI.

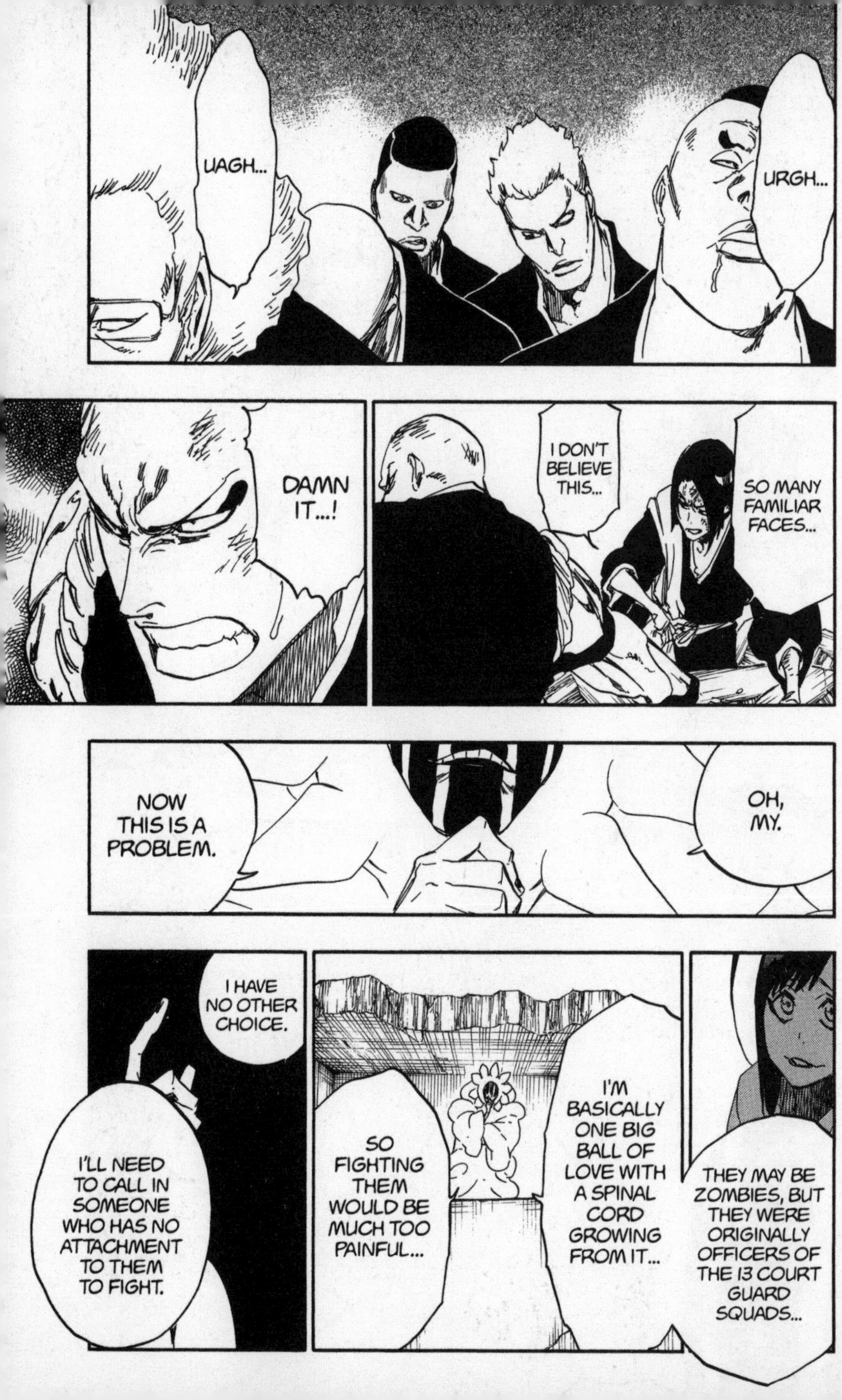
URGH...
UAGH...
SO MANY FAMILIAR FACES...
I DON'T BELIEVE THIS...
DAMN IT...!
OH, MY.
NOW THIS IS A PROBLEM.
THEY MAY BE ZOMBIES, BUT THEY WERE ORIGINALLY OFFICERS OF THE 13 COURT GUARD SQUADS...
I'M BASICALLY ONE BIG BALL OF LOVE WITH A SPINAL CORD GROWING FROM IT...
SO FIGHTING THEM WOULD BE MUCH TOO PAINFUL...
I HAVE NO OTHER CHOICE.
I'LL NEED TO CALL IN SOMEONE WHO HAS NO ATTACHMENT TO THEM TO FIGHT.

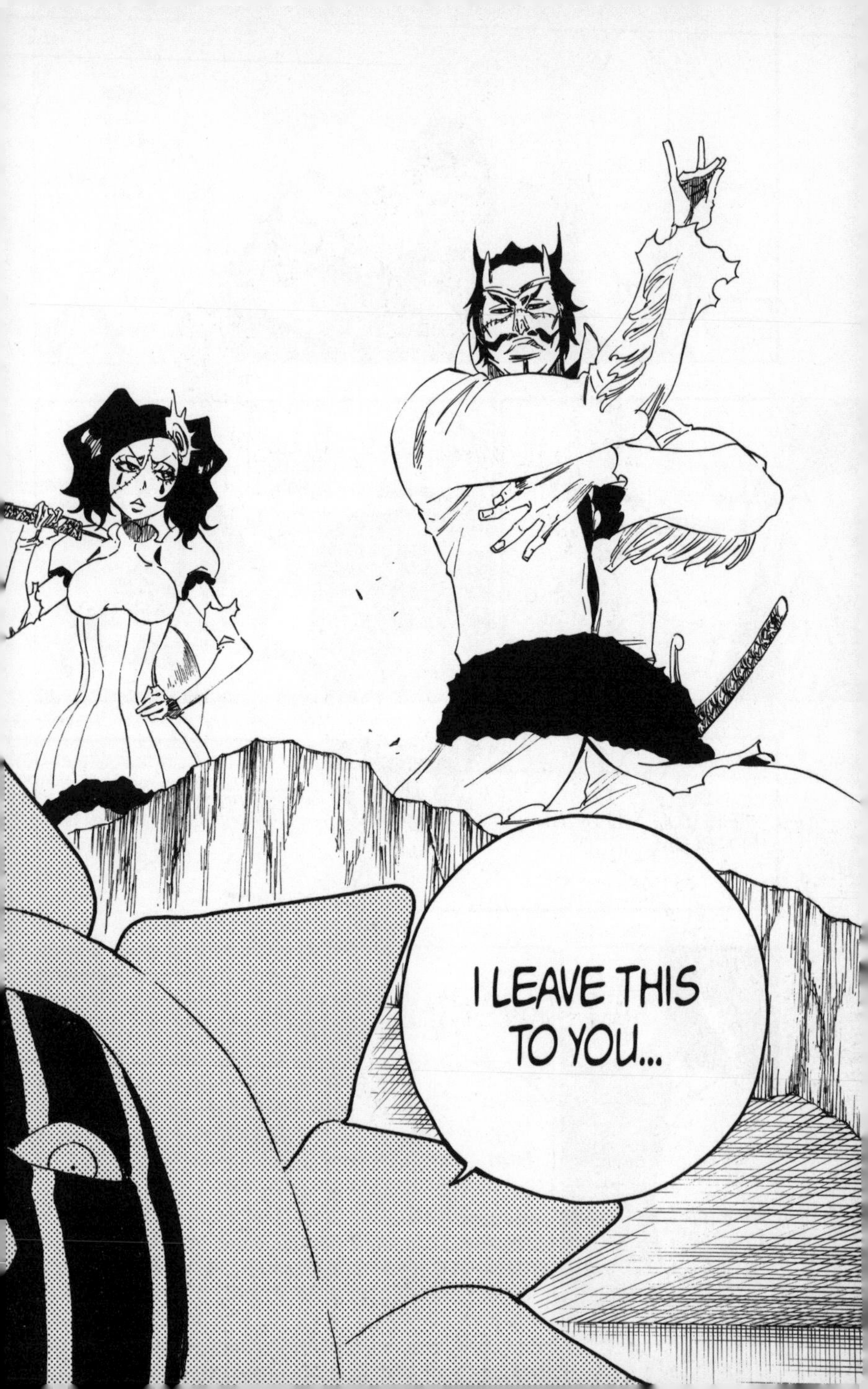
I LEAVE THIS TO YOU...

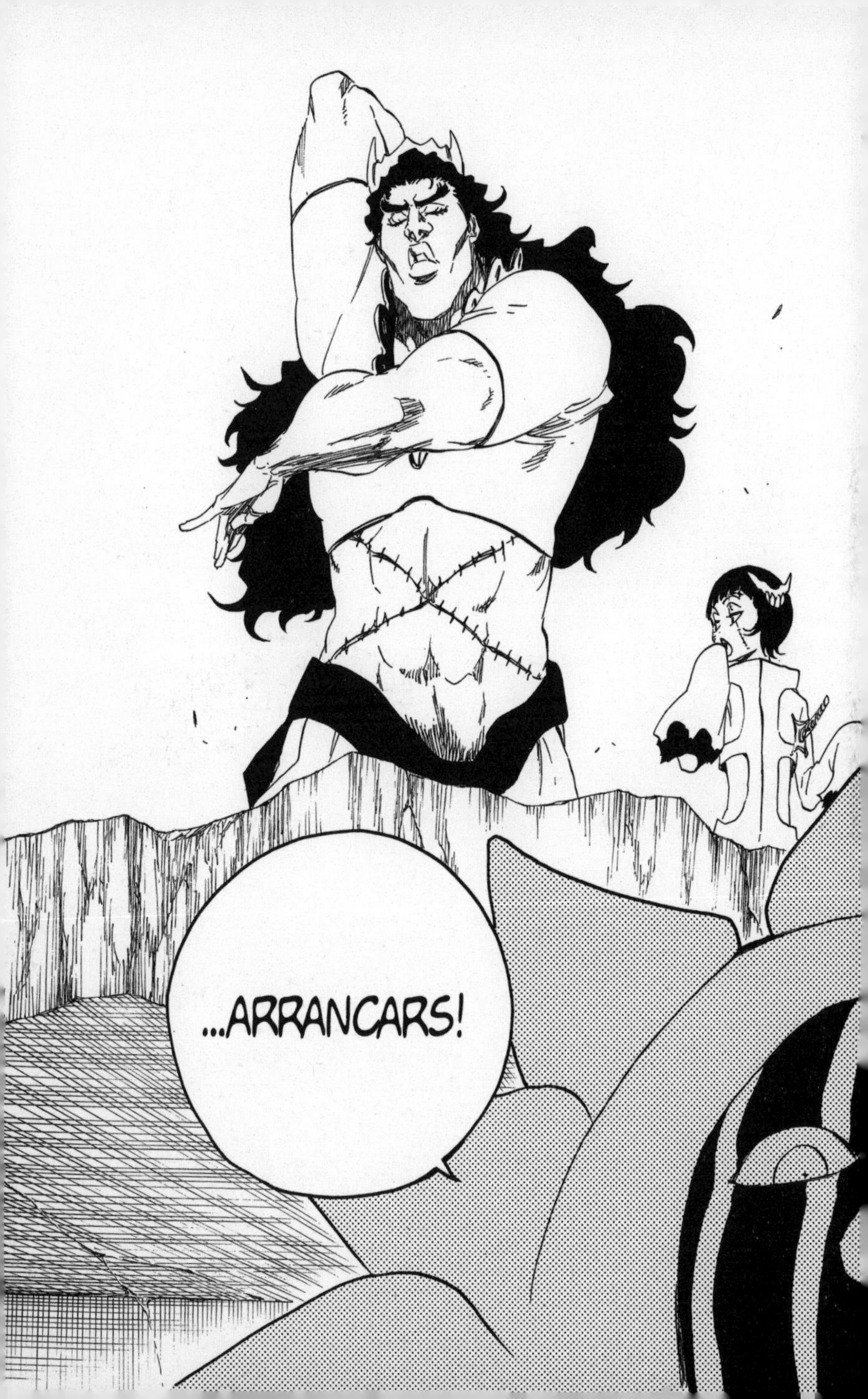
...ARRANCARS!

YOU'RE
PROBABLY
WONDERING HOW
I WAS ABLE TO
PREPARE ALL
THIS ON SHORT
NOTICE...

I KNOW...

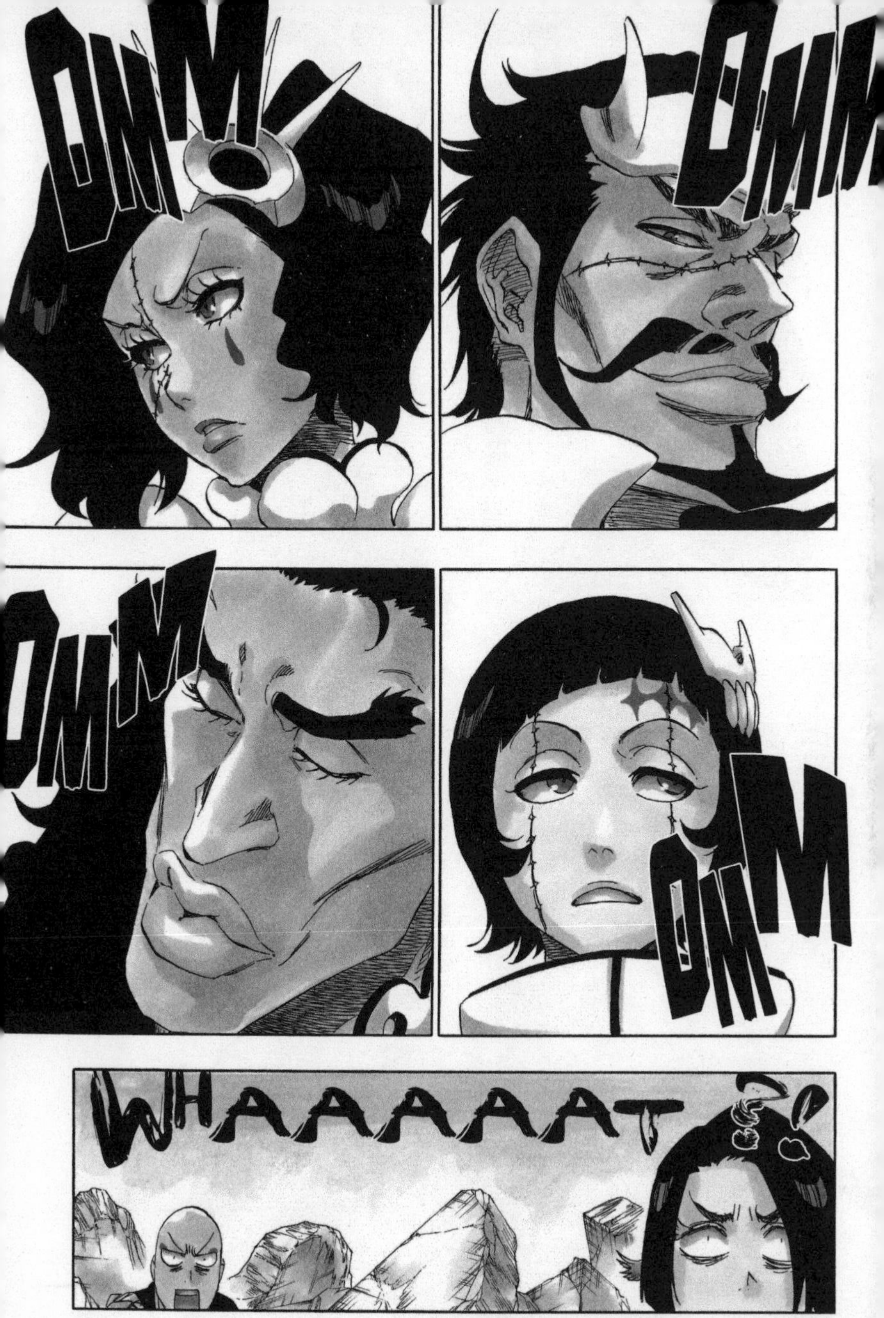
WHAAAAAT?!

591. MARCHING OUT THE ZOMBIES 2

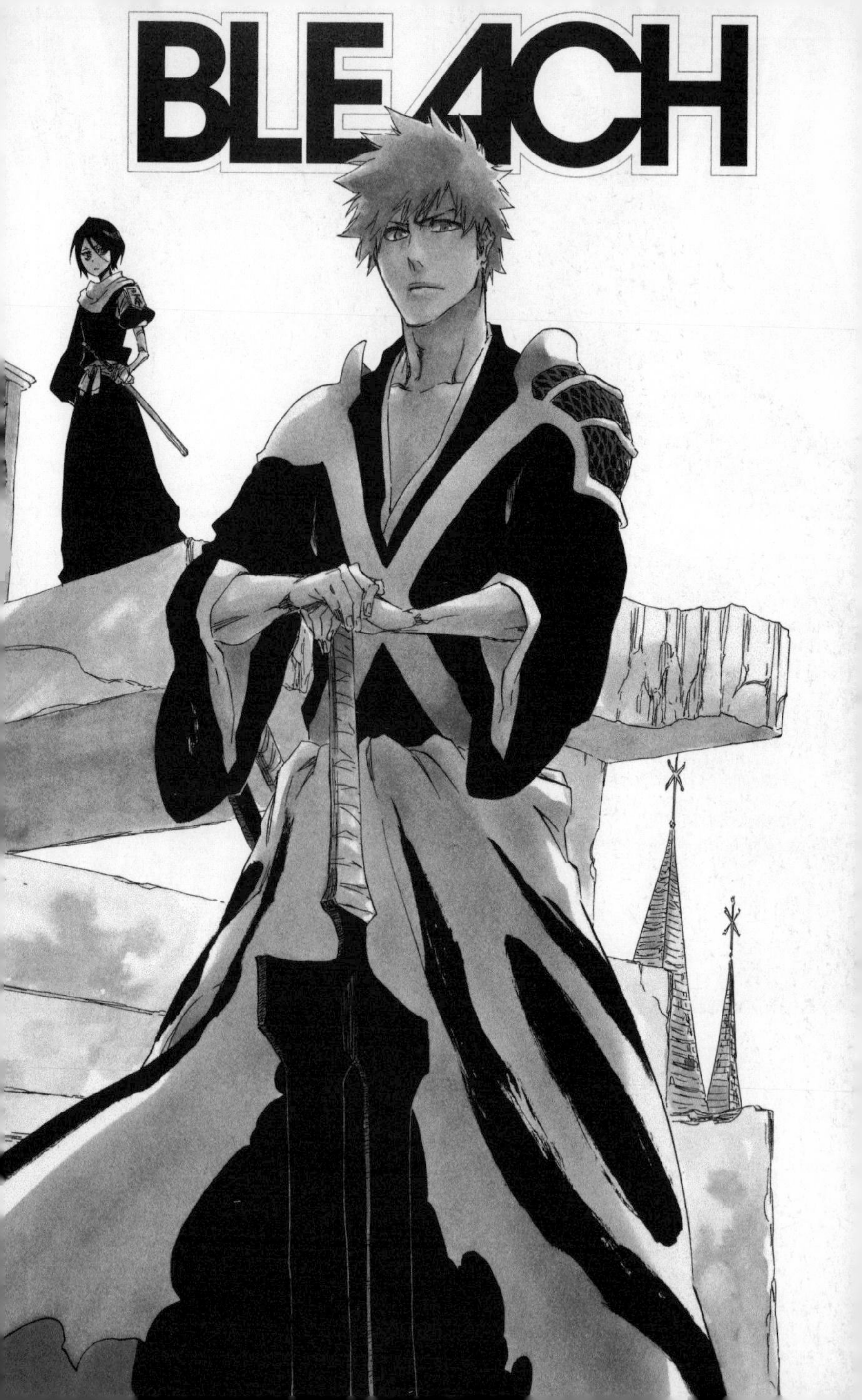
BLEACH

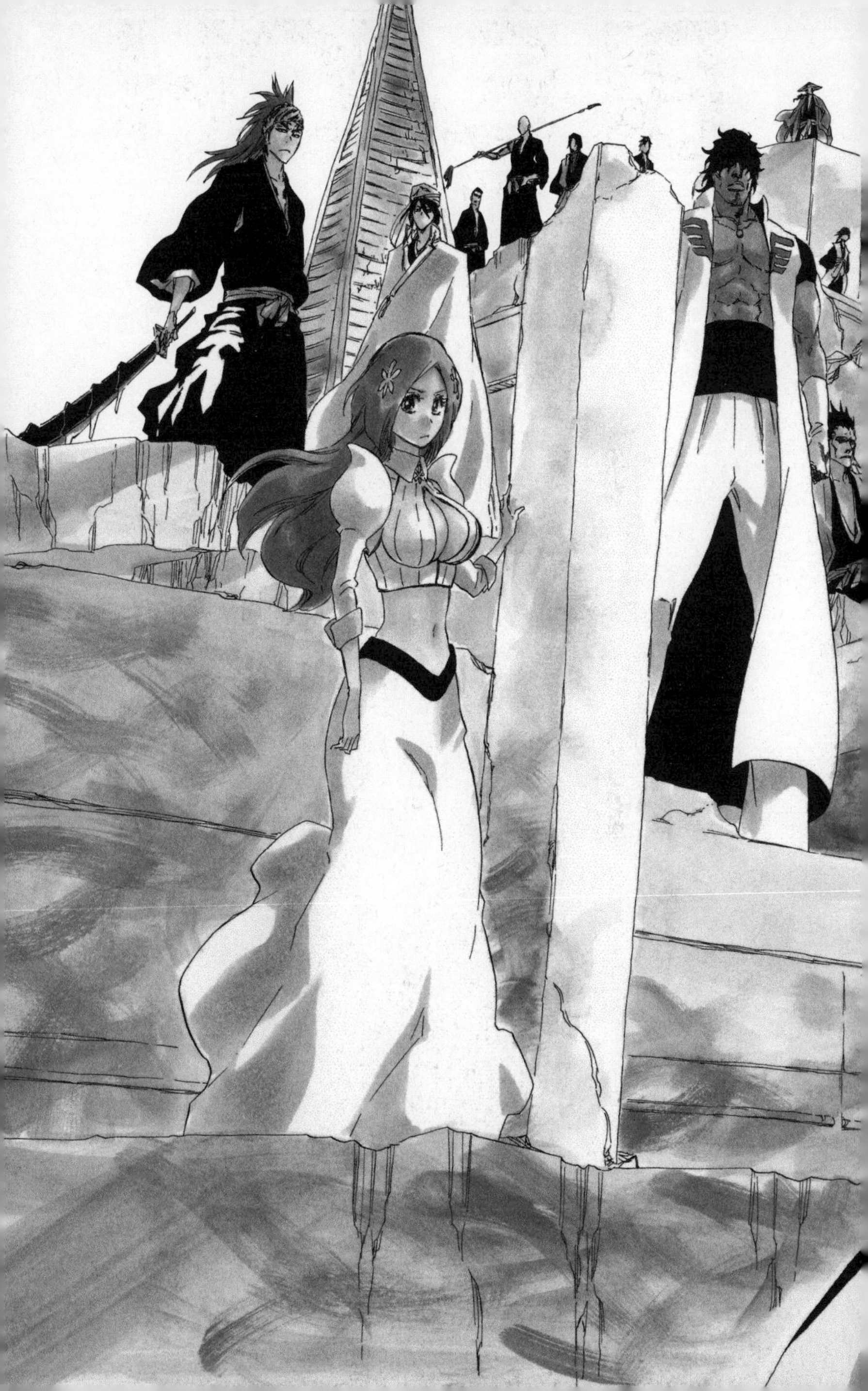

BLEACH
ブリーチ

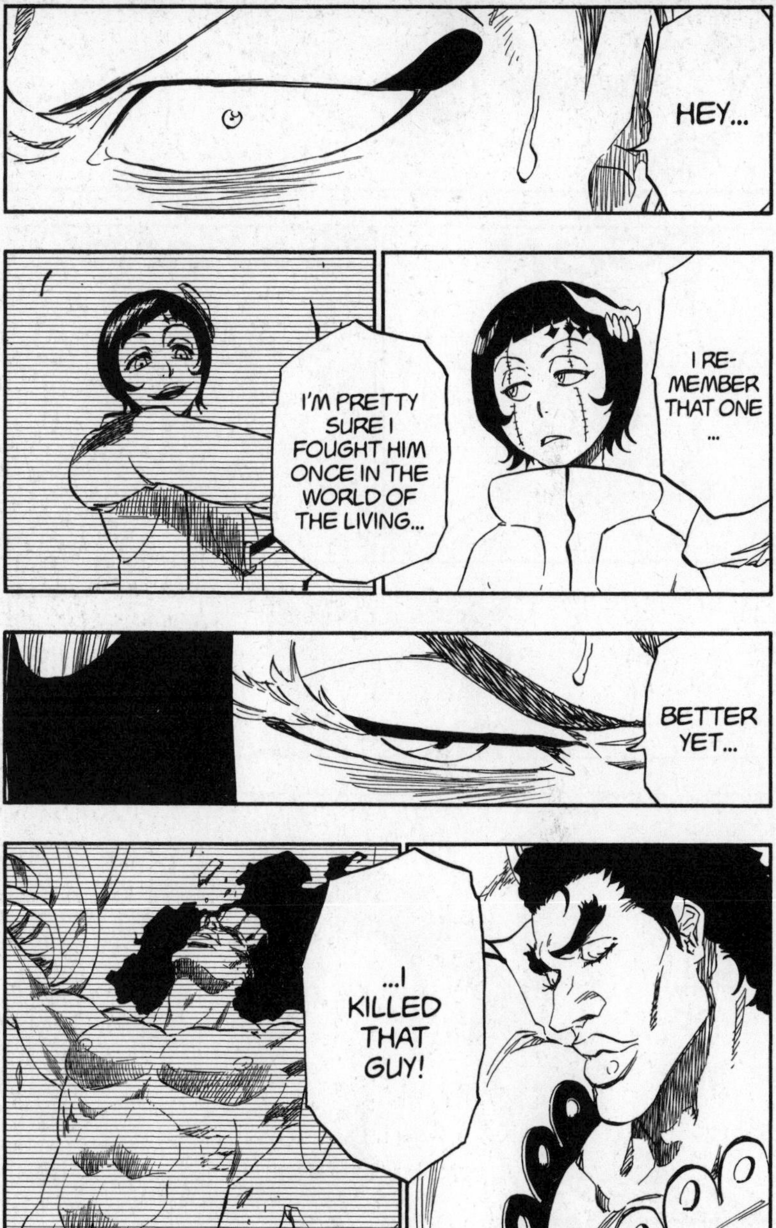
HEY...
I RE-MEMBER THAT ONE ...
I'M PRETTY SURE I FOUGHT HIM ONCE IN THE WORLD OF THE LIVING...
BETTER YET...
...I KILLED THAT GUY!

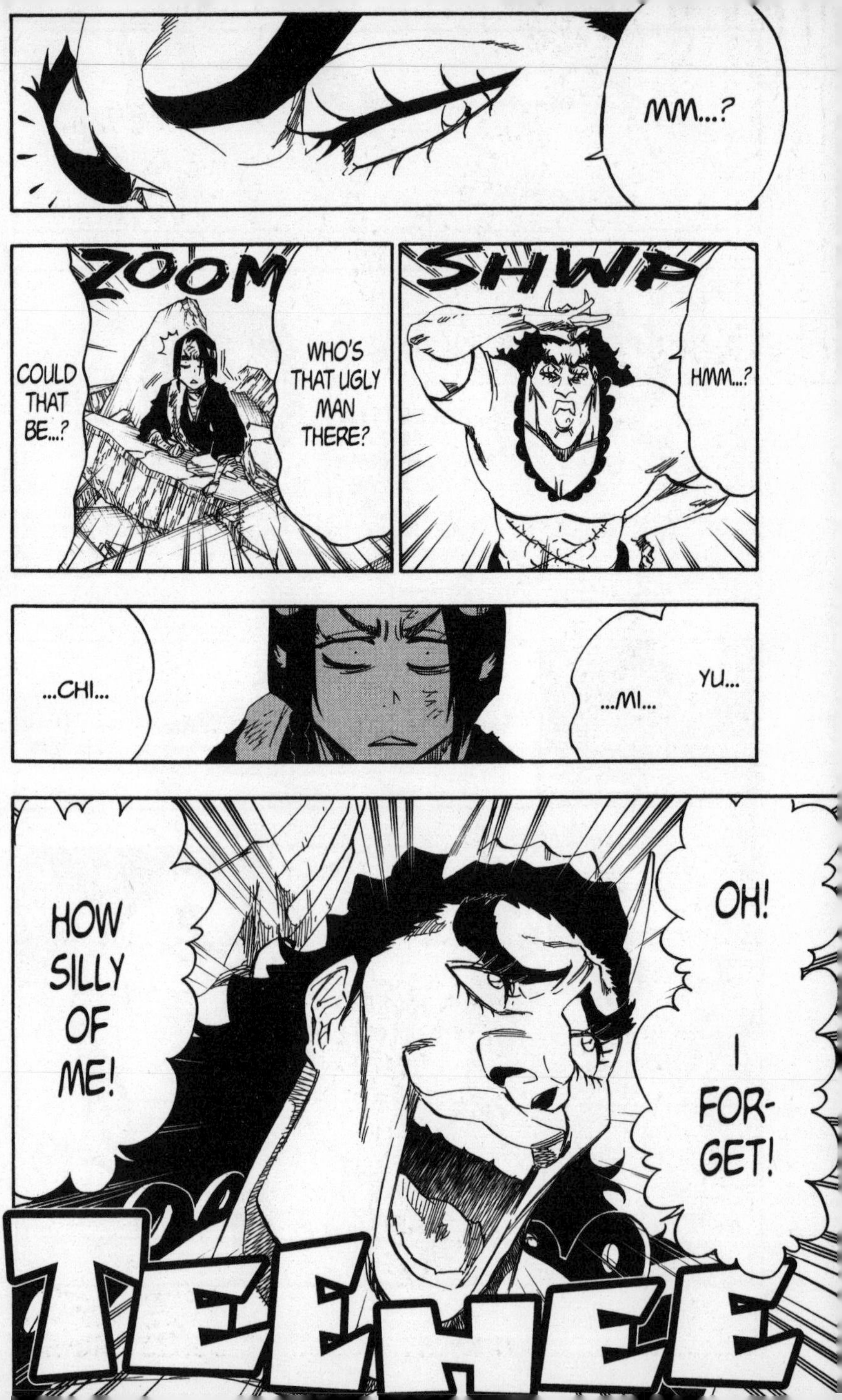
MM...?
SHWP
HMM...?
ZOOM
WHO'S THAT UGLY MAN THERE?
COULD THAT BE...?
YU...
...MI...
...CHI...
OH! I FOR-GET!
HOW SILLY OF ME!
TEEHEE

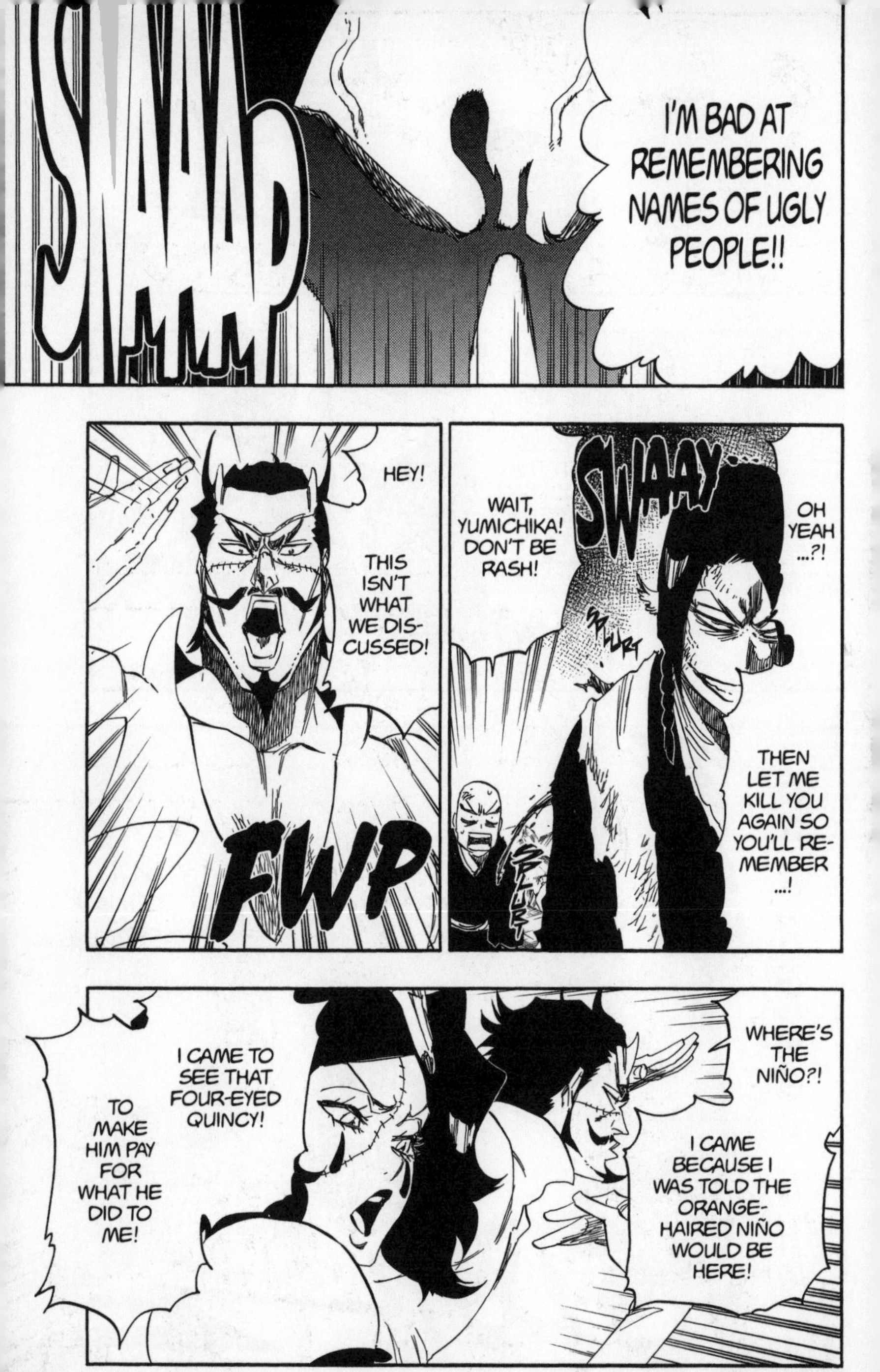
I'M BAD AT REMEMBERING NAMES OF UGLY PEOPLE!!
SNAAP
OH YEAH ...?!
SWAAY
WAIT, YUMICHIKA! DON'T BE RASH!
SPLURT
THEN LET ME KILL YOU AGAIN SO YOU'LL RE-MEMBER ...!
SPLURT
HEY!
THIS ISN'T WHAT WE DIS-CUSSED!
FWP
WHERE'S THE NIÑO?!
I CAME BECAUSE I WAS TOLD THE ORANGE-HAIRED NIÑO WOULD BE HERE!
I CAME TO SEE THAT FOUR-EYED QUINCY!
TO MAKE HIM PAY FOR WHAT HE DID TO ME!

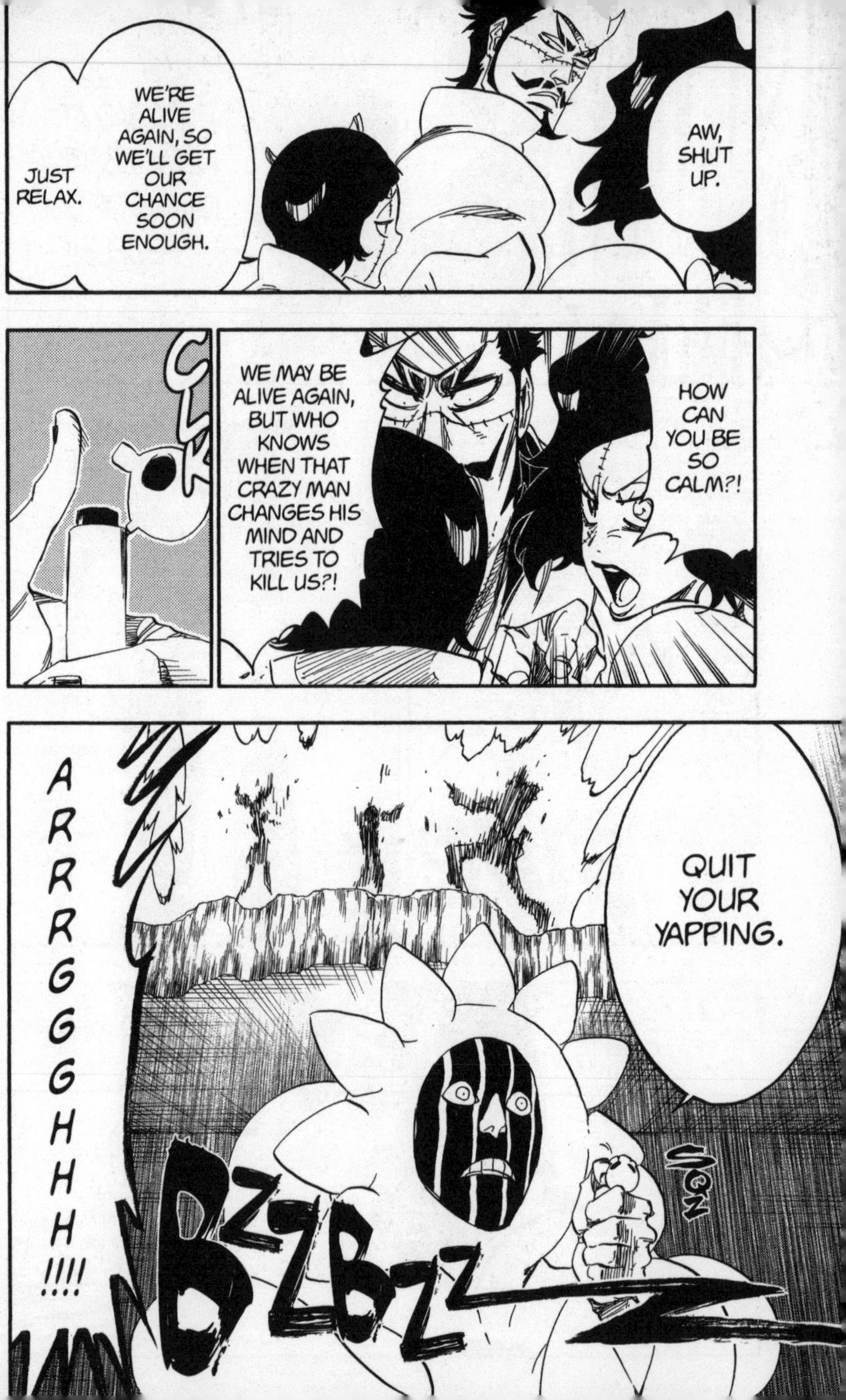
AW, SHUT UP.
WE'RE ALIVE AGAIN, SO WE'LL GET OUR CHANCE SOON ENOUGH.
JUST RELAX.
HOW CAN YOU BE SO CALM?!
WE MAY BE ALIVE AGAIN, BUT WHO KNOWS WHEN THAT CRAZY MAN CHANGES HIS MIND AND TRIES TO KILL US?!
CLK
QUIT YOUR YAPPING.
ARRRGGGHHH!!!!
BZZBZZ

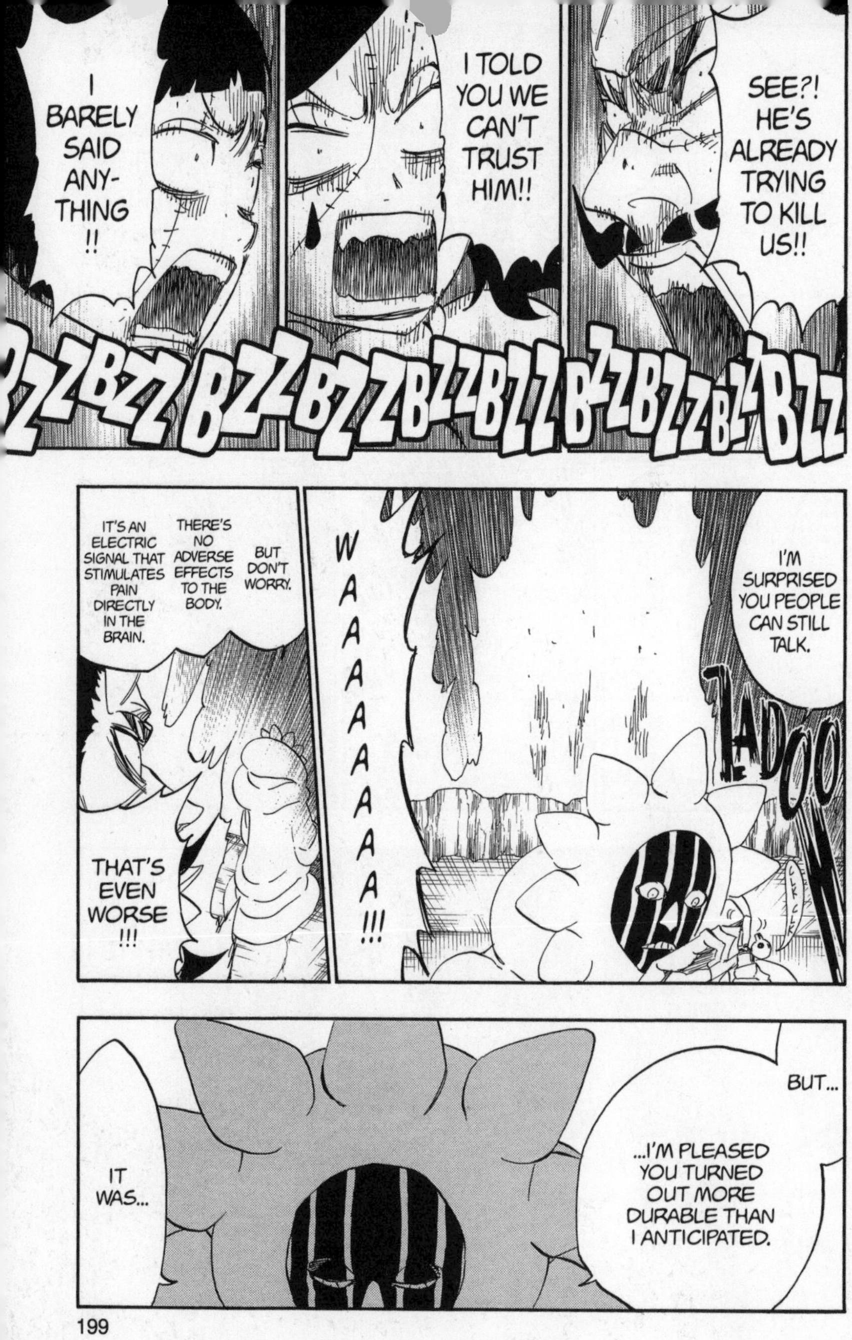
SEE?! HE'S ALREADY TRYING TO KILL US!!
I TOLD YOU WE CAN'T TRUST HIM!!
I BARELY SAID ANYTHING!!
BZZ
I'M SURPRISED YOU PEOPLE CAN STILL TALK.
TADOOM
WAAAAAAAAAAA!!!
BUT DON'T WORRY.
THERE'S NO ADVERSE EFFECTS TO THE BODY.
IT'S AN ELECTRIC SIGNAL THAT STIMULATES PAIN DIRECTLY IN THE BRAIN.
THAT'S EVEN WORSE!!!
BUT...
...I'M PLEASED YOU TURNED OUT MORE DURABLE THAN I ANTICIPATED.
IT WAS...

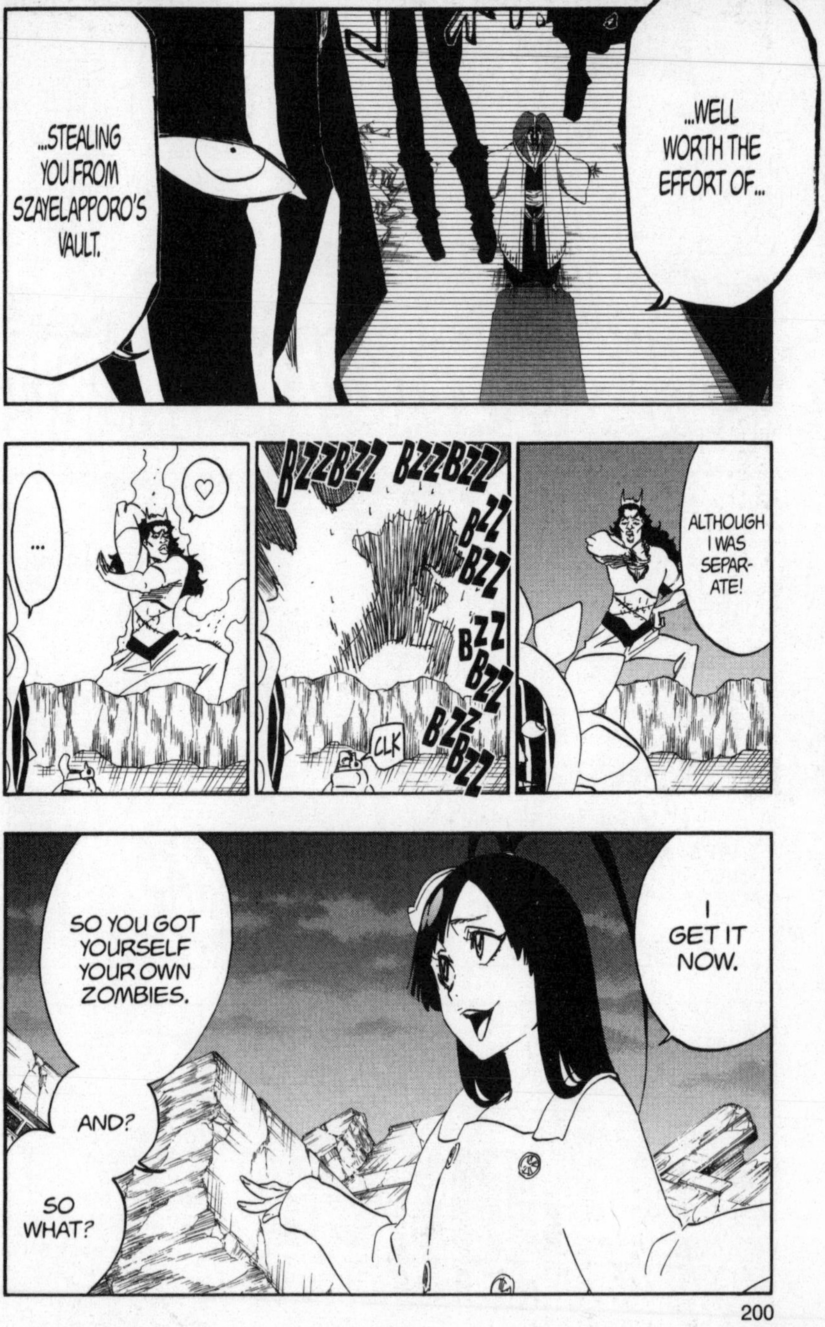
...WELL WORTH THE EFFORT OF...
...STEALING YOU FROM SZAYELAPPORO'S VAULT.
ALTHOUGH I WAS SEPAR-ATE!
BZZBZZ BZZBZZ
BZZ
BZZ
BZZ
BZZ
BZZ
BZZ
CLK
♡
...
I GET IT NOW.
SO YOU GOT YOURSELF YOUR OWN ZOMBIES.
AND?
SO WHAT?

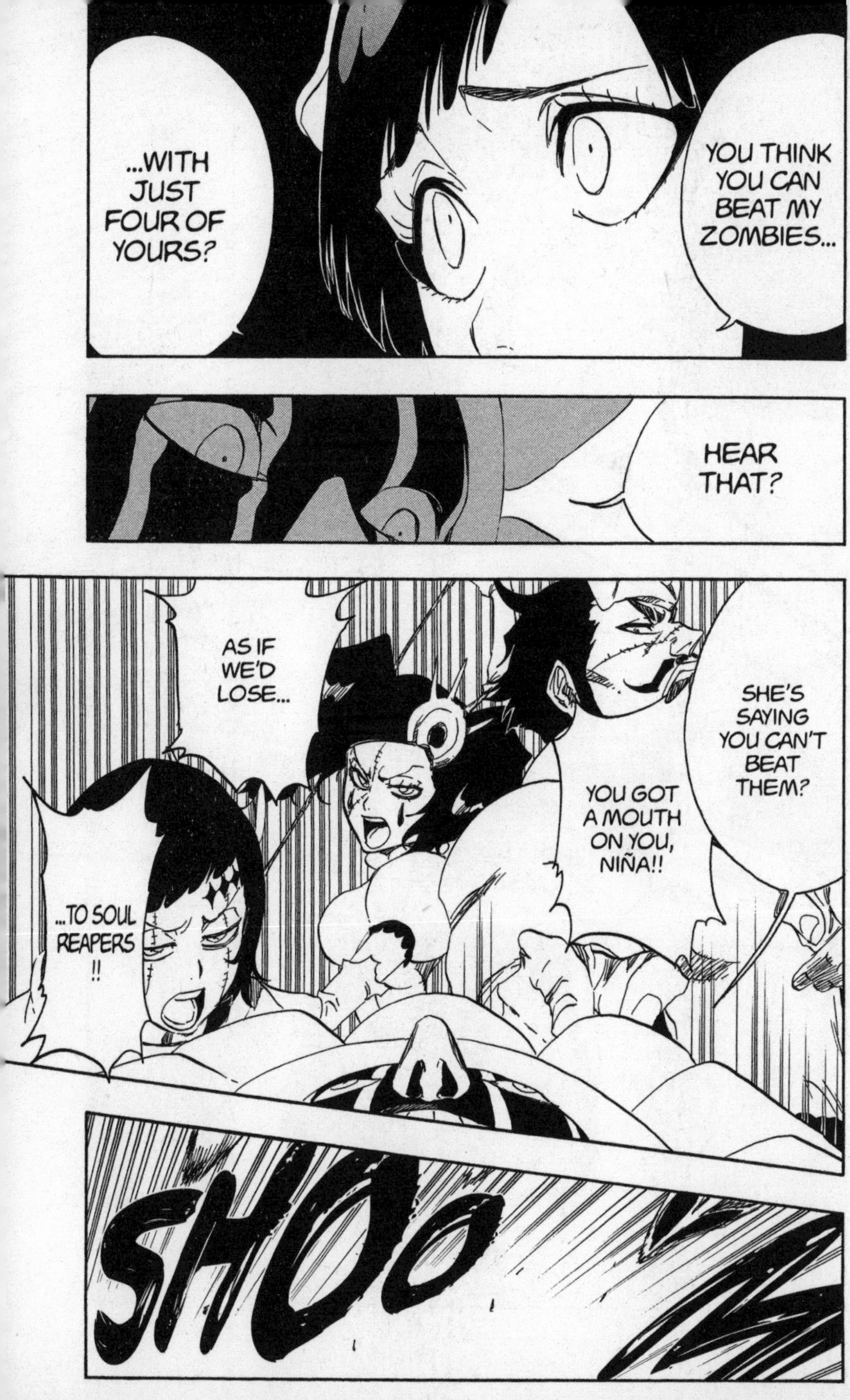
YOU THINK YOU CAN BEAT MY ZOMBIES...
...WITH JUST FOUR OF YOURS?
HEAR THAT?
SHE'S SAYING YOU CAN'T BEAT THEM?
YOU GOT A MOUTH ON YOU, NIÑA!!
AS IF WE'D LOSE...
...TO SOUL REAPERS !!
SHOOO

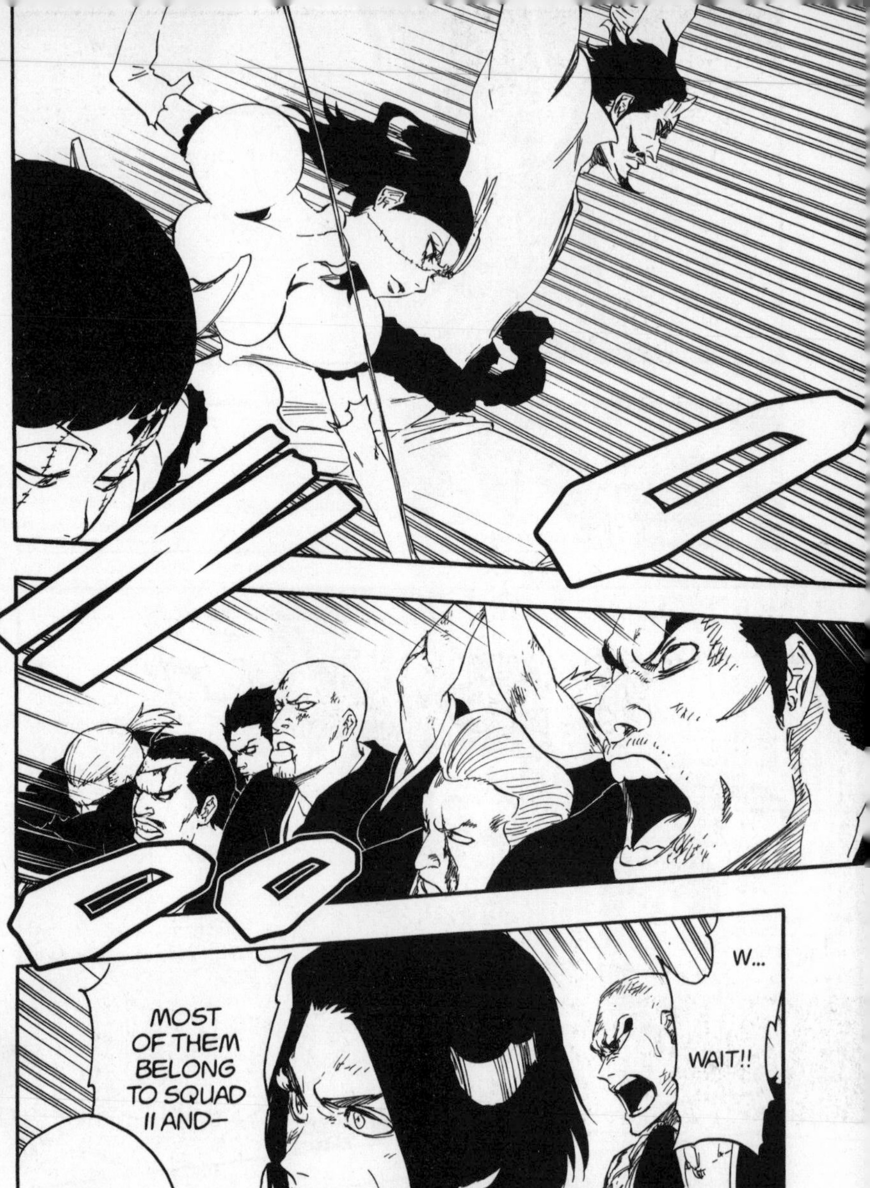
W...
WAIT!!
MOST OF THEM BELONG TO SQUAD II AND—
WHAT ABOUT IT?

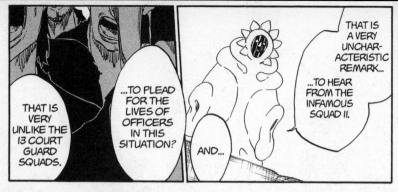

THAT IS A VERY UNCHAR-ACTERISTIC REMARK...
...TO HEAR FROM THE INFAMOUS SQUAD II.
AND...
...TO PLEAD FOR THE LIVES OF OFFICERS IN THIS SITUATION?
THAT IS VERY UNLIKE THE 13 COURT GUARD SQUADS.
"PROTECT THE SEIREITEI"...
SINCE WHEN HAVE THE COURT GUARDS...
...GONE SO SOFT?
AN OFFICER SHALL DIE IN THE COURT GUARD.
IF ONE HARMS THE COURT GUARD, ONE SHALL TAKE ONE'S OWN LIFE.
BLEACH
THOSE WERE THE WORDS OF...
591.

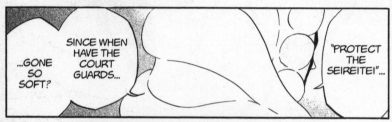

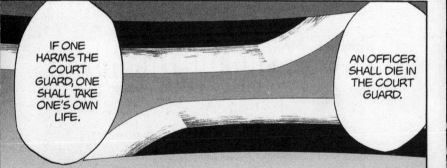

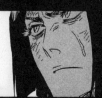

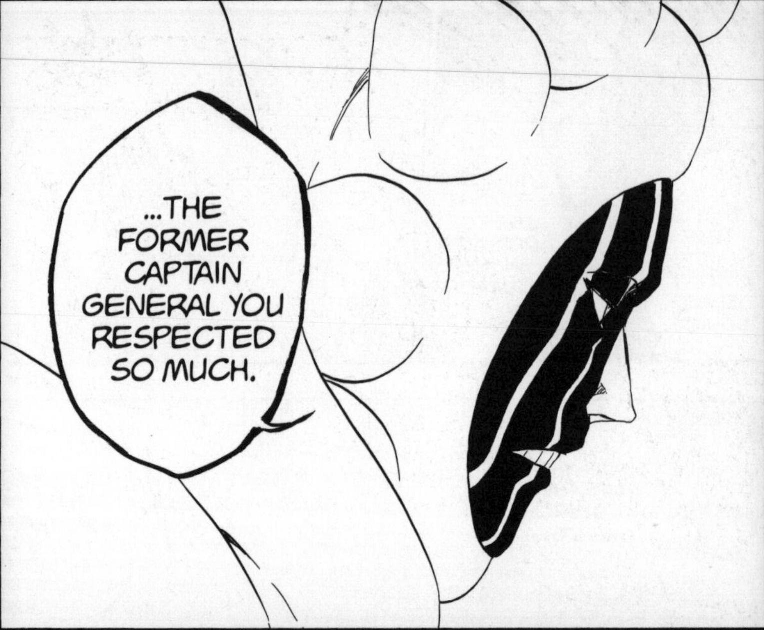
...THE FORMER CAPTAIN GENERAL YOU RESPECTED SO MUCH.

Marching Out the ZOMBIES 2

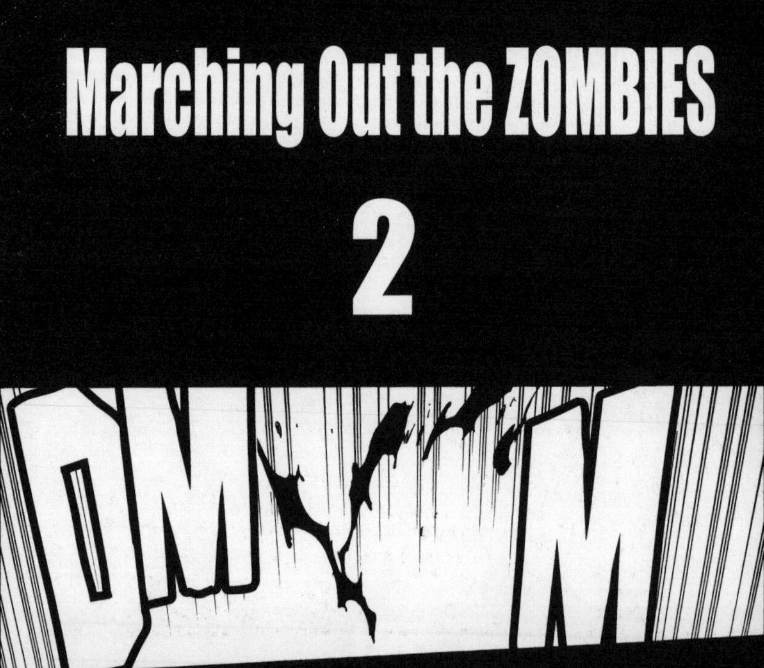

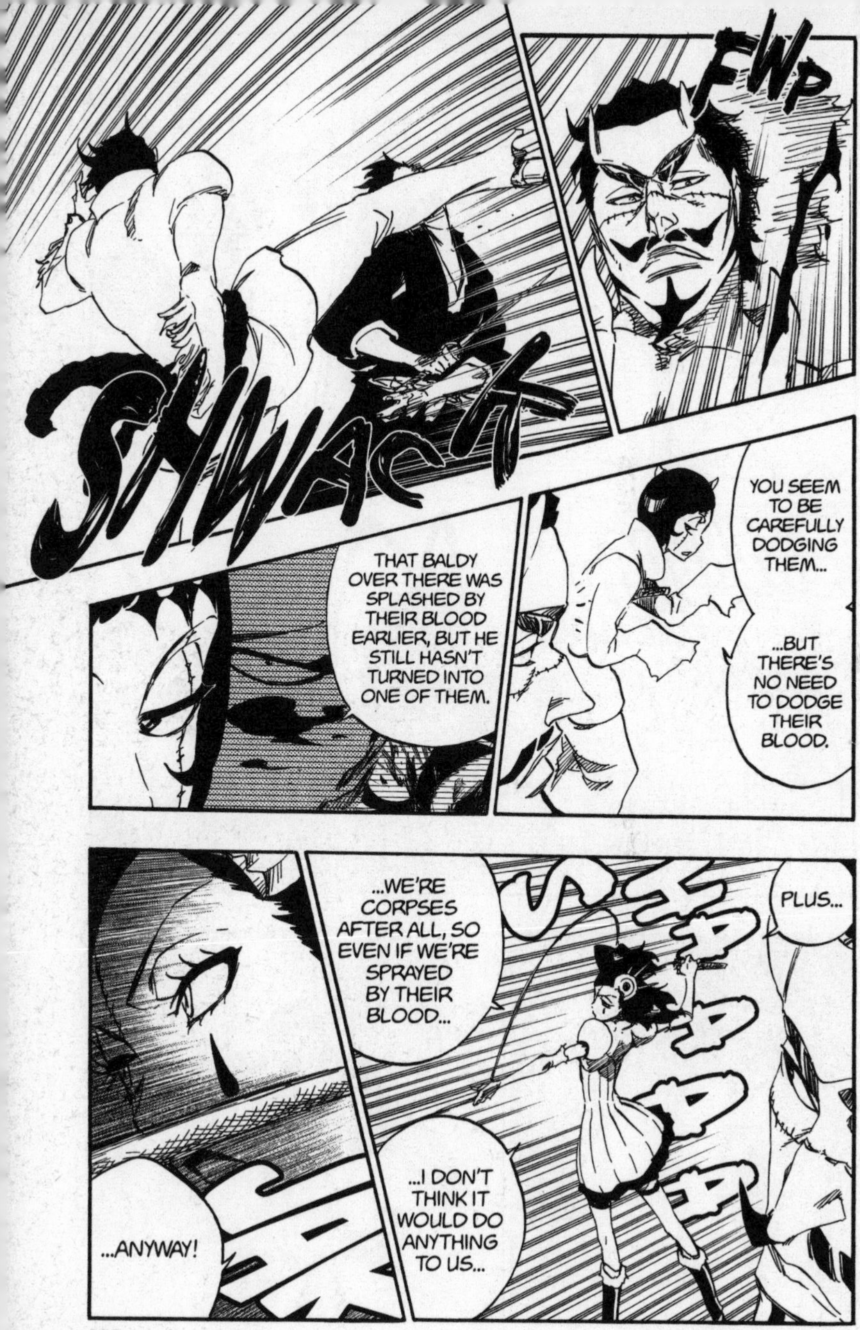
FWP
SHWACK
YOU SEEM TO BE CAREFULLY DODGING THEM...
...BUT THERE'S NO NEED TO DODGE THEIR BLOOD.
THAT BALDY OVER THERE WAS SPLASHED BY THEIR BLOOD EARLIER, BUT HE STILL HASN'T TURNED INTO ONE OF THEM.
PLUS...
...WE'RE CORPSES AFTER ALL, SO EVEN IF WE'RE SPRAYED BY THEIR BLOOD...
...I DON'T THINK IT WOULD DO ANYTHING TO US...
...ANYWAY!

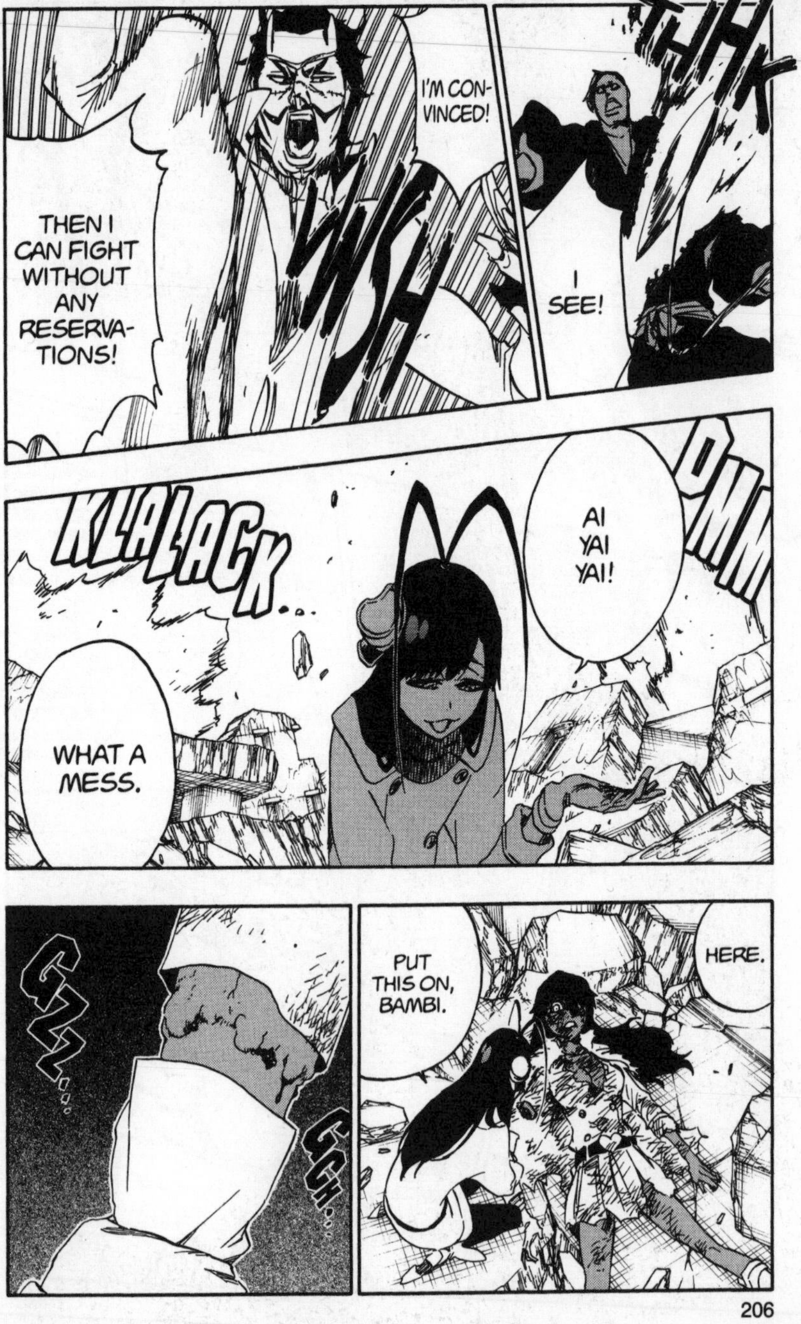
THHK
I SEE!
I'M CON-VINCED!
WSH
THEN I CAN FIGHT WITHOUT ANY RESERVA-TIONS!
DMM
AI YAI YAI!
KLALACK
WHAT A MESS.
HERE.
PUT THIS ON, BAMBI.
GZZ...
GCH...

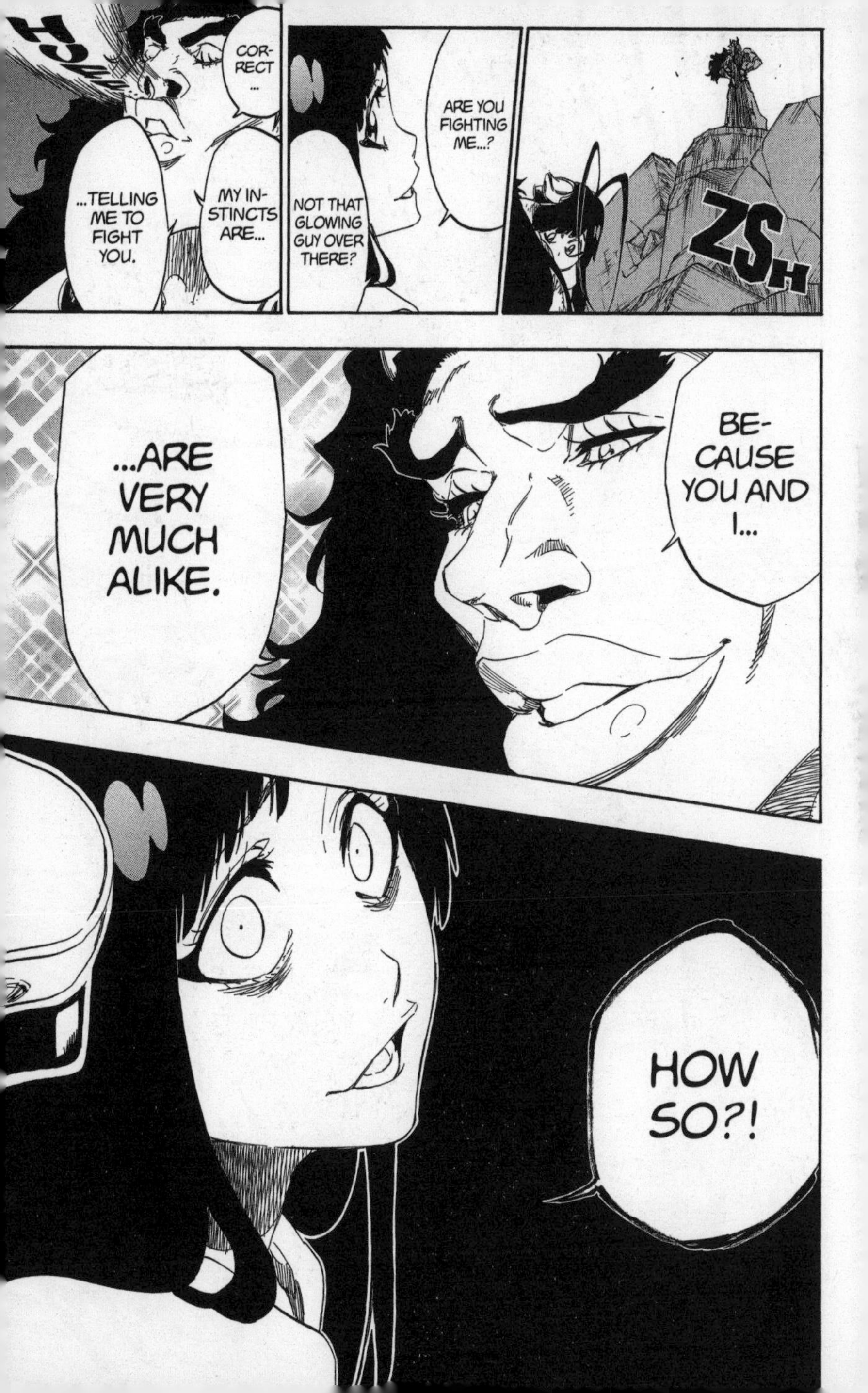
ZSH
ARE YOU FIGHTING ME...?
NOT THAT GLOWING GUY OVER THERE?
COR-RECT...
MY IN-STINCTS ARE...
...TELLING ME TO FIGHT YOU.
BE-CAUSE YOU AND I...
...ARE VERY MUCH ALIKE.
HOW SO?!

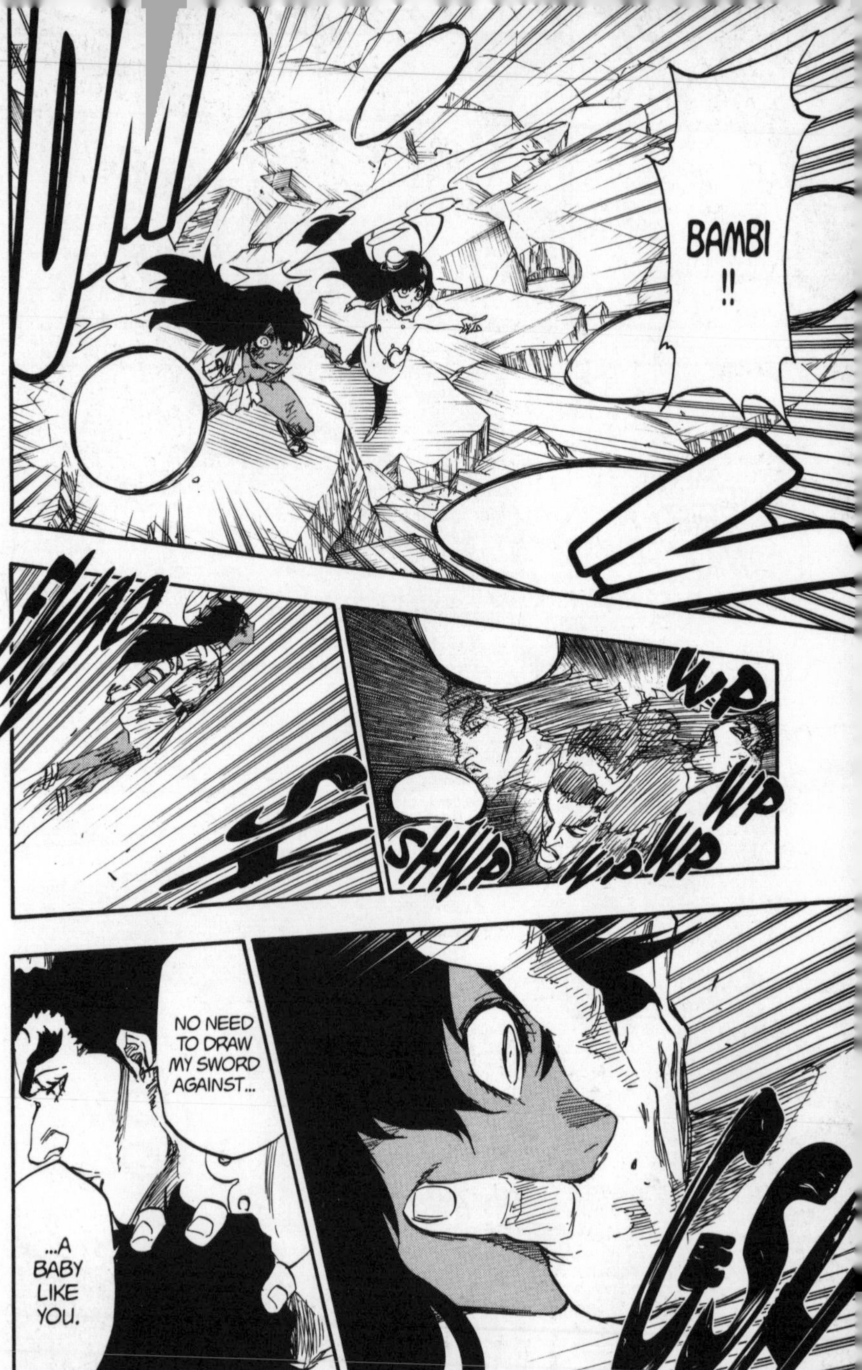
BAMBI !!
WP
WP
WP WP
SHWP
NO NEED TO DRAW MY SWORD AGAINST...
...A BABY LIKE YOU.

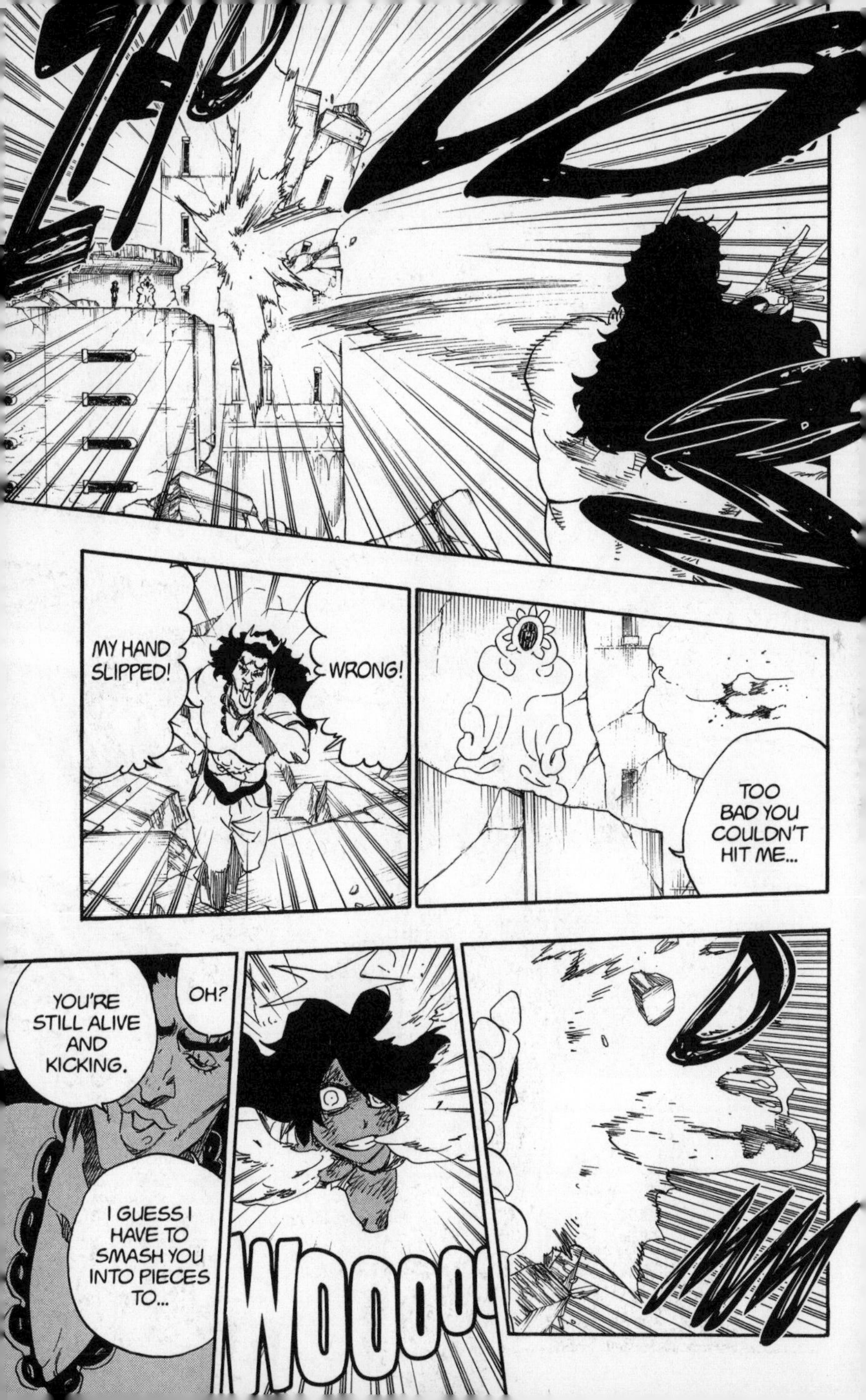
TOO BAD YOU COULDN'T HIT ME...
WRONG!
MY HAND SLIPPED!
WOOOOO
OH?
YOU'RE STILL ALIVE AND KICKING.
I GUESS I HAVE TO SMASH YOU INTO PIECES TO...

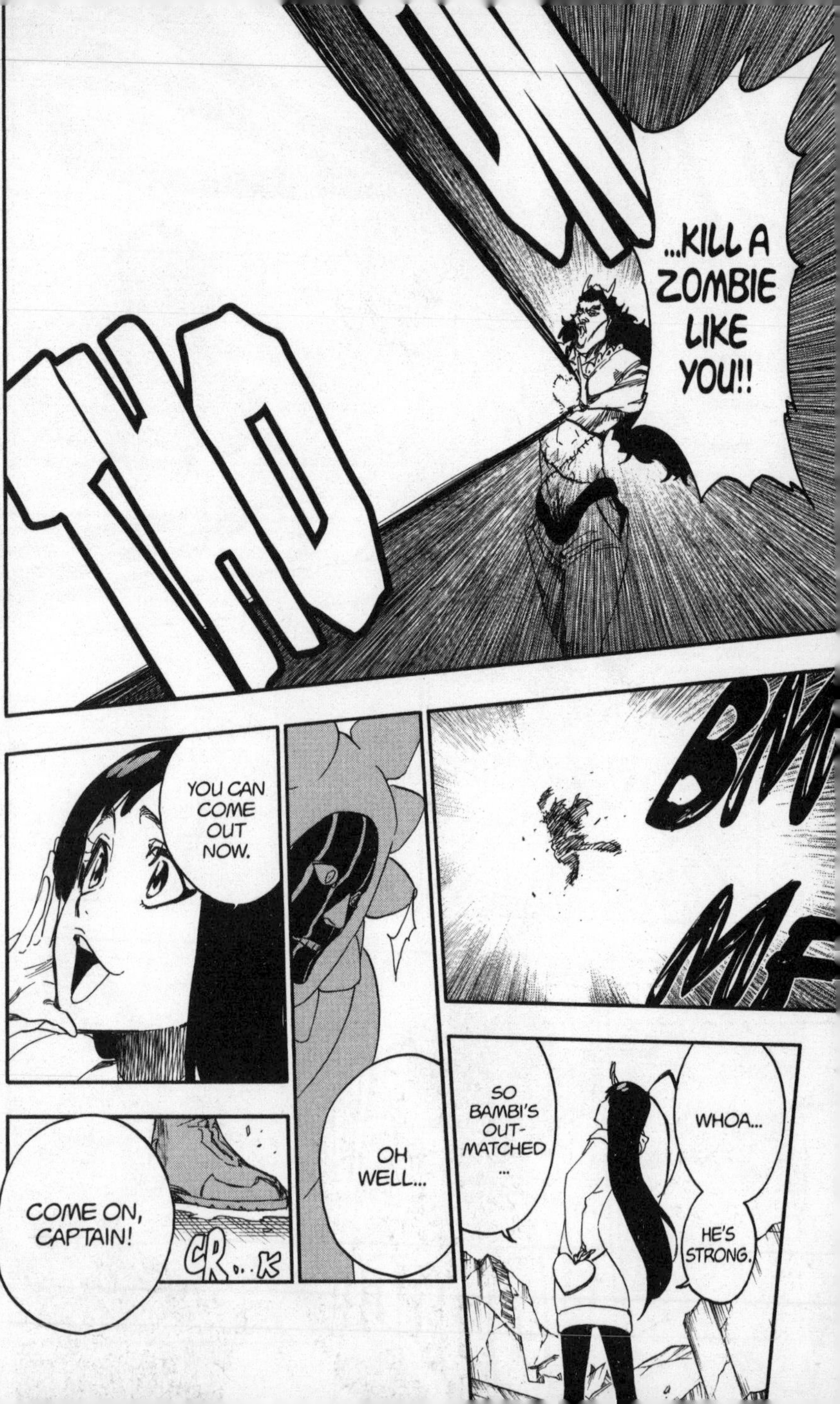
...KILL A ZOMBIE LIKE YOU!!
WHOA... HE'S STRONG.
SO BAMBI'S OUT-MATCHED...
OH WELL...
YOU CAN COME OUT NOW.
COME ON, CAPTAIN!
CR...K

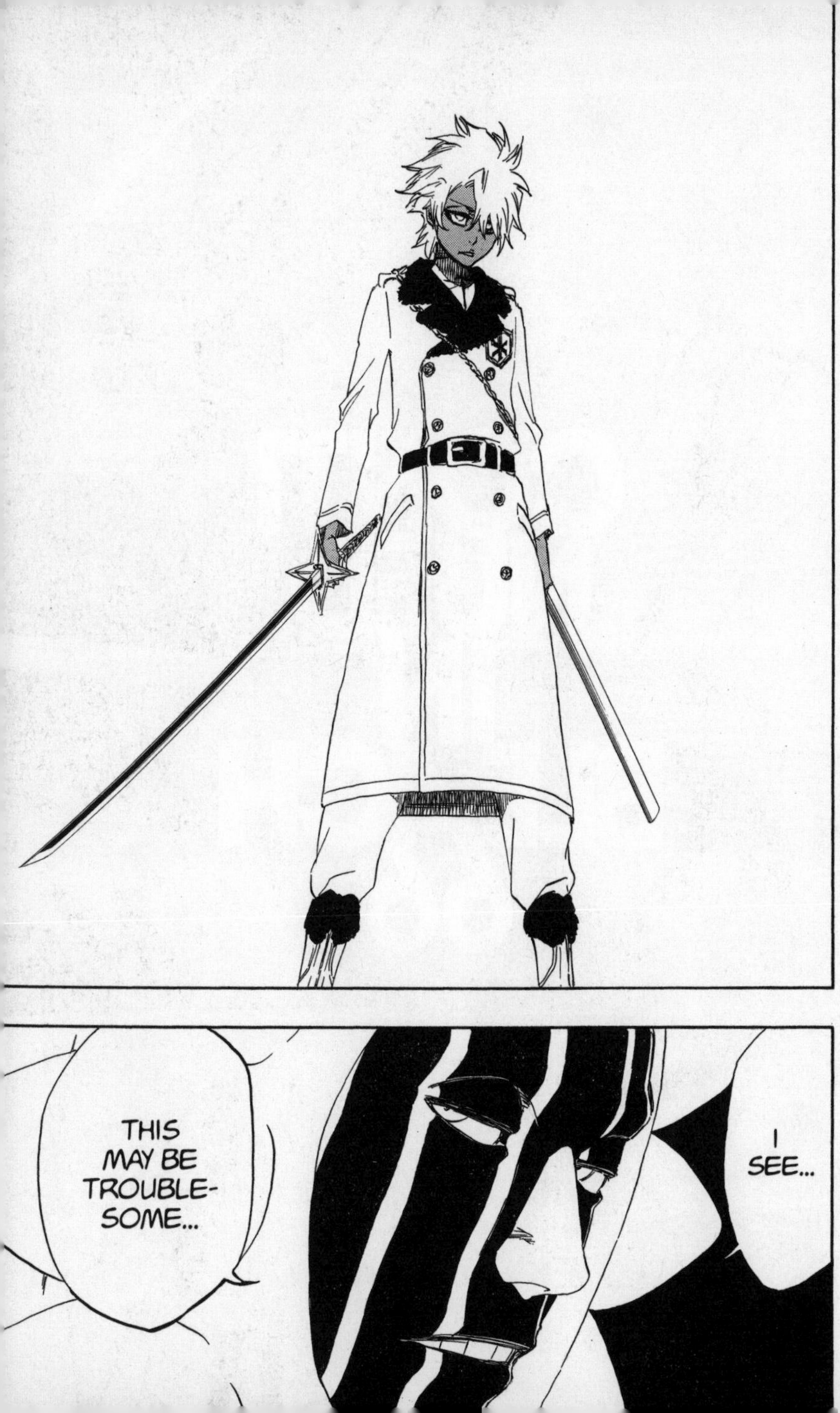
I SEE...
THIS MAY BE TROUBLE-SOME...

CONTI
NUED
IN
BLEACH
66

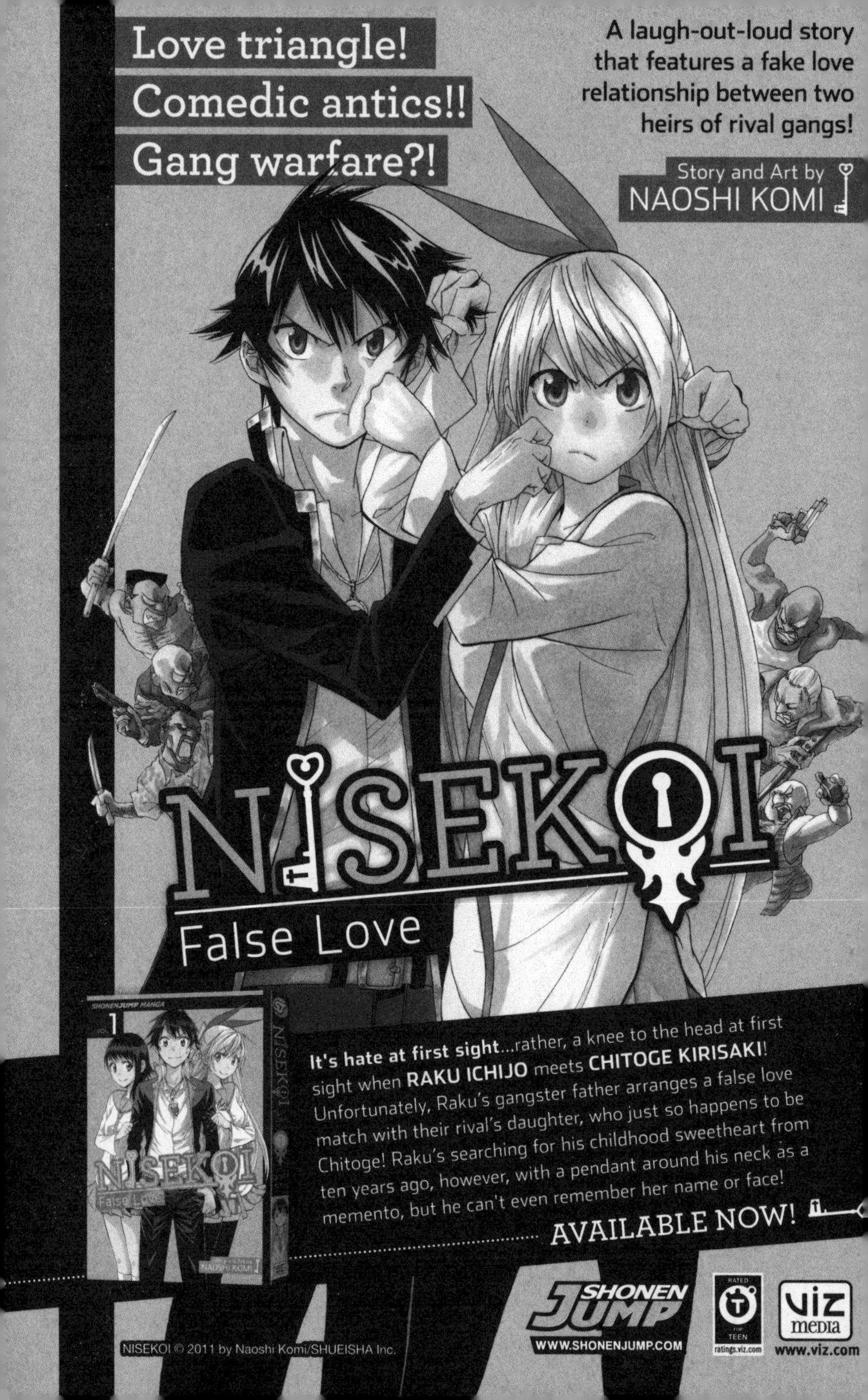
Love triangle!
Comedic antics!!
Gang warfare?!
A laugh-out-loud story that features a fake love relationship between two heirs of rival gangs!
Story and Art by
NAOSHI KOMI
NISEKOI
False Love
SHONENJUMP MANGA
VOL. 1
NISEKOI
False Love
NAOSHI KOMI
It's hate at first sight...rather, a knee to the head at first sight when RAKU ICHIJO meets CHITOGE KIRISAKI! Unfortunately, Raku's gangster father arranges a false love match with their rival's daughter, who just so happens to be Chitoge! Raku's searching for his childhood sweetheart from ten years ago, however, with a pendant around his neck as a memento, but he can't even remember her name or face!
AVAILABLE NOW!
SHONEN JUMP
WWW.SHONENJUMP.COM
RATED T FOR TEEN
ratings.viz.com
viz media
www.viz.com
NISEKOI © 2011 by Naoshi Komi/SHUEISHA Inc.

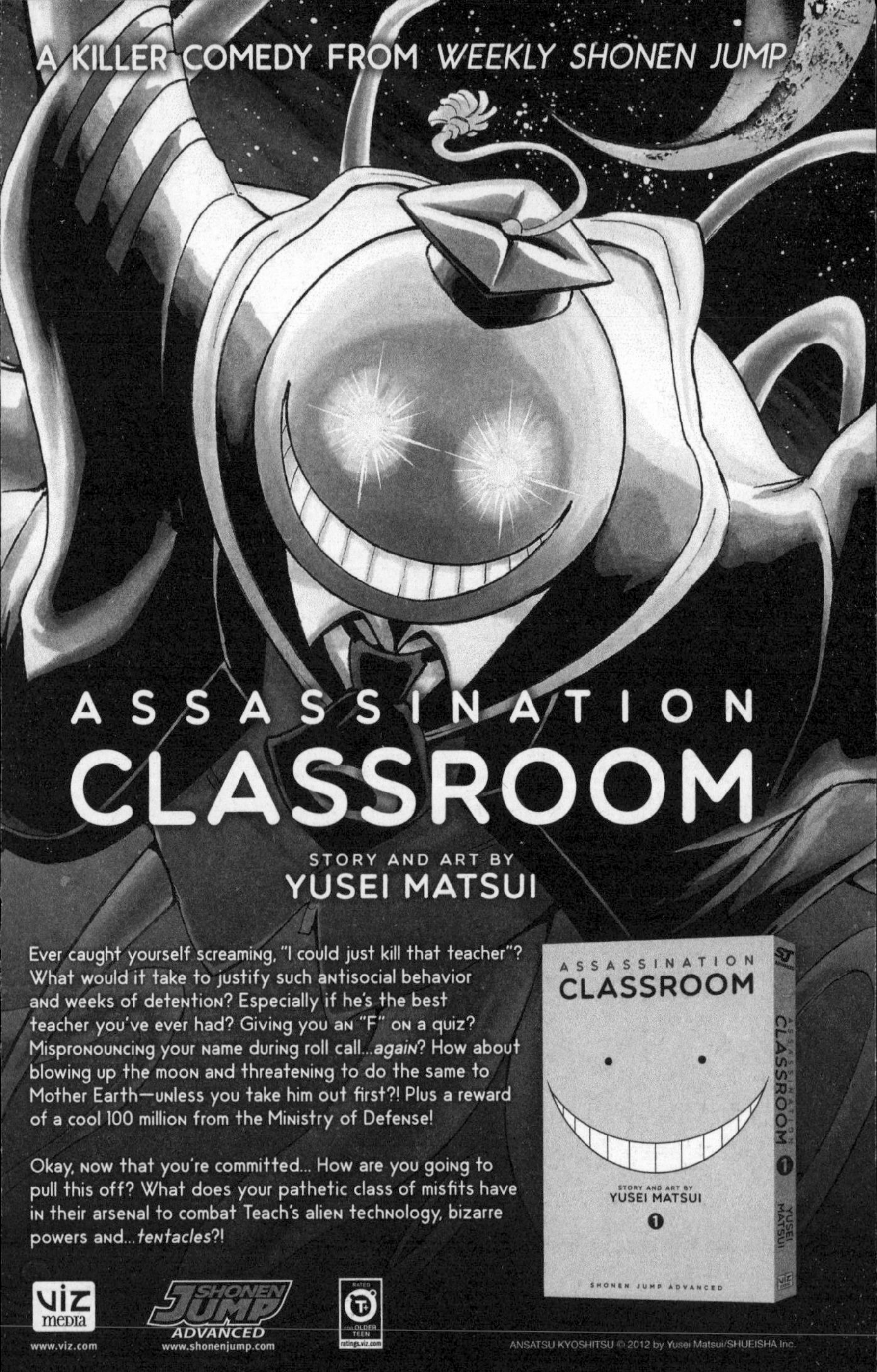
A KILLER COMEDY FROM *WEEKLY SHONEN JUMP*
ASSASSINATION
CLASSROOM
STORY AND ART BY
YUSEI MATSUI
Ever caught yourself screaming, "I could just kill that teacher"? What would it take to justify such antisocial behavior and weeks of detention? Especially if he's the best teacher you've ever had? Giving you an "F" on a quiz? Mispronouncing your name during roll call...*again*? How about blowing up the moon and threatening to do the same to Mother Earth—unless you take him out first?! Plus a reward of a cool 100 million from the Ministry of Defense!
Okay, now that you're committed... How are you going to pull this off? What does your pathetic class of misfits have in their arsenal to combat Teach's alien technology, bizarre powers and...*tentacles*?!
ASSASSINATION
CLASSROOM
STORY AND ART BY
YUSEI MATSUI
1
SHONEN JUMP ADVANCED
viz media
www.viz.com
SHONEN JUMP ADVANCED
www.shonenjump.com
RATED T+ FOR OLDER TEEN
ratings.viz.com
ANSATSU KYOSHITSU © 2012 by Yusei Matsui/SHUEISHA Inc.

You're Reading in the Wrong Direction!!

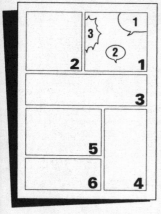

Whoops! Guess what? You're starting at the wrong end of the comic!

…It's true! In keeping with the original Japanese format, **Bleach** is meant to be read from right to left, starting in the upper-right corner.

Unlike English, which is read from left to right, Japanese is read from right to left, meaning that action, sound effects and word-balloon order are completely reversed… something which can make readers unfamiliar with Japanese feel pretty backwards themselves. For this reason, manga or Japanese comics published in the U.S. in English have sometimes been published "flopped"—that is, printed in exact reverse order, as though seen from the other side of a mirror.

By flopping pages, U.S. publishers can avoid confusing readers, but the compromise is not without its downside. For one thing, a character in a flopped manga series who once wore in the original Japanese version a T-shirt emblazoned with "M A Y" (as in "the merry month of") now wears one which reads "Y A M"! Additionally, many manga creators in Japan are themselves unhappy with the process, as some feel the mirror-imaging of their art skews their original intentions.

We are proud to bring you Tite Kubo's **Bleach** in the original unflopped format. For now, though, turn to the other side of the book and let the adventure begin…!

—Editor